ReFocus: The Films of Shyam Benegal

ReFocus: The International Directors Series

Series Editors: Robert Singer, Stefanie Van de Peer and Gary D. Rhodes

Board of advisors:
Lizelle Bisschoff (Glasgow University)
Stephanie Hemelryck Donald (University of Lincoln)
Anna Misiak (Falmouth University)
Des O'Rawe (Queen's University Belfast)

ReFocus is a series of contemporary methodological and theoretical approaches to the interdisciplinary analyses and interpretations of international film directors, from the celebrated to the ignored, in direct relationship to their respective culture – its myths, values and historical precepts – and the broader parameters of international film history and theory.

Titles in the series include:

Susanne Bier Edited by Missy Molloy, Mimi Nielsen and Meryl Shriver-Rice

Francis Veber Keith Corson

Jia Zhangke Maureen Turim

Xavier Dolan Edited by Andrée Lafontaine

Pedro Costa Nuno Barradas Jorge

Sohrab Shahid Saless Edited by Azadeh Fatehrad

Pablo Larraín Edited by Laura Hatry

Michel Gondry Edited by Marcelline Block and Jennifer Kirby

Rachid Bouchareb Edited by Michael Gott and Leslie Kealhofer-Kemp

Andrei Tarkovsky Edited by Sergey Toymentsev

Paul Leni Edited by Erica Tortolani and Martin F. Norden

Rakhshan Banietemad Edited by Maryam Ghorbankarimi

Jocelyn Saab Edited by Mathilde Rouxel and Stefanie Van de Peer

François Ozon Edited by Loïc Bourdeau

Teuvo Tulio Henry Bacon, Kimmo Laine and Jaakko Seppälä

João Pedro Rodrigues and João Rui Guerra da Mata Edited by José Duarte and Filipa Rosário

Lucrecia Martel Edited by Natalia Christofoletti Barrenha, Julia Kratje and Paul Merchant

Shyam Benegal Edited by Sneha Kar Chaudhuri and Ramit Samaddar

edinburghuniversitypress.com/series/refocint

ReFocus:
The Films of Shyam Benegal

Edited by Sneha Kar Chaudhuri and
Ramit Samaddar

EDINBURGH
University Press

Edinburgh University Press is one of the leading university presses in the UK. We publish academic books and journals in our selected subject areas across the humanities and social sciences, combining cutting-edge scholarship with high editorial and production values to produce academic works of lasting importance. For more information visit our website: edinburghuniversitypress.com

© editorial matter and organisation, Sneha Kar Chaudhuri and Ramit Samaddar, 2023, 2024
© the chapters their several authors, 2023, 2024

Edinburgh University Press Ltd
13 Infirmary Street
Edinburgh EH1 1LT

First published in hardback by Edinburgh University Press 2023

Typeset in 11/13 Ehrhardt MT by
IDSUK (DataConnection) Ltd

A CIP record for this book is available from the British Library

ISBN 978 1 4744 5286 1 (hardback)
ISBN 978 1 4744 5287 8 (paperback)
ISBN 978 1 4744 5288 5 (webready PDF)
ISBN 978 1 4744 5289 2 (epub)

The right of Sneha Kar Chaudhuri and Ramit Samaddar to be identified as editors of this work has been asserted in accordance with the Copyright, Designs and Patents Act 1988 and the Copyright and Related Rights Regulations 2003 (SI No. 2498).

Contents

List of Figures	vii
Notes on Contributors	ix
Acknowledgements	xiv
Introduction	1
Sneha Kar Chaudhuri and Ramit Samaddar	
1 *Ankur*: Multiple Narratives of Protest	12
Sarani Ghosal Mondal	
2 *Nishant* and the New Dawn: Towards a Sacerdotal–Secular Modernity?	29
Nikhila H	
3 Churning Out Change: A Moment of Reading *Manthan*	48
Ritu Sen Chaudhuri	
4 Where Labour is Performed: The Public/Private Dichotomy and the Politics of Stigma in *Bhumika* and *Mandi*	64
Suchitra Mathur	
5 Adaptation and Epistemic Redress: The Indian Uprising in *Junoon*	83
Ana Cristina Mendes	
6 Cause and Kin: Knowledge and Nationhood in *Kalyug*	100
Somak Mukherjee	
7 The Ascent in *Arohan*	118
Partha Pratim Sen and Arunima Ray (Chowdhury)	
8 From Fidelity to Creativity: Benegal and *Suraj Ka Satvan Ghoda*	135
Sudha Shastri	
9 *Mammo* and Projections of the Muslim Woman: Indian Parallel Cinema, Partition and Belonging	154
Omar Ahmed	

10	Adapting Gandhi/Kasturba in *The Making of the Mahatma* *Vivek Sachdeva*	171
11	In Search of Zubeidaa *Ramit Samaddar*	185
12	Subversive Heroism and the Politics of Biopic Adaptation in *Bose: The Forgotten Hero* *Sneha Kar Chaudhuri*	196
13	The Rural in the Glocal Intersection: Representation of Space in *Welcome to Sajjanpur* and *Well Done Abba* *Aysha Iqbal Viswamohan and Sayanty Chatterjee*	208
14	Shyam Benegal in Conversation *Anuradha Dingwaney Needham*	223

Index   244

Figures

1.1	The mirror scene	18
1.2	The trial scene (Rajamma before the village council)	19
2.1	The distraught schoolmaster chides the priest for his otherworldly concerns	35
2.2	The climactic moment – a remorseful Susheela and a puzzled Vishwam	40
3.1	Dr Rao surrounded by the sceptic villagers	50
3.2	Bindu and the other women members of the co-operative society	55
4.1	Usha as defined by Brahmanical patriarchy: sexualised performer and stigmatised wife	66
4.2	Caught between stigmatisation and protectionism: sex workers and the discourse of 'social reform' within Brahmanical patriarchy	75
5.1	An exasperated Sarfaraz protests: 'The country is aflame and all he does is fuss over pigeons'	93
5.2	Ruth dreams she is being raped by Javed	94
6.1	Karan looks at the cityscape of Bombay from the balcony of his apartment	109
6.2	The sequence featuring the viewing of the wedding video	114
6.3	Brothers confronted by their mother	116
7.1	Hari and the reluctant Bolai come to Bibhutibhushan for a loan	126
7.2	Schoolmaster Halder Babu leading a procession of All India Kisan Sabha along with Hasan	127
8.1	Jamuna is filled with disgust at the thought of her prospective bridegroom	143
8.2	The visual medium potently suggesting the intimacy between Jamuna and Ramdhan	145

9.1	Mammo recounts her memories of the Partition to Riyaz	161
9.2	Mammo is dragged away by the police	165
9.3	Mammo is deported from India	165
9.4	The final shot of *Mulk*	167
9.5	The final shot of *Mammo*	168
10.1	Gandhi reads out the letter to Kasturba	177
10.2	Kasturba saying to Gandhi, 'Just because I am your wife . . . I have to put up with this non-sense?'	179
11.1	Fayyazi forcibly takes baby Riyaz from a visibly distraught Zubeidaa	188
11.2	Zubeidaa argues with Mandira over royal conventions	192
12.1	Bose in conversation with Gandhi and Nehru after he is elected president in the Tripura Convention, 1939	201
12.2	Bose's interactions with Hitler in Germany as he seeks help against the British in India, 1942	202
12.3	Bose with his wife Emilie and daughter Anita before leaving Germany in 1942	204
13.1	Mahadev reads a letter in the open space under the banyan tree of his rural village	213
13.2	Arman Ali and Muskan sitting on the site of their unbuilt *bavdi*	218
14.1	A scene from *Mandi*	230
14.2	A scene from *Bhumika*	232
14.3	A scene from *The Making of the Mahatma*	238

Notes on Contributors

Omar Ahmed is a UK-based film scholar who has been teaching Film and Media Studies for over thirteen years. He was formerly Head of Film at Aquinas College, Manchester. He is currently completing a PhD at the University of Manchester and was awarded funding by The Arts, Humanities and Research Council (AHRC) in 2015 to focus on the Indian Parallel Cinema movement. He published his first book, *Studying Indian Cinema*, in 2015 and contributed several essays to *The Directory of World Cinema: India* (2015). He wrote the first monograph on *RoboCop* (1987), published in 2018, and is curating a season of Indian independent films titled 'Not Just Bollywood' for HOME in Manchester.

Sayanty Chatterjee graduated in English literature from Bethune College, University of Calcutta, holds an MA in English from Lady Shri Ram College, University of Delhi, and an MPhil in Translation Studies from the University of Hyderabad. Presently, she is enrolled in a PhD programme at the Department of Humanities and Social Sciences in Indian Institute of Technology Madras, India. Her broad research areas consist of popular culture and Indian films. Currently, she is working on the representation of small-town spaces in contemporary popular Hindi films.

Sneha Kar Chaudhuri is Associate Professor of English at West Bengal State University, Kolkata. She holds a BA (English Honours), an MA and a PhD (as UGC-Junior Research Fellow) from the Department of English, Jadavpur University, Kolkata. Editorial board member of the international peer-reviewed journal *Neo-Victorian Studies*, her recent publications include a volume (co-edited with Chandrava Chakravarty) entitled *Tagore's Ideas of the New Woman: The Making and Unmaking of Female Subjectivity* (2017) and a chapter on Tagore's adaptations in *Tagore's Drama in the Perspective of Indian*

Theatre (2020). Her research interests include Neo-Victorian studies, gender studies, adaptation studies, historical fiction and cinema.

Ritu Sen Chaudhuri is Professor and former Head, Department of Sociology, West Bengal State University, Kolkata, India. She received her UGC NET Junior Research Fellow and joined The Centre for Studies in Social Sciences, Calcutta as an ICSSR PhD Research Fellow. She completed her PhD while teaching in the Department of Sociology at Mahishadal Girl's College, Kolkata. She has worked for an India Government AIDS project covering the different red-light areas of Kolkata and its surroundings. She also had a voluntary association with an NGO (Jabala) working with the children of sex workers while completing her masters. She has delivered many lectures at a number of universities and research institutes and presented papers in national and international talks, seminars and conferences. She is a Guest Lecturer at the Women's Studies Research Centre, University of Calcutta; School of Women's Studies, Jadavpur University; Department of Education, University of Calcutta; and the Departments of History and English, West Bengal State University.

Nikhila H is Professor and Head of the Department of Film Studies in the EFL University, Hyderabad, India. She teaches courses and supervises research on the different language cinemas in South India, and on contemporary visual culture. Her areas of research interest are gender and cinema, and various forms of cinematic and intermedial transformations, such as remakes and adaptations.

Suchitra Mathur, Professor of English at Indian Institute of Technology Kanpur, India, works in the areas of feminist studies and cultural studies with a special focus on Indian popular culture. She has published articles on detective fiction, science fiction and graphic narratives as well as Hindi film, where her focus has been on investigating the politics of cross-cultural adaptation from a postcolonial feminist perspective. She is the co-editor of the volume *Reading With a Difference: Gender, Race, and Cultural Identity* (1993).

Ana Cristina Mendes is Assistant Professor of English Studies at the School of Arts and Humanities, University of Lisbon. Her areas of specialisation are cultural and postcolonial studies, with an emphasis on the representations and reception of alterity in the global cultural marketplace. Her latest publications include the co-edited special issue 'New Directions in Rushdie Studies' (2017) of *The Journal of Commonwealth Literature*, articles in *Continuum* and *Journal of Postcolonial Writing*, and the co-edited volume *Transnational Cinema at the Borders* (2018). She serves on the board of the Association of Cultural Studies and is a research affiliate at the Amsterdam Centre for Globalisation Studies (ACGS).

Sarani Ghosal Mondal is Associate Professor of English in the Department of Humanities and Sciences and Dean of Inter-Institutional Relations and Alumni Affairs at the National Institute of Technology, Goa, India. She is the author of *Poetry and Poetics of Walt Whitman and Sri Aurobindo* (2012) and the co-editor of *Indian Responses to Shakespeare* (2017). Her areas of interest are comparative literature, comparative mysticism, applied linguistics and creative writing. She has presented papers on comparative literature and applied linguistics at different universities in India as well as overseas. She has also collaborated in University Grants Commission-funded projects under the scheme of e-Pathshala.

Somak Mukherjee is currently a fifth-year doctoral candidate in the Department of English and Research Fellow at the Global Latinidades Project at the University of California, Santa Barbara. At UCSB, his research focus has been on postcolonial literary studies, environmental media studies, global modernisms, visual culture and urban studies. He is the current holder (2021–2) of the UCSB Interdisciplinary Humanities Center (IHC) Dissertation Research Fellowship. At UCSB he has received the Graduate Division Research Accelerator Award (2020) and the Dean's Prize for Teaching Fellowship (2021–2). His public writings have appeared in leading Indian print and digital platforms, such as *Scroll*, *The Citizen*, *Huffington Post*, *Humanities Underground*, and *Anandabazar Patrika*.

Anuradha Dingwaney Needham is Donald R. Longman Professor of English at Oberlin College. She is the author of *Using the Master's Tools: Resistance and the Literature of the African and South Asian Diasporas* (2000). She is editor, with Carol Maier, of *Between Languages and Cultures: Translation and Cross-cultural Texts* (1996) and more recently, with Rajeswari Sunder Rajan, of *The Crisis of Secularism in India* (2007). She has published on Anglophone literatures of the 'Third World', including the work of writers like Salman Rushdie and Arundhati Roy, on cross-cultural and interdisciplinary pedagogies, and on feminist theory and practice. During her year of Research Leave in 2010–11, she was completing a monograph on a filmmaker associated with New (Parallel or Art) Cinema in India entitled *New Indian Cinema in Post-Independence India: The Cultural Work of Shyam Benegal's Films*, published in 2013. Her teaching interests include: Anglophone Third World literatures; British Romanticism; post-structuralist theory, postcolonial theory and feminist theory. A recent entry in her teaching schedule includes Feminist Research Methodologies for the Gender, Sexuality and Feminist Studies (GSFS) Institute, of which she was the inaugural director, and she is developing a course on Popular Indian Cinema to teach in the near future.

Arunima Ray (Chowdhury) is Associate Professor of History at Vidyanagar College, University of Calcutta, India. She received her BA from Lady Brabourne College, Kolkata and MA from the University of Calcutta. She also received her MPhil and PhD degrees from University of Calcutta. Her areas of interests include socialism in India, international relations and American history. She received grants for minor research projects from the University Grants Commission (UGC), India, twice for her works on (a) socialism and its influence on Indian literature, and (b) the Islamic state and society in fifteenth- and early sixteenth-century Bengal. Her recent publications include *Socialist Thought and the Indian Intellect: Bengal in the First Half of the 20th Century* (2018).

Vivek Sachdeva is Professor of English, Guru Gobind Singh Indraprastha University, New Delhi, India. He was formerly Lecturer in English, B.P.S. Mahila Vishwavdyalaya, Khanpur Kalan, Sonepat, Haryana and Lecturer in English, D.A.V. College, Amritsar, Punjab. His book *Fiction to Film: Ruth Prawer Jhabvala's The Householder and Heat and Dust* was published in 2017. He has also translated two books of Hindi poetry into English and is presently translating Punjabi poetry into English. He has published several articles on the films of Shyam Benegal and is now working on a project exploring Benegal's cinematic representation of India in postcolonial times.

Ramit Samaddar is Assistant Professor of English at Jadavpur University, Kolkata. He received his BA (Honours), MA, MPhil, and PhD degrees in English from the same university. His areas of research interest are Romanticism, Victorian studies, travel writing, Hindi literature, and Bollywood cinema. His publications include a co-authored chapter on Bollywood war films in *A Companion to the War Film* (2016) and an entry on Charles Reade in *Companion to Victorian Popular Fiction* (2018).

Partha Pratim Sen is Associate Professor of Political Science at Vidyanagar College, University of Calcutta, India. He did his PhD on West Bengal politics at the Department of International Relations, Jadavpur University, Kolkata, India. His areas of interests include Bengal politics, security studies and international relations. He has completed a research project on 'suicide terrorism' funded by the University Grants Commission (UGC), India. His recent publications include *Terrorists' World* (2014) and *M. N. Roy: Ideas, Practices and Possibilities in Indian Politics* (2017), both of which he co-edited.

Sudha Shastri is Professor of English in the Department of Humanities and Social Sciences, Indian Institute of Technology Bombay, India. Her teaching and research interests lie in the areas of intertextuality, narratives, Shakespeare, Indian writing, and film. Her doctoral dissertation, *Intertextuality and Victorian*

Studies, was published by Orient Longman in 2001; and an edited volume of the refereed conference that she organised was published by Orient Blackswan in 2015 as *Disnarration: The Unsaid Matters*. She has presented papers at several national and international conferences and published articles in journals and chapters in books. She is a two-time recipient of Indian Institute of Technology Bombay's *Excellence in Teaching* Award, and her talk on 'Why Read Literature' can be viewed on YouTube.

Aysha Iqbal Viswamohan works as Professor at the Department of Humanities and Social Sciences, Indian Institute of Technology Madras, India. Her areas of research interest are drama, film studies and popular culture. She has a PhD in American drama. She has an MPhil and Post Graduate Diploma in Teaching English from EFL University, Hyderabad (India). She was the recipient of Canadian Faculty Enrichment Programme Grant in 2009 and spent some time at Simon Fraser University Vancouver, Canada researching in the field of film studies. In 2010, she carried out a research project on cinema for societal benefits with Simon Fraser University through the Partnership Development Seed Grant. In 2012, she was invited to give a series of lectures at Simon Fraser University on Hindi cinema. She has published widely in a number of peer-reviewed international journals such as *ELT J*, Oxford, *English Today*, *South Asian Review*, *Studies in Theatre & Performance* and *South Asian Popular Culture*. Her books include *Post-liberalization Indian Novels in English* (2013) and *Behind the Scenes: Contemporary Bollywood Directors* (2017).

Acknowledgements

Working on this book project has been a most fulfilling research experience for both of us in the past few years. There are many people whom we would like to take the opportunity to thank. When we conceived of this edited volume, we approached many scholars working in film studies to write for us and also posted a call for papers at the University of Pennsylvania website. The support and response we received were very encouraging.

We have a long list of people to thank and we begin with by thanking our series editors Robert Singer, Gary Rhodes and Stefanie Van de Peer, particularly Robert, who had all the timely suggestions and advice ready for us and always gave us unflinching support and kind encouragement. Without their faith in us, this work would not have been possible.

Then, we would extend our cordial thanks to the great maestro himself, Shyam Benegal, who has given his valuable interview for this book. A special thanks to Anuradha Needham for arranging this special interview.

We would also like to thank all our contributors for their perseverance and effort in framing the various drafts of their chapters and providing us with necessary inputs from time to time to improve the same. The final version of the volume would not have been possible without their relentless effort and sense of goodwill towards us. In this regard, the comments and suggestions of our readers and endorsers – Aparna Sharma, Meenakshi Bharat and Noel Brown – have been most useful and indispensable. Thank you to Shohini Chaudhuri for giving us some important suggestions at the beginning of the project.

A special thanks is due to our young proofreader, Aldish Edroos, who showed a lot of patience and enthusiasm in helping us to prepare the final draft. Our sincere thanks go to the former Commissioning Editor at EUP,

Richard Strachan, and the current Commissioning Editors, Sam Johnson and Gillian Leslie, for helping us with great warmth and sincerity. Many thanks to the entire production team at EUP.

Finally, we would also like to thank our parents for providing us with all the love, affection and support we needed in putting together such an ambitious volume. This book is sincerely dedicated to them.

Sneha Kar Chaudhuri
Ramit Samaddar
January 2022

Introduction

Sneha Kar Chaudhuri and Ramit Samaddar

Shyam Benegal is universally perceived as one of the most influential filmmakers from modern India. Yet his voluminous body of work remains relatively understudied in contemporary film scholarship. To help fill this critical lacuna, *The Films of Shyam Benegal* undertakes a closer look at the oeuvre of Benegal, a trailblazing auteur who has successfully redefined the contours of non-commercial Hindi-language cinema. This addition to the *ReFocus* series on international directors considers how Benegal, in the course of a scintillating career spanning over forty years, has made use of cinema as a powerful medium to faithfully narrate the story of a nation in a state of perennial transition. While Benegal's peers, the makers of *masala*[1] potboilers, have created rosy images of India, airbrushing the not-so-pleasant realities of post-Independence[2] life, Benegal has unflinchingly drawn attention to the same with the aim of raising the moral consciousness of the viewer. In fact, it would not be wrong to assert that always looming over Benegal's mind has been the inescapable presence of popular cinema, against which his alternative cinema could be said to have presented itself. For instance, as his debut feature *Ankur* (*The Seedling*) was being filmed in 1973, the lush romance *Bobby*, helmed by Raj Kapoor, widely regarded as the greatest showman in the annals of the Indian entertainment industry, appeared on celluloid and took the country by storm. In 1973 India also witnessed the release of Prakash Mehra's *Zanjeer* (*Shackles*), a crme-action drama that marked the introduction of the iconic Amitabh Bachchan as the angry young man and which turned out to be a blockbuster. Both *Bobby* and *Zanjeer* offer striking contrasts to *Ankur* and work as apt examples of the kind of cinema in opposition to which Benegal envisioned his own. As he himself candidly declares, '[t]he existing formal style of [movie making] was not suitable – I had no wish to work on design-made films.'[3] According to Benegal, these 'design-made films' were:

> A kind of Procrustean bed that shaped its content to fit its form. On the one hand it had the magpie-like ability to accumulate a great deal of variety to the entertainment it offered, but on the other hand the compulsion to picturize songs and dances in every film tended to circumscribe the subject matter of the films themselves. Often this form was a hindrance to cinematic self-expression.[4]

Small wonder, then, that Benegal spiritedly championed what is now hailed as parallel cinema, celebrated for its serious socio-political content, realistic aesthetic, and repudiation of clichéd song-and-dance sequences that typify mainstream Hindi movies (although a few Benegal films do contain creative continuities with mainstream films, two examples being the 1996 *Sardari Begum* and the 2001 *Zubeidaa*, which have mellifluous yet meaningful songs well-integrated into their plots). The fourteen chapters in the present collection are sincere tributes to Benegal's contribution to parallel cinema – a genre that has effectively painted a compelling and vivid portrait of India. The films considered in these chapters have unquestionably shaped the parameters of good cinema and moulded the way educated Indian audiences learned to look at life. In addition to these chapters, the book contains a full-length interview with the director himself that brings out his perspectives on the art of filmmaking. This is the first edited volume on Shyam Babu (as he is lovingly addressed by his admirers) and it showcases the wide array of thought-provoking contexts in which his films, surprising in their variety, can be examined.

Benegal was born on 14 December 1934 in Trimulgherry, then a British cantonment town about 15 km from Hyderabad, India. Belonging to a lower middle-class, but progressive Saraswat Brahmin[5] household, Benegal has been familiar with the magic world of images since his early days. His Gandhian father, Shridhar Benegal, was a professional photographer who had a knack for filming his children – he had ten – with his 16mm Paillard Bolex. He made films at festivals, fairs, picnics and army parades, which he would often screen on his three-gauge projector for his large family. These rudimentary homemade films were part and parcel of young Benegal's merriment. Benegal started school shortly after the breakout of the Second World War. He went to Mahbub College High School and matriculated from there in 1951. One of his uncles, Benegal Dinkar Rao, was a formative influence on Benegal during this time. Rao would often take Benegal and his brother Sadanand to watch Hollywood films at the Garrison, a nearby theatre. Afterwards, Benegal and his brother managed to befriend the Garrison projectionist and watched many films there. Here Benegal discovered cinematic legends such as Tyrone Power, Errol Flynn, William Wyler, Billy Wilder and

John Huston. So great was the impact of the audio-visual medium on Benegal that at the mere age of twelve, he made a film, *Chuttiyon Mein Mouj Mazha (Fun in the Holidays)*, with his father's cherished 16mm camera. As per Benegal,

> It had all sorts of little trick things. Train arrives at platform, all my cousins getting off the train, and then the train would go in reverse. The story very simple, the cousins go for a picnic, one child gets lost and we go seeking the lost child. That was basically the story of the film. This was seen by the family.[6]

From Mahbub College High School, Benegal went to study Economics at the renowned Nizam's College, Osmania University, where he established the Hyderabad Film Society. During these college years, Benegal followed the illustrious career of his director-producer-actor cousin, Guru Dutt, who dominated the 1950s Bombay (Mumbai) film industry with classics like *Mr. and Mrs. '55* (1955), *Pyaasa* (*Thirsty*, 1957), and *Kaagaz Ke Phool* (*Paper Flowers*, 1959):

> My cousin Guru Dutt was making films in Bombay. But I didn't know how I could start with my films. I didn't have enough money to travel to Bombay. So when I finished college I taught for a while. I was given a one-way third-class ticket to Bombay by a friend, whose brother worked in the Indian railways. This was the end of 1958, and I was looking for work in Bombay. Guru Dutt asked me to join his directorial department as his assistant, but that did not interest me. Luckily I found a job as a copywriter within three days![7]

In Bombay, Benegal joined Lintas, a posh advertising agency, as a copywriter for six months and then moved to its film department where he wrote scripts and made short films. By 1959, he had 150 such films to his credit, each characterised by a remarkable economy of expression. When he left advertising, Benegal had already made more than 1,000 films. In 1962, he received a lucrative offer to direct a Gujarat documentary about the Mahi Dam project. This marked a new innings in Benegal's life as he started making documentaries. One of his initial documentaries, *Child of the Streets* (1967), was seen by the French auteur Louis Malle and won him wide praise. His later documentaries, *Nehru* (1983) and *Satyajit Ray* (1984), both critical triumphs, are testimonies of his abiding love for the craft of documentary making. Benegal taught mass-communication skills between 1966 and 1973 at Bhavan's college in Bombay. Between 1970 and 1972, he learnt about children's television under the Homi Bhabha Fellowship and also worked with WGB Boston in the United States.

In 1975, Benegal made his own children's film, *Charandas Chor (Charandas, the Thief)*, which was produced by the Indian Children's Film Society.

A year before *Charandas Chor*, *Ankur* was released and immediately came to be recognised as a consummate example of parallel cinema, winning three National Film Awards[8] and a coveted Golden Bear nomination at the 24th Berlin International Film Festival. The Government of India bestowed two of its most prestigious awards on Benegal – the Padma Shri in 1976 and the Padma Bhushan in 1991. Benegal made some phenomenal 'new Indian cinema' in the 1970s and films like *Nishant* (*Night's End*, 1975), *Manthan* (*The Churning*, 1976) and *Bhumika* (*The Role*, 1977) all belong to this category of realistic films that were exposing and critiquing the various aspects of social, economic, political and patriarchal oppression in India. By the 1980s the popularity of this kind of cinema had subsided a little, but Benegal continued to make intellectually stimulating, independent films like *Junoon* (*The Obsession*, 1979), *Kalyug* (*The Mechanical Age*, 1981), *Mandi* (*Market Place*, 1983) and *Trikal* (*Past, Present and Future*, 1985). These were backed by actors and producers who had a great amount of respect for Benegal's brand of filmmaking. In the 1990s, he directed four of his most outstanding films – *Suraj Ka Satvan Ghoda* (*The Sun's Seventh Horse*, 1992), *Mammo* (1994), *Sardari Begum* (1996) and *The Making of the Mahatma* (1996). These were followed by the spectacular biopics *Zubeidaa* (2001) and *Bose: The Forgotten Hero* (2005) in the new millennium. At the end of this decade his two very powerful social satires based on the village community were released: *Welcome to Sajjanpur* (2008) and *Well Done Abba* (*Well Done Father*, 2009). Benegal's work on the small screen is as impressive as on the big screen. *Yatra* (*Travel*, 1986) is a fifteen-part serial filmed on the Himsagar Express, the longest-running train of Indian Railways. *Katha Sagar* (*A Sea of Stories*, 1986–91) is a series featuring stories by writers from around the world that aired on Doordarshan, India's state-owned television network. However, Benegal's masterpiece on television is *Bharat Ek Khoj*, a fifty-three-episode drama modelled on the book *The Discovery of India* (1946) by Jawaharlal Nehru, the first Prime Minister of India, which traces the long history of the country from its beginnings to its independence from the British in 1947. It has been said that 'Benegal has arguably made movies enough to retire on'. However, it seems he is not quite ready, and 'is now hard at work on his latest project, a biopic of Bangladesh's first president Sheikh Mujibur Rahman, *Bangabandhu*'.[9] Indeed, in a recent interview with Benegal we have learnt about this latest project. What is more, Benegal has emphatically added that *Bangabandhu* is hardly a final project. 'As long as I can keep reasonable health and my mind is also capable, I will keep making films.'[10]

What is noteworthy about these against-the-grain films is how the narratives are rendered authentic through Benegal's masterly delineation of the complex relationships between the characters and their environments. These films indisputably cement Benegal's reputation as an ace storyteller as well as a perceptive interpreter of the Indian milieu, a milieu caught in a state of constant flux. What is also noteworthy about these films is the fact that they feature eminent dramatic actors who breathe life into their author-backed roles through their naturalised style of acting. Gifted with an unerring casting eye, Benegal has discovered Shabana Azmi, Smita Patil, Naseeruddin Shah and Om Puri – the four acting pillars of parallel cinema – and introduced them to Hindi filmdom. These thespians appeared and reappeared in his productions, demonstrating their strengths as credible performers. About him Om Puri had said: 'Shyam is not just a feature film-maker, he is an activist with films on various subjects, always trying to tell a story, using narrative devices to underscore an issue.'[11] Girish Karnad, who starred in *Nishant* and *Manthan*, said:

> Shyam has a great casting eye, a terrific feel for the role and the actor. Once he accepted you in the team – he kept the team going, we were tied by a feeling of loyalty to him. Shyam had this great father feeling about his unit – he would be the father confessor, talk to all the unit members about their lives. One of the reasons why Shabana and Smita never got along was that both of them were in love with him – I mean as a father figure, not as a lover figure.[12]

What easily transpires from Karnad's unvarnished opinions is that one of the strongest points of Benegal as a filmmaker is his aptitude to handpick talented actors and keep them in a repertory of films, while maintaining the democratic spirit of the unit. What Govind Nihalani, Benegal's favourite cinematographer, said about him is equally significant and worth quoting in some detail:

> A fine combination of passion and the cerebral, he is one director who struck a balance between personal experience and ideology in his films. Shyam's contribution has been immense, he . . . did not succumb to mainstream formula, gave viewers an intelligent choice of films, also proved that art films can be economically viable.[13]

Despite his four-decade-long career and immense popularity both in India and overseas, only two book-length studies of Benegal have appeared thus far: Sangeeta Datta's *Shyam Benegal* (2002) and Anuradha Dingwaney Needham's *New Indian Cinema in Post-Independence India: The Cultural Work of Shyam Benegal's Films* (2013). Datta's book, the first Benegal-centric study, is essentially a rather simple journalistic introduction to the filmmaker, offering an elementary account of his life, his association with parallel cinema, and potted summaries of his films. *The Films of Shyam Benegal* has undertaken a rigorous scholarly approach, moving away from the traditional biographical thrust that characterises Datta's monograph so as to include fresh appraisals of Benegal's films from a range of diverse academic perspectives such as caste politics, labour studies, historiography, Marxism, gender criticism, adaptation studies and space theory. Needham's well-researched monograph teases out the cultural contexts of Benegal's films, but the main focus of the book remains the auteur's well-known films, and the volume makes no sustained engagement with his lesser-known cinematic ventures. Needham refrains from assessing the pertinent issues addressed in Benegal's 'minor' but significant films such as *Kalyug*, *Arohan (The Ascent)*, and *Suraj Ka Satvan Ghoda*; issues which will be discussed at length by the chapters in this volume. It is for these reasons that *The Films of Shyam Benegal* will have a competitive edge over Needham's work. Apart from the monographs of Datta and Needham, there exists a series of interviews of Benegal conducted by William Van der Heide in *Bollywood Babylon: Interviews with Shyam Benegal* (2006). The book contains extensive and detailed interviews with the master filmmaker under various thematic concerns and covers his views on his own films from *Ankur* to *Zubeidaa*. It has specific sets of interactions with Benegal on Indian cinema, Satyajit Ray, and Benegal's own films. The present volume contains an interview with Benegal by Anuradha Needham and focuses on issues left uncovered by Heide's book, especially Benegal's relation with commercial Bollywood and his films after *Zubeidaa*. The questions have been posed keeping in mind the focus of the chapters. Most recent books on Benegal and his cinema in the vernacular include Arun Kumar's *Shyam Benegal: Bharatiya Samvednaon Aur Adhikaron Ka Cinema* (Jaipur: Sahityagar, 2017) and Pramod Kumar Barnwal's *Shyam Benegal Aur Samantar Cinema* (Ghaziabad: Antika Prakashan, 2019). These might have failed to reach a global critical audience but nevertheless outline Benegal's unique contribution to parallel cinema in India and the rich humanitarian content of his films. The most recent book on Benegal, Vivek Sachdeva's *Benegal's India*, published in January 2020 by Routledge, is an ambitious attempt to address the nuanced and multifaceted representation of India in Benegal's cinema. It is significant to note what Sachdeva has said about Benegal's representation of India:

> Instead of presenting a romanticised image of the nation, he has looked at India as a nation from the point of view of the minorities, downtrodden and the under-privileged. The cultural and historical significance of his work lies in the fact that through his oeuvre one can also peep into issues troubling India at different periods of time.[14]

Samir Chopra's *Shyam Benegal: Filmmaker and Philosopher* (London: Bloomsbury Academic, 2020) also tries to do justice to Benegal's complex filmography with an emphasis on his guiding ideologies and philosophical outlook towards the interface of cinema and life.

INTRODUCTION 7

The aim of this *ReFocus* volume is to critically evaluate the eclectic films of one of post-Independence India's most feted directors. Given the sheer enormity of Benegal's oeuvre, the book has attempted to be as representative as possible in its scope by choosing to examine the auteur's 'major' as well as 'minor' cinematic ventures. This collection has chapters on Benegal's award-winning films, such as *Ankur*, *Nishant*, and *Manthan*, all credited for their hard-hitting portrayal of grass-roots problems in rural India, especially Benegal's engagement with poverty, caste discrimination and sexual exploitation. The book also has insightful chapters on Benegal's representations of the nation's past in *Junoon*, *Kalyug*, and *Trikal*. Benegal's fascinating renditions of complex female subjectivities in films such as *Bhumika* and *Mandi* and in his trilogy on Muslim women – *Mammo*, *Sardari Begum*, and *Zubeidaa* – will be explored in detail. The collection also offers contributions on Benegal's biopics on Mahatma Gandhi and Subhas Chandra Bose, which illustrate how Benegal has revised the lives of these legendary political leaders. Analyses of lesser-known but pivotal films, namely *Arohan* and *Suraj Ka Satvan Ghoda*, as well as Benegal's recent directorial endeavours *Welcome to Sajjanpur* and *Well Done Abba*, also fall under the purview of this volume. In addition to studying these seventeen films, the book features an interview with Benegal. As far as critical approach is concerned, each chapter defines the theoretical and contextual frameworks with which it has worked and applied closely in its film analysis. A rigorous effort has been made by the contributors to implement the tools and methodologies currently in use within film studies so as to make certain that discussions of Benegal are not merely limited to narrative and film content. The worth of a volume such as *The Films of Shyam Benegal* is immense, for an English-language assessment will invariably make the postcolonial filmmaker and his impressive body of work available to an international readership.

In Chapter 1, '*Ankur*: Multiple Narratives of Protest', Sarani Ghosal Mondal focuses on Benegal's first feature film *Ankur* (1974) and discusses the need to protest against oppression and to register protest on various levels, vocal and silent, explicit and symbolic, and at every level in society against injustice and oppression. This chapter looks at the diverse forms of protest that Benegal weaves into his narrative about southern India's victimised subalterns, particularly focusing on the position of subaltern women, their sufferings and struggle. In Chapter 2, '*Nishant* and the New Dawn: Towards a Sacerdotal–Secular Modernity?', Nikhila H argues that *Nishant* (1975) can be interpreted as the saga of the end of feudalism, an order that is characterised as expropriating the labour and enslaving the bodies of the toiling peasant classes. Thus, when the labouring classes rise in rebellion and kill the landlord and his family in *Nishant*, their deaths symbolically mark the end of the dark feudal night. But, *Nishant* also appears interesting for the way in which the new dawn is brought about: a dawn where the sacerdotal and the secular needs buttress and aid each other. With this backdrop, the two questions that this chapter addresses are: (1) does the critique of feudalism from the position of modernity re-inscribe the sacerdotal, and thereby work to reinstate caste?; and (2) how much of the anxiety surrounding the figure of the upper-caste woman who (forcibly or by volition) cohabits with a lower-caste man comes from the contemporary theatre of the time, where such scenarios of female crossovers and transgressions of caste boundaries were being staged? (This latter question is pertinent since Vijay Tendulkar, a leading Indian playwright with liberal leanings, wrote the original screenplay of *Nishant*). In Chapter 3, 'Churning Out Change: A Moment of Reading *Manthan*', Ritu Sen Chaudhuri explores Benegal's engagement with the idea of social change as represented in *Manthan* (1976), a film set around a milk-producing village in Gujarat, India. It also traces the politically charged message of change in *Manthan*. The chapter also explores the ways in which the film creates mass awareness about the changing face of rural India grappling with the often contradictory claims of tradition and modernity. In Chapter 4, 'Where Labour is Performed: The Public/Private Dichotomy and the Politics of Stigma in *Bhumika* and *Mandi*', Suchitra Mathur uses this intersectional framework to study Shyam Benegal's *Bhumika* (1977) and *Mandi* (1983), both of which deal with women's performance of stigmatised labour in the public marketplace. While *Bhumika*, through its exploration of the personal life of an actress, foregrounds the public–private dichotomy in the relationship between 'work' and 'respectability', *Mandi*, with its focus on a house of prostitutes, problematises the very distinction between domestic space and the 'public' marketplace in the performance of sexual labour. This chapter will attempt to look at these issues through an analysis of the political economy that structure and shape the performance of labour in the two films.

Chapter 5, 'Adaptation and Epistemic Redress: The Indian Uprising in *Junoon*', by Ana Cristina Mendes, discusses, using various theoretical approaches from adaptation and Neo-Victorian studies, Benegal's screen adaptation of Ruskin Bond's novella *A Flight of Pigeons* (1978) by particularly focusing on issues of trauma, historical memory and transmedial adaptation concerning the content and form of the film, respectively. In Chapter 6, 'Cause and Kin: Knowledge and Nationhood in *Kalyug*', Somak Mukherjee looks at the use of the epic plot and narrative strategies in *Kalyug*, a modern-day *Mahabharata* which tries to negotiate with the challenges of corporate modernisation and the traditional structures of societal and familial kinship in Indian society. In Chapter 7, 'Decoding the Political Spectrum of *Arohan/ The Ascent*', Partha Pratim Sen and Arunima Ray broadly examine the ways in which Benegal's early films consciously engaged with urgent political matters, such as class struggle. The chapter critically discusses *Arohan* (1982) as one such filmic experiment in which Benegal faithfully documents the triumph of class struggle, assisted by a state government committed to Marxist–Leninist ideology. Sudha Shastri in Chapter 8, 'From Fidelity to Creativity: Benegal and *Suraj Ka Satvan Ghoda*', examines Benegal's adaptation of Dharamvir Bharti's *Suraj Ka Satvan Ghoda* (first published 1952) into a film (2001), focusing primarily on the changes that the film has made to the story and investigating the outcomes of these changes. The novel, which predates the film by almost half a century, was hailed for its technical experimentation and inventiveness, in which a narrator seemingly tells the story of three women he has known, but which may well be the same story told three times, from three different entry-points into the narrative. In light of this being an adaptation, the focus of the chapter is on the ways in which the film is mindful of its medium while addressing and developing the themes and techniques of representation deployed by the book.

Chapter 9, Omar Ahmed's '*Mammo* and Projections of the Muslim Woman: Indian Parallel Cinema, Partition and Belonging', critically discusses Benegal's *Mammo* (1994), the first film in his 1990s trilogy on Muslim identity in a post-secular India, and explores the ways in which the film mourns the demise of secularism, functioning as a site of grief and loss in a transmuting Indian society and how this resonates with Benegal's authorial concerns. This is followed by a reading of how the secularist address is problematised, returning to the lingering memories of Partition in the 1970s, demonstrating how and why the film re-enacts the trauma/wounds of Partition. In Chapter 10, 'Adapting Gandhi/Kasturba in *The Making of the Mahatma*', Vivek Sachdeva discusses how the critical tools and strategies of adaptation studies can be deployed to study this biopic. Sachdeva also sees the film as a strong narrative about the apparently docile yet firm and assertive presence of Gandhi's wife, Kasturba Gandhi, making this biopic a film about the contradictions of female empowerment and the assertion of the self.

Chapter 11, 'In Search of Zubeidaa', by Ramit Samaddar, explores Shyam Benegal's portrayal of the free-spirited and beautiful Zubeidaa who remains an enigmatic and elusive character trying to figure out her individuality in a patriarchal world. It is also the third and most powerful instalment of his celebrated trilogy on Muslim women. Chapter 12, 'Subversive Heroism and the Politics of Biopic Adaptation in *Bose: The Forgotten Hero*', by Sneha Kar Chaudhuri, analyses Benegal's *Bose: The Forgotten Hero* (2005) as a celluloid tribute to one of the most controversial political leaders of India during the fight for independence against the British in the 1940s. It foregrounds the qualities of leadership, courage, honesty and wisdom in Subhas Chandra Bose's character and tries to create a space for him in the popular imagination. This chapter thoroughly critiques how Benegal appropriates the tropes and conventions of political celebrity biopics in Indian cinema to make a film that highlights the goodness of Bose even as a subversive hero who challenges the British by creating his own army, the Indian National Army. It uses the theoretical dimensions of biopic adaptations articulated by adaptation studies critics and critically analyses Benegal's cinematic attempts to salvage Bose's ambiguous political image. In Chapter 13, 'The Rural in the Glocal Intersection: Representation of Space in *Welcome to Sajjanpur* and *Well Done Abba*', Aysha Iqbal Viswamohan and Sayanty Chatterjee examine the production of a social space as it is closely intertwined with topographical and political space in the satiric films *Welcome to Sajjanpur* (2008) and *Well Done Abba* (2009). Here, Benegal paints a picture of two fictional villages, Sajjanpur and Chikatpally respectively, as they constantly negotiate their terms with globalisation. The interpenetration of the global and the local renders a peculiar shape to the representation of the rural areas as depicted in these two films. Finally, there is an expansive and authoritative interview with the great maestro himself, as conducted meticulously by Anuradha Needham, which throws fresh light on his life and works.

Noted film critic Saibal Chatterjee is of opinion that

> It's easy to write off his kind of films in these profit-driven times, but the very fact that Benegal, as active as he has ever been in his career, continues to project his humanist, socially informed vision on the big screen – and on his own terms at that – is cause enough for unstinted applause.[15]

Benegal has continued to critique Indian socio-political, economic and cultural realities at the intersection of tradition and modernity and has produced a consistently good and substantial body of work to challenge the clichés and stereotypes of mainstream commercial Hindi cinema. Benegal himself has firmly asserted that '[O]ne has to find a way to be seen and heard with the kind of film one makes.'[16] This book is a critical tribute to his kind of cinema, one that has established his uniqueness as a director, visionary and thinker.

NOTES

1. *Masala* films are those films that freely amalgamate action, comedy, romance and melo/drama. This distinct genre of Indian cinema derives its name from *masala*, a mixture of spices in Indian cuisine.
2. On 15 August 1947, India became an independent country, freeing itself from 200 years of British rule.
3. Sangeeta Datta, *Shyam Benegal* (New Delhi: Roli Books, 2008), 3.
4. Shyam Benegal, 'Making Movies in Mumbai', in *Bollywood: Popular Indian Cinema*, ed. Lalit Mohan Joshi (London: Dakini, 2001), 202.
5. Saraswat Brahmins are upper-caste Hindus of India who claim their ancestry to the banks of the ancient Sarasvati river.
6. Datta, 54.
7. Ibid., 58.
8. The National Film Awards is the most prestigious film award ceremony in India.

9. Nandini Ramnath, 'Why Filmmaking for Shyam Benegal is both "a microscope and a Telescope"', accessed 1 September 2021, <https://scroll.in/reel/1004175/interview-why-filmmaking-for-shyam-benegal-is-both-a-microscope-and-a-telescope>
10. Ibid.
11. Cited in Datta, 241–2.
12. Datta, 74.
13. Cited in Datta, 239.
14. Vivek Sachdeva, *Shyam Benegal's India: Alternative Images* (London: Routledge, 2020), 22.
15. Saibal Chatterjee, 'An Indian *Samar*', *Outlook*, 23 August 1999, 58.
16. Cited in Datta, 45.

CHAPTER 1

Ankur: Multiple Narratives of Protest

Sarani Ghosal Mondal

Shyam Benegal's *Ankur* (*The Seedling*, 1974) marks the arrival of 'alternative cinema' or 'parallel cinema' in India. The wave of such films was an initiative taken by the Film Finance Corporation (FFC). The body was formed in 1969 with the objective of promoting national culture, education and a healthy entertainment by offering loans for offbeat films.[1] However, Benegal's *Ankur* was not financed by FFC. The first two of his films were financed by Blaze Advertising Agency, for which he had already made a good number of commercials. His experience in the field of advertising films had taught him the lesson of economy of expression and that made him stand apart from his contemporary filmmakers in Bombay. Right from the beginning, Benegal wished to make films rooted in the 'regional-nationalist' spirit.[2] He had composed the short-story version of *Ankur* more than a decade earlier, when his cousin Guru Dutt had been a prominent director in Bollywood with a string of commercially successful films. Sangeeta Datta, in her book *Shyam Benegal*, selects an excerpt from Benegal's interview, where the filmmaker reveals his intention with a gesture of candour:

> Connect film making to the environment in which you lived. I felt we should make films that are closer to our sense of reality, closer to the Indian experience, closer to the kind of lives we lead. Both advertising and film have everything to do with communication . . . a film according to me, must provide an artistic experience to the audience and have a kind of social communication . . . which gives an insight into life . . .[3]

Benegal justifies his claim in the first three of his films, which are considered to be the 'emblematic trilogy' of new cinema in India.[4] These three films project the exploitation of villagers in a feudal socio-political set-up with an emerging conflict between tradition and modernity. In each of the three films, the entry of a city-bred educated protagonist poses a threat to the age-old system, and especially in *Ankur* the lure of modernity makes the plot more complicated than in that of *Nishant* (*Night's End*, 1975) and *Manthan* (*The Churning*, 1976), as the metaphor of modernity problematises the plot by negotiating with the patriarchal ideology of feudalism.

M. Madhava Prasad in his book *Ideology of the Hindi Film* refers to Aruna Vasudev claiming that before *Ankur*, 'new modes of perception and technique for both film makers and audience were still hazy and barely formulated. In the context of its time *Ankur* was a major step.'[5] Following its realist aesthetics, the film is set against the backdrop of peasant unrest in southeast India, especially in the Telangana region. To many viewers, the film reveals a strong influence of Satyajit Ray's neo-realism in its use of the outdoor location, available light and amateur actors.[6] The majority of contemporary filmmakers of parallel cinema preferred outdoor locales over the studio. Girish Karnad explains this motive as a 'ruralist drive', which portrays the image of real India after Independence. He also adds that this drive reduced the budget, as crowd scenes were made without any expenditure.[7] It is difficult to accept Karnad's argument with regard to the budget issue as Benegal's objective was to make the film look real and to address the populist issues, as well as to bring it 'closer to our sense of reality'. Benegal's approach comes very close to that of André Bazin, Siegfried Kracauer, Cesare Zavattini and others of the realist school of film theory. Critic James Dudley Andrew in his book on film theories quotes Bazin's proclamation on the realistic film, 'Cinema attains its fullness in being the art of the real.'[8] According to Andrew, realist filmmakers depend on the material world and record the visible reality. Reality appears to them as raw material, which is photographed and then shown on celluloid. Here, we have to remember that we see the tracings left by reality or the duplicate version of visible reality on the screen and that visible reality takes the shape of montage after the editing and manipulation by the filmmaker as per the demands of the script.[9] Robert Stam in his book *Film Theory: An Introduction* also argues in line with Andrew:

> Against those like the Formalists, who saw art as inescapably conventional and inherently different from life, Zavattini called for annihilating the distance between art and life. The point was not to invent stories which resembled reality, but rather reality into a story. The goal was a cinema without apparent mediation, where facts dictated form, and events seemed to recount themselves . . . Zavattini also called for a democratization of the cinema, both in terms of its human subjects and in terms of what kinds of events were worth

talking about . . . Indeed, the cinema made it possible for ordinary people to know about each other's lives, not in the name of voyeurism but in the name of solidarity.[10]

Benegal, like Bazin, Kracauer and Zavattini, relied very much on reality as raw material and shot his film in a remote village with available ambient light and sound. The striking aspects of his technique are the ethnographic details such as the landscape, dress code, rituals, rustic folk music and the Dakhni dialect, all of which are region specific. The aptness of such usage of *mise-en-scène* creates the realist aesthetics of *Ankur*. This also indicates the influence of Italian neo-realism on the filmmaker. The trend had begun with Bimal Roy and Satyajit Ray in India. Later, Benegal adopted this trend and successfully exploited it in his first three films.

Nehru formed his government in 1952, the first International Film Festival was held in Bombay, Madras and Calcutta by the Films Division . . . The films of Vittorio De Sica made a tremendous impact, and neo-realism had a lasting influence on Indian film-makers.[11]

Followers of Italian neo-realism had always preferred the outdoor location over the studio. Cuban filmmaker Walfredo Piñera once remarked that the most famous films in the world were being made in the streets.[12] Benegal's *Ankur* may also be termed third-world cinema, as the objective of the third-world cinema, according to Robert Stam, is to express 'national themes in a national style'.[13] It is surprising that many critics find third-world cinema too propagandist to be termed universal, since it addresses local issues.

Ankur's opening scene begins with a combination of extreme long and long shots showing a procession of men and women, especially the village folk, walking across the arid undulating land towards a temple. Such shots had been used in classical Western films. Lakshmi, the central character of the film, prays to the goddess for a child. The barren and stony landscape exemplifies her agony of not having an offspring, which is more acute than her poverty. She prays, 'Mother, I do not want anything; just a child' ('*Mereko kuchh nahin hona, bas ek bachha hona*'). After this, the camera focuses closely on the grief-stricken face of Kishtaya, the deaf and mute husband, as if Lakshmi's desire for motherhood will be fulfilled by him. Critic M. K. Raghavendra in an essay in his book *50 Indian Film Classics* makes a controversial comment on Lakshmi that she is a 'strikingly beautiful woman'. At another place in the same essay he says, 'casting Shabana Azmi as Lakshmi is perhaps a mistake because she stands out amid others and it is difficult to accept her as belonging to the class that she is meant to represent'.[14] This view is not really acceptable as it refers to the politics of Brahmanical patriarchy, which discriminates and oppresses Dalit women on the basis of gender, caste and class. Caste and class do not determine one's looks. Benegal's *Ankur* thoroughly projects the issue of manifold exploitation: caste, gender, sexual and psychological. At the same time, it also constructs a metaphor of protest from the feminist standpoint.

There is now a shift from the arid pasture of the country to the city and the spectators are introduced to Surya, the son of the landlord, who has just completed his education in the city. He returns to the village after his examination and the plot moves forward with the dichotomy of country and city; the feudal tradition and modernity. This further augments the director's liberal humanist approach. With the forward movement of the plot, the characters voice their opinions in their individualistic ways.

Meanwhile, the spectators are guided to the interior of the feudal manor, where the presence of Kaushalya, the mistress of the landlord, and her illegitimate son, along with the family members of the *zamindar* (feudal landlord), represents the first instance of transgression of the societal codes. Kaushalya is not ashamed of her illegitimate liaison. Her subversive attitude rather compliments Rajamma, who wishes to stay with a man of her choice rather than her husband. The narratives of Kaushalya and Rajamma forge the film's subplots, which run parallel to the developing romance between Lakshmi, the Dalit heroine, and Surya, the upper-caste hero. The plot deploys Lakshmi as the maid of Surya's household while Kishtaya manages to survive by doing odd jobs. In the dynamics of their personal relationship, Lakshmi appears to be strong and serves as 'a phallic support' to her jobless, alcoholic, impotent, deaf and mute husband, who is a symbol of the 'de-phallicized husband'.[15] But she is quite vulnerable in the power dynamics of this context due to her socio-economic plight. Dalit women experience oppression from three forces: oppression by the upper-caste men, oppression by men of the same caste, and class-based oppression. Most Dalit women survive on menial jobs as the system denies them the opportunity to take up respectable jobs, even if they are fit for them. In the context of the present plot, Lakshmi is a victim of the first and the third categories as her husband is not in a position to subjugate her due to his physical disabilities. Therefore, she assumes the role of a caregiver to Kishtaya, though her apparent strong appearance is merely a mask of stoicism. At times, the lens focuses on her helpless face as she is unable to cope with the daily drudgery, hardship and poverty. Her gesture of silence and stoic expression may be linked to Chandra Talapade Mohanty's remark about the 'silent subaltern.'[16] Her voice is already stifled by her misfortune and the system.

Surya, the city-bred male protagonist, enters the scene and exhibits his liberal ideology within the rigid set-up, and proclaims that he has no qualms in partaking of food cooked by the Dalit maid, Lakshmi, as he does not believe in caste. Such a liberal stance gives the viewers an apparent hint that he may be an agent of change. The village priest cautions Surya about the violation of the societal codes of hierarchy. Benegal's portrayal of Surya initially poses a contrast to his father's stance. Gradually, he starts exercising his power over the villagers in his own way and threatens the villagers of dire consequences should they be found stealing anything either from his fields or ponds or plantation. He also stops the supply of water to the fields of his half-brother, Pratap, and punishes Kishtaya for stealing toddy from his palm tree. As an act of punishment, Kishtaya is shaved and made to sit on a donkey and paraded across the village. Unable to bear the public humiliation, he leaves the village without anyone noticing. This incident is a turning point in the plot. Lakshmi is now completely left alone under Surya's gaze. However, Lakshmi has been shown to be an object of sexual attraction to Surya in three scenes: the grinding scene, the bathing scene, and the mirror scene.

The grinding scene takes place prior to the incident of Kishtaya's punishment. The subsequent scenes take place after Kishtaya's disappearance. In all the three scenes, Lakshmi has been made into a spectacle for male gratification. This relates to Laura Mulvey's theory of scopophilia as explained in her seminal essay 'Visual Pleasure and Narrative Cinema'. Mulvey argues that there are three aspects of the gaze: the camera, the viewer and the characters in the film. Contrary to Mulvey's opinion, Vasudevan cites Rajadhyaksha in the introduction of his book: '[the] spectator's look is not separate from, but overlaps and develops in close relationship to that of the camera'.[17] The role of the camera is akin to negotiating with the spectators. The position of the spectators in the dark theatre hall amounts to voyeurism. Mulvey's aspect of gaze operates on multiple levels. Bindu Nair observes that in Hindi cinema the woman is made to be a spectacle as the camera focuses on the selective parts of the body.[18] *Ankur* is not an exception. The aspect of scopophilia has been thoroughly exposed by Benegal's camera concentrating on the stealing looks of Surya towards Lakshmi's gestures and paralinguistic movements projecting the woman as an object of visual pleasure and male gratification. The grinding scene plays a crucial role in this aspect, followed by the bathing scene and the mirror scene. In the grinding scene, the camera takes a long shot of the front part of Lakshmi's toiling body from afar. The spectators and Surya see her grinding spices with a wooden pole, making her body sway in a rhythmic manner. The eye of the camera strategically captures the unconscious paralinguistic gestures of her body and face and thus objectifies her for Surya and the spectators.

Surya's constant gaze towards Lakshmi is captured with close-up and reverse angle shots. The close-up shot reflects the intense urge on Surya's face and the reverse angle shot intensifies Surya's desire for Lakshmi. Surya walks towards her slowly and asks if she is crying. Confused, Lakshmi looks at Surya and enquires if there is anything wrong. Here, one may doubt the long female gaze of Lakshmi towards Surya, which may be interpreted as her sense of astonishment since she did not expect her master's sudden presence right next to her. The following two-shot scene captures the spatial proximity of the duo and indicates Surya's secret sexual attraction.

After the deliberate disappearance of Kishtaya, Lakshmi begins to share considerable space in Surya's house. The viewers, however, are only provided with subtle details of the interior of the house. The striking aspect of Lakshmi's character is her survival instinct. She wishes to live amid poverty, hardship and humiliation. That is why we hear her humming a tune in the grinding scene. She wears kohl, bindi (red dot on the forehead) and attires of bright colour. All these add up to her survival instinct as well as her defiance of caste oppression. She has the right to live on her own terms, irrespective of her marginalised position.

The bathing scene is a high-angle shot, where Surya watches Lakshmi drying her hair standing in the pond. The sari is not draped properly around her bust. Afterwards, Surya, the camera and the spectators follow her into the house with a voyeuristic curiosity. Lakshmi adjusts her sari and looks at herself in the mirror to apply a bindi. This close-up scene may be compared to the Lacanian concept of the mirror phase. The mirror reflection helps us in building up the self-image. Lakshmi is aware of herself and her image. Class, caste and gender cannot really dampen her spirit of optimism. Unlike Kishtaya, she is hopeful and wants to conceive a child. Kishtaya takes recourse to alcohol when his pottery business faces ruin. The trope of the mirror image also refers to a kind of narcissistic approach. For instance, Sushila in *Nishant* repeatedly longs for a mirror, which, according to Madhava Prasad, is an example of 'disruptive narcissism'.[19] Unlike Sushila, Lakshmi appears to be subtly narcissistic, which leads to the disruption of societal codes as well in subsequent scenes. Surya stands just behind her and touches her shoulder. The viewers are shown their reflection in the complex mirror shot, where they look at each other in the mirror (Figure 1.1). This gives a clue to their growing intimacy by creating a frame within the frame.

'The complex mirror shots thus put the viewers in an equivocal and protean attitude.'[20] The viewers are yet to apprehend the matrix of their relationship. Lakshmi gives a scornful glance to Surya and retreats silently to her hut; this may be considered as an example of mild protest.

Benegal has strategically shown the hut and the house in a depth-of-focus shot, where the lush green paddy field sprawling over an area of about 500 metres appears between the two. The hut is indicative of Lakshmi's subalterneity while the house stands for economic security. Surya cajoles her back to the house under the pretext of domestic chores. Poverty works here as a catalyst to lure Lakshmi to the house of opportunities and wish fulfilment. Despite knowing Surya's desire for gratification, Lakshmi agrees to work in his house due to her survival instinct. Anuradha Needham adds more, saying:

Figure 1.1 The mirror scene.

> Lakshmi as a sexual object and as sexually objectified... Her awareness of his gaze (and she is often, though not always, aware that he is looking at her) recognizes and seems to acquiesce to his right to view her thus, and thereby concedes a species of *droit du seigneur* to their situation... Lakshmi in her hut, presumably having rejected his advances. But when Surya comes in pursuit, complaining – 'who will make my tea? ...' Lakshmi remains silent. As he departs, the camera offers a close-up of her face with a smile full of sensual knowledge that makes clear she grasps the sub-text of his complaints, which has more to do with his sexual needs and expectations regarding their fulfilment than work left unattended. Arguably, Surya's need of her suggests she has some power over him, much as the glance she returns implies a degree of reciprocity, but Lakshmi's smile also suggests her acknowledgement and acceptance of the situation as it exists, and this is a function of his structurally defined (feudal/patriarchal) power and her (subaltern) powerlessness.[21]

Anuradha Needham's argument highlights the socio-psychological politics that governs the relations in a feudal set-up. Lakshmi is compelled to yield to her landlord as she is economically dependent and that makes her reciprocal.

The spatial proximity draws them closer and their growing romance re-enacts the illegitimate liaison between Kaushalya and her father. Her economic insecurity, powerlessness and survival instinct push her to the extreme to transgress the imposed societal restraints. Her powerlessness is intensified by her silence. Though she submits to Surya, her mind is in a state of moral dilemma. The 'sub proletariats' are unable to articulate.[22] Here one may point out that Lakshmi's subtle make-up, the bright face and the ever-present red dot on the forehead (bindi) pose a sharp contrast with the poverty and despair inside the hut. If we examine her actions with empathy, they do not seem to be unusual. To be with a deaf and mute husband is quite frustrating for a woman. She does not have any support systems around. Lakshmi's bright and sophisticated face may be Benegal's deliberate projection of the aspiration of a Dalit woman to rise above the dirt and live well like upper-caste women.

The intrusion of Rajamma's trial scene at the village council (*panchayat*) is extremely important for the evolution of Lakshmi's subjectivity. She attends the trial scene out of curiosity. Rajamma, the runaway wife, speaks out boldly in front of everyone that she is unwilling to stay with her husband (Figure 1.2). She wishes to conceive and her desire is not fulfilled by her husband. Material prosperity is not all that one looks for in a marriage. She proclaims with a rebellious tone of protest – 'Food is not enough to gratify the hunger (*bhookh sirf pet ki nehin hoti hain*).'

Figure 1.2 The trial scene (Rajamma before the village council).

Rajamma's statement reflects a strong subversive feminist attitude. No societal code can hold her back from expressing her desire to live with her lover. In response to her protest, the choric voice of the villagers concludes that her act of transgression will ruin the world ('*tere jaisa aurat duniya ko dubayenge ek din*'). Rajamma's situation is analogous to that of Lakshmi to some extent, but Lakshmi is yet to break her silence. She witnesses the humiliating trial scene silently with a frown on her forehead and the close-up shot of her face speaks to that. It may be either her moral dilemma or her apprehension of consequences similar to those faced by Rajamma. Surya observes Lakshmi's reaction in the trial scene with a long gaze, though unaware of her inner crisis. According to Anuradha Needham, this scene is instrumental to the development of Lakshmi's subjectivity:

> The narrative enclosed within the tableau involves a woman's transgression: The runaway wife has not only left her husband to live with another man, but this man also, it is suggested, belongs to a lower caste. Her husband's family sees this transgression in terms of a socially unacceptable desire: 'What *more* does this woman *want?*' demands one brother-in-law after enumerating all the material benefits she enjoys as part of her husband's family. The wife reframes the ideological valence of her 'want' by asserting first that her husband 'is not a man' and then she 'wants a child' . . . thus the 'more' that this woman 'wants' incorporates a desire for both: a child and sexual satisfaction.[23]

The entire scene and the didactic instruction by the villagers also relate to the metaphor of the 'castration threat'.[24] The villagers try to adjudicate this domestic conflict by defaming Rajamma in the village council. Rajamma, on the contrary, does not offer a passive image to be looked at, but rather she speaks her mind and acts according to her will. She has not been sexually objectified by the filmmaker. In spite of being a male filmmaker, Benegal understands the complex matrix of the female psyche and its subjective voice. Rajamma's bold stance breaks the asymmetrical power politics. Benegal's apparent calmness and simplicity conceal a dense texture of psychological patterns in his female protagonists, who are individual case studies in the context of a vast sociological change in the offing. The technique of Benegal's narrative has the masterful fusion of diverse aspects of protest along with his interest in the female psyche rising up with an assertive voice. Benegal has spoken of his standpoint with regard to women-oriented films:

> It has been a growing awareness of women's centrality to life and society, although I do not subscribe to the Western concept of feminism. I didn't consciously choose to portray women characters; it is my predilection.

Indian women – if they have to survive and function – are forced to become strong and resilient. A lot of demands are made on them; they use strategies to keep alive and survive. I hate to represent women simply as victims, the *sati* syndrome [women as self-sacrificing martyrs] that warms the cockles of our hearts in paternalistic society. We need to see things not with filter of what is given but to see things as they are . . .[25]

Ankur exemplifies Benegal's message; where all the minor and major female characters are aware of their subjectivity and sexuality. The central metaphor of the film is protest – protest on various levels, vocal or silent, open or symbolic like the repeated reference to and projection of a belligerent woodpecker seeking to penetrate into the hard body of a palm tree. It is a study of both the submissive and the subversive female. Almost all the women exemplify two aspects: the voiceless and the vocal. Kaushalya is the cleverest of all the females in the film. Her success story is open to the viewers. She is a veteran in the art of life both in age and in experience. She acquires the right of a mistress from the feudal landlord (*zamindar*) and he also does at least some justice by her and their illegitimate son Pratap following the unwritten feudal code of protection, which dictates that the landlord will take care of his tenants. The landlord's wife (Surya's mother) is helpless before her husband, though her voice has a tone of suppressed subversion in the kitchen scene. Unlike Kaushalya, Lakshmi is young and inexperienced. She speaks through her silence in the first part of the film. Also, she appears to be a somewhat wavering character that is yet to decide the course of her journey. Despite her attraction to Surya, she is full of sympathy for her husband and displays a sincere gesture of protectiveness. After the trial scene, she gradually acquires a voice, though not that of a rebel.

> One could say the significance of this tableau is not just restricted to the development of Lakshmi's subjectivity, but incorporates the spectator's as well, rendering it co-extensive with Lakshmi's. This process, in turn, helps secure the spectator's identification with Lakshmi.[26]

With reference to Rajamma's trial and death (by suicide or murder), Lakshmi understands her position in the contemporary social milieu. The society does not authorise freedom of existence to a woman. The village court gives priority to the opinions of Rajamma's two brothers-in-law and husband. Lakshmi realises that her vulnerability and basic feminine insecurity push her back to the house instead of the hut since Surya being her master symbolises security and opportunity. But her moral dilemma continues in her dialogues with Surya: 'I wish to return to my husband, master' (*main apni marad ke paas jaungi, sarkar*). She tries to resist the temptation, though she is clueless about Kishtaya. Surya assures her he will provide shelter and care. 'I will take care of you forever (*main tera khayal rakhunga . . . hamesha ke liye*). This tone of assurance traps Lakshmi in Surya's house. She is too simple to examine Surya's words beyond their face value. Surya's flirtatious comments on her beauty make her genuinely happy. She seems to be content as her wants are fulfilled. But it is like a 'brief interlude'.[27] Anuradha Needham opines, 'by becoming Surya's mistress she is reproducing a socially accepted, if not socially sanctioned, relationship'.[28]

The filmmaker has incorporated another tableau of the card game followed by the objectification of another woman. In the card game scene, one of the villagers keeps his wife (known as Amlamma) as a pawn and loses her to his friend. The furious wife refuses to leave her household to be with another man. She quarrels violently with her drunken husband and his friend and the large kitchen knife in her hand symbolises the rise of women to overturn the dynamics of power politics.

Both the trial and the card game scenes exemplify how the voiceless females gradually start voicing their opinions with regard to their safety, psychological well-being and survival. Rajamma and Amlamma are not going to submit to the male command. Together with Kaushalya, they prepare the ground for Lakshmi to stand on her own feet. The arrival of Surya's wife and her pregnancy slowly transform Lakshmi from submissive to subversive. Being jealous and insecure, Surya's wife drives Lakshmi out of the house. She returns to her hut lonely and betrayed. The close-up shot in the hut reflects pain and despair on Lakshmi's face. She lies on the ground with a vacant look.

Surya repeats his father's history, but unlike his father is neither bold nor intelligent. His father did not care about society. Surya is educated in the city, in a society where codes have changed. Keeping two women, the wife and the mistress, used to be normal in his father's times, but in the context of a changing era, Surya is afraid of society. He is shown by Benegal to be shy, shaky and helpless before Lakshmi when she refuses to abort the child. Protecting the honour of a mistress is unthinkable for the college-educated modern man. He is arrogant and also a weak character. His appearance in the country from the city signalled the entry of modernity and liberal thinking in the patriarchal feudal set-up. He boldly proclaims that he does not believe in caste and class and accepts food from Lakshmi, which establishes Surya as an agent of change in the first part of the film. He is fond of cigarettes and modern music and also brings along a record player and a collection of records of film music, which seem to be quite fascinating to Lakshmi. The sound of the record player is a symbol of technological advancement and modernity, which intrudes upon the ambient sound of the woodpecker. Surya's liaison with Lakshmi bridges the gap between modernity and rustic feudal ideals. However, that does not really bring in any change in the set-up as was expected in the beginning.

In response to Surya's repeated and desperate demand that she either leave the village or abort the child, Lakshmi remains silent and resilient. Her silence is a productive silence as she does not bow down to Surya's demand. For the sake of survival, she resumes her work in the paddy field. The police *patel* (village police) urges her to negotiate with Surya for her material well-being, the way Kaushalya had done with the senior landlord. Lakshmi ignores his suggestion because she does not wish to repeat history. Without calculating the consequences, she undertakes the challenge. In the scene by the river bank, Surya, in a tone of utter desperation, almost pleads with Lakshmi, but she looks at him with a sense of contempt and spits into the water.[29] Surya becomes almost hysterical. The camera focuses on the confident face of Lakshmi. She walks with determination ahead of Surya with a bundle of fire logs on her head. She replies quietly to Surya's questions one by one: 'Did I ask you to look after the child? Should I be the one to be ashamed? I wish to keep the child.'

The change in Lakshmi is obvious now. She is no more a weak and wavering character. Her subjective self takes the lead of her being. The transformation of Lakshmi from submissive to subversive heralds the arrival of a new woman, who speaks for herself in order to sustain herself in a feudal patriarchy. Surya and his seduction by pseudo-liberal modernist ideas morphs Lakshmi from the silent subaltern to the vocal subaltern who does not wish to deprive herself of motherhood, whoever may be the father. It is not necessary that the husband has to be the biological father. Lakshmi's protest against the feudal command unsettles Surya psychologically. She inverts the oppressor/oppressed balance by questioning his sense of judgement.[30]

The metaphor of protest is also hidden in the diegetic sound of the woodpeckers continuously striking the hard stem of the palm tree. It offers a contrasting note to the apparent serenity of the village: the lush green fields, the line of palm trees, the women sowing seedlings of paddy and the smiling kids around. The scene of the woodpeckers striking the tall palm tree is juxtaposed with the scenes of Surya's and Lakshmi's intimacy, and Amlamma's fierce denial to leave her home after her husband's defeat in the card game. The symbolic diegetic sound is used in two subsequent scenes. On the first occasion, Lakshmi greets Surya's wife with a garland when she arrives in the village, but she does not appear to be warm towards Lakshmi. With her natural feminine instinct, she suspects something is going on between Lakshmi and her husband. Lakshmi watches her entering the house from outside with a gesture of helplessness and the incessant sound of the bird is audible as if to encourage Lakshmi to strike back against the impenetrable system. The scene dissolves into the interior of the house, which is now under the control of the wife. Unlike Surya's mother, who is totally submissive and speechless, Surya's wife is unwilling to submit to his directives. She raises her voice against the presence of Lakshmi. Suddenly, the camera focuses on an embroidery displaying the message 'best of luck', which seems to be somewhat ambiguous. Does the message in the tableau foreground the ensuing conflict or does it just wish filial luck to the woman of the house, or does it maybe do both? The mistress is displaced by the wife. Surya's voice is too meek to protect the dignity of Lakshmi before his father and his wife. Despite his repeated requests to keep Lakshmi as a maid for her survival, Surya's wife turns a deaf ear.

On the second occasion, Surya's wife, being curious about the continuous whistling sound, enquires about the name of the bird. The close-up shot reflects a gesture of shock on Surya's face as he once asked the same question to Lakshmi after the scene of their consummation. This time the sound of the woodpeckers begins to be annoying to Surya and he tries to muffle it by playing modern Bollywood music on his record player. This may be interpreted as Surya's attempt to stifle the voice of Lakshmi. The view of the belligerent woodpeckers from the window and the lonely tall palm trees creates a perfect *mise-en-scène* for Lakshmi to acquire a voice of her own.

Even though Surya's wife does not tolerate Lakshmi's presence in the house, at times she is sympathetic to Lakshmi's agony and offers her food out of a basic caregiving instinct. It is reminiscent of the scene in *Nishant* where the wife, Rukmini, offers food to the abducted mistress Sushila. Lakshmi's journey from the hut to the house and back has been projected by Benegal purely to convey that she is an outcaste in the feudal power structure. Kaushalya makes room for herself within it. Lakshmi fails to do so. If women are disaccommodated within the hegemonic structure, it necessitates the process of social transformation. What ensues, as Sundar Rajan explains, is 'the process of exorbiation', which of course assures inevitable change.[31]

Towards the close of the film, Kishtaya's sudden reappearance in the hut with some money is another turning point in Lakshmi's life. Seeing her husband back, Lakshmi cries uncontrollably out of her feeing of guilt. Anuradha Needham explains the act of sobbing as a 'therapeutic event'.[32] Kishtaya thinks it is his own child in Lakshmi's womb. Overjoyed, he goes to Surya for work. Surya, out of his guilty conscience, misunderstands Kishtaya's arrival with a stick and starts beating him mercilessly. Lakshmi runs out of her hut to protect Kishtaya. The villagers, the police *patel*, Pratap and Surya's wife in the beating scene form a choric voice against the new feudal male, whose conduct is unacceptable to all from various standpoints. Surya's father treated his mistress with an element of justice. But the younger landlord is unable to live up to that expectation. Society has advanced since the time of the old principles of the feudal system. To Surya's modern wife (who arrives in the village from the city in a car), the beating is an act of immorality. Her scornful and penetrating looks in the final scene are also a revealing protest against the husband's wrongful acts of exploiting a Dalit woman and beating her husband ruthlessly. The climactic beating scene reveals a fierce and subversive feministic voice in

Lakshmi. She curses Surya in public and cries out loudly that they are no more his servants as she also demands justice. The assertive voice of Lakshmi shatters the power structure completely. An ashamed and afraid Surya hides in the house, indicating a weakening feudal power.

The film finally ends with a boy hurling a stone at the window of the house and the screen turns red, symbolising the seedling of revolt against the oppressors. For Benegal, the window symbolises realisation and emancipation. It offers Lakshmi the different sides of feudal oppression – Rajamma being dragged to the village court like a stubborn animal, the procession after her unnatural death and the continuous pecking of the woodpeckers. As soon as the window breaks, the birds flutter around with a cry of freedom. According to Sangeeta Datta, the climax reflects Benegal's leftist views:

> Benegal's leftist vision is unambiguously stated in this complex tale of oppression. Behind the film lies a humanist film-maker's vision of an egalitarian society, devoid of class and caste divides and gender oppression.[33]

The ending of *Ankur* announces the message of the beginning of a potent revolt of the peasants against the feudal order and that is why it may seem to be abrupt to the critics. It lacks a proper closure. Datta says: 'The absence of closure and the act of defiance by a silent witness effectively point to the future developments and subversions of the power equation.'[34] Madhava Prasad offers a similar argument and says,

> the abrupt ending of *Ankur* was more important to the effectivity of the text than a conclusion deriving from the 'natural' propensities of the narrative ... The motivation for the ending derives from the representational dynamics of the preceding narrative and the extra-textual 'demand' for the spectacle of peasant revolt that the film promised to satisfy ...[35]

The similar issue of caste discrimination had been portrayed by Franz Osten in *Acchut Kanya* (*Untouchable Maiden*, 1936) and Bimal Roy in *Sujata* (1959), many years before the release of *Ankur*. And in both these films, we find the Brahmin boy falling in love with an untouchable girl. The spirit of liberalism was always there in Hindi films, but the metaphor of protest against the system is not very strong in the earlier films. The character of Kasturi in *Acchut Kanya* fails to transgress the barriers of class and caste for a romantic union with Pratap and the film ends on a tragic note. The titular character of Sujata in Bimal Roy's film does not face the discrimination as acutely as Kasturi or Lakshmi. She is brought up in the upper-caste household as an adopted daughter and so suffers from an identity crisis. Her silence and Kasturi's mild transgression ('*Tum Brahmin ho, main acchut*') do not really trigger any spark when compared to the way in which Rajamma and Lakshmi in the later part of *Ankur* project the assertive and subversive tone in their dialogues. Unlike Kasturi and Sujata, the other two characters appear to be quite vocal and concerned about self-empowerment and the fulfilment of desire. Kaushalya, despite being a mistress of the landlord, manages to obtain land to sustain herself and her son. Rajamma is not at all ashamed of speaking out before the village court (*panchayat*) about her husband being unable to satisfy her desire. Lakshmi also acquires a voice of her own later in the film. The daily drudgery and the scornful gesture of the villagers make her strong enough to withstand the oppressive blows of patriarchy. The apparent calmness in the characters and the serenity of lush green paddy fields offer a counterpoint to hunger, deprivation and denial.[36] Robert Stam's discussion of the objective of early film feminism in his 'The Feminist Intervention' is relevant here:

> Early film feminism focused on practical goals of consciousness raising, on denunciation of negative media imagery of women, as well as on more theoretical concerns. As the 'Womanifesto' of the 1975 New York Conference on Feminists in the Media put it: 'We do not accept the existing power structure and we are committed to changing it by the content and structure of our images and by the ways we related to each other in our work and with our audience.'[37]

Shyam Benegal had already anticipated this message a year prior to the conference and shown us how the voiceless female entities acquire a voice of their own. It is worth noting here that long before the publication of Mary Ann Doane's seminal text *The Desire to Desire* (1987), Benegal had boldly dealt with the issue of female desire, which is not a sin to be sublimated. Doane argues that films often foreground the subversive woman and in the course of the film they are ultimately 'circumscribed'.[38] This is to some extent relevant in the present context as well, but in spite of being a male filmmaker, Benegal does not portray his women as akin to transvestites, who had limited agency and self-expression in rural communities. In the caste-ridden society of rural Andhra Pradesh, underprivileged women speak and support one another with an awakened consciousness. It is, however, not just the portrayal of the underprivileged, but also of privileged women. Their collective voice puts up a strong note of resistance against the patriarchal and the Brahmanical hegemony.

Note: All dialogue translated by the author.

NOTES

1. Ashish Rajadhaksha, *Indian Cinema: A Very Short Introduction* (Oxford: Oxford University Press, 2016), 84.
2. Rajadhaksha, 78.
3. Sangeeta Datta, *Shyam Benegal* (New Delhi: Roli Books, 2002), 60.
4. Anuradha Dingwaney Needham, *New Indian Cinema in Post-Independent India: The Cultural work of Shyam Benegal's Films* (New York: Routledge, 2013), 19.
5. M. Madhava Prasad, *Ideology of the Hindi Film: A Historical Construction* (Oxford: Oxford University Press, 2016), 189.
6. Datta, 22.
7. Ibid., 29.
8. J. Dudley Andrew, *The Major Film Theories: An Introduction* (New York: Oxford University Press, 1976), 137.
9. Andrew, 106–78.
10. Robert Stam, *Film Theory: An Introduction* (Massachusetts: Blackwell Publishers, 2000), 72–82.
11. Datta, 21.
12. Stam, 92–102.
13. Ibid.
14. M. K. Raghavendra, *50 Indian Film Classics* (Noida: HarperCollins Publishers, 2009), 174–8.
15. Sundar Kaali, 'Narrating Seduction', in *Making Meaning in Indian Cinema*, ed. Ravi S. Vasudevan (New Delhi: Oxford University Press, 2000), 184.
16. Arpita Mukhopadhyay, 'Postcolonial Feminism and Third World Feminism', in *Feminism*, ed. Sumit Chakrabarti (Hyderabad: Orient Blackswan, 2016), 90–105.
17. Ravi S. Vasudevan, ed., introduction to *Making Meaning in Indian Cinema* (New Delhi: Oxford University Press, 2000), 26.
18. Bindu Nair, 'Female Bodies and the Male Gaze: Laura Mulvey and Hindi Cinema', in *Films and Feminism: Essays in Indian Cinema*, ed. Jasbir Jain and Sudha Rai (Jaipur: Rawat Publications, 2002), 52–8.
19. Prasad, 204.
20. Julian Hanich, 'Reflecting on Reflections: Cinema's Complex Mirror Shots', in *Indefinite Visions: Cinema and the Attractions of Uncertainty*, ed. Martine Beugnet, Allan Cameron, and Arild Fetveit (Edinburgh: Edinburgh University Press, 2017. Edinburgh Scholarship Online, 2018), <doi:10.3366/edinburgh/9781474407120.003.0009>
21. Needham, 26–7.
22. Gayatri Chakravorty Spivak, 'Can the Subaltern Speak', in *Colonial Discourse and Post-Colonial Theory: A Reader*, ed. and intro. Patrick Williams and Laura Chrisman (New York: Columbia University Press, 1994), 66–111.
23. Needham, 28.
24. Christine Gledhill, 'Recent Developments in Feminist Criticism', in *Film Theory and Criticism: Introductory Readings*, ed. Leo Braudy and Marshall Cohen (New York: Oxford University Press, 1999), 261–72.
25. Datta, 6.
26. Needham, 28.
27. Ibid., 29.
28. Ibid., 28.
29. Ibid., 29.

30. Datta, 66.
31. Needham, 31.
32. Ibid., 31.
33. Datta, 66.
34. Ibid., 78.
35. Prasad, 198–9.
36. Datta, 67.
37. Stam, 169–79.
38. Ibid., 175.

CHAPTER 2

Nishant and the New Dawn: Towards a Sacerdotal–Secular Modernity?

Nikhila H

INTRODUCTION

The ability to define, demarcate and identify the 'past' as distinct from the 'present' is a significant way in which history manifests itself. Parallel cinema has often been described, both in journalese and in academic discourse, as social realist; the fictional world created by the films that are identified under this category seems to imperceptibly flow into the present, and meld into the contemporary social world. Parallel films such as *Samskara* (*Funeral Rites*, 1970), *Kaadu* (*Forest*, 1973), *Ghatashraddha* (*The Ritual*, 1977), to arbitrarily name a few, or even *Ankur* (*The Seedling*, 1974), do not explicitly mark the events as historical, or demarcate the fictional world as the past or as something that prevailed in the past, which has since ceased to be so in the present (that is, the present when the films were made in the 1970s). This is not to suggest that the issues that they deal with such as caste, the practice of keeping concubines, or feudal land relations, were of the past, and the films erroneously make them seem contemporary. Rather, my point has to do with the method of treatment of their subject, whether it is caste, or feudalism, which is approached and critiqued as a contemporary problem.

It is here that Shyam Benegal's *Nishant* (*Night's End*, 1975) appears to me to be slightly different from the films named above, or even many other parallel films. Not only in the title does it indicate an 'end' (*anth* in Hindi means end/cessation) to the darkness that it delineates, but in the film too, right at the outset, the time of the film's action is clearly marked as 1945, that is, some thirty years before the time of the film's making. To mark out the film's action world as a specific time in the past is not necessarily to posit a break with the present; as opposed to a seamless, unmarked flow of time, it is to conceptualise a change that has taken place between a 'then' and a 'now', maybe even drawing from the past to transform the present.[1]

Therefore, it may be more appropriate to identify *Nishant* as a historical realist film. The film begins with the disclaimer: 'All the characters and names in this film are fictitious and bear no resemblance with any person living or dead.'[2] The overt function of this disclaimer since the time cinema was involved in litigation in 1932[3] has been to avoid the charge of libel. But the disclaimer in *Nishant* is also indicative of (1) the film's realism, that the events in the film could well be read as corresponding with actual events; and (2) its suppressed claims as history of the region.[4] Immediately after the credits, right at the outset comes the verbal-visual on the screen: 'In a feudal state . . . The year 1945'.[5] Though no place is specified here, the film throughout gives us plenty of cues to deduce where it is set. The year 1945 is also an indicator to fix the region, as that time period was momentous in the history of that region.[6]

So, the film has a connection with History which it would like to overtly disavow or suppress, preferring artistic licence over meeting demands of authenticity. It could also be read as a strategy of distancing itself from the political project of the Communist Party of India (Marxist–Leninist) at that time in the Telangana region, which was evoking the history of the Telangana Peasant Struggle of 1940s, and to make the film's concerns more general and gain wider acceptability. In such a scenario, how do we see this film's work vis-à-vis History? If we focus on the technique of realism that the film deploys, it seems that the film explores with great clarity the particular nature of modernity that was brought along with the end of the feudal order – a modernity that I have characterised in the title of this chapter as sacerdotal–secular modernity. On the other hand, if we focus on the fact that the original screenplay of the film was written by the well-known modernist playwright Vijay Tendulkar, whose many plays[7] question the hypocrisies of the patriarchal order in dealing with the issue of woman's desire and sexuality, it seems that the (feudal) past is a setting for staging contemporary anxieties around a modern man–woman relationship, particularly when the woman's desire is acknowledged.

In a review essay titled, 'Historiography meets Historiophoty[8]: The Perils and Promise of Rendering the Past on Film', Bryan F. Le Beau identifies two ways through which historians have approached films whose subject matter is History: (1) to see whether the films measure up to the standards set by professional historians to evaluate the histories that they film; and (2) to see how film, subject to the conventions of fiction, 'has been (or might be) employed as a vehicle for thinking about our relationship to the past'.[9] In a film that identifies itself as a historical film, it may be usual, though not necessarily productive, to see how the film falls short of, or is inauthentic in comparison with, orthographic history; but clearly the more challenging task for Le Beau, and also for the historians whose book Le Beau is reviewing, is 'to understand from the inside how a filmmaker might go about rendering the past on film'.[10] With Shyam Benegal's *Nishant*, which clearly disavows and deflects the possibility of comparison with the orthographic History of the Telangana peasant struggle of the 1940s and 1950s, the film invites the possibility of only the second approach, which is to see how the past is rendered on film.

With this broad framework, the following sections of the chapter delineate: (1) the language of the sacerdotal that translates itself into the secular language of public discourse and the secular that seeks endorsement and is propped up by the sacerdotal, that together oversee the end of the (feudal) night and the rise of dawn (modernity); (2) the language of the popular, which often hovers between the diegetic and extra-diegetic narrative space coming in the form of Telugu[11] folk songs and performative practices in the film, indicative probably of the film marginalising, or downplaying dissent and the larger social struggle; and (3) the language of woman's desire that ironically can only be fully articulated in death, in the form of the musical rendition of Quli Qutub Shah's verse; it is fleeting, half-articulated in the beginning, but when it becomes a background song sung in a full-throated manner, it can only appear as a terrible indictment of the violence and macabre twisting of woman's desire into a threat for the institution of the family, and destruction of the social order. Before going to these sections, however, I would like to clarify the term 'parallel cinema' that I have used in this chapter and offer an overview of the academic discourse within which *Nishant* figures.

I use the term 'parallel cinema' to locate Shyam Benegal's oeuvre simply as a convenient and well recognisable term, though there are many competing terms such as art cinema, arthouse cinema, New Wave cinema, alternative cinema, which are preferred by different writers. For the purposes of this chapter, I consider parallel cinema as referring to those films that are not star-driven, have no more than a tenuous link with the mainstream commercial film industry, and have their own trans-regional and trans-national networks of circulation. Although made in particular Indian languages such as Kannada, Bengali, Malayalam, Hindi, etc., they are identified less with their particular language film industry and audience, and more with a pan-Indian viewership that accesses these films via English subtitles. They are also made by literati that mediated between different cultural forms such as literature, theatre and cinema, bringing into cinema texts sensibilities and styles of representation from other contemporary print (literary) and performative modes.[12]

While many scholars have identified the features of parallel cinema, here considering mainly *Nishant*, I identify three features of parallel cinema, each of which I will elaborate on in the aforementioned three sections. The three features are (1) the eschewing of the preliminary consecration rites/worship on screen, a tradition that comes from *poorvaranga* or *rangapuja* in theatre, and which takes place elaborately in commercial cinema, often prior to the credit sequence and before entering into the diegetic world of the film; (2) the use of multiple languages and non-standard language varieties and folk forms as a part of the style of realism deployed in these parallel films; and (3) the use of songs, often in the background, not for creating the song-and-dance spectacle of commercial cinema that arrests narrative flow, but for layering the meaning of the unfolding visual narrative.

With regard to discussions of *Nishant* in academic discourse, a sample of which I will offer here, at least in two books the discussion of *Nishant* comes as part of the discussion of the filmmaker Shyam Benegal's oeuvre. In Sangeeta Datta's *Shyam Benegal* (2002), the director is contextualised as part of parallel cinema in India, and in Anuradha Dingwaney Needham's book (2013) Shyam Benegal's films are discussed as part of New Indian Cinema in post-Independence India, which is also the title of the book. While in the former *Nishant* figures as one element of the rural trilogy along with *Ankur* (1974) and *Manthan* (*The Churning*, 1976), in the latter *Nishant* and *Ankur* are uncoupled from *Manthan*, not least because of their common setting in the Telangana region. Sangeeta Datta reads the three films 'as third cinema'[13] in their deployment of an egalitarian agenda', albeit within the existing democratic structure of the nation-state.[14] For Needham, whose discussion emphasises the aspect of gender, transformation of feudalism can only come about through a 'long, arduous process of psychic transformation' that the victims of feudal oppression have to undergo, as particularly evident in the characters of Lakshmi in *Ankur* and Susheela in *Nishant*.[15] John Hood's discussion is part of a general introduction to ten major and some more minor filmmakers taken as representing Indian art cinema. Commenting on the ending of *Nishant*, which offers no simplistic vision of retributive justice in the wake of both innocent Rukmini and Susheela being killed by the mob of peasants, along with the cruel landlords, he views it as a 'warning on the futility of violence' and the 'inefficacy of religion' to contain popular fury.[16]

While Madhava Prasad offers an excellent discussion of the film, which along with *Ankur* and *Manthan* are seen as 'instances of an evolving developmental aesthetic employing a statist realism',[17] it was his brief and passing discussion of the issue of language used in the film (Dakhani Urdu), the controversy of credits acknowledgement, and the idea of a spectator-oriented realism rather than a pro-filmic realism as the defining feature of realism in Shyam Benegal's early films[18] that have been most useful for thinking through the issues in this chapter. Similarly, I have drawn much confidence from Kishore Valicha's discussion of the film as a commentary on the 'fragility of the middle class family' and also as the way in which 'sexuality . . . is seen not only as a form of debasement but also as a source of tension between social classes'[19] in pushing my argument about *Nishant* in the direction of the acknowledgement and disavowal of woman's desire.

While all these studies pay attention to the theme and plot of the film and offer excellent readings either in terms of the larger milieu that fostered parallel cinema in India or in terms of an auteur-driven style of filmmaking, in this chapter I focus on the multilingual manifestation in *Nishant*, which includes Dakhani Urdu, Hindi, Sanskrit, Telugu and English, and the layering of meaning that happens with these multiple languages. Also, I foreground those elements that are literally on the edges or margins of the film – the credit sequence, the closing moments or epilogue of the film, and those dimly heard voices that mostly occupy a curious space between diegetic and extra-diegetic realms in the film.

I THE ESCHEWING OF CONSECRATION RITES

As mentioned above, most commercial films of Indian cinema begin with some form, brief or elaborate, of consecration ritual, which involves the sustained frontal presence or worship on the screen of some deity, often accompanied by the chanting of Sanskrit *shlokas* (hymns). Tracing the origin of these visual practices to *poorvaranga* (prelude to the staged performance) and *rangapuja* (worship of the performance space), which are described in *Natyashastra* and later on taken into classical Sanskrit drama, and now into various forms of contemporary stage performances, such as dance, *yakshagana* and even modern theatre, Parciack (2016) notes that 'these rites symbolically differentiated theatrical time and space, and enabled a transition between the empirical world and the theatrical order'.[20] Taken into the cinematic world, 'they echo the intention to detach the aesthetic experience and order from the *samsaric* [this worldly], while endowing the medium with the status of intensified reality'.[21] Parciak then goes on to look at the preliminary consecration rituals employed in commercial films.[22]

Even a cursory look at the parallel films available on YouTube shows that most films begin immediately after the display of the Censor Board certificate, without any on-screen appearance of a deity or consecration ritual.[23] A question that arises in the absence of these is whether the consecration visuals were thought to go against the secular tone or space that the parallel films wanted to occupy, whether these films wanted to announce their modern form by eschewing the connection with theatrical tradition, or whether these films did not want to specifically call attention to their fictional realm, but would have liked the films to be seen as a continuum of the mundane or everyday social world inhabited by or known to the spectator. Also, if the screen deity or consecration ritual was inserted by the production house, that many of these films were produced by government bodies such as Film Finance Corporation or National Film Development Corporation may also be an explanation for their absence. In the case of Shyam Benegal's *Ankur*, *Nishant* and *Manthan*, the first two were produced by Blaze Advertising Agency and the last by 500,000 farmers of Gujarat, which appears in the form of a verbal-visual against a blank background.

A variant of the preliminary visuals is to make the visual of the deity or the worship part of the diegetic world of the film, rather than an unconnected precursor to the film. Here, the characters in the diegetic world would begin the proceedings with worship, which is part of the diegesis. Thus, in the film *Ankur*, we have the character Lakshmi (played by Shabana Azmi) in the opening scene, along with the credit sequence, worshipping and praying to the local deity Pochamma during the Bonalu festival.[24] In *Nishant*, it is interesting that worship is only indexically alluded to by the chanting of the *shlokas* in the background as the film credits float on the screen. After the credit sequence, the priest (played by Satyadev Dubey) walks to the temple for performing worship, only to find that the jewels of the deity have been stolen. So rather than consecration through worship, there is a desecration that follows the chants at the beginning of the film.

The chanting of the Sanskrit *shlokas* serves to establish him as a priest, or as belonging to the priestly order or caste (*brahmin*). After these loud incantations, which go on for over two-and-a-half minutes at the beginning along with the credit sequence,[25] we hear the priest chanting the Sanskrit *shlokas* two more times in the film: on one occasion, it is more like a meditative prayer that he is reciting alone,[26] and on the second occasion, he is chanting as part of a chorus, while a *yagna* (ritual fire sacrifice) is being performed.[27] The chants are not just priestly mumblings, but are used to add a layer of meaning to the visual and the diegetic context.[28] The priest is chanting in a language that is largely unintelligible to the people around him. He seems more like an anachronism. Like the other men of the village, he too is struck dumb by the excesses of the landlord (Amrish Puri) and his brothers (Mohan Agashe, Anant Nag and Naseeruddin Shah). So, though he can easily guess who the thieves of the temple jewellery are, when the landlord comes to the temple to retrieve the possible evidence against his brothers, he is meekly acquiescing. We rarely hear him speak in the early part of the film, as he seems bereft of a language to articulate in a manner intelligible to others what is happening around him.

The priest seems to find his voice when he translates himself to the language of the schoolmaster (played by Girish Karnad). After her kidnapping by the landlord's brothers, when the schoolmaster's wife Susheela (played by Shabana Azmi) visits the temple and finds the schoolmaster there, she ridicules his efforts at rescuing her from the landlord's house and goes away in a huff. The priest attempts to console the distraught husband, only to find the schoolmaster ridiculing his otherworldly orientation and pacification (Figure 2.1). This conversation seems to give a purpose to the priest to speak about the goings-on in the here and now, and he finds a language to converse with the villagers whose help is required to unseat the landlord.

Figure 2.1 The distraught schoolmaster chides the priest for his otherworldly concerns.

Theorists of secularism such as Jürgen Habermas (2009), Charles Taylor (2007) and Talal Asad (2003) have dispelled our notion of the secular being in an antonymous relationship with religion, and have spoken about the translation or osmosis that has happened over time in the making of the religious and the secular domains.[29] Drawing from these discussions, I find that in *Nishant*, it is only when the priest, representing the sacerdotal order, translates himself (literally he moves from mouthing Sanskrit to speaking in Hindi) that he becomes relevant and participatory in public discourse. Under the thumb of the landlord, he seemed to have lost his relevance, but almost as if comprehending his increased relevance and indispensability to the cause for which the schoolmaster is enlisting him, the priest seems to sufficiently secularise himself to become intelligible to his fellow villagers. In the early part of the film, he is all alone, confined to the temple, probably because of the constraints of caste in the form of purity and pollution. But soon, we see him in the public spaces of the village, shoulder to shoulder with the schoolmaster and other villagers. He also seems to employ moral suasion rather than fear to change the mind of the villagers, and to make them go against the landlord.

The schoolmaster with his love of English, which he tries to teach his young son, finds himself alien and unacceptable to the villagers to begin with, as he is from elsewhere. The villagers are unwilling to appear as witnesses to the landlord's brothers' act of kidnapping his wife, even though it unfolded before their eyes. Neither the English-speaking Collector, a government official, nor any of the personnel of the modern institutions, such as the police, lawyers, press, or his own higher officials, can help the schoolmaster to rescue his wife from the landlord's house. He thus draws on the power vested in the sacerdotal order, almost as a last resort, when this kidnapping crisis occurs. His cause requires endorsement by the priest. So only when the schoolmaster and the priest join forces can they inspire the villagers to rebel against the landlord.

I began this section pointing to the chanting of Sanskrit *shlokas*, unaccompanied by worship at the beginning of the film. Towards the end of the film, we see the priest officiating over a fire sacrifice with the villagers as participants and co-chanters. Again, in the beginning, as he climbs the steps after bathing in the river to walk towards the temple, we see him tottering, but he is suddenly of firmer footing as he walks out in a huff after a *Ramayana* performance in the village towards the end. So, if we revisit the question – why does *Nishant* eschew the preliminary ritual, the answer from within the diegesis could be that it is envisaging a different role and function for the priest as he is no longer an emissary between that world and this one; instead he exists in this and this alone. In the concluding part of this chapter, I will say more about how by its fictionalising work the film may be giving us an important insight into how the sacerdotal (as a form of Brahminism) made itself acceptable and relevant in the process of change. In this 1970s film, we see an unreflexive acknowledgement of the conditions of entry of the sacerdotal, the entry of which was made way for by an ineffectual secular, as part of its attempt at legitimacy for bringing about modernity and the new social order.

2 USE OF LANGUAGE VARIETIES AND FOLK FORMS

P. Sundarayya, who was part of the Telangana Peasant Struggle of 1946–51, and as the General Secretary of the Communist Party had prepared the historic report *Telangana People's Struggle and its Lessons* in 1972 in successive issues of the journal *Social Scientist* between February and May 1973, had published a four-part essay entitled 'Telangana People's Armed Struggle, 1946–1951', wherein he delineated in great detail the socio-economic conditions that gave rise to the movement. Sociologists such as D. N. Dhanagere (1974) and more recently historians such as I. Thirumali point to a land system that had created a class of landlords and disempowered and impoverished peasants. Dhanagere talks of how the land system had created a class of powerful *jagirdars* and *deshmukhs* (landlords), who were addressed as *dora* who under 'the *vetti* system [a system of forced labour and exactions] . . . could force a family from among his customary retainers to cultivate his land and to do one job or the other whether domestic, agricultural or official – as an obligation to the master'.[30] Further elaborating on the unparalleled power enjoyed by the *doras*, Thirumali says that 'there were even instances of punishment of people who built proper houses and wore shirts'.[31] Offering another dimension of the service extracted by the *doras*, Sundarayya says, 'slave girls were used by the landlords as concubines'.[32]

Given the widespread nature of the systemic exploitation and impoverishment of the peasants, it was only a matter of time before the peasants rebelled against the *dora*, and his strongmen. Organised under the communist banner into *dalams* (fighting units) and *sanghams* (political organisation), the peasants united and attacked the *doras* and seized control of lands; they aimed to create a *sangham rajyam* in place of a *dora rajyam* (rule of the people's collective to replace rule of the landlord). Thirumali also documents some of the folk songs through which people narrated their struggles and memorialised their heroes.[33] Men and women participated in the *sanghams* to defeat the *doras* and their strongmen.[34]

Right from the outset, *Nishant* refused this mantle of History; the film does not have to tie itself either to the chronology of events or to how it was initiated, or even what unfolded, in the course of its narrative. The film of course has scenes showing *vetti*, the landlord's seizing control of peasants' standing crop and harvest, dispossessing or turning out the peasants working on the land and taking away their livelihood, and the general way of the landlords' grabbing anything they think they should have as their entitlement, including women. There are also scenes in the film that point to the *dora*'s sanctioning and ceremonial power that he enjoyed during the wedding of the villagers, or during festivals and processions. While throughout the film we get a sense of the unbridled authority of the *dora* and exploitation of the villagers, the film hardly makes this the engine that drives the popular movement against the *dora*. There is no reference to *sanghams*, or even to the widespread and systemic nature of this exploitation. Instead, in *Nishant* we find that the people of the village seem to be taking on the landlord on behalf of, and at the behest of, the schoolmaster and the priest.

Is the voice of the people entirely absent, or does it come into the film in some marginal and muted form? In fact, the voice of the people, particularly the perspective of the peasants and sufferers of the landlord's excesses, comes in the form or folk songs or recitations. A close viewing of the film indicates some interesting layering of sounds, and use of the local Telangana variety of Telugu language for the recitation or singing, which is often barely audible, but nevertheless is an important presence in the sound structure of the film. The film deploys many aspects of local Telangana culture, either within the diegesis or in a space between the diegetic and the extra-diegetic levels, where the singing or recitation appears as a meta-commentary to what is happening at the diegetic level. For instance, there is a sequence in which a soothsayer enigmatically indicates the thief who has stolen the temple jewels. He recites:

One with strength/power
Don't ask again and again
One who is a drunkard
One without a wife.[35]

Though it is common knowledge who the thief is (even children know who is behind the theft, as they freely talk about it in the course of their games), the soothsayer's words are taken to mean some other common villager who is beaten and arrested.

Similarly, it is at *Sadar*, the buffalo carnival, and at the *Chindubhagavatha* folk performance of Ramayana that the villagers' unity against the landlord is forged by the schoolmaster and priest. But it is the *oggukatha* folk singing/ recitation in female voice, heard four or five times and punctuating certain key sequences in the film, which is most interesting. At around eight minutes into the film, when the villagers come to report the theft in the temple and call out loudly, 'Dora! Dora!' to the landlord who is getting himself massaged inside his mansion, there is a half-audible singing/recitation that picks up in the background about three brothers and the eating of bland *rotis* (flat bread, here made of corn flour) without salt and chilli. Whatever is being said, even if by way of criticism of the landlord's brothers, is only indirect and metaphorical here.

A second instance of this singing/reciting in the background in Telugu comes about thirty minutes into the film, when the schoolmaster and his wife, who have just moved to the village and taken residence in the house adjacent to the school, are getting up and dressed. As Susheela helps her young son with his morning rituals, the voice in the background sings about the changes that have come about, and how things are not the same anymore – with wandering minstrels being worshipped as holy men, with the mother turning poisonous, while the wife has turned sweet, with difficulty getting even a single meal, with children being born today with diminished powers of the senses, and with people being pierced with injections in the city and washing their face with soap and applying powder. Susheela and the schoolmaster, as we see them here, have moved from an ostensibly bigger town or city, and Susheela is clearly unhappy with the move to the village. She is a product of the new times – where people 'wash their face with soap and apply powder'. So, the song in the background is a meta-commentary, which characterises Susheela as part of the change that is taking place.

Two other more direct critiques of the landlord come at different points of the film, one around the thirty-fourth minute and the other around the forty-fourth minute. In both the sequences, we see the landlord in the foreground bearing a heavy hand against the peasants labouring in the fields. In the first instance, he orders that the crops be seized and the entire harvest sent to his house, thus depriving the peasant of any right over what is grown in the fields, even as a peasant pleads against this. In the second instance, when a peasant brings money to recover his land that has been taken away by the landlord for an unpaid loan, the landlord turns him away and orders his men to throw the peasant out. The Telugu song in the background narrates how the peasant's family is doing while the peasant has neither food nor clothing even as he works hard come rain or shine. Around the forty-second minute of the film, the landlord's brothers order the police *patel* (a policeman appointed by the government, but who works under the thumb of the landlord) to get the wide expanse of uneven land near the village school filled up using the unpaid labour of the villagers, to facilitate the smooth movement of their motor car; at that time the song in the background describes how the police *patel* collaborates with the *dora* in tormenting the people. An hour into the film, the kidnapped Susheela, who has been raped all night by the landlord's brothers, wakes up in the landlord's home while the singing/reciting voice in the background sings of the bastard children of the landlords and their unstoppable philandering ways even when the brother and sister-in-law have died. Finally, about 103 minutes into the film, we hear the voice addressing the rogue *dora*.[36]

An interesting aspect here is the language used, that is, Telugu, and the layering of sounds in the film. About the making of the earlier film, *Ankur*, which is set in the same context, Sangeeta Datta (2016) writes that Mohan Bijlani and Freni Varavia of Blaze Films, who were the producers of both *Ankur* and *Nishant*, were the ones who convinced Shyam Benegal to make the film in Hindi and not in Telugu as was the director's original plan.[37] So even though we have a few words and expressions uttered by some of the characters intermittently in Telugu, almost as an obligatory aspect of realism, for the most part *Ankur* is in Hindi/Dakhani Urdu. Here in *Nishant*, the use of Telugu, particularly in the form of these songs, is not only to establish the milieu, that is, as part of the technique of realism, but also because for those who would be cued into the history of the Telangana peasant struggle, these songs would be evocative of the larger struggle. While the diegetic movement of the film is to unravel the crisis brought about by Susheela's kidnapping (that is, a predicament suffered by one family), these Telugu folk songs, however minimally or indexically, serve to make their sorrow part of the larger sufferings of the peasants, which is what made them take on the landlords.

3 USE OF SONGS

One of the defining aspects of cinema in India is the importance and role of the song-and-dance spectacle in the films. Parciack sees the narrative and the musical layer structured hierarchically, with the narrative layer being tied to the phenomenal and societal order and the musical plane facilitating ascendance beyond the dramatic conflicts in the narrative plane. He then goes on to discuss at length the musical space as potentially transgressive and articulating its socially and morally forbidden aspects.[38]

Though *Nishant* does not have the song-and-dance sequence of commercial Hindi cinema, the film in the climactic moments breaks into song, an Urdu *ghazal*,[39] *Piya baaj pyaala* . . . (I cannot drink or breathe without my beloved) that we hear in the background, a composition by Mohammed Quli Qutub Shah.[40] When we hear the song near the end of the film, we realise that we have heard Susheela absentmindedly hum the tune a couple of times earlier in the film – as she bathed her son, and as she served food to her husband and son, before her abduction. The humming was only in the form of notes that had not yet been worded, almost as if they were her repressed, formless and unarticulated desires. But in the climactic moments of the film we hear Preeti Sagar's (the singer) full-throated rendition of the song in the background. This is when the landlord's younger brother Vishwam, who is infatuated with Susheela and had her abducted by his brothers from her home, runs away with her after the mob of peasants attacks the landlord's home to kill all of them; the two then take shelter in rocky terrain to avoid the attackers. When Vishwam is able to catch his breath and ask in shock and incomprehension how all this happened, Susheela's eyes fill with sorrow as she remembers her son; even as they share this pensive moment together, the mob of peasants steadfastly advances towards them to kill them (Figure 2.2). The *ghazal* that plays in the background then details a woman's desire and intense longing for her absent lover.

According to Parciack (2016), the musical layer elevates and takes one above the mundane and *dharmic* world into the realm of repressed desires; on the face of it, the lyrics of the *ghazal* certainly pertain to the realm of the hidden desires of woman, which have no space in contemporary societal or moral order. But what is interesting is the positioning of the song in the film,

Figure 2.2 The climactic moment – a remorseful Susheela and a puzzled Vishwam.

which comes in the last four minutes, virtually drowning out the sound of the advancing peasants who are baying for their blood, and the agitated, stoic and regret-filled conversation of Vishwam and Susheela.[41] Even as the song continues to play, the camera takes us to the interior of the landlord's home, where through the eyes of a young village boy, we see the unintended consequences of the violence on the landlord's family – the death of Rukmini, the kindly wife of Vishwam, before whose dead body the shell-shocked priest sits mournfully.

It seems as if retrospectively we have to evaluate the whole film differently after the appearance of this song, and once we realise that it was this song that we had heard Susheela hum earlier. Is the film indicting her for her desires, which however inchoate in the early stages have brought this upon her and the landlord's family? Are we meant to juxtapose the small innocent desires that she articulates to her husband, such as the desire for a full-length mirror and for a sari, against the enormity of the events which unfolded? Is she being blamed for her desires in the film, or is she being seen as a victim, for the cruel and twisted way in which things have ended for her?

As in much of modernist literature, and in modernist plays of the period by playwrights such as Chandrashekara Kambara, Girish Karnad[42] and Vijay Tendulkar, *Nishant* shows the representation of woman's sexuality that cannot be contained/regulated within the institution of monogamous marriage and the consequences in the form of the disintegration of the caste and class order. The acknowledgement of woman's sexuality in these plays is invariably ridden with crisis for the male or the husband. Most of the plays can then only envisage the social order dissipating into chaos as a result of woman's desire.

Because woman's desire is a sustained preoccupation in modernist drama and more generally in modernist literature, it is not surprising to see it manifest itself in this film, which is scripted by Vijay Tendulkar. It seems that the question of land for the peasants is turned into the question of woman's sexuality, which gives rise to tension between different social entities; or that central to the class question here is not so much land relations as sexual relations. The two classes are not the peasant and the landlord class, but the class that is emerging into modernity against the class entrenched in the feudal.

CONCLUSION

Feudalism, the system of making land grants to lords by the king in return for service (usually military service) and the working on land by semi-free labour, whose bonds with the landlord are forged by various kinds of obligatory services, has been much discussed in the European context; historically speaking, feudalism is seen as characteristic of the Middle Ages, which were called the

Dark Ages in the European context. It seems that those discussions have been transposed into the Indian, particularly Telangana, context by this film about the end of landlordism and via its title *Nishant* (*Night's End*). The Dark Ages were followed by the Enlightenment in Europe, but *Nishant* stops short of visualising the contours of the new dawn. The film seems to end in ambiguity rather than optimism about what will follow at the end of darkness. The film closes with a shot of the children of the village seated inside the temple even as the same *ghazal* in the background winds down to a conclusion. It seems that the young children sitting inside the precincts of the temple are awaiting the priest to come and show them direction; the priest, who is sitting shell-shocked before Rukmini's dead body in the landlord's house and has just witnessed the killings of the landlord and his brothers, has to get up when a young boy peers in and the scene suggests he will soon make his way to the temple and the children seated there.

The principal actors in the orthographic History, who strove to bring about the end of landlordism as it existed, have been represented on the periphery of this film, their voice and protest placed in the extra-diegetic space. This could hardly be attributed to the peasants' lack of consciousness about their exploitation; the Telugu folk songs can be taken as an articulation and also an acknowledgement by the film of their consciousness and protests against the evils of landlordism. But in the historiophoty of this film, their story seems too insubstantial, and they do not secure an author-backed role in the history that the film narrates. The key figures in this film that preside over the end of landlordism are the schoolmaster and the priest.

Given that the priest and the schoolmaster[43] would be expected to belong to the upper echelons of the social order, as would the landlord,[44] one would expect that they would have more in common with the landlord than to regard him as a class enemy. In fact, the initial silence of the priest regarding the theft of the temple jewels could be thought of as his complicity with the landlord; he neither chides the landlord nor even regards him as a wrongdoer. In other words, while the peasant and the landlord would be 'natural' class enemies, there would be little to suggest that the priest and the schoolmaster would be ranged against the landlord. The film has to contrive to show the schoolmaster as becoming an adversary of the landlord, so deploys the figure of the woman to drive a wedge between them, and to create a contradiction. Sexual competition among men, and the fear that this competition may be decided by the woman in favour of the more powerful, that is, on the side of the landlord, drives this change.

It is also important that by the time the film gets made, more than two decades have passed since the peasant struggle and history has pronounced its judgement in favour of the peasants, even if it means that their battle is not yet over. The film is retrospectively constructing the schoolmaster as a catalyst in ending the old order, and in being a harbinger of the new. Whatever has accrued in the name of modernity in the intervening decades is recuperated now as the legacy of the schoolmaster-initiated struggle. So, the modernity that gets instituted in *Nishant* comes out of collaboration between the schoolmaster pursuing a secular occupation and the priest assigned to the sacerdotal order in society.

Again, if we look retrospectively at what this film does, it does not see the priest as unacceptable or as an anachronism for the ushering in of modernity (though the schoolmaster chides him for his otherworldly concerns being useless in addressing the problems that are upon them); it is only the landlord who is seen as a contradiction to be overcome. So, the priest is enfolded into the new, while the landlord is retrenched, and dispensed with.

In the first section of this chapter, I looked at how the priest is transported across two time periods – the feudal, as the film identifies it, and the post-feudal. Whatever concrete form that takes, the film does not point to a future without the priest in the form of a controlling/ordering power. In the second part, I looked at how the film used the peasant struggle to prop up the sexual struggle that is at the centre of the film. In the third part, I looked at how the film deploys the woman's desire as destroying the old order (as also the woman in the process) – it seems to suggest that the woman's desire has the limited role of bringing what existed to an end, but cannot offer a vision of the new or even go along with forces that are going to bring about the new order.

Finally, what can we say about the narrative work being carried out by the film? The film seems to constitute a particular kind of modernity – what I have termed in this chapter the sacerdotal–secular modernity – and legitimise its act of constitution by giving a narrative past to it. Unlike in a social realist film that locates itself in a present, in *Nishant*, the present is brought into being and legitimised by being given a historical narrative. History in the form of historiophoty appears 'real' and 'true' to us not simply because it resembles the world as we know it, but because it tells us how it came to be (and in doing so, performatively brings it into being). The film is not committed to the past of the 1940s, and so disavows its connection to that History. It is, however, committed to the present's past, whose history will serve to legitimise the present that is being constituted.

Note: All dialogue translated by the author.

NOTES

1. Ashish Rajadhyaksha, *Indian Cinema in the Time of Celluloid: From Bollywood to the Emergency* (New Delhi: Tulika Books, 2009). Rajadhyaksha in his essay 'Gautam Ghose's "Maabhoomi": Territorial Realism and the "Narrator"' tries to account for the location of

what he calls the New Cinema of Shyam Benegal, Gautam Ghosh Mrinal Sen and others in Telangana (formerly Hyderabad state) and says that these filmmakers saw this region as quintessentially feudal India, which had seen the peasant uprising between 1946 and 1951. He further points to how it was the 'location of the sequel Communist Party of India (Marxist–Leninist) action [in the 1970s], which traced a direct and conscious ancestry to the late 1940s, and was a defining presence at the time that the New Cinema films were being made' (Rajadhyaksha, 358). In a note, he further points out that Vijay Tendulkar, who is credited with writing the original screenplay for *Nishant*, had recalled to him in private conversation that the presence of the intellectuals of CPI (M-L) was substantial on the sets of the film (Rajadhyaksha, 358).
2. *Nishant*, directed by Shyam Benegal (1975), accessed 1 September 2021, <https://www.youtube.com/watch?v=nEZMvixYP7w, 0:11–0:19>
3. The origins of this disclaimer in cinema are traced to the litigation against the 1932 film *Rasputin and the Empress*, when the Russian princess Irina Alexandrovna sued MGM Studios for libel as the film seemed to insinuate that princess Natasha (intended to represent Irina Alexandrovna) had been raped by Rasputin.
4. Towards the end of 1972, just three years before *Nishant* was made, the Communist Party of India (Marxist) had published a comprehensive report on the Peasant Struggle in Telangana between 1946 and 1951, prepared by P. Sundarayya, entitled *Telangana People's Struggle and Lessons*. It is unlikely that Vijay Tendulkar, who wrote the original screenplay and who had 'accepted the leadership of the Committee for the Protection of Democratic Rights, a leading pro-People's War civil liberties group in Bombay' (Rajadhyaksha, 358) and Shyam Benegal, who hailed from Hyderabad and spent his formative years there (Datta, 47–63) would have been unaware of Sundarayya's definitive work.
5. *Nishant*, Benegal (1975), 2:57–3:01.
6. For instance, P. Sundarayya, 'Telangana People's Armed Struggle, 1946–51', Parts 1–4, *Social Scientist* 1, no. 7–10 (1973), and I. Thirumali, 'Dora and Gadi: Manifestation of Landlord Domination in Telangana', *Economic and Political Weekly* 27, no. 9 (1992): 477–82, accessed 1 September 2021, <https://www.jstor.org/stable/4397664>
7. Vijay Tendulkar, *Collected Plays in Translation, Kamala, Silence! The Court is in Session, Sakharam Binder, Etc.* (New Delhi: Oxford University Press, 2004). At least three plays of Vijay Tendulkar (2004) which explore the hypocrisies relating to woman's sexuality and desire come immediately to mind – *Sakharam Binder* (1972), *Silence! The Court is in Session* (1967) and *Kamala* (1981).
8. Hayden White, 'Historiography and Historiophoty', *The American Historical Review* 93, no. 5 (1988): 1193–9, 93. Historiophoty is a term coined by the postmodern historian Hayden White in the essay to describe the 'representation of history and our thought about it in visual images and filmic discourse'.
9. Bryan F. Le Beau, 'Historiography Meets Historiophoty: The Perils and Promise of Rendering the Past on Film', *American Studies* 38, no. 1 (1997): 152, accessed 1 September 2021, <http://www.jstor.org/stable/40642863>
10. Le Beau, 154.
11. Telugu is a language spoken largely in the states of Telangana and Andhra Pradesh in India.
12. See Pradip Krishen, 'Knocking at the Doors of Public Culture: India's Parallel Cinema', *Public Culture* 4, no. 1 (Fall 1991): 25–41, accessed 1 September 2021, <https://read.dukeupress.edu/public-culture/article-pdf/4/1/25/455780/ddpcult_4_1_25.pdf>, and Ira Bhaskar, 'The Indian New Wave', in *Routledge Handbook of Indian Cinemas*, ed. K. Moti Gokulsingh, Wimal Dissanayake and Rohit Dasgupta (London and New York: Routledge, 2013), 19–33, for a detailed discussion and overview of parallel cinema and

its characteristic features. See Film India, *The New Generation: 1960–1980* (New Delhi: The Directorate of Film Festivals, 1981), and John W. Hood, *The Essential Mystery: Major Filmmakers of Indian Art Cinema* (New Delhi: Orient Blackswan, 2009), for an elaborate listing of filmmakers and films under this category. For understanding the place of parallel cinema in Film Studies in India, see Manas Ghosh, 'Alternative Cinema: Response of Indian Film Studies', *Journal of the Moving Image* (2011): 51–60; for a more sustained discussion on the terminology, see Rochana Majumdar, 'Art Cinema: The Indian Career of a Global Category', *Critical Inquiry* 42, no. 3 (Spring 2016): 580–610, <doi:10.1086/685605>; for one of the early discussions of the state's role in fostering parallel cinema, see Mira Reym Binford, 'State Patronage and India's New Cinema', *Critical Arts* 2, no. 4 (1983): 33–46, <doi:10.1080/02560048308537566>; for a sharper critique of this cinema as not being sufficiently anti-imperialist, see the chapter '"New Wave" Cinema: Limits of Reformism', in Pranjali Bandhu, *Black and White of Cinema in India* (Thiruvananthapuram: Odyssey, 1992).

13. For more on Third Cinema, see 'Third Cinema' at <https://www.britannica.com/art/Third-Cinema>, accessed 1 September 2021.
14. Sangeeta Datta, *Shyam Benegal* (New Delhi: Roli Books, 2002), 99.
15. Anuradha Dingwaney Needham, *New Indian Cinema in Post-Independence India: The Cultural Work of Shyam Benegal's Films* (London and New York: Routledge, 2013), 46.
16. Hood, 205.
17. Madhava M. Prasad, *Ideology of the Hindi Film: A Historical Construction* (New Delhi: Oxford University Press, 1998), 25.
18. Prasad, 195.
19. Kishore Valicha, *The Moving Image: A Study of Indian Cinema* (Hyderabad: Orient Longman, 1999), 103–4.
20. Ronie Parciack, *Popular Hindi Cinema: Aesthetic Formations of the Seen and Unseen* (London and New York: Routledge, 2016), 50.
21. Parciack, 50.
22. Ibid., 50–6.
23. I cannot vouch for the version of the films uploaded on YouTube as the original or authentic version of the films; so, it may well be that the consecration ritual has been edited out of the YouTube version. But, at the same time, if we look at any commercial film of Indian cinema on YouTube, we find the initial consecration ritual to be very much there, or even embellished further with new ones. The one exception I found was in the parallel film *Kaadu* (Forest, Kannada, 1973), directed by Girish Karnad, which begins with a montage of the temple *gopura* (pyramidal tower) and the deity Lakshmi-Narasimha. The production Company's name 'LN (Lakshmi-Narsimha) Films' then appears in the form of a verbal-visual in the foreground, but there is no worship as such.
24. For more details on *Bonalu*, see <https://en.wikipedia.org/wiki/Bonalu>, accessed 1 September 2021.
25. *Nishant*, Benegal (1975), 0:17–2:49.
26. Ibid., 18:25–18:41.
27. Ibid., 1:55:14–1:55:45.
28. The priest recites about nine *shlokas* at the beginning of the film, the first lines of which are: (1) *Karagre Vasthe Lakshmi* – a chant that accompanies looking at one's palms when waking up in the morning, for it is the abode of gods and goddesses; (2) *Mukam Karoti Vachalam* – a chant in praise of god who can make the dumb turn eloquent and the lame cross mountains; (3) *Guru Brahma Guru Vishnu* – a chant in praise of the teacher as equivalent to the gods; (4) *Punyashloko Nalo raja* – a chant in praise of the good men in mythology; (5) *Ahalya Draupadi Kunti* – a chant in praise of the five women in mythology

extolled for their virtue; (6) *Krishnaya Vasudevaya* – a chant paying obeisance to god; (7) *Gange cha Yamunechaiva* – a chant praying to the rivers to consecrate the surroundings; (8) *Papoham Papakarmaham* – a chant seeking protection from sinful deeds; (9) *Om Suryayanamaha* – chants in praise of the sun. Each of these *shlokas* at the beginning is interesting for prefiguring the events to follow in the film. For instance, the *shloka Mukam Karoti Vachalam* mentioned above appears as a prayer for turning people struck dumb by the landlord's cruelty to find their voice and fight for themselves. The *shloka Guru Brahma Guru Vishnu* would be ironic in the context of the film, as far from being respected as god, the schoolmaster is shamed and his family life disintegrates because of the cruelty of the landlord's family. Similarly, the *shloka Ahalya Draupadi Kunti* in praise of the five virtuous women in mythology provides an interesting blueprint or frame for looking at Susheela, a married woman and mother in the film, who is cruelly kidnapped by the landlord's brothers and turned into chattel. In the second instance, the priestly mutterings of the Sanskrit *shlokas* occur after the discovery of theft in the temple, when the priest is sitting desolately at the temple altar and his lips are automatically muttering the *Gayatri Mantra* – where he is meditating on the glory of the sun to inspire intelligence and banish darkness. In the last instance in the film, while performing fire sacrifice before taking the deities out in procession, we hear the priest chant in chorus the *shloka – Purusha Evedam Sarvamyadbhutamyachabhavyam*. This is the *purushasukta* chant delineating what is required of a man, which in the context of the film is to kill the landlord's family and put an end to the feudal order.
29. See Mohammad Golam Nabi Mozumder, 'Interrogating Post-Secularism: Jürgen Habermas, Charles Taylor, and Talal Asad' (master's thesis, University of Pittsburgh, 2011), for a comprehensive discussion of these three theorists on secularism.
30. D. N. Dhanagere, 'Social Origins of the Peasant Insurrection in Telangana (1946–51)', *Contributions to Indian Sociology*, no. 8 (1974): 112.
31. Thirumali, 'Dora and Gadi', 479.
32. P. Sundarayya, 'Telangana People's Armed Struggle, 1946–1951. Part One: Historical Setting', *Social Scientist* 1, no. 7 (1973): 11, <doi:10.2307/3516269>
33. I. Thirumali, *Against Dora and Nizam: People's movement in Telangana 1939–1948* (New Delhi: Kanishka Publishers, Distributors, 2003), 172.
34. For an account of their participation in this movement by women, see Lalita K., Vasantha Kannabiran, Rama Melkote, Uma Maheshwari, Susie Tharu, Veena Shatrugna, and 'Stree Shakti Sangathana', *'We Were Making History . . .' Life Stories of Women in the Telangana People's Struggle* (New Delhi: Kali for Women, 1989).
35. *Nishant*, Benegal (1975), 13:18. All translations of the Telugu songs/recitations are by Yamini Krishna C., who has also helped me understand the context of the folk performances. I have also discussed with Allakonda Sampathkumar the folk songs and the cultural movement fostered by the Jana Natya Mandali during the Telangana Peasant Movement of the 1940s.
36. It is unclear whether these songs were specifically composed and sung for this film, or chosen from an available repertoire of such folk songs which were an inseparable part of the peasant movement in Telangana in the 1940s and were used widely for mobilising peasants against the landlords; they may have been inserted into the film during editing and post-production, rather than in the course of location shooting. See Hitendra Ghosh, 'Sound', in *Indian Cinema: A Retrospective 1987* (New Delhi: Vikas Publishing House, 1988), 75. Ghosh, who was the sound recordist for the film, says in an interview: '*Nishant* (1975) was a great experience. Benegal gave me a free hand and tremendous support. For instance, I remember once in a night schedule, when everything was totally dark except for the shooting lights, I was picking up a strange moan on my mike. Using the Senheiser Rifle microphone, I tracked it down gradually almost for a furlong, and came upon a hut.

There was a woman crying and a lot of other women were bereaving their fortune. There must have been a bereavement or something. When I entered they set upon me with whips and I had to make a run for it . . . Anyway when we were editing that sequence in which Mohan Agashe's men [the landlord's brothers] come and abduct Shabana [Susheela in the film], we were stuck for what sound to use. Vanraj Bhatia [music director of the film] said that he would not like to have music for that abduction. So I made a loop of the sound I had recorded on location, and kept repeating it over and over again throughout the scene. That sound made a tremendous impact, it was like a foreboding of what would happen.'

37. Sangeeta Datta, 'Shyam Benegal's "Ankur" and the Beginning of a Film Movement', *Scroll.in*, 14 December 2016 <https://scroll.in/reel/823176/shyam-benegals-ankur-and-the-beginning-of-a-film-movement>, accessed 1 September 2021.
38. Parciack, 57–63.
39. For a quick introduction to this form of poetry, see *Ghazal*, accessed 1 September 2021, <https://en.wikipedia.org/wiki/Ghazal>
40. Mohammed Quli Qutub Shah (1565–1612), a Sultan of the Qutub Shahi dynasty and founder of the city of Hyderabad is celebrated for his love for Bhagmati, and for not only being a patron of poets in this court, but for himself being a poet in Urdu, Persian and Telugu. For more, see <https://en.wikipedia.org/wiki/Muhammad_Quli_Qutb_Shah>, accessed 1 September 2021. Given below is first the transliteration into the Roman alphabet of the Urdu *ghazal*, and then its English translation, available at <https://anisr.wordpress.com/category/translations>, accessed 1 September 2021.

> *Piyabaajpyalapiya jai na*
> *Piyabajektiljiya jai na*
> *Kahithepiya bin saburikaroon*
> *Kahhiya jai ammakiya jai na*
> *Nahiishqjis wo badakoodhai*
> *Kadhen us se mil bisiya jai na*
> *Qutub Shah na de mujhdiwanekupund*
> *Diwanekokucchpunddiya jai na*

> I can't drink, my drink, without my love
> I can't breathe; I sink, without my love
> I should be patient, you say, without my love
> How easy to say, how hard to live, without my love
> A boor, indeed, is one who does not love
> Can I ever be a boor to live without my love
> No counsels, Qutub Shah! None to this crazy one
> None indeed! I'm the crazy one, without my love

41. *Nishant*, Benegal (1975), 2:12:40.
42. See Nikhila H., 'Forays into Folk: Recasting Womanhood in the Kannada Drama of the 60s and 70s', *Journal of Karnataka Studies* II, no. 1 (2004–5): 159–71, for an extended discussion of the aspect of sexuality of woman and its representation in the modernist plays of Chandrashekara Kambara and Girish Karnad.
43. While the priest would be a Brahmin following his traditional occupation, the schoolmaster in all likelihood would be a Brahmin who had benefited from English education, and had moved into secular occupations, such as school-teaching and other kinds of clerical positions.
44. See Thirumali (1992), 479–80 for the caste composition of the landlord class and the peasant and labouring classes which ranged itself against the landlord class.

CHAPTER 3

Churning Out Change: A Moment of Reading *Manthan*

Ritu Sen Chaudhuri

This chapter animates the concerns of caste as they are being churned out in the film *Manthan* (*The Churning*, 1976). In the film, the caste politics, operating around a milk-producing village of Gujarat called Sema, are traversed by the dilemmas of nation-building. The film also takes up some issues concerning gender and in certain ways subsumes them within the wider questions it addresses. *Manthan* provokes change. It opens the seemingly idyllic village up to the statist project of development. Calling upon an initiative of setting up a dairy co-operative society, it eventually stirs up the whole village. Beginning with an effort to confront the deceitful business terms between the local milk-producers and the profiteering middle-men (selling the low-priced milk in urban markets at an inflated rate) the 'society' eventually goads the feudal caste-class edifice of the village. This chapter is an attempt to posit the film and its dealing with the caste processes within three specific discourses on the 'village' initiated by M. K. Gandhi, Jawaharlal Nehru and Dr B. R. Ambedkar. As a self-declared Nehruvian, Benegal upholds a socialistic pattern of nation-building. Socialist development absorbs the village into the wider project of planned economy and industrialisation, electoral democracy and secularism. More than an analysis of the cinematic structure of the film, the point here is to ponder on the thematic nuances through which Benegal's ideological engagement with liberal democracy is being depicted. In tandem with its content, the film also bears the mark of a change in the genre called Hindi cinema.

Shyam Benegal, one of the pioneers of parallel cinema, a pan-Indian event of the rise of realist film in the 1970s and 1980s, comes up with a rural trilogy early in his career. His debut film *Ankur* (*The Seedling*, 1974) is followed by *Nishant* (*Night's End*, 1975) and *Manthan*. All three films address the transformative processes of feudal India in terms of ownership and power.[1] Going beyond the Bollywood formulae, parallel cinema adapted realist aesthetics, psychological depth and regionalism to represent people striving against post-colonial predicaments. Financed by the members of the Gujarat Co-operative Milk Marketing Federation, each of whom contributed two Indian rupees, the film upholds the incredible power of cinema. The film's energy incited several villagers to establish their own co-operatives. It narrates the groundwork laid down in Gujarat by Dr Verghese that led to the founding of the first dairy co-operative in India, Amul, in Anand, and the materialisation of Operation Flood or the White Revolution. The co-operative movement involves the production and distribution of milk and its by-products by the farmers themselves, evading the corrupt middle-men. The movement altered India's status from a milk-deficient nation to the world's leading producer of milk.

Dr Rao, the protagonist of the film, embodies Dr Verghese. Yet he exists in his own right. Memories and deeds come alive and get layered together through the narrative of the film. Embodying Kurien and his interactions with the villagers, Dr Rao wanders into situations, reaches a remote village of Gujarat and sets up a dairy co-operative. The question of untouchability formulates an essential argument of the film. Dr Rao persistently calls for the *harijans*[2] to join the co-operative to make it sustainable. The co-operative is implicated into an intricate interface of the tradition-bound locals and the elite intellectual with a critical and emancipatory life-world. It ignites a movement among the village 'untouchables'. This ravages the whole social edifice as well as the political and economic setting of the village. The caste system is disparaged, the feudal traditions are thrashed, the underpinnings of patriarchal–misogynist structure are exposed and the economy is forced out of indolence.

The opening sequence, as it scrolls up the credit title, reflects a train track under a blue sky and a yellow station board (in the right corner) inscribed with *Semla* in black. A long shot captures an inbound train gradually smoking up the clear sky (perhaps foretelling the dismal events about to occur) before it halts at a lonely village platform. Dr Rao and his companion have arrived just on time. Unable to foresee the timely arrival of the train, the villagers reach a little late with the garland. Not allowing it to adorn his neck, Dr Rao slips the garland around his fingers. The garland is about to swing its way with him, but just then he drops it on a wayside bush. He walks down the rural fields refusing to board an overloaded horse cart. The simple beginning of the film projects an idealistic young man trying to hold sway over his circumstances. As the film proceeds, things gradually spiral out of his control. Dr Rao is a veterinary doctor posted at the village to set up a dairy co-operative. The villagers refuse to buy his idea. For ages they have been habituated to selling their milk to the upper-caste businessman Mishra, though at a slashed rate. The situation changes when Dr Rao, violating his disciplinary limitations, comes to meet one of the villagers' urgent needs. His medicines save the life of a little boy. Due to the absence of the basic healthcare services, the village people now flock to his place seeking treatment for their ailments. He succeeds in registering the first member for the co-operative. However, the majority still stands against him. Especially Bhola, the angry young lower-caste man, who is strongly sceptical of the urban people and so worsens the situation with his sabotage attempts (Figure 3.1). Rather than an exhibition of his strength this aggression manifests his absolute helplessness and mortal fear. Bhola articulates his deep distrust of the rich and upper-caste sects who have always spat on them and made them work like cowering slaves. As the film proceeds, he is gradually drawn towards Dr Rao's mission. At the end, it is Bhola who, going to desperate lengths, salvages the co-operative. Bindu, the *harijan* woman occasionally left by her husband to fend for herself and the child, is another cornerstone of the film. Her life remains fraught because of her oppressive husband and the upper-caste men in the village. Bindu's voice and her silence, her vulnerability and defeat, and her unformed relationship with Dr Rao reflect a realistic yet partial dealing with the question of gender as it remains tangled with caste issues.

Before going deeper into the caste and gender insinuations within the backdrop of a village, let me talk first about the discursive category the 'Indian village'. Orientalist lines of thought, often backed by the colonial administrators, have epitomised India as an eternal land of village republics resistant to change.³ Following this cue, nationalist discourses have marked the village as an essential trope of the civilisational specificity of India – the basic unit

Figure 3.1 Dr Rao (extreme right) surrounded by the sceptic villagers (Bhola next to Rao, Moti and Bindu with the child on her lap).

of the Indian social formation. This subsequently has taken the most variegated turns. Often ignoring the material conditions of rural life that are striated with regional variations and historical particularities, the village is being reproduced as the upholder of ageless Indian values. On the other hand, the village, seen as the 'real' face of India (plagued with illiteracy, superstition, caste-class-gender-religious discriminations), also vindicates the necessity for social reform. Thus, the nationalists invert the orientalist–idealistic discourse on Indian villages into a direct allegation against colonial governance. They explain the problems afflicting the country as overt failures of the British rule. These seeds of the imaginations of a sovereign nation sprouted in at least three different nodes:[4] M. K. Gandhi, Jawaharlal Nehru and B. R. Ambedkar. For Gandhi the village is the abode of civilisational authenticity, for Nehru it happens to be a space of colonial backwardness, and for Ambedkar it remains as a field of caste oppression.[5] One must remember that all the three thinkers, albeit in three different ways, condemned caste (and gender) discrimination. If for Gandhi the concern was of morality, for Nehru it was progress and for Ambedkar it was justice (in formal constitutional terms). The commonality between the three stands, the call for reform remains.

Gandhi talks about a caste/class-less village society without vertical divisions. 'We are inheritors of a rural civilization' he avers, '. . . we must perpetuate the present rural civilization and endeavour to rid it of its acknowledged defects.'[6] He aspires for *swaraj*, for a harmonious, self-governed, self-sufficient village-centric nation uncorrupted by the modern Western ideological and technological advances. This, however, by no means keeps Gandhi 'as an outsider to modernity, an anomalous figure who stood completely apart from other nationalists . . . As a national claim over a territory configured by modern technics, swaraj was at once an intervention within modernity and an attempt to steer the nation in a different direction.'[7] Gandhi's criticism of the essential features of modern civil society cannot be reduced to a 'romantic' or 'idealistic' critique of the intemperance of modern Western material civilisation. Gandhi's idealism, in the mentation of a sovereign nation, has a political point to make. It is to harness an ideological concord, within the nationalist movement, among the caste–class oppositions between the subalterns and elites of India.[8] Nehru seems to work out the impracticality of the Gandhian scheme. I am not going into the complex detail of the debate between the Gandhian, Nehruvian and Ambedkarian ideas on the Indian village. I will quickly touch upon Nehru's position against Gandhi's reliance on village self-sufficiency and Ambedkar's position countering the Gandhian insistence on village self-governance. These two instances have some bearing on my reading of *Manthan*. The film avowedly keeps to the Nehruvian scheme of village development beckoning modern technology and dismissing archaic agrarian relations.

Nehru declares that the economic self-sufficiency of the village, grounded on community ownership and the co-operative system, has been ravaged by the colonisers. When India has been reduced to just 'a colonial and agricultural appendage of the British structure',[9] reversal is not a solution. The co-operative principle should be applied in renewed terms 'by developing collective and co-operative farms [and] ... establishing of the fundamentals of the socialist structure.'[10] It must be mentioned here that instituting a socialist state has never been the primary goal of Nehru per se. More than a decade before India's independence, he took up the task of modernising the nation. To achieve this, he called for a Fabian mode of social democracy and a Soviet pattern of centralised planning. The consequence was a 'mixed-economy'; a peculiar blend of centralised planning and private enterprise.[11] Building up village co-operative societies (in dairy, storage, processing sectors) constitutes a part of the first two five-year plans of independent India. Although closely related, co-operative is not essentially linked to socialism. Keeping the socialist states aside, co-operatives are also quite compatible with the Nehruvian model of a 'socialistic' state heading towards state capitalism. Even though he was a part of the Nehruvian government and strongly endorsed the agenda of modernisation, Ambedkar's take on Indian villages was different. He wanted to modernise the villages and unshackle them from the oppressive mechanisms of the traditional caste system.

Ambedkar exposes the Hindu upper-caste underpinnings of the Indian villages. Villages, he holds, are the abode of caste authority. They remain ever parochial and regressive. He deflates the glorification of village self-governance with a strike of distrust. In his October 1932 speech on the Village Panchayat Bill, Ambedkar declares,

> [a] population which is hidebound by caste ... infected by ancient prejudices ... dominated by notions of gradations in life ... can it be expected to have the right notions even to discharge bare justice ... it is not proper to expect us to submit our life and our liberty and our property to the hands of these panchas.

Adopting the parliamentary model of politics, the foundations of the sovereign state of India, Ambedkar advocates, should be grounded in democratic constitutionalism.

'Ambedkar not only relied on constitutional issues, he made one of his most important marks through the constitution, and he was convinced that "untouchables" could only thrive through constitutional negotiation around their status as an oppressed and disenfranchised minority.'[12] The Constitution of India, drafted under his chairmanship, does not refer to questions of local self-governance of villages. Also, Nehru desists from the enactment of the *panchayati raj* until 1957 (the first two terms of his prime ministership). The film *Manthan*, assuming a similar line of thought, aptly reflects that far from being neutral, village forums or *panchayats* operate strictly as caste councils.

Manthan addresses the caste question point-blank. From the very inception of the co-operative society Dr Rao appeals for the participation of the 'untouchables'. His perception of the viability of the co-operative is tied to anti-caste socialistic ideals. Rao's attention towards the lowest castes agitates his associates and the upper-class/caste villagers. His sharp rebuffs during occasional altercations with Deshmukh and other villagers reveal his resolute argument. The aim of the co-operative is to empower people, across caste-class-gender, with economic freedom and dignity. So long as the untouchable castes refrain from joining the society its goal cannot be accomplished. To emphasise the point, Benegal creates a short sub-text within the film. His documentary, *The Unquiet Revolution* (on Operation Flood), is screened before the villagers, educating them about dairy-processing.[13] The documentary allusion grounds the film within a context. As such, the viewers come to discern a correspondence between the film and the Nehruvian canon of building up a modern nation-state with socialistic ambitions. As Benegal makes the villagers watch the documentary, the viewer of the film catches a couple of scenes and voiceovers: 'in the milk centres religion, class and caste distinctions are wiped away. People from all castes wait in the same queue to put in their milk'. While the documentary narrates the success story of Kurien, the film places Rao within the real-life situation, thoroughly troubled by caste-class-gender issues.

In his essay 'Talkies, Movies, Cinema', Benegal talks about how a speech by Nehru, which he heard during his college years, had a deep impact on him. 'During the speech', he writes, 'Nehru mentioned that all communications had hidden messages . . . Nehru referred to these hidden persuaders as a component of change.'[14] This makes Benegal believe that cinema is not a mere means to entertainment. It facilitates social change. He trusts that 'film-makers had some kind of a role to play in helping to change our traditional hierarchically constructed feudal society to an egalitarian and democratic one'.[15] The auteur here has a very specific message to convey. The 'organic intellectual' (here the elite-bureaucrat) is the social agent to transport the wider message of socialistic development to the remote corners of the country. Yet, the success of the statist project, in the last instance, rests on the direct involvement of the lower-caste people. Perhaps at this very moment, Benegal moves a few steps beyond the Nehruvian order. Unwittingly though, he seems to verge on the contentions of Ambedkar. The point made here is subtle. For both Ambedkar and Nehru, participation of the lower/lowest castes in the national mission is imperative. However, there is a sharp qualitative difference between the two views. Nehru's critique of caste (or gender or class) is subservient to his wider goal of development through industrialisation. To accomplish modernisation, he has to eliminate the incidence of social discrimination in general. Contrarily,

Ambedkar's primary concern is caste. His engagement with caste is not just a political stance. Through an ethical-moral-academic lead, Ambedkar works out the means of its annihilation. The narrative structure of the film logically sustains the upfront participation of the untouchables as a pre-condition for the functioning of the society. Without rendering the issue of caste contingent to the project of nation-building the film has inverted the story. In an Ambedkarian stride, *Manthan* foregrounds the point that the work of the nation is implicated in the edifice of caste. Caste is a key impediment to development. To develop this, the narrative negotiates with the limitations of both centralised planning and the decentralised *panchayati* system. On the one hand, the state planning system, missing out the specificity of the caste question, fails to formulate strategies to combat caste. On the other, the *panchayat* itself works as caste body. I will follow the progression of the narrative to substantiate the argument I have made. While I do this I also focus on the question of gender and explicate why I think the film remains inadequate in its dealings of the subject.

Rao tests the fat content of the milk the villagers collect and offers them a reasonable price. Increasingly, he gains the confidence of Bindu and a few other women of the village (Figure 3.2). Also, a contained sense of mutual admiration springs up between Bindu and Rao before it gets truncated both by Rao's conscious non-indulgence and the sudden arrival of their respective spouses. Rao repetitively quizzes Bindu and accepts her help both to comprehend the nitty-gritty of village politics and to draw Bhola's attention. In spite of Bindu's tacit approval he avoids any personal conversation with her. Before going into Rao and Bindu's relationship, let us follow yet another course of events. Despite all of Rao's efforts, the membership of the co-operative does not increase. He realises that the majority will avoid the 'society' until the *surpanch* (the upper-caste headman) and Bhola (the assumed leader of the untouchables) become members. The morning after the documentary screening, the *surpanch* enlists himself. Though Deshmukh views this as a toe in the door, Rao remains jittery. Deshmukh advises him not to intrude into the local politics and to wait until things settle according to their natural course. Rao harps the same tune, that is, the poor *harijans* will never join if they get an idea that the 'society' belongs to the upper caste. Also, the upper caste may prohibit them from joining. Deshmukh turns caustic and does not understand why Rao reduces the whole aim of the co-operative into a *harijan* versus non-*harijan* dispute. Rao holds steady to his claims. He sacks Chandavarkar, one of his associates, for wooing and toying with an untouchable girl and gradually comes to win Bhola's faith. Bhola himself is a victim of such a deception. His mother was ditched by a city contractor. Rao also bails Bhola out of the lock-up when the *surpanch*, under Deshmukh's instigation, has him detained for going rogue. The series of events reassures Bhola as he tries to become accommodated into the 'society'.

Figure 3.2 Bindu and the other women members of the co-operative society.

Amid this, Rao's wife Shanta arrives from the town. Much to his surprise, she poses a query, 'Why do you mix with the *harijans*? They are beneath us.' Rao requests her to appreciate them, 'They too have certain virtues,' he affirms. Shanta replies, 'You like them because they consider you an important man ... they respect you.' Rao has no answer for this. Why? What exactly is the relationship between the elite outsider and the local men? The State Dairy Board has sanctioned Rao, on the basis of his education and expertise, with the task of setting up a co-operative society. Does this provide him with the authority to speak on behalf of the villagers? Is not this top-down approach presupposing a knower–known divide? Is it not that the man from the city is the bringer of knowledge and the humble villagers its recipients? Generating an inimitable energy among the untouchables to move forward on their own, the film ends up problematising this knower–known divide. Paradoxically, this is made possible through Rao's intervention. Rao tries relentlessly to help the villagers assume a pro-active role. He is seen constantly talking to them, both in public and private, raising consciousness.

The question of why he doesn't make even the slightest effort to help his wife understand the reality still remains. *Manthan* shows Rao and Shanta chatting cheek-to-cheek on an indoor swing chair, but the film never takes the wife outdoors (except to the station when they are leaving the village). Why? Is this not allowed for the upper-caste woman? On a later occasion, Shanta asks again: Why is Rao so attached to the untouchables? When Rao probes, 'Who told this to you'? Shanta replies, 'It is over the walls that I get to know this . . . who else have I been able to talk to in this desert?' This is quite literally true. The film does not allow Shanta to talk to anyone other than her husband. Also, the film underscores her only eye contact with an outsider, Bhola, by her abstinence from interaction with any other man. Rao reprimands her, 'you never realise . . . neither my responsibilities nor my helplessness'. How will she be able to 'realise' if she is neither a witness of the outside affairs nor a receiver of any news? Rao never involves her in any serious discussion, he grips her as if she is an infant. He fathers her in such completeness that she could stay a perpetual child. Rao's refusal to intellectually engage with his wife reflects his gross gender insensitivity. Perhaps this rejection of the woman (or the other in a generic sense) as a potential knower also echoes the patronising nature of the statist developmental project. Far from being participatory, it remains authoritative. And as such, it fails. The film finds a way to get to the bottom of this failure. Through the disruptive acts of the lower-caste people, it brings the co-operative society back to life. However, the question of gender, although it raised, remains unanswered. The narrative does not return to the wife with a resolution; maybe Shanta is just a static supporting character helping to delineate Rao's persona as a paternalist patroniser.

Now that both the leaders are associated with the co-operative, leading to a steady increase in its trade, the businessman Mishra becomes alarmed. He plans to save his business by paying more for the milk and defaming Rao and his 'society'. Rao tries to make people understand that Mishra might raise his rate even higher, but that should not by any means affect the 'society'. More than just offering a fair price, the co-operative has to engage in wider developmental activities. Village co-operatives must aim to take proper care of the cattle, construct roads, dig tube wells, open schools and hospitals. Through his small co-operative Rao links up the inconsequential village with the pan-Indian pursuit of development. Yet the lower-caste villagers remain hesitant. They fear the *surpanch* will soon arrogate the 'society' as his private property. Rao organises an election for the post of society-head, where along with the higher castes, the lowest castes are allowed to offer their candidature. Ignoring Deshmukh's repeated warnings he pushes the *harijans* to unite against the *surpanch*. Bhola declares, 'We will fight the elections . . . let the *surpanch* do whatever he can . . . we will fight our own battle!' Why is it that Rao never pays any heed to Deshmukh's cautions? He is always holier-than-thou; he is always dismissive. Deshmukh reproaches Rao for being partial, 'We must see the both sides equally . . . is it not unfair to take sides? The co-operative must maintain neutrality.' Rao replies, 'While one has money and power the other side is left with nothing . . . treat both at par . . . what do you mean!' Deshmukh can foresee that the election will bring a severe upheaval. The tension between Bhola and the *surpanch* will flare up the whole village. Rao candidly responses,

'I see no harm in it!' Rao is not wrong, but is too confident, self-righteous and impatient to judge the gravity of the situation. Can a longstanding structural challenge be solved overnight? It is already late when Rao realises that the co-operative would be ruined were the election to turn communal. Has Rao over-played his hand? The first election meeting is adjourned amid a brawl. The tension between the upper and lower castes ramps up. The co-operative election polarises the village into two opposing camps. Following the unexpected result, Rao gets caught up in nasty politics. Initially Moti, the *harijan* representative, and the *surpanch* get an equal number of votes. Later Moti takes victory over the *surpanch* in a tie-breaker. The *surpanch* cannot accept this insult. How can he be defeated by a 'sub-human untouchable?' Joining hands with Mishra and Bindu's husband, he conspires to take his revenge.

Bindu's husband has always been against Rao. He humiliates Rao by pointing at his alleged relationship with Bindu. She sternly retaliates and does not let him grope her as per his whims. The husband pounces on her and forewarns that he would not let a fallen woman go like that. Leaving her penniless, he poisons her buffalo, which is her sole source of livelihood. Bindu cries and her friend consoles her, 'While you marry, you have dreams; you will be a queen . . . who knows the future!' Like other lower-caste women Bindu lives a life of relentless toil and misery. She takes care of her buffalo, collects and churns milk, attends to her son, cooks the food, carries water, gets beaten up by the husband, and deceived by the moneylender. She is tired. As the background song reiterates a folk lyric, 'I am weary. No, I don't milk the cow. No, I don't collect water. I have no rest and no peace', Bindu along with Bhola runs to the co-operative seeking help. Rao says that the loan can only be arranged after a meeting. He personally offers her some money. Indignant, Bindu refuses his offer, perhaps because she cannot stand Rao's arrogance and because she never expected charity. She looked forward to some support from the co-operative. She believed Rao would understand her. But he fails to figure her out. He fails to comprehend exactly what she wanted. This is simply because on no occasion does he try to do so. He turns out to be 'just like any other man' (Bindu's enunciation). Unlike Shanta, Bindu is a significant character in the film; the narrative makes an attempt to develop her character as a strong woman. Yet, the narrative cannot handle the issues concerning her violation – to operate through a misogynistic ensemble of ideological and institutional arrangements – as a woman. *Manthan* fails to probe the specific concerns of gender, where an untouchable woman is violated by her husband, cheated by upper-caste men, underestimated by the elite patroniser just because she is a woman, and where her oppression as a woman is only intensified for her being a *harijan*.

The modern man Rao remains unfair in his interactions with women (both Bindu and Shanta). He rather takes for granted that they will be subservient to him and his noble mission. More than the women themselves, it is the very discourse of our modernity that conditions him that way and rationalises his problematic ideas.[16] In his first meeting with Bindu, when he has come to test the milk, he almost ignores her presence and seeks only the father of her child. In a typical thoroughly disgusted voice though, Bindu candidly identifies herself as the father, 'the father is just here', she says. Without paying any heed to her snapping remark, Rao goes on with his job. On several further occasions too, Rao takes a similar stance. Bindu is upright, often audacious in her terms. Perhaps the safest way to handle this unsophisticated lower-caste woman is to not give her any due attention. This is in no way a simple thing to do, for Rao cannot just blatantly ignore her. He needs her help to get to the brass tacks of the village community. He also has a liking for her. Nevertheless, he adopts an overtly hierarchised and self-possessed mode of interaction with her which provides him the opportunity to overlook her agency.

The world of men might go against her, she might get weary at times, but at the end of the day Bindu is indomitable. She moves on. A few days later, Bindu reaches Mishra's office. She remains sceptical though. In the presence of her husband, Mishra gives her a buffalo at zero per cent interest. She has to make her thumb impression on a court-paper, without knowing that it declares that Dr Rao has raped her. A lawyer, appointed by Mishra, approaches Dr Rao and gives him the prosecution notice. Rao becomes highly distressed. Mishra's goons set fire to the *harijan basti*. Everything burns to ashes and the same *harijans* are put behind bars. Mishra brings aids to the villagers and later bails out the *harijans* too. In spite of Bhola's cautioning, the horrified *harijans* accept the loans offered by Mishra. Once again, they come under his sway. Over the ruins of the co-operative Mishra recoups his business. Bhola continues yelling for quite some time, 'The society is ours, we have created it. We are rid of the *surpanch* . . . now you want Mishra to fix you. We admit we had some faults yet we all joined hands to bring something new.' No one cares when he departs alone.

In the middle of this mix-up the *surpanch* leaves for the town to buy out Rao's transfer order from the higher officials. Mishra sends the lawyer back to Rao conveying how he has persuaded Bindu to withdraw the false rape case. He also offers Rao compensation for the whole ordeal. Dr Rao is still not ready to be purchased. In an insane rage he promises to continue the co-operative against all odds. He returns home and receives a telegram stating that his transfer order has been issued. With a futile attempt of talking to Bindu for the last time Rao severs his links with the village. We see the semi-arid landscape around the train track once again. The train appears as Bhola comes running all the way across the barren fields and the grazing pastures, gaining speed before he reaches it. The very next day Mishra lowers the price of milk. Bhola frantically tries to remind his people about the co-operative; it belongs to them and together they can make it work again. A little procession, going from anguish to aspiration, follows Bhola and Moti heading towards the 'society'. Bindu joins up and the co-operative is set in motion. People's sense of autonomy and their initiatives cover up the limitations of centralised planning.

M. K. Gandhi was thoroughly suspicious of the centralised planning system. He thought it would lead to the beneficiaries becoming passive. He preferred individual sense of sovereignty and ethical conviction; preferences and practices were the real sources of change. He encouraged village self-governance. Does the film, at the end, take a Gandhian spin? Not really, for the untouchable's sense of autonomy is mediated by a statist project stopping because of the dedication of an individual state official, Rao. Had the village society been kept impervious to the national mission the lower-caste people would hardly have been able to challenge the upper-caste hegemony in the village *panchayats*. In the society versus state challenge, Gandhi takes the side of the society whereas Nehru and Ambedkar opt for the state. Both Nehru and Ambedkar are advocates of state planning. Ambedkar's unswerving effort is to administer a planned transformation on the basis of constitutional provisions defending minority/Dalit rights. Nehru fails to gauge, with as much precision as Ambedkar, the abysmal impact of caste in village societies and the line of attack the state will have to design to annihilate it. This delimits Nehruvian planning and consequently the accomplishments of Dr Rao. The primary impediment to the co-operative happens to be the oppositional interest of the upper and lower castes. It is not possible to put an end to this without the force of the people themselves. The elite intellectual Rao, the putative instrument of social change, is the respected knower and the *harijan* community is the object of his knowledge. His conscientious effort is logically circumscribed within this dichotomy. He creates the space, acting as a catalyst, leaving it open to transformations. This stimulation is a change in itself. He has educated, agitated and organised the people. Yet, far-reaching transformations require the intervention of the people themselves. They require a barefaced confrontation between oppositional castes, with the lower-caste claiming their rights from which they have systematically been forbidden. In the clearest of terms *Manthan* establishes the point that systemic caste oppression can be transcended through the everyday individual and collective initiatives of the lower castes. I read this as a turn analogous to Ambedkar. Let me clarify that the claim here is not of a one-to-one correspondence between Ambedkarian thought and the diegesis of the film. It is rather to think of a semblance between two disparate things – ideology and cinema.

The film could have ended at Rao's failure. Or else, it could have rendered him successful. Without choosing these predictable options *Manthan* has recourse to another figure. The narrative takes its time to work out the character arc of Bhola. Beginning as an unreasonable angry man he gradually transforms himself, coming to terms with the democratic principles introduced by

Rao and his co-operative. Prevailing over his otherness, he empowers himself to resolve the impasse manoeuvred by the system of caste. *Manthan* also raises the question of gender. Yet it does not deal with the specificities concerning it. Interestingly, the narrative seeks the resolution of Bindu's problems through her empowerment – she ignores her familial interdictions to join the movement kindled by Bhola. Bindu's liberation is marked by her participation in the wider call of the nation. The point here is to include the woman within the man's discourse of nation-building, which invokes self-determination, statehood, democracy, progress and modernity. Bindu's claustrophobia, generated both by the plot and the structure of the film, is rendered inconsequential in the face of the broader issues of nation-building. The question of gender thus gets accommodated within the historic goal of building up the independent nation.

In a way this resonates with the general concerns of post-Independence India. India witnessed an elusive shift of attention of the nationalist elites from the Hindu, urban, upper middle-caste/class women in the early nineteenth century to the common mass of women in Gandhian politics. Consequently, the Nehruvian era ended up exhibiting the archetypal image of the poor woman (with an under-fed child on her lap) as the icon of independent India. Setting the trend of India's development for almost forty years since Independence, this era also scripted the failure of the modernising projects of gender equity. India developed the five-year plans[17] and established several administrative bodies.[18] Yet most of these committees and their policy documents naively considered women as targets for household- and motherhood-oriented welfare services and perpetually failed to identify the real problems of the women.[19] *Manthan*, although portraying the poor woman, strides far ahead of the hegemonic discourse of nationalism. In spite of questioning the woman's role within the discourse of nation-building, it lets her make an independent move, disregarding the prohibitive family. However, remaining closer to the statist projects of Nehru, the film fails to engage with Ambedkar's concern about the structural complicity between caste and gender.[20] Delineating the means of reproduction of caste both at the level of everyday life and societal structure, the film does not get at the roots of the gendered nature of caste dominance. It does not show how the gender question remains entwined with the question of caste.[21]

Madhava Prasad labels *Manthan* an 'Emergency Film' and a 'mobilized state apparatus'[22] to strengthen the Congress agenda of socialistic change during the period of Emergency (1975–7) declared by the then Prime Minister Indira Gandhi. Anuradha Needham observes that though the release of the film coincides with the Emergency years, Benegal tends to convalesce an earlier historical moment (the independence of India), reflecting on what went wrong. He addresses the questions of equality and justice as the unaccomplished tasks of nation-building. Needham holds that rather than calibrate the statist project of development, *Manthan* offers a subtle critique of it.²³ Prasad holds a deep distrust of Benegal's representation of 'the rebellion of the oppressed as the result of a calculated intervention from above by a militant bureaucracy'.²⁴ It would be impetuous to reduce the film to an appeasement to the state, rendering the rise of the people fully amenable to its calculations or extended mechanisms. The obvious primacy of Bhola's intervention in the narrative of *Manthan* draws upon the limits of the state apparatus. Rather than accommodating radicalism within the discourse of nation-building, *Manthan* engenders a radical figure that will denigrate the state-sponsored project of development and find a resolution to it. In this chapter, I have attempted to follow such a politically charged message of change, where the common lower-caste villagers live up to a utopic moment of negotiating the grand narrative of nation-building.

Note: All dialogue translated by the author.

NOTES

1. Sangeeta Datta, *Shyam Benegal* (New Delhi: Roli Books, 2002).
2. Though the dialogues of the film refer to the untouchable lower castes as *harijan*, for reasons unknown, the English subtitles use the term Dalit. Following the script of the film the essay adheres to the term *harijan*. It is now common knowledge that though both terms denote people of the untouchable caste (*harijan* was coined by Gandhi, discarding his earlier coinage 'supressed classes', and Dalit was initially used by Jyotiba Phule, then taken up by Ambedkar and later by the Dalit Panthers), they cannot be used interchangeably. While *harijan* euphemises the oppressive nature of the Hindu society, the word Dalit upholds a sense of the anti-caste movement. It is interesting that though the film uses the term *harijan*, it does not stick to its Gandhian connotation. Rather, the narrative structure of *Manthan* takes the question of caste to an Ambedkarian height, depicting how the merit of a state policy (formation of the dairy co-operatives) remains grounded in the participation of the lowest castes.
3. B. S. Cohn, *An Anthropologist Among Historian and Other Essays* (Delhi: Oxford University Press, 1987). R Inden, *Imagining India* (Cambridge: Blackwell, 1990). Nicholas B. Dirks, *Castes of Mind: Colonialism and the Making of Modern India* (Princeton, NJ: Princeton University Press, 2001), 265.
4. There are several other strands of nationalist imaginations in elite and subaltern, literary and oral, sporadic and consistent quarters that are manifest and latent in the cartographic space of India over more than two hundred years. In this occasion, I talk about only three dominant discourses.
5. Surinder S. Jodhka, 'Nation and Villages: Images of Rural India in Gandhi, Nehru and Ambedkar', *Economic and Political Weekly* 37, no. 32 (2002): 3342–54.
6. M. K. Gandhi, *Gandhiji on Villages*, selected and compiled with an introduction by Divya Joshi (Mumbai: Mani Bhavan Gandhi Sangrahalaya, 2002), 15.
7. Gyan Prakash, 'Civil Society, Community, and the Nation in Colonial India', *Etnográfica* 6, no. 1 (2002): 37.
8. Partha Chatterjee, *The Nation and its Fragments: Colonial and Post-colonial Histories* (Delhi: Oxford University Press, 1993).

9. S. Gopal, *Jawaharlal Nehru: A Biography*, vol. III (Cambridge, MA: Harvard University Press, 1984), 303.
10. Gopal, 399–400.
11. S. Gopal, *Jawaharlal Nehru: A Biography*, vol. II (Cambridge, MA: Harvard University Press, 1980). B Parekh, 'Nehru and the National Philosophy of India', *Economic and Political Weekly* 26, no. 1–2 (1991): 35–48.
12. Dirks, 265.
13. Anuradha Dingwaney Needham, *New Indian Cinema in Post-Independence India: The Cultural Work of Shyam Benegal* (New York and London: Routledge, 2013).
14. Shyam Benegal, 'Talkies, Movies, Cinema,' *India International Centre Quarterly* 38, no. 3–4 (2011): 356.
15. Benegal, 357.
16. Dipesh Chakrabarty, 'Postcoloniality and the Artifice of History: Who Speaks for "Indian" Pasts?' *Representations*, no. 37 (1992): 1–26. Dipesh Chakrabarty has rightly observed that the Indian nationalists had smartly contorted the essential principles of modernity to retain the traditional patriarchal authority. The ideology of the extended Indian family purposely disqualified the woman as a 'free' modern individual who can befriend the modern man. Women experienced the typically modern phenomena including the advent of industry, print media, nuclear family, newer modes of time-space management and improved communication in gender-specific ways. One has to keep in mind that this indirect exclusion of women, from the realm of the modern, is grounded in the blatant exclusion of lower-caste women. At the cost of total abnegation of the lower-caste/class women, this discourse essentially addresses the Hindu, upper-caste/class women. I do not mean to say that Rao's moves can fully be accommodated within the dominant discourses of nationalism. His dealings with the *harijans* hold the capacity to question the paternalistic claims of nationalism. Yet when it comes to the question of women he adheres to a dominant/conservative position.
17. While the first two five-year plans (1951–61) organised women into *Mahila Mandals* to act as focal points at the grassroots level for the development of women, the third (1961–6) and the fourth (1969–74) five-year plans pinpointed female education as a major welfare strategy. The fifth five-year plan (1974–9) saw a shift in the approach to women's development from 'welfare' to 'development'. It coincided with the publication of the Towards Equality Report where Indian women were seen to be going through the most horrific experiences of declining sex ratios, increasing rates of mortality and morbidity, economic marginalisation and victimisation by discriminatory personal laws.
18. For example the National Planning Committee (1938), the Community Development Programme (1952) – each with a sub-committee concerning women.
19. N. Banerjee, 'Whatever Happened to the Dreams of Modernity? The Nehruvian Era and Woman's Position', *Economic and Political Weekly* 33, no. 17 (1998): WS-2–7.
20. At least two key moments allow one to read Ambedkar's dealing with the question of caste and gender. The first is an explicit move of translating the principle of gender equality in the Fundamental Rights Resolution (1931) to a constitutional measure guaranteeing 'equality between the sexes' (Articles 14 and 16). As the first Law Minister, he takes up the task of radically altering the patriarchal Hindu personal laws through the abolition of caste restrictions in marriage and legalising monogamy, divorce and equal property shares for women. However, in the face of the sturdy fight of the Hindu nationalists against the Hindu Code Bill (1947–8), Ambedkar has to resign in 1951. The second moment is more implicit. Dalit feminists – working according to the arguments of the Dalit feminist movements (since the 1990s) – have reclaimed Ambedkar to read the caste-gender interfaces. See also, Sharmila Rege, *Against the Madness of Manu: B. R. Ambedkar's*

Writings on Brahmanical Patriarchy (New Delhi: Navayana, 2013), 61. 'In Ambedkar's formulations', Sharmila Rege points out, 'three operations central to the origin and development of caste come on to light: intra-group organization of reproduction, violent control of surplus woman's sexuality, and legitimating control practices through ideology.'
21. See Ritu Sen Chaudhuri, 'Ambedkar Beyond the Critique of Indology: Sexuality and Feminism in the Field of Caste', in *The Radical in Ambedkar: Critical Reflections*, ed. Anand Teltumbde and Suraj Yengde (New Delhi: Penguin Random House, 2018), 359–74, for a detailed discussion on caste gender complicity.
22. Madhava Prasad, *Ideology of the Hindi Film: A Historical Construction* (New Delhi: Oxford University Press, 1998), 209.
23. Needham. For example, the didactic state imperative of 'family planning' (outrageously clinging to the Emergency) has been ridiculed through the voices of Mishra and Bindu. Mishra in his attempt to dissipate Rao advises him that instead of bothering the milkmen he should take up the task of teaching them hygiene, decent practices and family planning. In her first meeting with Rao, Bindu shoos him away saying that she has seen enough of the family planning publicist. What exactly was he looking for?
24. Prasad, 215.

CHAPTER 4

Where Labour is Performed: The Public/Private Dichotomy and the Politics of Stigma in *Bhumika* and *Mandi*

Suchitra Mathur

In recent years, the Hindi film industry has seen a number of 'women-oriented' films that create narratives of women's empowerment. From *Queen* (2013, directed by Vikas Bahl) to *Lipstick Under My Burkha* (2016, directed by Alankrita Shrivastava), such films usually define women's liberation in terms of their challenging the boundaries of their roles as defined by marriage/family and often, in the process, exploring female desire. Such conceptualisation of feminist agency, however, implies an unquestioning acceptance of the domestic/public binary as the defining feature of patriarchy, which raises some troubling questions when examined through the lens of socialist Dalit feminism. As socialist feminists have pointed out, the idea of the 'breadwinner husband' with his economically dependent 'housewife', which underpins this gendered domestic/public binary, far from being a natural phenomenon is, in fact, the creation of capitalist patriarchy which is a relatively recent and ongoing historical process. Within the specifically Indian context, the formulation of this domestic/public division has been further complicated by anti-colonial Brahmanical nationalism which re-visioned this division in terms of the inner/spiritual versus the outer/material.[1] In this formulation, women became the protectors and transmitters of 'Indian culture' that was preserved within the familial domestic sphere while men provided the necessary material sustenance through their engagement with the world of the colonisers. And this 'Indian culture' was defined in upper-class/upper-caste terms whereby this domesticated 'Indian' woman was carefully distinguished from the lower-class/lower-caste women who necessarily worked outside their homes and were, as such, seen as unchaste.[2] Within the Indian context, therefore, the gendering of the domestic/public binary is both class and caste specific, making any idea of women's liberation premised simply upon crossing the *lakshman rekha* of marital domesticity potentially complicit with casteist capitalism.

Interestingly, this complexity of the 'woman's question', while largely glossed over in contemporary Hindi cinema, is evident in the 'women-oriented' films of the so-called parallel cinema from the 1970s and 1980s. Shyam Benegal's *Bhumika* (*The Role*, 1977) and *Mandi* (*Market Place*, 1983) exemplify this earlier phase of Hindi feminist cinema. While *Bhumika* focuses on the life of an actress struggling to define her sense of selfhood in relation to the various public and private roles imposed upon her by a patriarchal society,[3] *Mandi* focuses on a house of prostitutes where women negotiate with the economy of sex work within a society structured by capitalist patriarchy.[4] In both cases, the protagonists are working women, but their access to spaces outside the confines of marital domesticity, while seeming to provide a modicum of economic and sexual agency, is not presented as being empowering in itself. Though both films offer a strong critique of patriarchy, they do not offer any simple narratives of women's liberation through entry into the public sphere of work. The labour these women perform, in fact, problematises any easy distinction between the domestic and the public in terms of either tradition versus modernity or dependence versus independence as presumed in contemporary Hindi films. Instead, the politics of work in these films is seen to be gendered in terms of stigma versus respectability, highlighting the class/caste specificity of the domestic/public binary. Coming from disenfranchised communities, these labouring women are caught between an enforced entry into the public sphere of work that stigmatises them as unchaste and an embrace of marital domesticity to attain respectability through acceptance of male protection. This complicates the notions of choice and agency that underpin contemporary narratives of women's liberation. Do the women in *Bhumika* and *Mandi* then remain victims, or do these films also provide an alternative narrative of liberation that takes into account the intersection of class and caste with gender? In this chapter, I will attempt to answer this question through a close reading of both films in terms of their representation of women as workers.

BHUMIKA

Based on the autobiography of Hansa Wadkar,[5] a doyenne of early Marathi cinema, *Bhumika* traces the life of Usha through two parallel intertwined narratives – her film career and her personal life – both of which are seen to be mutually constitutive in determining the scope and meaning of women's work. The film opens with Usha in a *tamasha* performance as part of a film shooting. *Tamasha* is a Marathi folk art specifically associated with erotic dance performances by lower-caste women, making it part of a tradition of sexualised performative labour that continues to structure lower-caste women's employment opportunities in the public sphere.[6] The opening sequence of the film, therefore, immediately associates Usha's work with stigmatised lower-caste labour. The implications of this association are made evident in the next scene when Usha, upon returning home, is confronted by her husband's suspicions regarding her relations with a fellow actor who had come to drop her home since her own transport had been unavailable. When, in response to this implied accusation of sexual promiscuity, she decides to leave, taking her daughter with her, the husband taunts her with, '*Le jayo, banao apni tarah. Doosron ke ghar padi rahegi*' ('Go on, take her, make her like yourself so that she never has a home of her own'). Not only does this taunt reinforce the idea of stigma through association ('make her like yourself'), but it also clearly establishes the framework of Brahmanical patriarchy wherein the chaste wife who has a home of her own is opposed to the unchaste 'public' woman who remains outside the framework of such respectable domesticity (Figure 4.1).

The casteist aspect of this mapping of the stigma versus respectability binary onto public performance versus private domesticity becomes even more evident in the following flashback sequence that takes us to Usha's childhood and introduces us to her grandmother, a professional singer, who lives with her daughter (Usha's mother) who is married to a *brahmin*. Though the term is never used in the film, it is clear that Usha's grandmother is a *devdasi*, a woman whose caste-mandated labour as a public performer effectively marks her sexual availability which precludes marital domesticity. Her daughter (Usha's mother) has attempted to overcome the stigma associated with her mother's sexualised labour through her marriage to a Brahmin, thus acquiring not only a higher caste status through marriage, but also the respectability associated

Figure 4.1 Usha as defined by Brahmanical patriarchy: sexualised performer and stigmatised wife.

with marital domesticity. The child Usha is seen to be caught between the two, with the grandmother encouraging her to learn singing to ensure that she has a means of livelihood in her old age, while the mother insists that she learn household tasks to best prepare herself for a respectable marriage. However, the sudden death of the husband, which leaves the entire family destitute, forces the mother to agree to use her daughter's skill as a singer as a means of economic sustenance. The child Usha is thus pushed into following in her grandmother's footsteps by becoming the breadwinner for the family through the use of her performative labour. Though technically not a *devdasi*, it is this heritage – characterised equally by artistic skill and casteist stigma – that paves the way for her entry into the film industry. It is instructive to remember at this point that many of the actresses who became the stars of early Indian cinema came from similar backgrounds; the film world was not seen to be a space for 'respectable women'.[7] In *Bhumika*, one of Benegal's intended aims is to invoke the history of Hindi cinema, and though this aspect of caste-based gendered labour in the early years of the film industry may not be the focus of his ironic tribute, it nonetheless exposes the dark underbelly of the glamour-based power often associated with these divas of Indian cinema.

This backstory regarding Usha's association with the film industry not only undermines any easy equation of work in the public sphere as a matter of empowering choice or agency, but also foregrounds patriarchal control over women's labour. As Nirmala Banerjee points out, 'a woman is moulded into a woman worker by patriarchal forces which control, regulate and direct how, where and how much a woman should work'.[8] And while this control operates primarily at the level of 'private patriarchy' wherein 'women provide the family with its most flexible and elastic resource',[9] it is also reproduced in the public realm where 'the appropriation particularly of women's labour is on a more collective level'.[10] In *Bhumika*, exploitation of women's labour at both levels is evident in the case of Usha. As noted above, she is pushed into films to support her family, but while her mother and grandmother agree to this use of her labour, it is Keshav who is instrumental in getting her into the industry and later managing her career. A neighbour's son who appears to have become a de facto member of Usha's family through his practical assistance while her father remained incapacitated by alcoholism, Keshav quietly takes charge of the three-woman household once the father dies. Throughout, the focus of his interest is clearly Usha; he pesters her to sing for him, coerces her into promising to marry him when she grows up and entices her through the excitement of watching a film shooting to sing for a film producer known to him. Despite being of a lower caste than Usha's Brahmin father and lacking any independent source of income, Keshav nevertheless wields patriarchal power over Usha's labour simply by virtue of being a man, which gives him direct access to the public world of the film industry.

The fact that Usha's work as an actress is completely mediated by Keshav from the beginning not only indicates patriarchal control of women's labour at the familial level, but also the patriarchal structure of the industry itself. The latter is evident throughout the film, most obviously in the fact that the producers, directors, cinematographers, choreographers – all those who control the performance of Usha's labour – are exclusively men. It is these men who not only dictate how Usha acts, what she wears and how she is seen, but also the films that are made. They are the ones who determine the shape of the narratives that are brought to life through Usha's acting; they write the scripts that she performs. From the Sita and Savitri kind of self-sacrificing victims to the enticing temptress who is the object of her lover's desire, the roles she is made to enact re-inscribe the idea of women as embodiments of patriarchal notions of dharma and desire.[11] At the same time, Usha's labouring body itself is exploited through its subjection to the voyeuristic male gaze, be it through careful arrangement of her limbs by a choreographer, by drenching her costume on the orders of a director, or via the intrusive lens of the camera through which a cinematographer focuses on her heaving bosom. Thus, as a worker in the patriarchal film industry, Usha is subjected not only to the control of her labour by men, but also its sexualisation. This process of appropriation transforms the woman worker Usha into the star commodity Urvashi – the name plastered across billboards advertising her films. As one reviewer of the film points out:

> The heroine's two names are telling as well. Apart from the not-uncommon household name Usha ('dawn,' the name of a Vedic goddess), she also carries the stage name Urvashi, that of an *apsara* or celestial courtesan celebrated for her mythological seduction of a great king. In Hindu mythology, apsaras were dancing girls in Indra's heavenly paradise; unmarried, and perpetually available for casual liaisons with men whom they (or Indra) might choose to tempt or favor; indeed, Indra used them regularly to keep the chastity-derived powers of saintly ascetics in check, lest they threaten his own cosmic dominance. In the ancient origin myth of Sanskrit drama, such celestial callgirls became the first actresses, and they also became the prototype of the *vaishya* or 'professional woman' of classical and medieval times, the courtesan who was both a highly educated and glamorous entertainer and a potential mistress to well-to-do patrons.[12]

The parallels with the *devdasi* are unmistakable. While at one end it is familial economic compulsions combined with gendered caste-based skill that structure Usha's entry into the professional workforce, on the other side, the patriarchal workplace reinforces Brahmanical ideas regarding the sexual accessibility of such public performers through her transformation into

Urvashi. The material and the ideological thus come together in this intersection of caste, class and gender that constrain and control Usha's performance of stigmatised labour in the public sphere.

It is against this patriarchal appropriation of her public labour that we need to understand Usha's repeatedly expressed desire for domesticity. This aspect of Usha's characterisation has drawn much critical attention. While one reviewer finds that, 'Usha's motives for stubbornly pursuing this relationship (culminating in a pre-marital pregnancy) with the unattractive and much older Keshav – who appears to have lusted after her since childhood – are not spelled out',[13] a more scholarly analysis of the film's gender politics understands Usha's 'desire for home and middle-class respectability' as an indication of her internalisation of patriarchal norms that then conflicts with her desire for 'freedom and autonomy'.[14] A careful reading of the film with a focus on the mechanics of Brahmanical patriarchy's control of women, however, belies these claims. As a young adult female worker in the film industry, Usha appears to harbour no interest in marital domesticity; she, in fact, finds Rajan's (a fellow actor) sudden declaration of love for her in the midst of a shooting quite amusing, and is visibly upset by Keshav's assertion of his rights over her as his betrothed in front of her colleagues. In this particular confrontation with Keshav, he also berates her for enjoying herself with other men in her capacity as an actress, making Usha acutely aware of the stigma associated with her sexualised performative labour. She accompanies Keshav after this interaction only out of concern for her grandmother. At home, however, she is once again subjected to patriarchal control, this time in the voice of her mother, who tries to enforce 'middle-class respectability' on her by forbidding her from going out with a lower-caste boy like Keshav. It is in revolt against this imposition of Brahmanical patriarchal norms that Usha decides to get pregnant by Keshav as a sure-fire way to make her mother agree to this relationship. Far from acceding to the notion of patriarchal respectability, Usha wilfully challenges it through this assertion of her sexual agency. It is this desire for control over her own body and its labour, sexual and otherwise, that makes Usha declare her intention to get married, after which she will leave films and focus on children and housework.

It is instructive here to return to Needham's reading of Usha's choice, which is couched in terms of the mainstream feminist idea of liberation outlined at the beginning of this chapter:

> The source of Usha's conflicts derives from her desire, on the one hand, for the security of a domestic sphere defined by marriage, husband, and children, and, on the other, for the freedom to live her life as she chooses . . . Thus, although her status as a professional woman provides her with some independence, work is not what she most wants. She wants, instead, to assume the role of a housewife . . .[15]

This idea of the 'housewife' as someone who does not 'work' and who is confined to the 'domestic sphere defined by marriage' is very class-caste specific. This idea is associated with respectability within the Brahmanical patriarchal framework, and in *Bhumika*, it most clearly governs the life of Shantabai, Usha's mother. Her pride in being the wife of a Brahmin, evident in her dismissal of Keshav as a prospective husband for Usha because of his lower caste, makes her subservient to her husband during his lifetime (quietly accepting physical abuse at his hands) and, even after his death, keeps her confined to the house (now her daughter's) where she unquestioningly accepts her role as the near invisible cook and childcare provider. Usha, on the other hand, neither seeks out nor accepts this idea of the subservient housewife. It is important to note that her idea of marriage is related to the attainment not of respectable wifehood, but of a home that frees her from compulsive stigmatised labour in the public sphere and provides a space for her own control over her body and its labour. It is Keshav's assertion of his patriarchal control over both – by making her go back to work in films and, later, by forcing her to undergo an abortion – that makes Usha walk out of this marriage repeatedly. As she says to Rajan, '*apne hi ghar mein dam nahin ghutna chahiye*' ('one shouldn't feel suffocated in one's own house'). Instead, she claims, '*main sahi maine mein gharwali banana chahti hoon*' ('I want to become a *gharwali* in the true sense of the word'), where '*gharwali*' needs to be understood less as a meek housewife and more as the respected household organiser. Here it is important to distinguish between the idea of respectability with its specific Brahmanical patriarchal associations and that of self-respect associated specifically with Dalit women's reclamation of their body by denying its presumed accessibility by upper-caste men. Usha's desire to be a *gharwali* needs to be understood in this caste-specific context of claiming self-respect, of 're-mak[ing]' herself 'in dress, deportment, attitudes, rather than uphold[ing] custom and faith'.[16]

In the film, this idea of self-respect, as opposed to respectability, is most obvious in Usha's relationship with Vinayak Kale. As mentioned earlier, the first sequence in the film ends with Usha walking out of her marital home to move into a hotel where she can live on her own terms. It is in this hotel that she meets Vinayak Kale, a successful businessman, who is staying in the room opposite hers. She goes to his room when she hears a song recorded in her grandmother's voice playing there. This first encounter is significant not only for showing Usha's disregard for conventional patriarchal respectability, but also for revealing the terms for Usha's assertion of her self-respect. The room is occupied by Kale and a male friend, a fact explicitly pointed out to her, but ignoring this impropriety (in patriarchal terms), Usha goes in to listen to the song after identifying the singer as her grandmother. The acknowledgement of this relationship along with her complete concentration on the song while in the room indicate Usha's attempt to reclaim an artistic heritage that, in her case, was appropriated and stigmatised as sexualised performative labour. Her conscious distancing of herself from the latter is evident in her rejection of the male friend's attempts to interact with her as the well-known actress; instead, she immerses herself in the song, responding to it purely as aesthetic expression and thus, implicitly re-affirming the song as an embodiment of what Marx calls 'unalienated labour' whose production is intended only for the affirmation of the producer as well as the user.[17] Interestingly, it is Kale who seems to share this aesthetic pleasure in the song, and also refuses to recognise Usha in her public identity as an actress, acknowledging her only as a woman deserving of basic gentlemanly courtesy (he immediately puts on his shirt when Usha enters the room to listen to the song). Usha's decision to go and live with Kale in his ancestral home, therefore, far from being an attempt at gaining domestic respectability, is premised on a rejection of the wife/whore dichotomy that defines women within Brahmanical patriarchy. She barely hesitates when she finds out that Kale is not only already married, but also has a son, choosing instead to stay with him, which seems to allow her to put her past, which identified her only in terms of her stigmatised performative labour, behind her.

But this retreat into the private domestic world is not premised on a rejection of work itself. While rejecting public performative labour, Usha chooses to embrace private labour in Kale's house by taking over the running of the entire household. The element of choice appears to be of paramount importance here; Kale neither tells her, nor even seems to expect her, to undertake the tasks of domestic management which she gradually takes over largely as a way of making herself part of the extended family unit. It is the domestic work of caregiving that allows Usha to create affiliative bonds with Kale's mother, his paralysed wife, and her son, while her supervision of household food requirements builds her relationship with various vendors who come to deliver provisions to the house. Within this domestic economy, therefore, Usha's labour seems to remain under her own control, used only to provide a sense of affirmative self-fulfilment through the comfort it brings to others and the sense of community it fosters without any apparent dependence upon her relationship with Kale. In this, Usha's 'unalienated' performance of domestic labour may be seen in contrast to Shantabai's performance of the same labour under the strict control of a patriarchal regime. In Shantabai's case, the performance of tasks such as cooking and caregiving is clearly seen as the discharge of domestic duties that are implicitly required for the maintenance of her position within the patriarchal household. First as a dependent housewife whose value is measured by the services she provides to her husband and later as a dependent widow whose position in her daughter's household is defined in terms of the domestic service she provides in place of Usha who works outside the home, Shantabai is the most ostensible example in the film of patriarchal appropriation of women's domestic labour. This appropriation, as Sangari argues, is simultaneously structural and ideological:

> An affiliation between domestic labour and this complex of sacrificial ideologies is structured both into the nature of the work and into its positioning within familial relationships. The religious and cultural rationales for motherhood, wifehood and non-dissoluble marriage may be seen as trying to not only to [sic] underwrite this source of labour but to guarantee a private domain of non-alienated labour, or rather what can often be made to appear as a domain of non-alienated labour being itself unmeasurable and occurring in the frame of lasting 'non-contractual' personal relationships.[18]

This appearance, however, is deceptive since 'patriarchies build personal relationships into exploitation, operate *inside* the sphere of relationships of love, nurture and sexuality, are indeed inseparable from them'.[19] Consequently, 'women themselves find it difficult or impossible either to separate the personal from the structural or to see themselves outside the orbit of such relationships'.[20]

It is Shantabai's inability to see herself outside these familial relationships that structures her performance of domestic labour; Usha, on the other hand, steps outside the prescribed limits of both motherhood and wifehood for women when she goes to live with Kale and denies having any children. And yet, the domestic labour performed by Usha as a matter of 'personal' choice is equally structured by patriarchal forces. This is brought subtly to our notice in a scene where a simple look from Kale takes Usha from the companionable bedside of Kale's mother to Kale's bed. Not only does Kale have access to her sexual labour on demand, but this aspect of her domestic work clearly has priority over any other self-willed use of her labour. In fact, seen in this light, all aspects of Usha's domestic labour are ultimately controlled by Kale, who is also their ultimate beneficiary since her effective household management frees him from all domestic responsibilities, allowing him to focus exclusively on his business interests. It is in this way that women's unpaid domestic labour is an essential though invisible aspect of capitalist economy; men's ability to engage in the public world of material production is premised upon women's work of social reproduction within the private realm of home and family. In handing over the household keys to Usha, therefore, Kale's mother enacts only a transference of stewardship that endows her with no consequential decision-making powers. Control over all domestic resources, material and human, remains with Kale. Usha is confronted with this brute patriarchal reality when the driver, under orders from Kale, refuses her the use of the car to take Kale's son to a nearby fair. Kale's subsequent blunt statement that women of his household have no right to step outside its prescribed limits shatters Usha's illusion of choice and control that had underpinned her relationship with Kale. Recognising that her private domestic labour is as much under patriarchal control as her earlier public performative labour, Usha immediately decides to leave, using the resources of the law and her official status as a married woman to escape Kale's domestic prison. It is, of course, supremely ironic that it is the patriarchal state, with its laws enforcing restitution of conjugal rights, which rescues Usha from Kale's patriarchal home.

Bhumika, thus, clearly shows that Brahmanical patriarchy completely controls women's labour in all spheres – within the family, in the industry, and even at the level of the state (the legal protector of the patriarchal family). It is not surprising then that Usha's final decision is to withdraw herself and her labour from both spheres of circulation. While her refusal to either return to her marriage with Keshav or to live with her now married daughter indicates her complete rejection of the domestic sphere, her turning a deaf ear to Rajan's invitation to return to the film industry marks her refusal to re-enter the public sphere of work. The film ends with Usha alone in a hotel room, listening to a recording of her grandmother's song, determined to deal with her '*akelapan*', her individual isolation from the world, on her own terms. Is this indicative of what Sangari calls 'individuation' – the claiming of an individual independent identity wherein women's labour is subject neither to direct familial control nor to indirect appropriation through public patriarchal economic structures?[21] It is important to remember here that Usha does indeed have the material means for such independence; her opening up of a bank account in her own name was another reason for Keshav's anger in the first sequence of the film. And her grandmother's record could possibly be seen as pointing towards a future skill-based source of income wherein the aestheticisation rather than sexualisation of women's performative labour allows for a de-stigmatised entry into the public sphere of work. How far these very subtle hints constitute a viable alternative narrative of female liberation may be better understood by exploring their development in *Mandi*, the next film in which Benegal put women working in the public sphere centre stage.

MANDI

Based on Ghulam Abbas's short story 'Anandi', *Mandi* is a comic satirical critique of capitalist patriarchy that, through its wife/whore dichotomy, asserts its control, both material and ideological, over women's sexual labour. While the film's primary focus is on a group of sex workers, it also contains a parallel narrative about the marital alliance between two business families in the city, and these two together thoroughly undermine the gendered private/public binary created by capitalist patriarchy. Despite the significant tonal differences between *Mandi* and *Bhumika*, it is this exploration of the relationship between the inner domestic realm and the outer realm of public exchange in terms of the valuation and control over women's labour that connects the two films. *Mandi*, in fact, may be seen as an extension of *Bhumika* in this regard; while in *Bhumika* the private/public performance of labour is presented primarily through the experiences of one woman's negotiations with the respectability/ stigma binary, in *Mandi*, the same dynamics of women's labour are explored in relation to larger socio-economic structures that reformulate respectability/ stigma in terms of protection versus exploitation as a framework for the organised public control of women's labour.

In *Bhumika*, the stigmatisation of women's public performative labour was linked implicitly, through caste associations, with sexual accessibility; in *Mandi*, this implicit assumption of Brahmanical patriarchy is made explicit by presenting women's public labour *as* sex work. This literalisation of the wife/ whore dichotomy is emplotted through Phoolmani, a tribal village girl who is brought to the house of sex workers as a wife by her husband and transformed into a whore when her husband leaves her there. It is interesting to note here that in Phoolmani's case, this change in status does not entail an actual change in location – the same room is 'private'/respectable when shared with her husband, but becomes 'public'/stigmatised when he leaves her there alone. The stigma of sexual accessibility, therefore, is linked here not to stepping outside of the house, but to a withdrawal of protection sanctioned by Brahmanical patriarchy even within the house. This is premised on what Sangari identifies as the 'construction of binary oppositions between procreative and non-procreative sexuality-good wives and "others" such as widows, prostitutes' which enables 'a hierarchical differentiation of labour and services' whereby these '"other" women provide a pool for the collective appropriation of labour and services wherein sexuality is unfenced by marriage'.[22] In other words, being bereft of the protection offered by marriage, women such as Phoolmani are ripe for exploitation unless they can find an alternative socially sanctioned protector.

In the film, the latter, that is, unmarried women, is represented by Nari Niketan, a state-sanctioned women's shelter run by Shanti Devi, the khadi saree-clad social worker whose own entry into the public sphere is endowed with respectability by her commitment to the preservation of *'hamari paanch hazaar saal purani sanskriti'* ('our 5000-year-old [Indian] culture') defined in terms of a patriarchal social morality. It is Shanti Devi who starts a campaign to rescue Phoolmani, and in the process, close down the house of sex workers that occupies a prime location in the city's marketplace. Here it is instructive to recall that the main law related to prostitution that was on the books when *Mandi* was made was the Suppression of Immoral Traffic in Women and Girls Act, 1956.[23] Tellingly known as 'SITA' (the name of the wife of the god

Rama who embodies the ideal of the chaste wife in Hindu mythology), this law, according to D'Cunha, 'was not the outcome of an independent, sustained, consolidated mass movement in the country, but rather the result of India being a signatory to the United Nations International Convention for the Suppression of Traffic in Persons and of the Exploitation of others, passed in New York in 1950'.[24] As such, it exemplifies state patriarchy, evident in its definition of prostitutes in two ways – as victims of trafficking in need of rescue and as criminals who endanger social morality through their public seduction of men. Shanti Devi clearly draws upon this formulation in her campaign regarding Phoolmani, identifying her as an exploited woman detained against her will in the brothel, which therefore needs to be shut down while state-sponsored patriarchal protection is provided to the victim(s) by Nari Niketan.

This discourse of protection from exploitation in relation to prostitution completely negates not only the aspect of these women's economic survival, but also their agency. The former is evident in an exchange that takes place when Shanti Devi is publicly condemning the existence of the brothel while standing in front of it (Figure 4.2). The sex workers, who are watching her from the window, interrupt her with '*phir roti kaise khaenge?*' ('then how will we eat?'), to which Shanti Devi makes the pious reply that '*roti hi sab kuch nahin hoti*' ('bread is not everything'), thereby attempting to subordinate material survival to ideological conformity. The sex workers (apart from Phoolmani

Figure 4.2 Caught between stigmatisation and protectionism: sex workers and the discourse of 'social reform' within Brahmanical patriarchy.

who is shown to have internalised this ideology, at least at this point in the film) repeatedly challenge this erasure of their identity as workers, as providers of a labour that is essential to the survival of society; as Rukmini Bai (the one in charge of the house of sex workers) proudly claims, '*hum hain to samaaj hai*' ('society exists because we exist'). She then goes on to remind Shanti Devi that '*mard khareedta hai tabhi aurat bikti hai*' ('women sell sex only because men buy it'), foregrounding sex work as part of the economy of market exchange. At the same time, and somewhat contradictorily, Rukmini Bai also emphasises that '*hum kalakaar hain, kalaa hamari saans hai*' ('we are artists; our art is our life'), which glosses over the sex work by making the dance and musical skills of the women the chief source of their demand in the market. Such an assertion of artistic agency tries to place these women outside the entire sexualised protection/exploitation framework by defining their work in terms of performative labour whose value is aesthetic. This may be seen to parallel the kind of value that is associated with the grandmother's song at various points in *Bhumika*. But while in the latter film this idea of aesthetic value appears to be validated through the de-sexualised presentation of the song as a recorded voice rather than live performance, in *Mandi* the film seems to ironically undermine such claims of the primacy of the aesthetic through the overtly sexualised body language of the performing women. And even if this assertion of the aesthetic merit of their work is taken at face value, there is no implicit invocation of the idea of 'unalienated labour' that gains value only from the fulfilment it offers to the producer as well as the user of the product as seen in *Bhumika*. Instead, the women themselves are clear that the real value of their art lies in its market price as a commodity, in the return it gets them in terms of money and, possibly, fame. What they assert is their choice to enter the market as free agents selling a self-owned commodity, be it their art or their bodies.

In terms of the contemporary feminist debate regarding prostitution,[25] therefore, *Mandi* clearly weighs in on the side of seeing those engaged in this industry as sex workers wherein the focus is on their labour and how it functions within the marketplace rather than seeing them exclusively as victims of trafficking who need to be rescued and rehabilitated. In fact, the film's positive representation of the house of sex workers has led certain reviewers to see it as representing an almost utopian 'cooperative matriarchal culture' where 'women reign supreme. They make their own decisions, run their own lives, and together (or singly) decide whether they will get involved with men, with which men, and on what terms.'[26] Furthermore,

> For the girls, the brothel is their own home as much as it is a source of their income . . . Rukmini Bai is their mother, and they treat her as such. The girls are close friends with each other and spend a lot of their time gossiping about the happenings in the house and the neighbourhood.[27]

Seen in these terms, the community of sex workers appears to represent not only agential empowerment, but also an alternative to the Brahmanical patriarchal family. The latter, as discussed earlier, is defined by its strict demarcation between the private and the public in terms of gendered labour, which is tied to control of female sexuality as a means to ensure the patrilineal bloodline. In *Mandi*, this idea of the family is exemplified through two prominent citizens of the city – its mayor Mr Agarwal and the businessman Mr Gupta. Mr Agarwal, conveniently, has no wife (she is dead), and he already has the required son, while Mr Gupta's wife and daughter are never seen to step outside the house. The two fathers have arranged the marriage of their respective children as a way to cement a business relationship, asserting full control over the children's lives with no consideration for their desires. Of course, these respectable family men have intimate connections with the brothel in town – Agarwal has sired a daughter with one of the sex workers, while Gupta has bought the house that the sex workers inhabit. But this 'illegitimate' daughter is carefully kept away from the Agarwal family home (she is not even aware, through half the film, that Agarwal is her father) and is allowed entry into the Gupta house only as a paid entertainer whose stigmatised labour clearly differentiates her from the shrinking virginal daughter of the house who is not even able to take pleasure in such entertainment, thus reinforcing the whore/wife binary.

Given the fact that 'the film's primary affective allegiance is with [this] world inhabited by the courtesans',[28] Benegal does appear to be offering it as an enabling alternative for women from the patriarchal ideology that 'positions women within the domestic sphere, with no power to determine how they should live'.[29] The community of sex workers not only seems to offer choice and agency to its members, but is also more inclusive since it does not uphold the stigma-creating domestic/public binary. It is in this house that the 'illegitimate' daughters find a home, and where women of different communities – Hindu and Muslim – live together companionably, pursuing domestic caregiving activities alongside the performative sexual labour that earns them their livelihood. Even the distinction between the affective and the economic appears to be blurred here; while Rukmini Bai, as the 'madam' of the brothel, claims a part of the earnings of the other women, she is also the object of Zeenat's (the illegitimate daughter) affectionate concern and care when she appears unwell. Similarly, while the *havaldar* (policeman) provides a modicum of protection to the brothel from the law in exchange for payment from Rukmini Bai, he also shares a personal relationship with Kamli (one of the sex workers) who is clearly pregnant with his child. As such, the sex-worker household does seem to provide a liberating alternative to the constricting idea of the Brahmanical patriarchal family.

But how far does this alternative exist outside the ambit of capitalist patriarchy? As Needham herself points out, 'Benegal's film establishes the equivalence of these two ostensibly opposing worlds'[30] through the idea of the marketplace (the 'Mandi' of the film's title) which governs the transactions as much in the sex-worker household as it does in the 'respectable' homes of the middle-class city fathers. The relationship, in fact, is not just one of equivalence or even of negotiations between two equal worlds as represented by the transactions between Rukmini Bai and Agarwal as well as Gupta. In material terms, it is the latter – the capitalist patriarchs – who control the former through their ownership of the resources necessary for the sex workers' productive performance of their labour. These women may own their bodies and their artistic skills, but it is Gupta who owns their house and Agarwal who heads the municipal council that dictates town policies. At an individual level, the women may decide the who/when/where of their sex work, but collectively as prostitutes their place and ability to work is governed by the state (and its capitalist backers), which has the systemic power to render the sex workers homeless and thus jobless. Though the film does not show the sex workers as helpless victims of this system, they are definitely not equal partners in it; they can only negotiate for their survival which ultimately requires patriarchal protection. Rukmini Bai is able to extract certain sums of hush money from both Gupta and Agarwal to vacate the centrally located house without creating a scandal, but ultimately, for creating their alternative living/working space outside the city, they need Gupta's patronage; it is only when he asserts his economic clout that the new brothel is built quickly. In the process, Rukmini Bai is replaced by Nadira as the madam of the brothel, rendering the former homeless and jobless once again. At the same time, the three women who decide to leave the new brothel to pursue their own desires also do so under male sponsorship – Kamli decides to leave sex work to be the *havaldar*'s wife; Basanti leaves with her photographer boyfriend with whose help she hopes to get into the film industry; Zeenat elopes with Sunil, Agarwal's son, who offers her love and the security of a considerable cash reserve stolen from his father. These women are not direct victims of exploitation, but their individual choices exhibit an agency that remains contained within a capitalist patriarchal structure wherein women's labour is controlled by men, be it within the domestic or the public sphere.

The ending of the film, however, does appear to offer an alternative through Zeenat's decision to leave Sunil to head out on her own, and Phoolmani's escape from Nari Niketan to return to Rukmini Bai who sees in her the possibility of starting her business again. Neither domesticity nor male patronage appears anywhere on the horizon here, which seems to 'assert the difference that a courtesan culture can make in the lives of women, including potentially alternate modalities of being women that can and do raise serious questions about gender relations in the "respectable" world'.[31] It appears, then, that if *Bhumika* concluded with only a rejection of the terms for women's labour within a casteist capitalist patriarchy with barely a hint of an alternative through the grandmother's recording,

Mandi combines this rejection with the detailed portrayal of an alternative which, through constantly under threat by the dominant system, has the potential to empower women through removing the stigma associated with women's engagement in public performative labour.

But is this narrative of liberation any different from the idea of women's empowerment found in contemporary Hindi films described at the beginning of this chapter? Benegal's films do undoubtedly provide a more complicated understanding of patriarchy as a system than seeing it simply as women's sexual subordination through their confinement to the domestic. Taking into account the intersection of class and caste with gender and recognising how the politics of stigma needs to be negotiated as women enter the public sphere of work, *Bhumika* and *Mandi* do not offer any easy escape route to women; they only reclaim women's agency and assert their right to choose how and where their labour is deployed. As such, the films offer a significant challenge to the control of individual women's labour by individual patriarchs – at the films' conclusions Usha rejects Keshav's offer of marital domesticity as well as a Rajan-sponsored re-entry into films, while Zeenat, Rukmini Bai and Phoolmani reject all individual patriarchal protectors to make their own way in the world. And yet, given the systemic patriarchal structures in place at all levels – society, state, industry – which have been shown by the films themselves, how far does such assertion of individual freedom by women actually prevent the collective appropriation of women's labour by 'public patriarchy' which 'does not exclude women from certain sites, but rather subordinates women in all of them'?[32] Both films leave this question hanging, making their narratives of women's emancipation provisional and suggestive rather than affirmative and celebratory.

It is this unfinished aspect of such individual narratives of women's liberation that make Benegal's films act as an important counterpoint to the contemporary crop of self-proclaimed feminist films. And yet, even though *Bhumika* and *Mandi* recognise the limited scope for individual women's assertion of their right over their own body and its labour, the films are unable to indicate any paths of resistance to these underlying structures of capitalist patriarchy. In fact, while in *Bhumika* at least Usha's strategy of retreat indicates an awareness of this unavoidable structure of exploitation, in *Mandi*, Zeenat's bold march into the unknown with just a bag full of money shows no such awareness; similarly Rukmini Bai's plans to re-open a brothel with Phoolmani actually participate in perpetuating this system. Since the films leave these women with nothing but their individual resources to deal with this entrenched system, the women have only three choices – to withdraw from it, to negotiate with it for their survival, or to buy into its logic and use it for their personal benefit. What is never even hinted at as an option is any collective resistance to this system. While *Bhumika* remains focused on Usha in isolation, *Mandi*, even though concerned with a community of sex workers, ultimately presents them as discrete individuals with no possibility of building solidarity among themselves as workers.[33] Interestingly, Benegal's own *Arohan* (*The Ascent*, 1982), made between *Bhumika* and *Mandi*, includes a powerful representation of farm labourers' collective resistance to landlord oppression, even while revealing its tragic consequences.[34] Is it then the focus on women and the gender issue that makes it difficult to envision such collective struggle in these women-oriented films? Divided by familial and community affiliations, women, as mentioned earlier, do not constitute an identifiable 'class'; any gender-based solidarity appears to be compromised by their entrenched self-interest in perpetuating a patriarchy that allows them isolated pockets of power. Be it Shantabai's attempt to control Usha's sexuality as a means of maintaining her own respectability, or Shanta Devi's offensive against the sex workers as a way of consolidating her own socio-economic position, women in *Bhumika* and *Mandi* are shown to be too much a part of the system to offer any collective resistance to it. Is there then no possibility of collective resistance to capitalist patriarchy? Two films – one emerging from the same parallel cinema movement that includes Benegal, and the other a contemporary independent production – provide enabling representations of such a possibility, offering an important contrast to the feminist films of Benegal as well as contemporary mainstream Hindi cinema.[35] Ketan Mehta's *Mirch Masala* (*Hot Spice*, 1987) concludes with a powerful sequence of labouring women coming together to resist sexual exploitation by ruling-class men.[36] Ektara Collective's *Turup* (*Checkmate*, 2017) portrays the complex forging of solidarity across class, caste, community and gender to resist the powerful nexus between political parties, business and religion.[37] Though a detailed analysis of these films is beyond the scope of this chapter, it is important to note that in both films solidarity is built through work, through the performance of labour with a mutual recognition of its social value, and the emergent sense of dignity/self-respect. It is this liberating potential of women and work that remains missing in *Bhumika* and *Mandi*, even as they provide an insightful critique of the structures that constrain women's labour within Brahmanical capitalist patriarchy.

Note: All dialogue translated by the author.

NOTES

1. Partha Chatterjee, *The Nation and its Fragments: Colonial and Postcolonial Histories* (Delhi: Oxford University Press, 1994), 147.
2. See, for instance, Sumanta Banerjee, 'Marginalisation of Women's Popular Culture in Nineteenth Century Bengal', in *Recasting Women: Essays in Colonial History*, ed. Kumkum Sangari and Sudesh Vaid (New Delhi: Kali for Women, 1989), 131.
3. *Bhumika*, directed by Shyam Benegal (1977; Mumbai: Shemaroo Video Ltd., 2006), VCD.

4. *Mandi*, directed by Shyam Benegal (1983; Mumbai: Shermaroo Video Ltd., 2006), VCD.
5. Hansa Wadkar, *You Ask, I Tell*, ed. and trans. Jasbir Jain and Shobha Shinde (New Delhi: Zubaan, 2013).
6. Meena Gopal, 'Caste, Sexuality and Labour: The Troubled Connection', *Current Sociology* 60, no. 2 (2012), 228, accessed 1 September 2021, <https://journals.sagepub.com/doi/10.1177/0011392111429223>
7. For a detailed analysis of the gender and class politics of early Hindi cinema, see Neepa Majumdar, *Wanted Cultured Ladies Only: Female Stardom and Cinema in India, 1930s–1950s* (New Delhi: Oxford University Press, 2010). Majumdar examines the various strategies used by the 'reformist voice' in the film industry to provide a sense of respectability to its female actresses – it 'promoted the image of their hard work, recommended that educated women become actresses, and critiqued old prejudices against the profession' (69). Interestingly, Benegal appears to participate in this 'reformist' agenda even while creating his ironic tribute to early cinema in *Bhumika*. This is evident is his careful excision of any ideas that may seem morally dubious to middle-class respectability in his presentation of Usha. Though based on Hansa Wadkar, Usha's character neither struggles with alcoholism nor evinces any 'addiction' to the profession of acting, both of which are part of Wadkar's autobiographical narrative.
8. Nirmala Banerjee, 'A Note on Women as Workers', in *Mapping the Field: Gender Relations in Contemporary India*, ed. Nirmala Banerjee, Samita Sen and Nandita Dhawan (Kolkata: Stree, 2011), 195.
9. Banerjee, 210.
10. Nirmala Banerjee, 'Analysing Women's Work Under Patriarchy', in *From Myths to Markets: Essays on Gender*, ed. Kumkum Sangari and Uma Chakravarti (Shimla: Indian Institute of Advanced Study, 1999), 328.
11. Patricia Uberoi, *Freedom and Destiny: Gender, Family, and Popular Culture in India* (New Delhi: Oxford University Press, 2006), 123. According to Uberoi, 'In the Hindi cinema, as has often been observed, the opposed dimensions of wifehood – procreativity and sexuality, love as duty and love as sexual passion – have typically been separated into distinct social roles and assigned to different social spaces.' But 'popular cinema constantly plays with the challenge of bringing about a seamless fusion of wifeliness and sexuality, *dharma* and desire'. In *Bhumika*, Usha embodies this attempted fusion through the roles she is asked to enact in different films.
12. Philip Lutgendorf, 'Bhumika', *Indian Cinema*, The University of Iowa, accessed 3 December 2018, <https://uiowa.edu/indiancinema/bhumika>
13. Lutgendorf.
14. Anuradha Dingwaney Needham, *New Indian Cinema in Post-Independence India: The Cultural Work of Shyam Benegal's Films* (New York: Routledge, 2013), 55.
15. Needham, 51.
16. V. Geetha, 'Dalit Feminism: Where Life-Worlds and Histories Meet', in *Women Contesting Culture: Changing Frames of Gender Politics in India*, ed. Kavita Panjabi and Paromita Chakravarti (Kolkata: Stree, 2012), 248.
17. Cited in Kumkum Sangari, 'The "Amenities of Domestic Life": Questions on Labour', *Social Scientist* 21, no. 9/11 (September–October 1993), 5, accessed 1 September 2021, <http://www.jstor.org/stable/3520425>
18. Sangari, 5.
19. Ibid., 4–5.
20. Ibid., 5.
21. Ibid., 14–15.
22. Sangari, 16.

23. This act was amended and changed to the Immoral Trafficking (Prevention) Act, 1986, which is currently the only law in India that deals directly with prostitution.
24. Jean D'Cunha, 'Prostitution in a Patriarchal Society: A Critical Review of the SIT Act', *Economic and Political Weekly* 22, no. 45 (November 7, 1987), 1919.
25. A good summary of this debate is provided in Annie George, U. Vindhya and Sawmya Ray, 'Sex Trafficking and Sex Work: Definitions, Debates and Dynamics – A Review of Literature', *Economic and Political Weekly* 45, no. 17 (April 24–30, 2010), 64–73, accessed 1 September 2021, <https://www.jstor.org/stable/25664387>. Nivedita Menon also provides a concise analysis specifically within the Indian context. See Nivedita Menon, 'Sexuality: Politics of Sex-Work and Counter-Heteronormative Movements', in *Mapping the Field: Gender Relations in Contemporary India*, ed. Nirmala Banerjee, Samita Sen and Nandita Dhawan (Kolkata: Stree, 2012), 573–8.
26. 'Shyam Benegal's "Mandi"', *Elite-Irony: The Blog*, last modified July 11, 2009, <http://elite-irony.blogspot.com/2009/07/shyam-benegals-mandi.html>
27. Sunaina Bose, 'Mandi Film Review: A Marketplace Of Empowerment', last modified 16 November 2017, <https://feminisminindia.com/2017/11/16/mandi-film-review>
28. Needham, 59.
29. Ibid., 64.
30. Ibid., 60.
31. Ibid., 64.
32. Sylvia Walby, 'Theorising Patriarchy', *Sociology* 23, no. 2 (May 1989), 213–34, accessed 1 September 2021, <https://www.jstor.org/stable/42853921>. This aspect of public patriarchy is clearly brought out in the source story for the film; Abbas's 'Anandi' ends with the new brothel itself facing attack by the municipal council with the sex workers being thrown out of the town once again. Benegal chooses to ignore this inevitable patriarchal control over women's collective labour by focusing on the possibilities indicated by the individual actions of Zeenat, Rukmini Bai and Phoolmani.
33. Interestingly, both films show instances of failed solidarity among women. While in *Bhumika*, the affective bond that Usha forges with the women of Kale's household does not provide her with any support to challenge Kale's patriarchal control, in *Mandi*, the seeming camaraderie among the sex workers is completely undermined by their pursuit of their individual self-interest in the face of the changes related to the establishment of the new brothel.
34. *Arohan*, directed by Shyam Benegal (1982; Kolkata: West Bengal Film Development Corporation Ltd).
35. It is important here to distinguish between the ideas of sisterhood and solidarity. The former, based simply on women's bonding in reaction to patriarchal control, is an important trope in most contemporary self-proclaimed feminist Hindi films. However, such bonding does not translate into a solidarity that recognises the class/caste divisions among women and forms a politically conscious collective that takes these differences into account while offering resistance to patriarchal exploitation as seen in *Mirch Masala* and *Turup*.
36. *Mirch Masala*, directed by Ketan Mehta (1987; Mumbai: National Film Development Corporation of India [NFDC]).
37. *Turup*, directed by Ektara Collective (2017).

CHAPTER 5

Adaptation and Epistemic Redress: The Indian Uprising in *Junoon*

Ana Cristina Mendes

INTRODUCTION: INDIA – THE LOCUS OF ENUNCIATION AND ADAPTATION

> If a memory wasn't a thing but a memory of a memory of a memory, mirrors set in parallel, then what the brain told you now about what it claimed had happened then would be coloured by what had happened in between. It was like a country remembering its history: the past was never just the past, it was what made the present able to live with itself.[1]

Our interest – curiosity, even – in the Victorian Age has resulted in a continued investment in ventriloquising the Victorians themselves, as in the case of the various adaptations of Victorian novels and afterlives of Victorian literature in contemporary settings as well as through neo-Victorian renditions. Towards an epistemic reading of adaptation, this chapter discusses the Hindi film *Junoon* (*The Obsession*, 1979), directed by Shyam Benegal and produced by Shashi Kapoor, a screen adaptation of the neo-Victorian novella *A Flight of Pigeons* (1978) by Anglo-Indian author Ruskin Bond, set during the 1857 Indian uprising against British rule, as a creative exercise of epistemic redress whose locus of enunciation and adaptation is a former colony of the British empire. Bond[2] admits to being inspired by Victorian authors such as R. L. Stevenson and Charles Dickens; nonetheless, *A Flight of Pigeons* was based on Anglo-Indian writer J. F. Fanthome's 1896 novel *Mariam*.[3]

Junoon follows *A Flight of Pigeons* closely plot-wise. Bond's novella was chosen by Benegal and actor-producer Shashi Kapoor (*Junoon* was Kapoor's first film as producer) to be adapted for the big screen following its publication.

This double adaptative movement can be characterised as trans-temporal ventriloquism,[4] as Benegal's screen adaptation of Bond's neo-Victorian novella is an instance of postcolonial epistemic remediation of Victorian mutiny fictions whose enunciators were British. In *A Flight of Pigeons* and *Junoon* the location of knowledge production about the 1857 uprising is post-Independence India. Miles Taylor explains that various causes led to this 'widespread, organised revolt' in northern India, reaching beyond the localised military mutinies: '[s]ocial change, modernised communications, religion, new taxes and old grievances.'[5] As such, the epistemic remediation of *A Flight of Pigeons* and *Junoon* involves issues of archive, memory and trauma, setting out to restate a sense of historical continuity. Such reading is based on a clear link established between British imperialism and textuality; as Elleke Boehmer argues, 'Present-day readers . . . experience Empire textually, through the medium of nineteenth- and twentieth-century novels and periodicals, travel writings, scraps of doggerel.'[6] In fact, invested in bringing into practice a 'grammar of difference',[7] the British Empire was itself 'a textual exercise' sustained by a vast array of texts.[8]

The Victorian textual experiences of the events of 1857–8 in India represented, for the most part, one of the most impactful episodes of the Indian freedom struggle (also known as the Sepoy Mutiny) as a vexatious mutiny, or the outcome of 'the acts of ambitious Men, who have deceived their Countrymen, by false reports, and led them to open Rebellion', in Queen Victoria's textualisation in her 'Proclamation, by the Queen in Council, to the Princes, Chiefs and People of India' (published by the Governor General at Allahabad, 1 November 1858).[9] The fears brought on by the military uprising against British rule in India, emanating from home in the metropole but also from colonial settlers, were articulated in popular Victorian mutiny fictions. These ranged from best-selling colonial adventure tales such as G. A. Henty's *A Pipe of Mystery* (1898), which tells the story of the rebellion involving the Indian regiments of the colonial British army during May and June 1857 as another 'old story' of 'foolish confidence and black treachery'[10] to short stories such as Charles Dickens's and Wilkie Collins's *The Perils of Certain English Prisoners* (1857), a collaborative writing project for the Christmas edition of *Household Worlds* inspired by, in Dickens's view, the courage of the English women during the mutiny and the image of the treacherous sepoy who had revolted against his commanding officers.[11]

Of note also is the celebratory narrative poem 'The Defence of Lucknow' (1879) by Alfred, Lord Tennyson, which depicts the successful defence of the capital of the state of Uttar Pradesh, where the British Residence was located, under a 'ghastly siege' following the uprisings. The poem praises the persistence and courage of the British soldiers when defending the garrison of Lucknow in the face of pain and death, based on the accounts of General James Outram and Colonel William Inglis. The racial and cultural superiority of the British soldiers, supported by their wives and children over a period of more than three months, is underscored by the refrain: 'And ever upon the topmost roof our banner of England blew!' This eulogy of the strength of English collective cultural identity (of the quality of 'Englishness' that corresponds to the ability to command, obey and endure as the poem suggests in Part IV) also includes the 'faithful Indians brothers' who helped the English cause: 'Praise to our Indian brothers, and let the dark face have his due! / Thanks to the kindly dark faces who fought with us, faithful and few, / Fought with the bravest among us, and drove them, and smote them, and slew' (Part V). These are set in stark opposition to the 'spies', 'rebels', 'dark pioneer[s]', 'fiend[s]', 'foe[s]' and 'traitors' (Parts II, III and IV). Narratives such as Tennyson's advocated for the British imperialists 'an unambiguously heroic image of themselves as conquerors and civilizers of the world'.[12] There were also visual representations, such as the oil painting *The Relief of Lucknow* (1857) by Thomas Jones Barker, which was only seen by Queen Victoria and Prince Albert three years later.[13] Commissioned by Queen Victoria, the Swedish court painter Egron Lundgren went to India and depicted the relief of Lucknow by the British; these sketches served as a basis for Barker's painting, which is currently on display at the National Portrait Gallery, London. Besides, Victoria had access to other representations of the events in India, such as photographs by Dr John Murray and Felice Beato, as well as to the ink drawings and watercolours by Charlotte Canning. Textual, discursive practices such as these, 'infused with imperial ideas of racial pride and imperial prowess',[14] produced the necessary distinctions between the coloniser and the colonised, and accounted for changes in their power relations crafted over centuries, when, in Catherine Hall's words, 'the "docile and loyal sepoy" of the pre-1857 British imagination, became the "treacherous nigger" of the Mutiny.'[15]

Both Bond and Benegal draw on the potential of adaptation as an act of trans-temporal ventriloquism to act as remediation or reparation of this traumatic event in Indian and British colonial histories. As such, this chapter focuses on postcolonial adaptation as a strategy of epistemic redress, working with Sandra Ponzanesi's argument, when considering the 'marriage of adaptation and postcolonial critique', that '[i]n the transposition of semiotic codes, languages, genres, audiences and markets something is as often lost as gained in translation.'[16] On the reasons for making *Junoon*, Benegal observes:

> It's a good example of communities living together under stress in India today. The melting-pot theory doesn't hold. People don't give up their culture and dive in. It's better for them to survive within a framework that finds arrangements and explores possibilities to live in peace.[17]

Satyadev Dubey, who wrote the dialogue for the film, notes: 'This film is revolutionary not only in content but as a beacon for the future. For the first time, a famous film star has found the courage to invest in a film with a social point.'[18] Bond and Benegal's texts relate to a contemporary moment of post-Independence, catering to present identity politics and representational needs. Trans-temporal ventriloquism hence becomes a strategy of political intervention.

ADAPTING VICTORIAN MUTINY FICTIONS

The permanent interaction between literature and cinema has given rise to numerous studies and a substantial amount of critical debate.[19] Irrespective of the various theoretical conclusions that have resulted from the approximation of the two media, it is recognised that cinema, from an early age, used novels as a source of inspiration, at a diegetic level, and continuously as a structural support. Filmmakers have also used adaptation in a conscious attempt to extend the prestige of the novel to film, a condition that will favour, from the outset, the commercial success of the production. The reciprocal influence between literature and cinema is also confirmed by the fact that the high profile of the author of the novel is almost inevitably transferred to the film adaptation (a case in point being the successive attempts to adapt Salman Rushdie's 1981 *Midnight's Children*).[20] With the sale of the rights to literary works to the cinema there is a similar phenomenon: not only does the film benefit commercially by being an adaptation of a bestseller, but the novel is also revalued with an adaptation that may enable successive re-editions.[21]

The key aspect of the intertextual reading of an adaptation is that in it may cohabit several texts: a work can interact not only with a source, but also with other novels, older adaptations and a variety of texts in other media. In addition, intertextuality is not linear but multidirectional, so this critical perspective recognises that although the novel precedes the film, the individual may find the adaptation first. The intertextual approach is therefore interested in the convergence between the arts and identifies the multiplicity of links between them. A broader understanding of intertextuality has led to the understanding that there is no single source for a given work. Each film, in fact, each representational artefact, can be seen as an adaptation of many previous artefacts. Indeed, poststructuralism and postmodernism have been commonly employed by theorists in order to question the idea that the literary work has an essence. Relating to this question of intertextuality, Robert Stam suggests the Bakhtinian notions of intertextual dialogue and transtextuality of Gérard Genette as a way to challenge the pitfalls of fidelity. Presenting the five types of transtextual relations pointed out by Genette, Stam sees hypertextuality as the most useful of these relations to study film adaptation.[22] In this context, filmic adaptations are understood as hypertexts derived from pre-existing hypotexts, with the various prior adaptations forming a cumulative hypotext available to the filmmakers. Adaptations are here seen in the complex and broader context of intertextual reference and transformation, where texts create other texts 'in an endless process of recycling, transformation, and transmutation, with no point of origin'.[23]

Explicitly following an intertextual reading of adaptation, this chapter looks at postcolonial adaptation, using as case study the film *Junoon*, as a strategy of epistemic redress through trans-temporal ventriloquism. The use of the metaphor of ventriloquism differs according to whether its positive or negative attributes are evoked in the analysis. For example, David Goldblatt[24] points to the positive use of ventriloquism as a concept and tries to rehabilitate it in the context of contemporary discussions in the humanities. Alternatively, using an example from media and cultural studies, David Morley and Charlotte Brunsdon discuss 'populist ventriloquism' with reference to the television news magazine programme *Nationwide*, broadcast on BBC1 from 1969 to 1978, as 'a crucial strand in the way the programme attempts to forge an "identification" with its audience' which, paradoxically, 'is actively denied in the programme: the presenters appear as "just like us", just ordinary people – who happen to be "on telly", doing the talking, while we listen.'[25] The use in this analysis of the concept of trans-temporal ventriloquism supports the argument that, as a concrete socio-cultural object that ventriloquises Victorian mutiny fictions, Benegal's screen adaptation of Bond's neo-Victorian novella is an instance of postcolonial remediation and epistemic redress.

The adaptation of Victorian and neo-Victorian texts is one of the many contexts in which knowledge about India has been produced (or invented). Adaptation, as an instance of rewriting, is a practice of creating imaginaries; as such, it is important to trace and interrogate the inventions of India. The many globally imagined Indias, and the many consequences of these inventions, have occupied the attention of several academics, going back at least to the landmark book published in 1990 by Ronald Inden, *Imagining India*. Inden's Foucauldian study details the extent to which knowledge of the Indian sub-continent, whose production was located in the West, was based on European imperial desires of world conquest, as well as fantasies about its own rationality. Inden argues that the West, or rather the 'Anglo-French Imperial Formation', imagined Hinduism as illuminating the 'feminine' 'mind of India'; India was perceived in the Western imagination as the society of caste and 'Divine Kingship', and as the land of idyllic communities materialised in villages. For Inden, India was invented as a land of 'dreamy imagination' rather than governed by 'practical reason'.[26]

Historians of religion, Indologists, Britons 'in empire' and at home, and commentators who believed in the grand narrative of social progress entailed by Europe's civilising mission seemed to have imagined India along these lines during the Victorian and Edwardian periods. Their India is represented as a stable homogeneous community (regardless of minor differences) and rooted in superstition. An illustrative example of this is Karl Marx's justification of British rule in India, of its 'civilising mission' governed by rationality – even if the 'social revolution' that resulted from this rule in *Hindostan* was, in Marx's words, 'actuated by the vilest interests':

> We must not forget that these idyllic village communities, inoffensive though as they might appear, had always been the solid foundation of Oriental despotism, that they restrained the human mind within the smallest possible compass, making it the unresisting tool of superstition, enslaving it beneath traditional rules, depriving it of all grandeur and historical energies ... We must not forget that these little communities were contaminated by distinctions of caste and by slavery, that they subjugated man to external circumstances instead of elevating man the sovereign of circumstances, that they transformed a self-developing social state into never changing natural destiny, and thus brought about a brutalizing worship of nature, exhibiting its degradation in the fact that man, the sovereign of nature, fell down on his knees in adoration of *Hanuman*, the monkey, and *Sabbala*, the cow.[27]

In the twenty-first century, examples still abound of this imagined India. For instance, in Michael Winterbottom's *Trishna*, released in 2011, pastoral nineteenth-century England is relocated to contemporary India – first to fast-paced Mumbai, then later to palatial Rajasthan. This British film is an adaptation of a key text of Victorian literature – Thomas Hardy's *Tess of the d'Urbervilles* (1891), which uses twenty-first century India as a setting to convey the idea of the traditional, rural social order of Hardy's invented rural nineteenth-century Wessex.[28] Setting *Tess* in modern-day India, reimagining the novel in the India of the much-hyped economic boom, would be more faithful than recreating 1870s rural England. This hauntingly takes us to Inden's survey of how the 'wild fabrications of the nineteenth-century European imagination' – particularly knowledge of India's 'strange' rural 'political economy',[29] 'idyllic but static'[30] – were also used to justify the West's imposition of rule over India, and whose remains are still visible today.

WHAT IS IN A NAME?

With the onset of colonisation, power was exercised via the creation of knowledge, and the forging of new discourses – for instance, through naming and historiography – and its correlative epistemicide constituted a form of exerting and maintaining colonial power. As Boehmer argues: 'Sometimes called orientalist or Africanist, depending on the categories of representation involved, colonialist discourses thus constituted the systems of cognition – interpretative screens, glass churches – which Europe used to found and guarantee its colonial authority.'[31] Epistemicide occurred, for example, when the European travellers and colonisers claimed to discover a place 'that was already there'.[32] It was essential to attribute conceptual form to the diversity, the otherness, encountered by European travellers and colonisers, that is, 'to use known rhetorical figures to translate the inarticulate'. In a Eurocentric account of history, European reference points were necessary to make a place theoretically knowable. This travelling movement of concepts and names undergirding a colonial organisation of space was elaborated in Edward Said's idea of 'imaginative geographies', where the:

> Imaginative geography of the 'our land – barbarian land' variety does not require that the barbarians acknowledge the distinction. It is enough for 'us' to set up these boundaries in our own minds; 'they' become 'they' accordingly, and both their territory and their mentality are designated as different from 'ours'.[33]

Naming (or re-naming) happens in the contact zone of imperial expansion and is premised on the incorporation and disciplining of indigenous narratives, such as narrative space and time. Naming is not only an expression of imperial desire, but also an active tool of colonial conquest in the context of the institutionalisation of colonial power.

It has been a master trope in postcolonial writing to undermine the very idea of 'discovery' and 'ownership' of land. As an example, in the perspective of postcolonial writers such as Rushdie in the novel *The Moor's Last Sigh* (1995), the 'discovery' of India by Vasco da Gama (rather, the sea route to India) was in fact the beginning of the cultural encounters between the East and the West; recently, we find similar revising, revisiting, and reparation of imperial narratives featuring da Gama in the Indian writer Manu S Pillai's 2015 historical novel *The Ivory Throne: Chronicles of the House of Travancore* (the opening paragraph from the chapter 'Introduction: The Story of Kerala' is illustrative in this respect).

In his role as a commentator of European imperial rule, Marx was one of the most visible contributors to the heated debate in colonial historiography surrounding the appropriate designation for the events taking place in 1857–8, which extended to postcolonial historiography and cultural memory studies in recent decades. Writing from London for *The New York Daily Tribune* on 4 September 1857 (in an issue published on 16 September), Marx notes:

> However infamous the conduct of the Sepoys, it is only the reflex, in a concentrated form, of England's own conduct in India, not only during the epoch of the foundation of her Eastern Empire, but even during the last ten years of a long-settled rule. To characterize that rule, it suffices to say that torture formed ail organic institution of its financial policy. There is something in human history like retribution: and it is a rule of historical retribution that its instrument be forged not by the offended, but by the offender himself.[34]

Nonetheless, Marx's support of British imperialism was conflicted, as he believed in the 'civilising mission' to be undertaken in India by the English:

> Indian society has no history at all, at least no known history. What we call its history, is but the history of the successive intruders who founded their empires on the passive basis of that unresisting and unchanging society. The question, therefore, is not whether the English had a right to conquer India, but whether we are to prefer India conquered by the Turk, by the Persian, by the Russian, to India conquered by the Briton. England has to fulfil a double mission in India: one destructive, the other regenerating the annihilation of old Asiatic society, and the laying the material foundations of Western society in Asia.[35]

As Crispin Bates observes in his discussion of the recurrent uprisings in India against British rule in the early nineteenth century, the 'so-called Pax Britannica in India was . . . very much a myth'.[36] If European colonial naming and historiography hold within them the spectre of epistemicide under the form of repressed indigenous knowledge claims, counter-naming and counter-historiographical accounts have reasserted this repressed content – naming back against the colonial power structures. The naming of the rebellion of 1857–8 in India, whether designated as a rebellion, a revolt, a struggle for emancipation, the First War of Independence, a sepoy mutiny, or an uncivilised uprising, mirrors power negotiations as much as it imparts disjunctures and a crisis in colonial authority. Speaking to the tensions and relations of power inherent in acts of colonial and postcolonial acts of (re)naming, the designation 'First War of Independence' in particular is an ideological label which aims at decentring the privileged historical position Europe wrote for itself in the nineteenth century.

EPISTEMIC REDRESS IN *JUNOON*

While in Inden's *Imagining India* and Winterbottom's *Trishna* the location of knowledge production about India is the West, in *A Flight of Pigeons* and

Junoon the locus of knowledge production or enunciation is post-Independence India. Setting the scene for the action that will follow, the audiences of *Junoon* are reminded of the story of the martyr Mangal Pandey – a sepoy from the thirty-fourth Bengal Native Infantry who attacked his British sergeant during a parade in the Barrackpore cantonment in West Bengal and was then hanged for rebellion against the East India Company on 8 April 1857. Aided by local newspapers and the advent of the telegraph, news of sepoy discontent spread outwards from Meerut, where a mutiny began on 10 May 1857 involving the third Light Cavalry, triggering other military rebellions across northern India towards the Punjab region and around Bhopal and Gwalior. Information about the uprising reached Queen Victoria in July. Over the black screen prior to the beginning of *Junoon*, the voiceover reads:

> 29 March, 1857. Sepoy Mangal Pandey fires the first shot against British oppression. He is hanged.
> 10 May, 1857. The Indian garrison at Meerut revolts.
> 11 May, 1857. The sepoys from Meerut arrive in Delhi. Soon after, they proclaim Bahadur Shah Zafar, Emperor of Hindustan.[37]

The action of *Junoon* is set in late May in a 'small British cantonment town in the Indian plains' in Shahjahanpur. It was constructed as a period film – in Benegal's cameraman Govind Nihalani's words, 'a conscious effort' was made 'to see that the frames are balanced, that the light is soft enough to capture that special atmosphere in the paintings of the period . . . the brilliance of the Indian summer'.[38] The film entwines the threads of personal narratives and family bonding with the British colonial enterprise in India, Indian national history, and independence movements. For example, the character of the 'crusading rebel' Sarfaraz Khan (performed by Naseeruddin Shah), the brother-in-law of the protagonist Javed Khan, the leader of the rebels (as they are referred to throughout the story), belongs to Mangal Pandey's thirty-fourth Bengal Native Infantry. Sarfaraz references Mangal Pandey directly: 'We Indians have suffered enough from these foreigners. They squeezed us dry and we accepted it. But insulting our honour and respect still wasn't enough. It drove Mangal Pandey to turn his gun on them.'

The first frame of the film is of a flock of pigeons flying in a circular pattern above domes and pillars in Shahjahanpur;[39] they will circle the area until all are together and regrouped. This swirling movement of pigeons will be repeated throughout the film, offering circularity to the narrative, taking the audience back to the beginning of the film.

This circularity is also undergirded by the overbearing presence of a *fakir* at the beginning and end of the narrative, with the result that they mirror each other. In the early scene where a wild dance by an entranced *fakir* takes centre stage, a succession of medium shots of the *fakir*, *ghazal* performers, and sepoys culminate in ecstasy, zooming in on the titular character – the Pathan Javed Khan,[40] performed by Shashi Kapoor. Linking the white pigeons to the Europeans residing in Shahjahanpur, before collapsing on the ground the *fakir* ominously declares:

> Strange events you foresee through me! He says all will be read. Bathed in red. I am being plunged into a river of blood. He says it is the blood of outcast foreigners! The foreigners will be wiped out! Fate decreed they would rule for one hundred years. Now it will end! They will fly away like pigeons! They will depart . . . a flight of pigeons.

The rebel soldiers in *Junoon* want to purge the existence of Europeans from their town, putting an end to their bondage. From the perspective of the British settlers, this desire is echoed in Victorian texts such as *Cawnpore* (1866), an alternative script of the events of 1857–8 by G. O. Trevelyan. *Cawnpore* details the siege of Cawnpore (now Kanpur, near Meerut where the rebellion had already spread), when a British garrison surrendered to Nana Sahib, the leader of rebel forces. In Trevelyan's account,

> The Bengal sepoy desired with a nervous and morbid anxiety to get quit of the Sahibs by fair means or foul. He did not care to expose us to unnecessary misery and humiliation; to torture our men, or to outrage our women. His sole object was to see the last of us: to get done with us for good and for ever. Ignorant beyond conception of European geography and statistics, he had convinced himself that, if once the Anglo-Indians of every sex and age were killed off, from the Governor General to the serjeant-major's baby, there did not exist the wherewithal to replace them.[41]

After the opening scene, which establishes the tone and the setting, it is precisely on an Anglo-Indian family that *Junoon* places the focus. After a massacre in St Mary's church, three women of the Labadoor family, the daughter Ruth (performed by Nafisa Ali), the widow Mariam (performed by Jennifer Kendal), and the ailing grandmother, take shelter from the rebels with the wealthy Hindu family of Lala Ramjimal (performed by Kulbhushan Kharbanda), who feels indebted to the British family. Ruth is traumatised after having witnessed the killing of her father, a clerk in the British magistrate's office, during the Sunday worship, together with the local British congregation massacred by rebels led by Sarfaraz. 'From now on,' audiences are told, 'the East India Company's rule has ended in this area. It is again ruled by His Majesty King Bahadur Shah of Delhi.'

Javed, already obsessed by Ruth to the point of madness before the church massacre (hence the title of the film *Junoon*, meaning 'obsession'), takes her and her family by force from Lala's house to his own. This act saves the British women's lives, as only they escape the purge led by the rebel soldiers. Despite the protests of Javed's wife, Firdaus,[42] the Labadoor family is now under the protection of the Pathan, who dresses them in Indian clothes and sends them to live with his aunt. Previously, Javed's only obsession had been breeding carrier pigeons; as Sarfaraz says to Firdaus at the beginning of the film, 'The country is aflame and all he does is fuss over pigeons' (Figure 5.1).

Firdaus sees the pigeons as her rivals, but a new rival enters the scene. Javed is now also obsessed with Ruth and wants to make her his second spouse. Mariam withholds her consent over the union. The outcome of the battle for Delhi – by now the epicentre of the revolt – is to resolve this issue between Mariam and Javed in terms of ownership. Mariam promises to allow the marriage of Ruth to the rebellious native on the condition that the Indians win over the British: 'If Delhi is yours, then Ruth is yours.' Mariam feels that 'the enemy is always suspect', but also fears the pollution and contagion of the interracial relationship between her daughter and the Pathan as the British are bound to win the battle in Delhi. Mariam's intense emotional response issues from the fear that her family is under threat of dissolution, a threat that is primarily sexual, and a fear of the other that can be extended as a metaphor for the family that is the empire. In this respect, Boehmer notes how the period of

Figure 5.1 An exasperated Sarfaraz protests: 'The country is aflame and all he does is fuss over pigeons.'

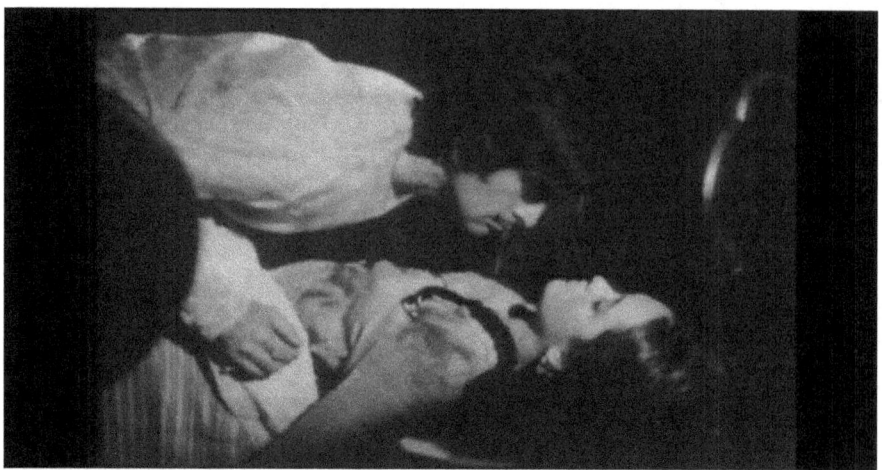

Figure 5.2 Ruth dreams she is being raped by Javed.

Victorian high imperialism witnessed 'the formalization of imperialist ideologies, especially those pertaining to race, encouraged by the spread of Social Darwinist thought'.[43] The other of colonialism is hence a constituent part of the coloniser, who constructs herself in opposition to this imaginary other. Therefore, the subject is herself and the non-other.

At this point in *Junoon*, both families – Mariam's and the Empire – seem to be safe from attack, as the ill-organised Indian forces are fighting a lost battle. Nonetheless, Ruth dreams she is being raped by Javed (Figure 5.2) in a scene filmed in a purpose-built building resembling the original church that stood next to it, as the Church of England did not allow it to be used as a setting for this rape scene.

Jenny Sharpe notices how, in this context of Victorian high imperialism, the dissemination of narratives 'of the violated bodies of English women' was a strategy by British rule to manage 'the violation of colonialism'. In this respect, English womanhood is instrumental 'for articulating a colonial hierarchy of race'.[44] Sharpe notes:

> Stories describing what rebels did to English women mirror the highly ritualized form of punishment and retribution that the British army executed. Captured sepoys were force-fed pork or beef and then blown from cannons; the heads of rebel leaders were displayed on spears; the roads down which an avenging army marched were lined with the dead bodies of villagers dangling from the trees as a warning of the consequences of insurrection; entire cities were looted and then reduced to rubble.[45]

The fear of desecration of the imperial body (the rape of the British woman) is textualised in mutiny fictions because the colonial structures of power are perceived as being irredeemably at risk. In Victorian Anglo-Indian fiction, as Sharpe posits, '*rape* is not a consistent and stable signifier but one that surfaces at strategic moments'.[46] Most relevantly, 'the idea of native men raping white women was not part of the colonial landscape in India prior to the 1857 uprising'.[47]

Victorian mutiny plays, such as Dion Boucicault's *Jessie Brown, or the Relief of Lucknow* (1858), also successfully memorialised in textual form the 'public outrage over the massacre of [British] women and children and the stereotypic lasciviousness of Indians'. In fact, it is suggested that that is what drives the actions of the protagonist, the leader of the rebellion in Cawnpore, Nana Sahib – 'hence the only motive suggested for the Mutiny as a whole – is to kidnap one Mrs. Campbell for his harem'.[48] Therefore, the cunning and licentiousness of a character based on the historical figure of an Indian Peshwa, who temporarily gained control of the British garrison in Cawnpore leading to the Bibighar massacre in 1857, and was construed in mutiny fiction as the 'Satanic locus of all Oriental treachery, lust, and murder',[49] synecdochally stands for the rebellion as a whole.

The colonial discourse at play here is that of rape, and in particular, the highly charged leitmotif of British women forever in danger of being (sexually) attacked by brown men – or black 'scum' that sometimes rises, in the words of Nana Sahib's henchman Achmet in Boucicault's *Jessie Brown*, responding to the words of Geordie McGregor, one of the officers in the English Service: 'Oh, the siege continues; but it will be taken, of course – these black rascals are mere scum.'[50] Likewise, the discourse of brown men who can't help being disloyal and lascivious in mutiny fiction is taken up and undermined by Bond's and Benegal's neo-Victorian works in ways similar to E. M. Forster's *A Passage to India* (1924) and *The Jewel in the Crown* (1966), and the first book of Paul Scott's *Raj Quartet*. Sharpe discusses how the rape of the English woman Daphne Manners by Indian men and the miscarriages of colonial justice that followed in Scott's novel came to represent the ravenousness of British rule in India in the years leading to Independence. Sharpe notes how Scott's use of the rape trope evokes a 'racial memory' that can be traced back to the events of 1857–1858, when 'the idea of rebellion was so closely imbricated with the violation of English womanhood that the Mutiny was remembered as a barbaric attack on innocent white women' (Sharpe, 2).[51]

In *Junoon*, after finding out that they have lost the battle for Delhi (which returned to British control in September 1857), following the siege of Cawnpore, Sarfaraz goes to Javed's house and destroys the pigeon coops: 'Hell and damnation of these pigeons! Birds of ill omen, they've caused the death of our soldiers. A thousand curses on them. They are profane!' The film ends with a voiceover informing the audience that Javed met martyrdom fighting the

British and that Ruth died unwed fifty-five years later in England, unable to forget the Pathan who offered her and her family sanctuary from the Indian rebel soldiers. Ultimately, the storyline goes beyond the simple opposition between victims and villains, bypassing the polarities frequently rehearsed in Victorian mutiny fiction.

CONCLUSION

This chapter refers to some of the ways in which the cultural memory of the events of 1857–8 in India was negotiated in Victorian mutiny fiction. The reconstruction of these events has inspired post-Independence creators, in both literature and cinema, as if the long nineteenth century served as a precursor to the late twentieth century. In literature, besides Ruskin Bond's novel, Mahonar Malgonkar's fictional autobiography of Nana Sahib, *The Devil's Wind* (1972) and G. D. Khosla's *The Last Mughal* (1989) have offered new cultural constructions of the 1857 uprising. In Bond and Benegal's texts, the uprising is understood as an event that exists extratextually and is represented as what 'actually happened.'[52] Their narratives are used as a reference to the 'real' past world, a time of anxieties, as described by Catherine Hall:

> The complex mix of power and vulnerability associated with being white, being a colonizer, was painfully obvious to the British in India in the wake of the Sepoy Rebellion of 1857. The shift that was taking place across many sites of Empire, the shift from the liberal humanitarian idea of the educable potential of all men to a harsher view of the ineradicable nature of racial difference, was particularly pronounced in India.[53]

At the same time, as with other neo-Victorian novels and their filmic adaptations, these texts generate renewed forms of knowledge about the narratives of the Victorian period. The reflexive nostalgia of neo-Victorian cultural artefacts is characteristically conscious of the limitations of any representation of a historical period, of the risks of the inaccuracy of absences. Indeed, as Bates notes, 'Most of the accounts of 1857 that have survived are unreliable as historical sources.'[54] The Victorian past represented in these neo-Victorian texts is a past that is known only through its cultural constructions or, as Boehmer would put it, through its textualisation. This chapter concludes that Bond's and Benegal's postcolonial narratives seek to reinstate India in a shared historical continuum, reflecting a desire for historical stability and the need for a shared narrative of Indian resistance and courage. In this context, film adaptation offers a frame of memory transmission and a medium of remembrance, even if, Andreas Huyssen notes, 'Memory as re-representation, as making present, is always in danger of collapsing the constitutive tension between past and present.'⁵⁵That the cultural act of engendering narratives about the past is a strategy of dealing with the present is emphasised in the epigraph to this chapter extracted from Julian Barnes's *England, England* (1998), which in turn calls attention to the need for the comparative study of memory as it takes an increasingly transcultural form.

Note: All dialogue translated by the author.

NOTES

1. Julian Barnes, *England, England* (London: Picador, 1999), 6.
2. Ruskin Bond, 'The Roadside Fire', *Outlook*, January 12, 2015, accessed 1 September 2021, <https://www.outlookindia.com/magazine/story/by-the-roadside-fire/292969>.
3. Clare Anderson, *Subaltern Lives: Biographies of Colonialism in the Indian Ocean World, 1790–1920* (New York: Cambridge University Press, 2012), 150.
4. Ana Cristina Mendes, 'Surviving *The Jungle Book*: Trans-temporal Ventriloquism in Ian Iqbal Rashid's *Surviving Sabu*', *Journal of British Cinema and Television* 15, no. 4 (2018): 532–52.
5. Miles Taylor, *Empress: Queen Victoria and India* (New Haven, CT: Yale University Press, 2018), 66.
6. Elleke Boehmer, *Colonial and Postcolonial Literature: Migrant Metaphors* (Oxford: Oxford University Press, 2005), 14.
7. Ann Laura Stoler and Frederick Cooper, 'Between Metropole and Colony: Rethinking a Research Agenda', in *Tensions of Empire: Colonial Cultures in a Bourgeois World*, ed. Frederick Cooper and Ann Laura Stoler (Berkeley: University of California Press, 1997), 1–57.
8. Boehmer, 14.
9. Following the East India Company Act, 1813 (Charter Act of 1813), the Proclamation for India establishes the royal prerogative regarding the Government of (British) India, transferred over from the East India Company, and is widely acknowledged as the 'Magna Carta' of Indian liberties. The document was first drafted by Lord Derby and his ministers, but the Queen asked for it to be amended, in her own words, bearing in mind that 'it is a female Sovereign who speaks to more than 100,000,000 of Eastern people on assuming the direct Government over them after a bloody civil war, giving them pledges which her future reign is to redeem, and explaining the principles of her Government. Such a document should breathe feelings of generosity, benevolence, and religious feeling, pointing out the privileges which the Indians will receive in being placed on an equality with the subjects of the British Crown, and the prosperity following in the train of civilisation'. ('Queen Victoria to the Earl of Derby', August 15, 1858).
10. G. A. Henty, *Among Malay Pirates: A Tale of Adventure and Peril* (London: Blackie and Sons, 1898), 237.
11. Lillian Nayder, *Unequal Partners: Charles Dickens, Wilkie Collins, and Victorian Authorship* (London and Ithaca, NY: Cornell University Press, 2002), 101.
12. Boehmer, 23.
13. Taylor, xxiv.
14. Boehmer, 14.

15. Catherine Hall, 'Of Gender and Empire: Reflections on the Nineteenth Century', in *Gender and Empire*, ed. Philippa Levine (Oxford: Oxford University Press, 2004), 50.
16. Sandra Ponzanesi, 'Postcolonial Adaptations: Gained and Lost in Translation', in *Postcolonial Cinema Studies*, ed. Sandra Ponzanesi and Marguerite Waller (London: Routledge, 2012), 172.
17. Pearl Padamsee, 'Love and Mutiny', *India Today*, last modified 16 February 2015, <https://www.indiatoday.in/magazine/society-the-arts/films/story/19780415-filmmaker-shyam-benegal-brings-to-life-ruskin-bonds-a-flight-of-pigeons-822924-2014-12-23>.
18. Padamsee.
19. See, for example, Brian McFarlane, *Novel to Film: An Introduction to the Theory of Adaptation* (Oxford: Oxford University Press, 1996); and James Naremore, ed., *Film Adaptation* (New Brunswick, NJ: Rutgers University Press, 2000), for a history of adaptation studies.
20. Ana Cristina Mendes and Joel Kuortti, 'Padma or no Padma: Audience in the Adaptations of *Midnight's Children*', *The Journal of Commonwealth Literature* 52, vol. 3 (2017), 501–18.
21. An example of this is Danny Boyle's *Slumdog Millionaire* and Vikas Swarup's *Q&A*.
22. Robert Stam, 'Beyond Fidelity: The Dialogics of Adaptation', in *Film Adaptation*, ed. James Naremore (New Brunswick, NJ: Rutgers University Press, 2000).
23. Stam, 66.
24. David Goldblatt, 'Ventriloquism: Ecstatic Exchange and the History of the Artwork', *The Journal of Aesthetics and Art Criticism* 51, no. 3 (1993), 389–98.
25. David Morley and Charlotte Brunsdon, *The Nationwide Television Studies* (London: Routledge, 2005), 76.
26. Ronald Inden, *Imagining India* (Cambridge, MA: Blackwell, 1990), 3. This is an account which, while persuasive, is to some extent undermined by the effectual rule of the British and even the stability of this colonial power in India.
27. Karl Marx, 'The British Rule in India (10 June 1853)', in *The Marx-Engels Reader*, ed. Robert C. Tucker (New York: W. W. Norton, 1978), 658.
28. Ana Cristina Mendes, '"From Carts to Jet Engines": The Afterlife of *Tess of the d'Urbervilles* in Michael Winterbottom's *Trishna*', *Adaptation* 9, no. 2 (2016): 221–33.
29. Inden, 4.
30. Ibid., 151.
31. Boehmer, 48.
32. Mary Louise Pratt, *Imperial Eyes: Travel Writing and Transculturation* (London: Routledge, 1992), 28.
33. Edward W. Said, *Orientalism* (New York: Pantheon, 1978), 54.
34. See also Karl Marx and Friedrich Engels, *The First Indian War of Independence, 1857–1859* (Moscow: Foreign Languages Publishing House, 1959).
35. Karl Marx, 'The Future Results of British Rule in India (22 July 1853)', in *The Marx-Engels Reader*, ed. Robert C. Tucker (New York: W. W. Norton, 1978), 659.
36. Crispin Bates, *Subalterns and Raj: South Asia since 1600* (London: Routledge, 2007), 56.
37. Bahadur Shah Zafar was seen by the colonial administrators as leader of the revolt and was tried in January 1858.
38. Padamsee.
39. The actual filming location is the ghost town of Kakori, 14 km outside Lucknow, Uttar Pradesh, which was at the centre of the uprising against British rule in 1857.
40. On the culture of the northern frontier and the Pathans, Catherine Hall writes: 'In the period after 1857, the British mapped the races of India and contrasted "martial races" with the non-martial, to the detriment of the latter. The men of the North,

especially the Pathans, warlike antagonists of the British, were admired for their energy and independence. Seen as wild, pure-bred, and rebellious, the Islamic Pathans were favourably compared with the intelligent, educated, but effeminate Bengali middle class.' (Hall 2004, 74).

41. George Otto Trevelyan, *Cawnpore* (London: Macmillan & Co., 1886), 108.
42. The character of Firdaus is performed by Shabana Azmi, a leading actress of the Indian new wave parallel cinema.
43. Boehmer, 30.
44. Jenny Sharpe, *Allegories of Empire: The Figure of Woman in the Colonial Text* (Minneapolis: University of Minnesota Press, 1993), 4.
45. Sharpe, 6.
46. Ibid., 2.
47. Ibid., 4.
48. Patrick Brantlinger, *Rule of Darkness: British Literature and Imperialism, 1830–1914* (Ithaca, NY: Cornell, 1988), 206.
49. Brantlinger, 204.
50. Dion Boucicault, *Jessie Brown, or the Relief of Lucknow: A Drama in Three Acts* (New York: Samuel French, 1858), 4.
51. Sharpe, 2. See also,Nancy Paxton, *Writing Under the Raj: Gender, Race and Rape in the British Colonial Imagination, 1830–1947* (New Brunswick, NJ: Indiana University Press, 1999); Claudia Klaver, 'Domesticity Under Siege: British Women and Imperial Crisis at the Siege of Lucknow 1857', *Women's Writing* 8 (2001): 21–58; Catherine Hart, ''Oh What Horrors will be Disclosed When We Know All': British Women and the Private/Public Experience of the Siege of Lucknow.', *Prose Studies* 34 (2012): 185–96.
52. Alison Lee, *Realism and Power: Postmodern British Fiction* (London: Routledge, 1990), 35.
53. Hall, 72.
54. Bates, 63.
55. Andreas Huyssen, *Present Pasts: Urban Palimpsests and the Politics of Memory* (Stanford, CA: Stanford University Press, 2009), 10.

CHAPTER 6

Cause and Kin: Knowledge and Nationhood in *Kalyug*

Somak Mukherjee

WHY *MAHABHARATA*? EPIC FORM AND CINEMATIC REALISM

Over the course of Shyam Benegal's long career, *Kalyug* (*The Mechanical Age*, 1981) quite understandably holds a uniquely intermediary significance. This is not surprising because the film certainly marks a radical departure in the treatment of subjects in Benegal's cinema. This was not Benegal's first endeavour collaborating with a big studio. He had already worked successfully with Shashi Kapoor's production in *Junoon* (*The Obsession*, 1979), which enjoyed equally good critical response and perhaps greater commercial success.[1] Though one could argue that *Junoon* as a period piece was more experimental in its choice of casting, in many ways, despite the same RK Films banner, *Kalyug* is much more decisively expressive in its status as a multi-starrer. In addition to the choice of actors, the implications of itemised and locational uses of song-and-dance sequences reveal an unprecedented attention on Benegal's part to a specifically urban middle-class populism. At the same time, *Kalyug*'s complexity cannot be bounded by a narrow definition of commercial agenda. Rather, it is perhaps a very self-reflexively mainstream attempt on Benegal's part, and thereby tellingly representative of his larger reflections on the intellectual and professional milieu that informed Benegal's professional work in the preceding two decades.

On the one hand, *Kalyug*'s naming is well located in the heavily industrialised landscape of post-Nehruvian India's commercial capital, Bombay, with the opening credits establishing the mechanised rhythm of progress in the ever-moving factory setting. This is a movie of the machine age because the dispassionate and precise utility of relationships takes precedence over integrity of filial bonds. In this regard, the film reflects on a conflict between mechanistic inevitability of outcomes (the cause) and preordained integrity of biological bonds (the kin). Thus, the sense of foreboding and an almost prophetic inevitability of dehumanised subjects loom over the film from the very beginning. Yet, the epochal sensibilities and idiomatic use of the epic form also refers to a deliberative projection of disrupted temporalities. In epochal discourse, *Kalyug* indicates an infernal and terminal state of crisis, reaching a point of saturation. Thus, Benegal's attempt is not merely to adapt the epic form to manifest how it travels well across time, but rather to underscore the anxieties that arise out of this time-travel of medium and narrative. *Kalyug* is not about the time-tested truth of why brothers hate one another over their rights on inherited legacy, but rather about how potency in kinship ties are not even sufficient for agency, let alone integrity. The foreknowledge of kinship, *Kalyug* demonstrates, is about mistaking singularities of choices for singularities of commitments. Because, as it turns out, bonds of blood are not enough to stir up agencies of betrayal or violence.

So, what additional discourses of knowledge, anticipatory or supernumerary, are at work here to present to us a simmering and fractured imaginary of nationhood? This is fundamentally what my chapter aims to trace. Because these elusive operations of knowledge that drive the action in Girish Karnad (screenplay) and Satyadev Dubey's (dialogue) narrative also set apart Benegal's (who shares writing credits) treatment of contemporaneity in the film. From *Ankur* (*The Seedling*, 1974), through *Nishant* (*Night's End*, 1975), *Manthan* (*The Churning*, 1976) and even *Bhumika* (*The Role*, 1977), the commitment to contemporaneity is undoubtedly palpable. These films are tied together by a common commitment to social justice in narrative representation and a lateral movement of agencies that defies not only the norms and expectations of contemporary social settings but also the expectations of the viewer.

The quiet yet remarkably potent agencies of womanhood in all of the films mentioned above defy gendered norms even within the framework of the so-called 'New Cinema' movement, which arguably was underway before Benegal debuted as a feature film director. In temporal or geographical context, Benegal's works of the 1970s are quite diverse, yet all of them at least project a sense of the present that people were living in with deeply committed forms of storytelling. The directionality of the contemporariness runs in conjunction with the movement for attainable justice. This reparative and mobile force of justice is primarily responsible for the narrative energy of these early feature works: a subterranean yet pervasive and restless drive. In this context, the writing collaborators of Benegal play an equally important role.

In Benegal's debut film *Ankur*, the director himself wrote the screenplay, but the dialogue credit went to Satyadev Dubey. His next was a screen adaptation of Habib Tanvir's *Charandas Chor* (*Charandas, the Thief*, 1975), where he shared the screenplay credit with Shama Zaidi. Dubey returned as a writer for *Nishant*, but this time sharing the writing credit with noted playwright Vijay Tendulkar. Benegal kept on pursuing eclectic choices as his writers in his later movies as well. *Manthan* was jointly written by Kaifi Azmi (dialogue) and Vijay Tendulkar (screenplay). *Bhumika* marked the first collaboration between the trio of Girish Karnad, Dubey and Benegal. There was another surprise waiting for the audience in *Junoon*. The dialogue credits for the adaptation of Ruskin Bond's novella jointly went to Ismat Chughtai and Satyadev Dubey. This itself could be seen as a representative example of Benegal's motivation for going with such an eclectic writing team over the years. In addition to competence, authority and a certain intellectual growth of these stalwarts occurring at the same time as Benegal's (at least in the case of Dubey, Karnad and Tendulkar, a recurring inclusion), there was a rhetoric of justice in these writers' work in their respective medium which was profoundly rooted in the sense of the contemporary. Despite coming from different intellectual and even linguistic backgrounds, all of these writers conveyed a trans-regional understanding of the collision between developmental progress and social injustice in the Nehruvian welfare state. Even more importantly, the collective spirit of writing with such a diverse creative team also ensured a consistent search in Benegal's cinema for an assimilated and radically plural Indian identity that went beyond the specific context of the caste-gender-class identity in individual films. In *Kalyug* too, this integrity of writing collective was kept intact, wherein Karnad, Benegal and Dubey comprised the team. Yet, perhaps Benegal's ensemble acting team, resembling a theatre unit, was turned into a true multi-starrer not only because of the big studio banner of RK Films, but also because of an attempt to reflect on the role of mainstream cinema and popular culture in defining this search for a plural Indian identity. The form, narrative and idiom of *Mahabharata* became an ideal vehicle perhaps because Benegal was less interested in the time-tested appeal of conflict ingrained in the plot and rather more in the many modes of disintegration of these elements.

So, the immediate response of finding adaptive virtues in Benegal's narrative structure in keeping the thematic relevance of the Indian epic form intact could be a distraction. Benegal is less interested in seeing how relevant *Mahabharata* still is in contemporary Indian life or to what extent the disintegration of values as seen in the *Mahabharata* narrative seems utterly relevant today. Rather, he is much more invested in truly displacing the epistemic universe of the Indian epic in today's India. The unravelling or disintegration of different layers of values framed by a brutal pragmatism of the corporate sphere makes not only the adaptation much more subversive, but also the reflective commentary on contemporary mainstream cinema's melodramatic adaptation of these values quite significant. Therefore, the film quite deliberately, yet surreptitiously, manages to become a commentary on what constitutes the values of kinship in today's mainstream discourse. And the *Mahabharata* narrative is a good vehicle for conveying the unseemliness of ties and bonds in the eyes of today's public.

In an interview given to Bengali newspaper *Aajkal* (*Nowadays*) more than a decade after the release of the film, Benegal quite clearly said that it would be a misreading of *Kalyug* to merely see at as a modernised version of *Mahabharata*:

> I don't think in *Kalyug* I have tried to give any 'modern relevance' to any specific event of *Mahabharata*. Rather, there is certainly a presence of the fundamental thematic elements of the epic in my life. Actually what I adapted was certain archetypes presented in *Mahabharata*, rethinking them in the present context. The relevance of these archetypes is certainly eternal. True at any given age. Kalyug reminds you of these age old archetypes present in Mahabharata.[2]

In the same interview, Benegal quite strongly defended his casting of mainstream Bollywood actors in *Junoon*, not seeing it as a significant marker of change in terms of treatment. Time is the protagonist of the film, he claimed, and therefore inclusion of stars like Shashi Kapoor pragmatically responded to the demands of characterisation. At the same time, if we consider the quartet of *Ankur-Nishant-Manthan-Bhumika* together then one grasps a significant change of milieu and treatment of temporality in *Kalyug*. In the case of the latter, it is not time, unlike in *Junoon*, which is the protagonist of the narrative, but rather an immersive present that disrupts the directionality of justice. Therefore, an attempt to unpack the socio-temporal milieu of *Kalyug* is necessary to understand the significance of kinship in the film.

IN TRANSIT: MILIEU AND DISCURSIVE KNOWLEDGE IN *KALYUG*

Class conflict and exploitation of the rural poor by the feudal order has been a quintessential hallmark of Benegal's early works. The setting plays an important role in the heightening of this conflict. A significant and applauded single shot sequence from *Ankur* features Lakshmi (Shabana Azmi) running through the courtyard of her small village house to wake her husband, Kishtayya (Sadhu Meher) to alert him of the arrival of the village landlord's son, Surya, played by Anant Nag, in a motor car. Lakshmi then opens the gate of their house to Surya's honking car sailing through the green rural landscape. The arrival of the car not only implies a technological disruption affecting the daily cycle, but also establishes a feudal impunity that only sees people like Lakshmi and Kishtayya through an extractivist prism. This is an early indication of a recurring concern of Benegal in his early films: how feudal values and feudalism's fundamentally exploitative structure survive through a transition from colonial to independent welfare state and continue to intervene into a sustainable relationship between the people and their locale. The film ends on a note of fugitive resistance to this fragile survival of feudal domesticity when a young boy throws a stone at Surya's house and then escapes, breaking a glass window. This reversal of disruption in many ways is reflective of the transparency of violence inscribed in the relationship between Lakshmi and Surya. But Laskhmi's realisation of that potential of violence is the result of the emerging knowledge of both her pregnancy and of Surya's duplicity. However, while Surya's early arrival in a car is based on a correct estimation of social structure, Kishtayya's return to the village leads to Surya's false assumption that the former is driven by vengeance. In Kishtayya's humiliation, based on false knowledge, the social truth of the feudal autocracy is preserved. Yet, there is a web of entangled knowledge structures of social bonds at work: one based on debts of custodianship. In *Manthan*, on the other hand, the opening shot (accompanied by Preeti Sagar's melodious voice celebrating rural belonging) – the motif of the arriving train through the static grey landscape – bears promise of welfare and change. Veterinary surgeon Dr Rao's (Girish Karnad) car rides through the village symbolising the power of benevolent technology. Rao's mission of welfare begins with theft: he is accused of stealing the milk sample from Bindu's (Smita Patil) home. At a moment of confrontation, he is rescued by Mishra-ji (Amrish Puri), who gives him a ride in his car, saving him from angry and suspicious villagers. This sequence may well mark the motor car as a symbol of protectionist status quo. It also acts as a harbinger of hope when Rao and his colleague return after saving the life of a child at the crack of dawn. In both *Ankur* and *Manthan*, despite the ambiguity of intent, technology incurs a change that transforms the milieu. In *Bhumika*, the evolution of the protagonist's social identity is foregrounded against the technological change of Indian cinema in four phases.

Kalyug marks a significant shift. The film begins with a graphic introductory narrative of the family trees of the rival business clans, showing their familial ties. This may well set the narrative within the idiom of the all-too-familiar epic, but the static and inflexible visual chart is more like a stipulation and less an initiation. In fact, what is at the root of the success of these two business families is not really established, as if the successive family trees mark the banality of their tension as something given. Right after this, the shift in the optics of the power structure, from property-based feudalism to the much more opaque finance capital of corporate India, is complete with another act of arrival. But this time, it is much less spatially determined and thereby not confined to the trajectories of land and genealogical possession. Sandeepraj of Khubchand Firm receives the news of contract finalisation by fax machine and conveys it quickly. This is followed by opening credits where the factory environment filled with heavy machinery and the process of production implies a post-domestic space of productivity and prosperity. Bharat (Anant Nag) arrives, just like Sandeepraj, at his professional space, enraged at the prospect of a lost contract. Karan (Shashi Kapoor) and Dhanraj (a surprisingly sympathetic portrayal of Duryodhan, brilliantly played by Victor Banerjee) are introduced in the film, rather symbolically removing their protective welding gear in the factory in a warrior-like way. Thus, the expansion of rivalry transcends not only the domestic front, but also the predetermined values of land-based authority. In the factory space, the manufacturing in motion is a precursor to the prudential domain of finance capital. Here the potential for profit is potentially infinite and practically exponential. This shift of tension, right at the outset, to the professional space also strips any subsequent value of its connection to the original source.

Thus Benegal quite deliberately subverts the dichotomy of good and evil in giving legitimacy to the ambition of both sides, whereby one-upmanship is not seen as an evil strategy, but rather the hallmark of unsentimental corporatism. This indistinction between good and evil also precisely shifts the knowledge discourses on the legitimacy of one's action to a perpetually discursive space. Again, one such sphere is the space of transit. Pivotal sequences in the play are set against the bleak and smoggy post-industrial cityscape of south Bombay, be it Balraj's (Kulbhushan Kharbanda) chase of Sandeepraj or Karan's moment of frustrated stagnation being stuck in his car in the middle of a Ganesh Puja procession. Bharat, while on a car ride with Dharamraj (Raj Babbar) and Supriya (Rekha), passes on a key piece of information extracted from Bhishamchand (A. K. Hangal) that Karan has under-quoted the cost of the STS project by getting three high-precision imported machines through a contact from England for a government project a few years ago. These moments of strategic revelation are key to the plot development. Such instances of strategic interference also signify a shift towards a more transitory and discursive domain of knowledge. This seems to be both an act of reduction and of expansion, since if we grant a certain spiritual or providentiary value to the domestic space, the more liminal spaces of a restaurant or a car ride reduce only the premonitory materiality of action. At the same time, there is no reduction to the urgency of cause and action. It has merely been expanded to the more concretely strategic space of the board room. As Supriya sarcastically remarks when Bhishamchand advises Bharat to take business setbacks sportingly: 'Even after a football match defeat the clashing teams occasionally try to kill one another.'

KINSHIP AND THE LEGITIMACY OF BEING

One of the most interesting aspects of *Kalyug* is Benegal's counter-intuitive approach to the question of legitimacy. The film jettisons the moral binary well established between the Pandavas and Kauravas in the epic in favour of creating an ambivalent frame of legitimacy. In the narrative, it happens as a consequence of the chaotic evil surrounding Indian industry at the height of the Licence Raj of the 1970s. Benegal not only ascribes equal accountability to the sparring families in terms of moral lapse, but also reflects on this state of equity from the perspective of Karan's character. Nevertheless, the afterlives of Karna's character from the epic often generated a sympathetic view of his anti-hero status precisely because his heroism was often borne out by a sense of aggrieved self, which itself was the result of concealment and secrecies. This not only relates to the secrecy surrounding Karna's parentage, but also Karna's own act of concealment to Parashurama concerning his non-Brahmin social status. Such sympathetic portrayals of Karna's character include Tagore's long poem, 'Karna Kunti Samvaad' or Shivaji Sawant's Marathi masterpiece, *Mrityunjaya (Victory Over Death)*.[3] In *Kalyug*, however, no such self-exaggeration is pursued in the portrayal of Karan's character, though his list of accomplishments includes being a Rhodes Scholar. This was only mentioned in passing by Dharamraj in a discussion about his business acumen. Yet, within the limited range of the narrative, Karan's context for preparedness is not established. We see him right from the outset as a figure of perfection, even as Dhanraj's equal. Bharat, despite his resentment towards him, even tries to make Karan switch sides in a 'legitimate' manner by offering him senior management positions, much to the consternation of Dhanraj. These moments of moral manoeuvring once again remind us that the yardstick of legitimacy is much more flexible in the narrative.

I want to dwell more on this entangled relationship between kinship and legitimacy that emerges in the discourses on nationalism. In this regard an excellent text to draw insight from is Irish political scientist and historian Benedict Anderson's landmark treatise, *Imagined Communities: Reflections on the Origin and Spread of Nationalism* (1983). My intention here is neither to explore the importance of the book in the field of nationalism studies nor to delve into the critiques of its trans-historical arguments. Both have been well documented. Rather, for me it is interesting that right before providing the now landmark definition of a nation in the book in a self-declared 'anthropological spirit' ('it is an imagined political community – and imagined as both inherently limited and sovereign'), Anderson chooses to provide us with a necessary proviso. He writes while discussing the capacity of ambiguity embedded in the nationalistic discourse:

> One tends unconsciously to hypostasize the existence of Nationalism-with-a-big-N (rather as one might Age-with-a-capital-A) and then to classify 'it' as an ideology. (Note that if everyone has an age, Age is merely an analytical expression.) It would, I think, make things easier if

one treated it as if it belonged with 'kinship' and 'religion,' rather than with 'liberalism' or 'fascism.'[4]

This definitional shift towards nationalism's belonging to categories of material (one could even argue, largely domesticated) practices such as kinship and religion not only consolidates its potency, but also puts it in a more intimate economy of affect. Therefore, the shift is from ideological affiliation (liberalism of Fascism) towards a subterranean, but perpetually charged, force of emotions that is bound by kinship. In turn, these matrixes of emotions are also creating new principles of obligations and accountabilities, which are not born in what we capaciously define as the public sphere or civil society. Yet, Anderson's clarification regarding nationalism's definitional affiliation also helps us reflect on the principles of justice arising out of the bounded nexus of the private or familial sphere. Are they not equally responsible for the consolidation of nationalistic thought? It seems, with Benegal's transposition of the warring men of *Mahabharata* into post-Nehruvian industrial India, we are also being asked to consider alternative dimensions of belonging to the nation *away* from the constitutional capacities followed by the civil society. Therefore, although the polished bourgeoisie as depicted in the film belongs to the civil society in matters of taste and consumption (be it Karan's consumption of Bach concertos or Bharat's reluctant attention to Indian classical music on a date night with Subhadra), the code is blood ties, not the inscriptions of the Constitution. Thus, it is interesting to consider whether Benegal's consideration of the 'Age of Vice' as depicted in relation to its characterisation as an analytical expression by Anderson is borne out of a sense of continuity rather than transgression. One may wonder whether Benegal is leading us towards a more uneasy truth that in today's age of vice, blood ties continue to dictate principles of morality and transgress the post-familial consolidation of the principles of justice as enshrined in the Constitution. If that is the case, then his target is not the transgression of constitutional values, but the continuation of familial values that never even accorded the constitutional values their space in the public sphere. For the rivals of *Kalyug*, the Nation is a more innocent placeholder category for nexus.

Anderson writes further about this entrenched practice of meaning-making out of solidarities and loyalties beyond their transactional value:

> The pre-bourgeois ruling classes generated their cohesions in some sense outside language, or at least outside print-language. If the ruler of Siam took a Malay noblewoman as a concubine, or if the King of England married a Spanish princess – did they ever talk seriously together? Solidarities were the products of kinship, clientship, and personal loyalties.[5]

French Philosopher Étienne Balibar's essay on the history and ideology of the nation form also helps us see clearly through the confusion surrounding whether the continuity of values as referred to in the film is genealogical or affiliatory. Balibar himself takes a stand in defining genealogy in national societies as the archive of affiliations or alliances, and denies it too much importance as a body of knowledge that studies continuity formally or in a more intimate manner (such as in oral family history). This pushes me to look at the values of solidarity or loyalty as expressed in *Kalyug* as not something that laments a lost past in a feat of comparison, but rather as an utterly relatable currency of belonging. Therefore, when the families embody the spirit of the Pandavas or the Kauravas, they are instrumentalising the power of kinship and its extended nexus as a deeply contemporaneous force, not as an anachronistic force of resistance in the life of the republic. Balibar writes:

> Let us note here that in contemporary national societies, except for a few genealogy 'fanatics' and a few who are 'nostalgic' for the days of the aristocracy, genealogy is no longer either a body of theoretical knowledge nor an object of oral memory, nor is it recorded and conserved privately: Today *it is the state which draws up and stores the archive of filiations and alliances*.
>
> Here again we have to distinguish between a deep and a superficial level. The superficial level is familialist discourse (constitutive of conservative nationalism) which at a very early stage became linked with nationalism in political tradition – particularly within the French tradition. The deep level is the simultaneous emergence of 'private life,' the 'intimate (small) family circle' and the family policy of the state, which projects into the public sphere the new notion of population and the demographic techniques for measuring it, of the supervision of its health and morals, and of its reproduction. The result is that the modern family circle is quite the opposite of an autonomous sphere at the frontiers of which the structures of the state would halt. It is the sphere in which the relations between individuals are immediately charged with a 'civic' function and made possible by constant state assistance beginning with relations between the sexes which are aligned to procreation.[6]

The conflicting loyalty between the dharma of kinship and the dharma of labour is also acutely felt not only in moments where Karan faces critical knowledge surrounding his position in the family, but also in those which concern his position in the industry. The introductory graphics of family straightforwardly sets up Bharat and Subhadra as a couple, when the narrative naturally takes some time to establish that important plot development. This display of foreknowledge is not surprising if we consider the orders of relations in families. One might consider that everyone will fall under this framework of inevitability and expectations. However, two deliberate omissions break that order of expectation in Benegal's family index. First of all, there is no profile of Puranchand. Even if we consider that this omission is due to the fact that he plays no part in the film, one cannot escape the contradiction. In *Mahabharata*, the legitimacy of his offspring gaining the upper hand in the moral order also depended upon Puranchand's (Pandu) death against Dhritarashtra's disability. Dhritarashtra survives, but the trajectory of Pandu's fate is given enough background context. In the film, on the other hand, Puranchand is stripped of any visual presence. This omission, one might suspect, is not only because he is dead, but also because the foundational virtues of dynasties are impotent in forming sustainable ties in industrial space. Even more importantly, Karan's introduction is made only through his rank in the company and with a significant omission regarding his place in the family. The details will emerge later, but unlike Bharat and Subhadra's relationship, there is neither a background nor a foreknowledge established. This points towards a generic negation of the inevitability of origin in the relationship structures of the film (Figure 6.1).

Figure 6.1 Karan (Shashi Kapoor) looks at the cityscape of Bombay from the balcony of his apartment.

In an interview, Benegal provided the context for the ambivalent figurations of Karan's character in the film:

> In the *Mahabharata*, Karna is a very interesting figure because he was born before his mother was married and was then abandoned to be looked after by someone else. He did not know that he belonged to the same family as the Pandavas, that he was actually the eldest brother. When the battle took place he was the general of the opposing forces, the Kauravas, because he was a very close friend of Duryodhana. Karna was as great a general, a duelist and an archer as Arjuna was. And when his mother discovered that he was going to lead the Kauravas, she told him that she was his mother. He breaks down, because he can't fight his own brothers – so she really weakens him. The central issue that fascinated me and continues to fascinate me is that of a mother who has not been a mother at all, who then expects the loyalty of the son, placing him in a terrible quandary. Karna eventually accepts his loyalty to his mother without betraying his loyalty to the side he is on and so allows himself to be killed. That was the central feature of the *Mahabharata* story that is very exciting and very interesting. We often have people who are placed in situations of conflicting loyalties, where the only honourable thing to do is to be sacrificed. So this served as the basis for *Kalyug*.[7]

If Benegal's attempt was to familiarise characters to the audience within a framework of precedence then the family tree sequence was already helpful in situating roles for characters despite giving them different names, for example, Bharat for Arjuna; Supriya for Draupadi. But when the aspect of relating to characters is brought forth by Benegal himself, then the intimate connection between predetermined and cultivated recognition also plays an important part in how we perceive these characters going beyond their role in the family structure.[8] Bharat and Subhadra during their courtship phase attend a *kathakali* performance, but get bored quickly when the performance depicts the scene of Draupadi's humiliation by Duhshashana and eventually Bhima's violent slaying of Duhshashana. They leave the performance largely due to Bharat's reluctance and end up in a nightclub. Again, raw energies of kinship have no effect on Bharat, whose marriage to Subhadra resembles a corporate merger much more than an extension of ties between two families. Bharat's climactic outburst upon hearing the foundational illegitimacy of his own status is certainly violent and almost convulsive. But one might argue that what enrages him much more than the promiscuity of his mother is the new possibility of attachment with Karan, now essentially proven to be his blood brother. There is now a clear line of distinction in the cause of revenge itself. Killing a professional rival who harms Bharat's own family is different to the retrospective knowledge of killing one's blood brother, because the latter is akin to the destruction of one's own self that happens in conjunction with the dissolution of the business family. Bharat's realisation of his own moral bankruptcy also destroys the core speculative energy of a corporate executive in him. In this case the film does not go against the simple binaries of morality in *Mahabharata*, but rather underscores a somewhat remarkable tension present in the original *Mahabharata* narrative: between individual morality and social morality. One must note that while the relative goodness of the Pandavas over the Kauravas is far less ambiguous in the narrative development of the text, its larger spectrum is a very nuanced and self-reflexive take on the moral ambiguity of human action, as Benegal himself notes. He says regarding the complexity of this tension between individual and social morality:

> Social morality is often a convention adopted to keep a society stable. So when you talk about individual conscience and individual morality it is completely different from social conscience and social morality. The distinction is important because when you talk about honesty you have to ask who is he honest to. He should be honest with himself rather than be simply honest to society. If the two can merge it's perfect. But they don't always merge.[9]

This is very clearly reflected in the curious binary between two kinds of actions that are not guided by the expansion of constitutive knowledge of the state among citizens, but rather by its protective retreat from it. In fact, these networks of secret knowledge are what drive the potency of privilege in the plotline. Both the families are in the domain of advantage because they know what others (government ministries or factory workers) don't. Thereby the foundational current of fashioning the self's relationship to the nation-state is the hidden privilege of knowledge. This privilege is at first circumstantial, like the construction of self–state relation in *Mahabharata*, predetermined by contingencies of birth or caste. When the characters develop self-understanding, there is a rather absolute standpoint of moral action: Arjuna does what Arjuna should, while Karna is the exception. Moral action is determined by an accepted hierarchy of milieu. Yet, Benegal is operating under a framework of a modern nation-state where equality is at least constitutionally enshrined. It is equally true that even this theoretical dream of equality was quickly disintegrating as India entered a period of rampant economic inequality from at least the early 1970s, unprecedented even by the standards of the early years of the republic. Around the same time the media discourse was shifting to a more class-centric approach to the depiction of collectivity, as the credence of nationhood in manifesting a more singular collectivity (overcoming obstacles) was giving way to the visible faultiness of persistent class divisions.

How do the Puranchands and Khubchands of this India reorient themselves in this environment through continuity and change? On the one hand, there is a continuity of privilege associated with established business families. Some of this formerly landed elite made the shift from feudalism to corporatism with ease. The institutional recognition of management philosophy through the establishment of Indian Institutes of Management (IIMs) was often an attempt to set in motion the potentialities of privilege in the disguise of expertise. Rule of the upper-class elite was thus seen less through a prism of continuity and more through an emergence of a new industrial upper class. Obscuring this continuity was to the benefit of the ruling class. Therefore, the intimacy of kinship of the Puranchands and Khubchands is closely related to the intimacies of knowledge: a marker of a continued legacy where their relationship to nation-building is related to a closely guarded network of knowledge, which in turn validates privilege as a logic of choice. However, in addition to this, there is a manoeuvre of guarding and extracting secrecy that implicates a shiftier transitional 'licensing' of knowledge from the state to corporations.

This transitional privilege of knowledge operates precisely in recognition of the conceptual equality of the welfare state. This is why award contracts shift from one family to another, or the police threatens the Puranchands that they lodged false police complaints regarding the stealing of consignments from the docks only to reap the insurance money dishonestly. Enraging Bharat, the police officer scornfully tells the Puranchands, 'If the super rich like you engage in stealing then what will happen to the poor of this country?!' Surprisingly, the complicity of the state is relatively negligible in the film. The state, be it in the form of government or financial institutions, shifts its recognition of transparency based on circumstantial knowledge. When, towards the climax of the film, the tide of fortune shifts again, Dhanraj receives a phone call from his investor with the news that his projects will soon be questioned in parliament, with a call for the invocation of personal guarantee. Dhanraj receives the news with outrage, but it is clear that the state is taking over matters. Yet, we also witness backroom deals beforehand such as with informants who receive the 'reward' of a research opportunity in the United States from Karan, or with the union boss Bhavani Pandey (Om Puri) via the offer of a compromise from Bharat, depriving the striking labourers of a fair deal.

The transitional privilege of knowledge discourses from the dharma of dynasty (fulfilled by kinship) to the dharma of capital (fulfilled by executive knowledge) is one of the most essential components of *Kalyug*'s narrative development. The writing team in many ways traversed a sensitive path of connecting the collective disintegration of the family with the gradual alienation of an individual. This was the hallmark of the grim and nihilistic outlook of today's machine age. While the destruction of one's own would have made a little difference in Karan's path of relentless aspiration, the knowledge of kinship throws him off the rail completely. This is underscored in Karan's relationship to Bombay. His position as an affluent soloist is emphasised in his fondness for listening to the Western classical music in his spacious apartment or gazing wistfully at the vast urban horizon in front of him. As someone whose parentage is obliterated, the horizon of the city represents both a therapeutic limitlessness and a cynical morality. Karan's rapid progress was in essence a product of his successful reconciliation of this dual relationship to the city he held. Later, clarity of parentage wreaks havoc in this state of wistful reconciliation, wherein Karan's way of looking at the city constantly reminded us of a hopeless indeterminacy, stagnation and even rage. According to Sangeeta Datta:

> Benegal's depiction of the cityscape, the long sequences offering glimpses of South Bombay as characters drive in their cars, the religious processions on the streets – all work powerfully to site characters in the urban milieu. Karan's social isolation is established in the scenes where he silently contemplates the city from his high rise apartment. At a climactic moment, Karan is caught in a traffic jam as the street throngs with people joining the Ganapati (Hindu elephant god) immersion ceremony on the beach. The moment of claustrophobia potently conveys the sense of an individual caught in the web of larger forces. Immersions of clay images of Ganapati and of the mother goddess Durga signify that the gods have turned away from Karan, momentarily recreating a high moment of Greek Tragedy. This also intensifies Karan's sense of betrayal by his mother.[10]

One cannot help but notice the parallel between the estrangement of Bharat and Karan. The knowledge of his mother's infidelity also breaks the potency of Bharat's labour as there is little distinction between his position as a member of the Puranchand family and the Puranchand enterprise. This non-distinction also precisely drives his action. The difference is, after the destruction of his attachment to the patriarchal corporation, he retreats into the matriarchal authority of Subhadra. For Karan, unfortunately, there is no such shelter. This complete lack of emotional refuge for him is gradually built into his character development. Maybe in better times Karan kept himself functional by retreating into his carefully constructed private world of lonely dinners or Bach suites, but in the end for him there is no place to go. In the dharma of dynasty, Karan successfully positioned himself as an outsider other whose loyalty lies in gratitude. In the dharma of capital, he supplemented gratitude with sheer competence. In the end, Karan's abject alienation is symbolised by the fact that the truth of his inheritance can only be realised through a complete disenfranchisement from the corporate space.

CONCLUSION: KINSHIP FROM DOMESTIC TO CORPORATE SPHERE IN *KALYUG*

When we discuss *Kalyug* today both as a milestone in Benegal's filmography and as an idiomatic adaptation of an Indian epic, we should move beyond the disputatious discourses of tradition and modernity, or religion and secularity. Benegal himself thought that this conflict of tradition and modernity in art cinema was a bit over inflated. He thought that *Kalyug* as an adaptation works because it potently conveys a critique of materialism in modern India.[11] This materialist critique is set in a transition of ties and social networks from the domestic to the professional sphere. Therefore, the weapons of destruction which would be in action on the battlefield could also have ornamental functions as an essential part of the household. The film supplements this with the weaponisation of contracts. Social contracts are established through a family viewing of Bharat and Subhadra's wedding video (Figure 6.2). In the corporate space, the contract is clearly more legalised than the intimacies of family bonding. Thus, the hyper-masculine

Figure 6.2 The sequence featuring the viewing of the wedding video.

thrill of advantage is located in finding trusted sources in the government and financial institutions, through a variety of alumni networks. Philip Lutgendorf writes:

> The 'kingdom' over which the two families are struggling consists of a series of massive government contracts, presumably defense related, on which both have bid, and which, in the course of the film, they attempt to steal from each other, assisted by the tricks of bought out union bosses and hired thugs. The film thus effectively invokes the business climate of the pre-liberalization 'license raj,' when imported raw materials and technologies were strictly controlled, as well as the endemic labour unrest of the 1970s and the ensuing period of autocratic rule by Indira Gandhi (the Khubchand and Sons factory sports inspirational signboards of the sort that proliferated during the Emergency; for example, 'Prosperity Through Productivity'). Its equivalent of divine weapons are precision foreign machines, obtained by Bharat and Karan as a result of sojourns in the West (the 'heaven' of modern Indian elite), and its version of the Kaurava-instigated humiliation of the Pandavas takes the form of an income tax raid on the Puranchand brothers' mansion to uncover suspected 'black money,' during which the agents rifle through enraged Surpiya's wardrobe, fingering her jewelry and undergarments.[12]

I find this reference to Indira Gandhi's regime (when the film released she was back gloriously in power after electoral setbacks post-Emergency) by Lutgendorf to be quite interesting and a good note to conclude our discussion of the dynamics of kinship in *Kalyug*.

The return of a matriarchal authority exuded in the intimate embrace of Bharat and Supriya cannot be separated from the political implication of Indira Gandhi's political journey in the preceding decade (Figure 6.3). Gandhi, who was revered as a mother goddess after the victory in the Bangladesh War of 1971, also attempted to infantilise her polity during the Emergency by subsuming her political identity within a framework of infallible kinship. But Supriya's authoritative body language and attitude leads us to even more complex questions concerning the unique dynamics of power set in domestic space. The question is less about the absolute precedence of emotional authority over professional affiliation in domestic space and more about its strategic negation of hyper-masculine forces in the executive sphere. *Kalyug* helps us ask – what kind of knowledge, and received in which circumstance, leads to a legitimised resistance to the emotional authority of kinship?

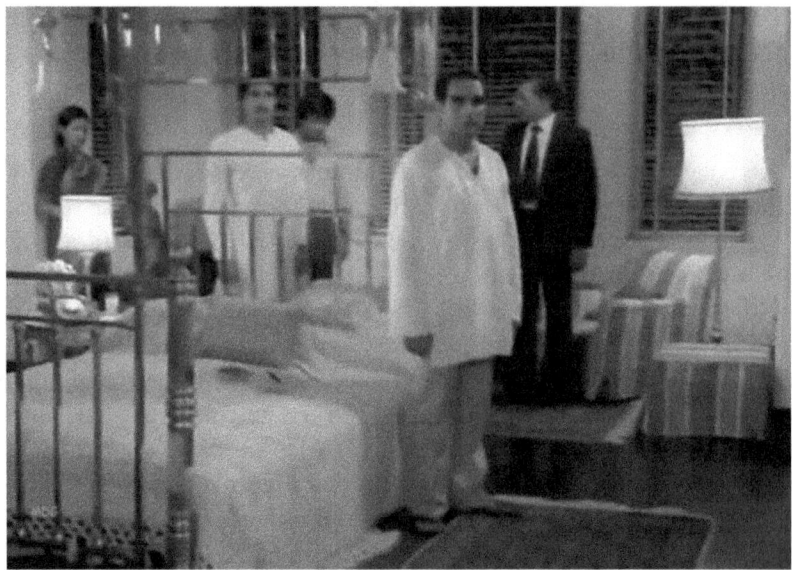

Figure 6.3 Brothers confronted by their mother.

Note: All dialogue translated by the author.

NOTES

1. Both *Junoon* and *Kalyug* won the Filmfare Award for best film, in 1980 and 1982, respectively.
2. Shyam Benegal, 'Chalachitra ke Shudhumatro Art Bhebey Chhobi Kore Kono Labh Nei', interview by *Aajkal*, 27 September 1992.
3. Kevin McGrath, *The Sanskrit Hero: Karna in Epic Mahābhārata* (Leiden: Brill, 2004), 243. Political psychologist and social theorist Ashis Nandy has also written significantly in several texts about the reinterpretation of *Mahabharata* from the perspective of Karna. In 2002, Nandy included *Kalyug* among a few 'brilliant' cultural works which has helped Vyasa's text acquire 'new shades of meaning after being a constant target of reinterpretations during the last hundred years'. Even earlier, Nandy had written how the character imagery of Karna had a 'special appeal among the parity elites of colonial India' and how thinkers like Jagadish Chandra Bose at the end of the nineteenth century considered Karna through a 'possible mythic paradigm for the modern Indian' (McGrath, 243). For Nandy, who has written extensively on Indian popular cinema, *Kalyug* is a commentary on the 'ambivalent fascination of the Indian middle classes with the character [of Karna]' (McGrath, 243).
4. Benedict Anderson, *Imagined Communities: Reflections on the Origin and Spread of Nationalism*, rev. ed. (London; New York: Verso, 2006), 5.

5. Anderson, 76.
6. Étienne Balibar, 'The Nation Form: History and Ideology', in *Becoming National: A Reader*, ed. Geoff Eley and Ronald Grigor Suny (New York: Oxford University Press 1996), 145.
7. William Van der Heide and Shyam Benegal, *Bollywood Babylon: Interviews with Shyam Benegal* (Oxford: Berg, 2006), 107.
8. Van der Heide and Benegal, 108.
9. Ibid., 109.
10. Sangeeta Datta, *Shyam Benegal* (London: British Film Institute, 2002), 130.
11. Van der Heide and Benegal, 108.
12. Philip Lutgendorf, 'Bending the Bharata: Two Uncommon Cinematic Adaptations', in *Indian Literature and Popular Cinema: Recasting Classics*, ed. Heidi R. M. Pauwels (London: Routledge, 2010), 25.

CHAPTER 7

The Ascent in *Arohan*

Partha Pratim Sen and Arunima Ray (Chowdhury)

INTRODUCTION

Class and class struggle have been profoundly dealt with in Indian cinema. This theme featured in Indian cinema whenever filmmakers tried to depict power struggles or power relations, be it in blockbusters or those films that simply made it to the various film festivals. However, it is not always that Indian filmmakers while dealing with power, power relations or class struggle, strictly adhered to the Marxist notion that the 'history of all hitherto existing societies is the history of class struggle'. Nevertheless, when it comes to critical analysis of these films, the Marxist perspectives indeed become 'profitable lenses',[1] which help us differentiate depictions of class struggle in the 'mainstream' from those in 'parallel' cinema. While looking into those parallel films where the central theme is struggle, oppression, power, and so on, we encounter some conscious adherence to Marxist thinking. The notion of class struggle culminating in a proletarian revolution similarly features in these films, but stops short of propagating a full-fledged revolution, given the parliamentary democracy practised in India. The democracy practised within an essentially bourgeois state tolerates Marxian narratives only within the purview of the Constitution. Thus, filmmakers who venture into depiction of class conflict and class struggle need to abide by the golden rule of the futility of armed struggle against the oppressor and the ultimate faith in the supremacy of the law of the land even if that is appropriated by the bourgeoisie.

While discussing the plight of cinema vis-à-vis the Indian bourgeois state, Anirudh Deshpande draws upon the understanding of the Indian bourgeoisie as depicted by Marxist critiques of the Indian cinema.[2] According to him, the Indian bourgeoisie comprises the lower middle class, the newly formed rich middle class and the traditional upper middle class. This division although utterly simplistic might give us an insight into the clientele of Indian films and the urge to depict the eventual futility of a protracted class struggle and a proletarian revolution. This desperation often leads the parallel filmmakers to end their films with a message of class reconciliation and the 'righteous' path of parliamentary democracy, where even communist parties can thrive and function.

The decades following India's independence, particularly the 1960s and the 1970s, witnessed socio-political turbulence, and the constant effort by the Indian state to manage such crises found an expression through Indian cinema. Filmmakers who were trying to depict Indian society and polity in a manner different from the hitherto popular 'hero-heroine-villain' formula found ample opportunity to depict and highlight the minds, aspirations and struggles of the common Indian men and women who comprised either the subaltern or the middle class consisting of the daily office-goers commuting on public transport who engaged in social and political dialogues and debates at local tea shops, but never directly became enmeshed in political activities apart from voting. The formula worked because it gave these people an opportunity to vent their desperation due to the gradual failure of the Indian state to fulfil their growing aspirations and expectations. On the other hand, there was a parallel stream of cinema-making that started as early as 1947 in Kolkata. Film aficionados comprised of artists, journalists, documentary filmmakers and even clerks got together to discuss, make and promote what was known as 'good cinema' in the city.[3] The aim was to constitute film societies along the lines of the cine clubs that were in vogue in Paris. Stalwarts like Satyajit Ray, Ritwik Ghatak, Mrinal Sen, Bimal Roy, Chidananda Das Gupta and Adoor Gopalarishnan were the pioneers of setting up such film societies, which were established between 1959 and 1981. They received direct patronage from leftist organisations such as the Progressive Writers Association, formed in 1936, and the Indian People's Theatre Association (IPTA), which came into being in 1942. Members of these organisations, which essentially had anti-capitalist, anti-fascist and pro-worker/peasant agendas, lost no time in associating themselves with the 'film society movement'. The idea was to highlight the plight of the common masses, which the profit-driven mainstream cinema could not fulfil, as well as to act as a mirror of the aspirations of these masses. The movement also aimed to transform cinema as a medium of mass entertainment into an art form for social, political and economic consciousness among the masses.[4] Ashish Rajadhyaksha has listed three films inspired directly by IPTA: *Dharti Ke Laal* (*Children of the Earth*, 1946) by K. A. Abbas; *Neecha Nagar* (*The Lower Depths*, 1946) by Chetan Anand; and *Kalpana* (*Imagination*, 1948), a musical dance-drama by Uday Shankar. In fact, IPTA even produced *Dharti Ke Laal*.[5] All the three films dealt, in their own way, with the conflicts between the haves and the have-nots, very consciously harping on the theme of class and class struggle. Each film ends with a triumphant note, where the proletariat wins albeit the revolution is kept partly silent, or at best, sublimated.

Shyam Benegal has been grappling with the issue of class and class conflict in rural India from his debut film *Ankur* (*The Seedling*, 1974). The film essentially deals with the story of the son of a landlord who comes to his father's 'estate' and poses as someone who does not believe in caste or untouchability, but essentially succumbs to all the values and vices of feudalism. Benegal's concern for the less privileged and his attempts to highlight the contradictions within the rich Indian upper class, which essentially is firmly rooted in the feudal value system, while all the time flirting with liberal capitalism, are evident in the films that followed *Ankur*, namely *Nishant* (*Night's End*, 1975) and later *Trikal* (*Past, Present and Future*) and *Kalyug* (*The Mechanical Age*, 1981).[6]

The present chapter tries to take a peek into Benegal's mind (or his heart), which constantly gets intrigued by the dynamics of class in Indian society. *Arohan* (*The Ascent*, 1982) was chosen as a case where Benegal deals with violent class conflict, which swept Bengal in the late 1960s and very interestingly gets reconciled by none other than a Marxist state government that accords land rights to the sharecroppers and also empowers the rural peasantry by enabling them to take on their erstwhile masters through the democratic process of election to the rural self-governments.

AGRARIAN RELATIONS IN BENGAL, A BRIEF OVERVIEW

With colonial rule came huge changes in the determination of agrarian relations in Bengal, and these had far-reaching consequences. The small peasantry was impoverished because of their increased dependence on the moneylenders. Pages of *Sambad Prabhakar*, a Bengali periodical, portrayed the dismal condition of the peasantry of the late nineteenth century. For Bengal specifically, as Partha Chatterjee writes, it was the permanent settlement that led the peasantry to dispossess their land, which became the property of the *zaminder* or the landlord (Chatterjee 1986: 170).[7] Again, commercialisation of production relations in agriculture led to the strengthening of semi-feudal forms of exploitation. Extensive control over the produce of the small cultivators began when the landlords, moneylenders and traders started using what Chatterjee calls the debt-credit mechanism. However, Chatterjee argues that the processes of commercialisation and exploitation of peasant labour were complex because exploitation of such labour could also be seen as a case of formal subordination of labour by capital. Again, although the small peasantry or sharecroppers were subjected to exploitation by the moneylenders, they retained partial control over their means of subsistence.

The nineteenth century, as Partha Chatterjee argues, saw one major problem regarding agricultural production in terms of a shortage of labour to cultivate the lands available in the northeast and south of Bengal. This was the time when parts of estates were sub-let to 'enterprising tenants who would undertake to mobilise cultivators to clear out and settle the new lands'.[8] Meanwhile, the Rent Act of 1859 was 'intended to set right the relations between the landlords and their tenants mainly by restricting the powers of the landlords to enhance rents and also clearly defining the rights of the raiyats/tenants particularly to sub-let lands'.[9] However, the act on the whole favoured the *zamindars* overlooking the interests of the 'sub-tenants' and the 'share-tenants'.

Between the Rent Act of 1859 and the Tenancy Act of 1885, a number of peasant rebellions came to be reported, foremost among which was the indigo rebellion (1859–62). It was primarily a clash between the peasants and the indigo planters. Peasant indignations had been on the rise and were becoming stronger by the late nineteenth century. B. B. Chaudhuri underlines the question of rent in the context of peasant disturbances. In 1873, the Pabna peasants in eastern Bengal revolted.[10] According to Chaudhuri, the late nineteenth-century movement suffered from an 'absence of what may be called a philosophy behind the programme of action of rebel peasants, which by relating the peasants' grievances to some fundamental social and economic institutions, could provide the rebels with a broad perspective for their movement'.[11] However, Ranajit Guha argues that the peasants had their own philosophy of political consciousness which was derived from their own political traditions and even interrogates the 'elitist paradigm'.[12] Again according to Guha, the popular mobilisation was 'realised in its most comprehensive form in the peasant uprisings'.[13] Partha Chatterjee is of the opinion that the 'Pabna Revolt of 1873 showed clearly that the economic context had changed enough to make it imperative for the colonial state to define more precisely, perhaps redefine, the legal rights of "property" among different agrarian classes.'[14]

From the beginning of the twentieth century, jute instead of indigo became the 'principal export crop in eastern and northern Bengal'. Partha Chatterjee argues that

> it was the gradual subsumption of peasant production under a market economy . . . that brought into operation the familiar process of indebtedness leading to increasing control by the creditor over the surplus product of the small producer, leading in turn to the transfer of the small peasants' land.[15]

The lands passed to the typical *jotedars*, who were rich peasants engaged in 'money lending, grain trading, and often also in small agricultural processing industries, such as rice mills'.[16] Following Partha Chatterjee, we can state that the declining landed proprietors faced conflict from the peasantry as well as from the new *jotedar*/moneylender/trader class. This *jotedar* class was trying to challenge the *zamindari* rights, seeking greater control over the produce and peasantry. The poor peasantry growing out of the 'small peasant' production, the colonial state which was facing increasing challenges while trying to maintain conditions for more economic appropriations, and finally, the middle-class intelligentsia – all were 'formed principally out of the ranks of the declining rentier classes, but play[ed] an independent role of leadership in the political sphere'.[17]

Furthering the discussions on agrarian relations and mass movements in Bengal, Chatterjee tries to compare the specificities of the movements of eastern Bengal and southwestern Bengal. Eastern Bengal consisted predominantly of upper-caste Hindu landlords and had a very high proportion of Muslim population where the principal sources of discontent were the illegal exaction known as 'abwab' and high interest on rent. This led to the Praja movement in eastern Bengal from the 1920s, with the following demands – '(1) abolition of illegal exactions, (2) reduction of rent, (3) reduction of interest rates and relief from indebtedness, (4) "honourable treatment of Muslim tenants in the *zamindar*'s office", and (5) abolition of the landlord's fee on transfer of *raiyati* land."[18] In the midst of such landlord–peasant antagonism the role of the colonial state was, as Chatterjee puts it, ambiguous. This conflict ended with the abolition of the *zamindari* system alongside Independence in 1947.

Southwestern Bengal, on the other hand, had an agrarian movement which, as Chatterjee argues, was directed against the colonial state. The movements were principally organised by the Indian National Congress and received support from the peasants of Tamluk and Contai in Midnapore on the question of increased taxes and against the formation of Union Boards in 1919. The richer peasantry was the primary mover behind the Union Board agitation, while the 'old *zamindari* classes were largely left by the wayside'.[19] However, although initially the entire movement was directed towards the colonial government, divisions arose within the peasantry mainly between the '*jotedar*/*mahajan*/trader class and a large mass of indebted small peasants and share croppers'.[20] The sharecroppers demanded the reduction of 'ad hoc impositions'[21] alongside a half-share of the produce. Although the Congress leadership tried to settle the problem, it cropped up again in the 1930s when there was renewed agitation among the sharecroppers, which became widespread in Tamluk. The demands of the *bhagchashi* or sharecroppers 'were now much more vociferous'.[22]

Meanwhile, by the mid-1930s, peasant organisations had begun to grow in different parts of the country. In the conference held in Meerut in 1936 under the presidentship of Kamala Devi Chattapadhyaya, a decision was taken to form the All India Kisan Congress. However, until the Tebhaga movement of 1946 conducted by the Communist Party of India through the Krishak Sabha in support of the demands of the sharecroppers, no significant uprising can be noted. The Krishak Sabha demanded an increase (*tebhaga*) in the *bargadar*'s (sharecropper) share from 50 per cent to 66 per cent. However, the movement could not gain ground in Midnapore, Burdwan, or in any part of southwestern Bengal. It did gain ground in northern Bengal and the Sundarbans areas of south Bengal where sharecropping was the norm. Then came the famine of 1943 which created a crisis in the rural economy, forcing the cultivators to take all the produce without sharing it with the *jotedars*.[23]

The Tebhaga movement was met with repression by the state. However, as Partha Chatterjee writes, the 'question of rights of sharecroppers was to become a major, perhaps the principal issue of Communist-led agrarian struggles in West Bengal after Independence and partition'.[24] It certainly provided the background for the enactment of the West Bengal Bargadar Act of 1950 which provided certain rights to the *bargadars*. Among other things, the act stated that if the landowner provided draft animals and agricultural implements then he would get one half of the harvest, otherwise the sharecroppers would retain two-thirds. However, the Bargadar Act could not solve the problems of the *bargadars* primarily because it

> did not provide security of tenure, there was no provision for recording of rights and obligations of the landowners and the tenant, and there was no possibility of making the bargadars the owners of the lands they cultivated in spite of their long standing status as tenants.[25]

The West Bengal Estates Acquisition Act (1953) dealt comprehensively with the structural problems that arose out of land laws under colonial rule. This act aimed to eliminate the *zamindari* and other intermediary interests through 'state acquisition on payment of compensation'.[26] But the act could not be implemented thoroughly.

The next most comprehensive measure in land reforms was the West Bengal Land Reforms Act of 1955, which tried to consolidate the rights of the *bargadars* and sharecroppers. The act underwent amendments in 1957 and 1977. In this act, the provisions of the West Bengal Bargadar Act were incorporated whereby the *bargadar* received protection against eviction and their right to cultivate increased to 1.0 hectares. From 1952 to 1967, that is, under the Congress regime, the parties on the Left such as the Communist Party of India/CPI, the Communist Party of India (Marxist)/CPI(M), the Revolutionary Socialist Party/RSP and the Forward Bloc/FB stood by the *bargadars* and the landless peasants in their fight with the *zamindars* and *jotedars*. The parties on the Left were no doubt gaining in strength until 1964 when the split in the CPI took place. The principal causes of the split were the 'Sino-Indian border dispute and the Sino-Soviet ideological conflict'.[27] Sahail Jawaid remarks that 'the dominant leadership of the CPI found in the Sino-Indian border dispute an occasion, and in the Sino-Soviet ideological conflict an alibi, for forcing a split to suit its interests'.[28]

Even after the rift between the CPI and the CPI(M), another extremist communist party, the Communist Party of India (Marxist–Leninist)/CPI(M-L), was formed based on Maoist lines and believing in a democratic revolution by building rural bases. Thus, the background was set for the Naxalbari movement in 1967, which aimed at the absolute annihilation of the *zamindars* and *jotedars*. On March 1967, peasants of Naxalbari, a small hamlet in Darjeeling district, and other adjoining areas launched armed struggle against the landlords. Incidentally, these peasants were organised by local CPI(M) leaders such as Charu Mazumdar, Kanu Sanyal and Jangal Santhal. This caused much embarrassment for the CPI(M), which was a part of the ruling United Front (UF) government. Consequently, when the CPI(M) tried hard to distance itself from such armed uprisings, China, who was providing moral and material support to the Naxalbari armed revolutionaries (the Naxalites), readily labelled the CPI(M) as revisionists and the armed peasants as revolutionaries.[29] These uprisings gained a brand name – 'Naxalism' – and those who adopted the ideology came to be known as 'Naxalites'. The Naxalites would spread violence in the days that followed and ultimately break away from the CPI(M) to form the CPI(Marxist–Leninist).

The movement initially started in three areas, namely Phanisdewa, Naxalbari and Khoribari, where more than half of the population were *bargadars*. Clashes occurred between the peasants and the landlords. The CPI(M-L) under the leadership of Charu Mazumdar and Kanu Sanyal led the violent movement with the principal objective of the annihilation of the old *zamindari* and *jotedari* systems thereby ending the existing exploitative semi-feudal system. What followed was an almost decade-long state reprisal through the police and the military, which ultimately led to the gradual demise of the Naxalite movement. The 1970s as the 'decade of liberation' dreamt of by Charu Mazumdar instead became a decade of repression. The enactment of anti-terror laws coupled with the national emergency of 1975 broke the backbone of the movement. The leaders and the armed rebels were either killed or put behind bars and subjected to custodial torture. Gradually the Naxalite movement waned and the West Bengal State Assembly elections of 1977 ushered in a new era in West Bengal politics when the CPI(M)-led coalition (comprising mostly of leftist parties) known as the Left Front came to power with a thumping majority, reducing the Congress presence to a mere twenty seats. This Left Front government would go on to rule West Bengal for the next three decades without a break.

CALCUTTA 71, PADATIK (THE GUERRILLA FIGHTER) AND PRATIDWANDI (THE ADVERSARY)

Naxalism and the Naxalite movement gave ample scope for filmmakers to ponder the issue of growing economic disparity and dissension among the youth of Bengal. Three films sought to capture the mood of the Naxalite movement sweeping Bengal between 1967 and 1975. *Calcutta 71* by Mrinal Sen is actually a compilation of four stories which highlighted the class divide, economic deprivation, oppression, erosion of human values and growing disparity among the masses. Sen takes us on a journey of class conflict between 1933 and 1971. *Calcutta 71* was made in 1972 and a year later Sen came up with *Padatik*. In *Padatik*, Sen dealt with the contradictions and conflicts faced by a Naxalite (played by Dhritiman Chatterjee) who questions the nature of the movement that at that time concentrated more on its programme of annihilation of class enemies than on its politics and resorted to violent murders, which proved counter-productive for the movement itself. *Pratidwandi* was made by Satyajit Ray who very subtly depicted the causes that could have acted as catalysts for the youth to take up arms. The protagonist, again played by Dhritiman Chatterjee, goes through the rigours of job-hunting and also witnessing the withering of middle-class Bengali values. These three films in our opinion sought to depict the Naxalite movement in a manner that explained its causes and the way in which it unfolded, and were also successful in creating a narrative whereby the filmmakers hesitatingly questioned the efficacy of a violent, armed struggle in a democratic set-up. Given a choice, perhaps they would choose the constitutional struggle even if they found some justification in the Naxalite movement.

AROHAN (THE ASCENT)

Shyam Benegal's depiction of class, class conflict and class struggle in *Arohan* is utterly convincing in nature since the film captures the real plight of the peasantry, especially the sharecroppers and their daily struggle to attain their rights over the land they till and the produce they harvest. The film is set between the years 1967 and 1979 during which time Bengal witnessed massive socio-political turmoil culminating in the establishment of a Marxist Left Front government. Benegal takes up the task of explaining the backdrop and thereby the need for making the film in the first place. He does this through Om Puri who plays the protagonist Hari Mandal, a *bargadar* or sharecropper in a village called Giripur in the district of Birbhum, West Bengal. The story begins with the death of the older landlord or *jotedar* and the passing of the land ownership to his wife. Bibhutibhushan Ganguly, the son of the dead *jotedar*, administers the land on behalf of his mother who is not keen to let Hari Mondal and his brother Bolai Mondal, both tillers of that piece of land, register their names as *bargadars* in the office of the local Junior Land Reforms Officer (JLRO). Therefore, when Hari and Bolai approach Bibhutibhushan for a loan of ₹2,000 for their sister's marriage, Bibhutibhushan directly orders Hari Mondal not to register his name in the JLRO office (Figure 7.1). Hari accepts the deal much to the annoyance of Bolai, who is reprimanded and ridiculed by the *jotedar*'s estate manager Mukunda Karmakar. Karmakar had already warned Hari that he should not come under the influence of the new schoolmaster Halder Babu who is a member of the All India Kisan Sabha (AIKS), the major peasant wing of the CPI(M).

Though Hari is successful in getting his sister married, his predicament grows when Bibhutibhushan strips him of his peasantry rights and converts him and Bolai to mere daily labourers on that land. Hari will no longer have to bear the burden of seeds and fertiliser. Bolai becomes furious and makes up his mind to travel to Kolkata, which he does eventually after being sacked by Bibhutibhushan. Hari also has two extra mouths to feed apart from his wife, two sons, and his brother and sister. They are Kalidashi, whom Hari calls aunt, and her unmarried daughter, Panchi. After Bolai departs, Kalidashi relocates herself to Kolkata with the help of Hari's neighbour Hasan Mollah, where she takes up the job of a housemaid in a middle-class family. Panchi, exasperated

Figure 7.1 Hari and the reluctant Bolai come to Bibhutibhushan for a loan.

with the constant imprecations from Hari's wife, decides to leave the place for a better life in Kolkata. She comes in contact with a pimp who lands her a job at a rich businessman's house as his mistress. She is content with all the so-called luxuries, which she could never even have dreamt of before.

The communists within the second UF government of West Bengal formed in 1969 tried to push forward the cause of the *bargadars* again. Halder Babu, the village schoolmaster, is shown leading an AIKS procession as Hari watches inquisitively (Figure 7.2). Working in the field along with his wife (now that Bolai has been sacked and is away), Hari delays taking the produce to Bibhutibhushan's farm house. Clearly Hari is in a dilemma. Karmakar threatens Hari and reminds him that if there are any further delays at all, and if Hari comes under the influence of the AIKS, he will invite the wrath of the landlord. The film captures just that moment of helplessness on the part of the *jotedar* since the crops are still in the field and he is unsure whether the 'deal' with Hari might be put off due to the increasing influence of AIKS and a left-leaning government in power.

Hari's neighbour Hasan comes to Hari's house with Halder Babu and Prabhudas Roy, a lawyer and an AIKS activist based in the district town of Siuri. Prabhudas and Halder convince Hari to file an appeal to restore his *bargadari* rights at the JRLO's office and ask him not to take the harvested crops to Bibhutibhushan's farm house but rather that he may just give the *jotedar* his

Figure 7.2 Schoolmaster Halder Babu leading a procession of All India Kisan Sabha along with Hasan.

share and if he refuses to take that share, Hari may deposit it at the JLRO's office. Hari reluctantly goes to the JLRO's office along with Prabhudas and Halder Babu and files an appeal with Prabhudas's help. However, Bibhutibhushan and Karmakar barge into the office along with their lawyer to file a counter application accusing Hari of fabricating facts; they claim that Hari is not a *bargadar*, but merely a labourer who has stolen the crops grown on the *jotedar*'s land. The officer, not impressed with Bibhutibhushan's accusations, promises to make a spot enquiry. However, before any such enquiry can be conducted Hari is accosted by Bibhutibhushan's goons who forcibly acquire his left thumb impression on a government-stamped paper, declaring a compromise between him and Bibhutibhushan. The JLRO, without checking the facts, declares before the Sub-Divisional Magistrate (SDM) that a compromise between Hari and Bibhutibhushan has been reached. The magistrate sees through the false papers, rejects Bibhutibhushan's claim and suggests that since the JLRO's enquiry had no basis, both parties should now seek the assistance of the Agricultural Extension Officer. He also asks the police administration to maintain the status quo. That very night, the police, acting on a complaint by Karmakar, raid Hari's house and confiscate all the grain and a pair of bullocks. Bibhutibhushan gets accosted by the villagers led by Halder Babu and he promises to withdraw the complaint against Hari. The SDM reprimands the police and restores the *bargadari* rights to Hari, and debars the *jotedar* from evicting Hari from the land he has been tilling for the past twenty years. The growing influence of the Naxalite movement is evident from the slogans praising Mao Zedong on the walls of the JLRO's office and later in a murder of an on-duty police officer on the streets of Kolkata. Meanwhile, President's Rule is imposed and the *jotedar* Bibhutibhushan is glowing with optimism. According to him, now that the UF government is no longer in power, the rule of law shall prevail and he will succeed in evicting Hari and making him his serf; after all, Hari has been a loyal servant of his family for years. He manages to acquire an interim order from the District Court (Munsiff Court) which debars Hari Mondal from visiting the premises of the *jotedar*'s land.

The President's Rule facilitated the return of the Congress Party, now known as Indira Congress or Congress-I. Hari again watches a Congress-I procession shouting slogans praising Indira Gandhi, the then Prime Minister of India. The procession includes Youth Congress leaders Priya Ranjan Das Munshi and Subrata Mukherjee along with the then Chief Minister of West Bengal Siddhartha Sankar Ray. This time the procession is also watched by a dejected Halder. Meanwhile, Bolai, who went to Kolkata to earn a living, ends up breaking a wagon and then becomes as a henchman (*mastan* in local parlance) of a well-known political leader, surly Congressman Dhiresh Babu.

One night, Bibhutibhushan's henchmen drag Hari out of his house, beat him mercilessly and set his house on fire. This assault leads to grievous injuries on Hari's body and he ends up with multiple fractures on his left leg. Both Halder and Prabhudas are arrested, obviously for being AIKS activists. This forces Hari to fend for himself. His injuries keep him away from court appearances and Bibhutibhushan's lawyer argues that since the interim order from the Munsiff Court has been procured, the SDM may kindly withdraw the benefits accorded by him to Hari. The sympathetic SDM refuses to do so. Then, when Hari is finally fit enough for an appearance, he does so without any legal representation. The SDM takes strong exception to the Munsiff Court's interim order and refers the case to the Calcutta High Court. The High Court sees this as contempt of court against the Munsiff Court and extracts an unconditional apology from both the SDM as well as from Hari Mondal. The whole judicial process, from the court summons to the proceedings in the High Court, make absolutely no sense to Hari since everything is conducted in English, a language which is alien to the peasants. Hence the so-called rule of law makes no sense at all to Hari. He loses his claim to his *bargadari* rights. When he tries to leave his village to work on another *jotedar*'s land, he witnesses a skirmish between the AIKS- and CPI(M)-backed peasants and those who were willing to work elsewhere. The skirmish results in the police firing on the warring peasants and killing a few of them.

Come 1977, Bengal sees another change in government led by a coalition of parties on the Left known as the Left Front (LF). The Left Front promises a new beginning for the *bargadars* like Hari. It brings about a change in the state *panchayati* system and holds elections. Hari is coaxed by Halder, now a government employee, to contest the *panchayat* polls against Mukunda Karmakar. Hari wins the polls and exhibits good leadership qualities when floods hit his village in 1978. By 1979, the LF has launched Operation Barga under which the rights of the *bargadars* are secured and the onus is now upon the *jotedar* to prove the invalidity of the claims made by any *bargadar*. Hari goes one step further and appeals to the peasants that merely attaining *barga* rights is not enough, and proposes setting up a co-operative system in farming which will benefit everyone. Hari ultimately gets back his *bargadari* rights. Meanwhile in Kolkata, Bolai, who became a henchman for a political leader, is charged with murder and is sentenced to life imprisonment. Panchi becomes pregnant and the rich businessman forces her to go through an abortion and later drives her away from flat. Panchi becomes insane and wanders the streets of the city. Kalidashi, who once witnessed Panchi's plight, dies of shock. Hari, ignorant of these developments, comes to the city to search for them, but returns empty-handed only to die two months later.

The film, almost a platform for LF propaganda, highlights the need for a more developed and beneficial programme for the sharecroppers. Operation Barga was a modified version of the radical slogan of 'Langol Jar Jomi Tar' (Land for the Tillers). Through this programme the government identified fifteen lakh (100,000) *bargadars* or sharecroppers and took steps to change the landlord–*bargadar* relationship.[30] A couple of the steps were:

1. Anti-eviction measures, through which landlords were largely prevented from forcibly throwing *bargadars* off the land. In fact, *bargadar* rights were made hereditary and thus perpetual.
2. A state guarantee that the *bargadars* would receive a fair share of the crop (75 per cent if the *bargadar* provided the non-labour inputs and 50 per cent if the landlord provided those inputs.)

The ultimate goal was to convert the sharecroppers into landowners through legislation because:

1. *Bargadars* would prefer working on land as landowners.
2. Many *bargadars* would negotiate voluntary and mutual deals with their landlords in which the *bargadar* would receive ownership of some portion of the *barga* land in return for giving up the *barga* rights on the rest of the land.
3. *Barga* rights would be retained even with a change in regime.

When the Left Front government launched 'Operation Barga' after it assumed power in 1977, it undertook the task of completing the recording of the *bargadars* within a time frame. The task of recording the *bargadars* was initiated by the previous Congress government under the 'Settlement Operation' programme. However, there were some constraints which impeded the process.[31] They were:

1. The ignorance of the *bargadars* about the process and benefits of recording their names; they never wanted to antagonise the landlords.
2. The landlords never wanted the *bargadars* to record their names at all. They used threats, intimidation and outright violence against the *bargadars*. Many were physically assaulted and their houses burnt.
3. The landlords in rural Bengal also acted as moneylenders and most of the *bargadars* were indebted to them. The *bargadars* did not want this source of cash or kind to dry up.

Besides, the government officials were indifferent to the objective of the whole operation and often held the registration camps within the premises of the properties owned by the landlords. The Left Front government sought to remove these impediments and restore the land rights to the *bargadars*. Results started to show within a year of launching Operation Barga. There was a threefold increase in the recording of *bargadars* under Operation Barga compared to under the Settlement Operation.

The Left Front in its 1977 election manifesto published on 19 May gave detailed plans and programmes, almost a like a governmental gazette, as to how the Front wished to undo the wrongs of previous Congress governments and also the steps it would take to usher in socio-economic development through the active mobilisation of workers and peasants. The manifesto contained a 36-point common minimum programme touching upon:[32]

1. The Economy
2. Labour
3. Land Reforms and Peasantry
4. Education
5. Local Bodies
6. Appointment of Inquiry Commissions
7. Minority and Weaker Sections

The two most important declarations in the manifesto deserve specific mention, namely:[33]

1. Nationalisation of all basic industries, takeover of foreign capital, ban on entry of multinationals and investment of private foreign capital, moratorium on foreign debt payments. Nationalisation monopoly of houses and certain specified industries in the interest of the masses. Nationalised sectors must be democratised, and clean and efficient administration ensured without making it subservient to the interests of monopolists.
2. Acquisition and distribution of surplus and *benami* (proxy) land to the landless and poor peasants and agricultural labourers free of cost. Radical changes in the land reform laws to do away with all forms of concentration of land holdings and to give substantial relief to *bargadars* (sharecroppers) and landless peasants and agricultural workers.

The newly elected Left Front government therefore faced a dilemma as to how to reconcile the ideological moorings of the government with the realities of a parliamentary federal system and with a bureaucracy which the Marxists always traditionally viewed as representative of the ruling class. In the case of India, the bureaucracy became an extension of the ruling party and therefore implementation of policies became more or less easy. However, the case of West Bengal was unique. The administration was mostly managed and manned by people who were rendered refugees due to the Partition and belonged to East Bengal, having no such connection with the landed class.[34] In fact, from the clerical to the middle-ranking officer level, the Left Front could easily establish its influence. Left Front leader Jyoti Basu confessed that '. . . although it is not possible to have radical change in administration now, many in the administration and police are quite alive to implementing our policies'. Therefore, the Left Front was successful in bringing about a change in the administration and the police.[35] Jyoti Basu made the government's policy towards business clear at the beginning of the first term of the Left Front government. He said, 'We believe in Socialism but we know it well that we have to work with capitalists. Socialism cannot be ushered in overnight. Let the capitalists understand us – our policy and our interest; we shall also try to appreciate their point of view.'[36]

POSTSCRIPT – DO WE NEED ANOTHER *AROHAN*?

In this film Benegal records some very significant events related to Operation Barga. Operation Barga was no doubt a success. Many Hari Mondals and their families benefited from it. The LF government continued to rule West Bengal for another three decades. Class-based political mobilisation in rural Bengal helped the peasantry gain a lot of dignity and a copybook-style de-classing of the erstwhile landlords (*malik-mai-baap*) began. Most of them initially held on to their allegiance to the Congress, but gradually buckled under the constantly growing influence of the Left in general and of CPI(M) in particular, and extended their support to them. The Left concentrated all their energies on rural Bengal since it constituted their primary support base. Through various frontal organisations the CPI(M) had made inroads into the lives of rural Bengali people and had more or less started controlling the lives of the peasants from the cradle to the grave. On the other hand, the culture of *gherao*, that is, preventing someone (mostly management staff of a factory) from leaving a place until one's demands are met, and *hartal* or total strike (also known as *bandh*) proved counter-productive after the Left assumed power. West Bengal started to witness an industrial exodus. Gradually lockouts overtook strikes. According to 'Labour in West Bengal', an official publication of the State Labour Department, there were 305 cases of lockout in the state in 2001, the highest since 1995. These lockouts accounted for 93 per cent of the total 211 for the country as a whole – seven lakh days lost during the year affecting twelve lakh workers.[37] The government was seen as anti-industry by industrialists, while the rural scene was getting more and more polarised with the erstwhile *bargadars* competing for loaves and fishes doled out by the Party, that is, the CPI(M). The lack of industry also meant a gradual depletion of urban votes. So, when the government tried to set up industries by way of land acquisition it was faced with tremendous resistance from the peasants who until then had extended their unflinching support. The scenes of unrest at Singur, Nandigram and Lalgarh were reminiscent of the period between 1967 and 1977. The tension was accentuated by the police firing at Nandigram and the influx of Maoists from the neighbouring states of Jharkhand and Odisha into these localities to lead and mobilise the peasants. These events proved that the protracted struggle of people like Hari Mondal no doubt reaped benefits and led to the empowerment of the rural proletariat, but the lure of power created more Bibhutibhushans and Karmakars out of the same Hari Mondals. It took another upheaval and another overthrow of an oppressive regime to provide justice to the Hari Mondals of Singur, Nandigram and Lalgarh. Hence, we may conclude that an *Arohan* is inevitable where there are Hari Mondals and Bibhutibhushans. The dynamics of class division, class conflict and class reconciliation through parliamentary democracy will continue for years to come.

Note: All dialogue translated by the author.

NOTES

1. Kevin K. Durand, 'Introduction: Marx, Critical Theory and the Cinema', in *Marxism and the Movies: Critical Essays on Class Struggle in the Cinema*, ed. Mary K. Leigh and Kevin K. Durand (Jefferson, NC and London: McFarland & Company, 2013), 3.
2. Anirudh Deshpande, 'Indian Cinema and the Bourgeois Nation State', *Economic and Political Weekly* 42, no. 50 (December 15–21, 2007), 99.
3. Rochona Majumdar, 'Debating Radical Cinema: A History of the Film Society Movement in India', *Modern Asian Studies* 46, no. 3 (2012): 731–3.
4. Majumdar, 731–3.
5. Ashish Rajadhyaksha, *Indian Cinema: A Very Short Introduction* (Oxford: Oxford University Press, 2016), 61.
6. Ben Sachs, 'First encounters with Shyam Benegal', *The Bleader*, last modified 12 April 2012, <https://www.chicagoreader.com/Bleader/archives/2012/04/12/first-encounters-with-shyam-benegal>
7. Partha Chatterjee, 'The Colonial State and Peasant Resistance in Bengal 1920–1947', *Past & Present*, no. 110 (1986): 169–204, accessed 1 September 2021, <http://www.jstor.org/stable/650652>
8. Chatterjee, 169–204.
9. P. Eashvaraiah, *The Communist Parties in Power and Agrarian Reforms in India* (Delhi: Academic Foundation, 1993), 160.
10. Benoy Bhusan Chaudhuri, 'Agrarian Movements in Bengal and Bihar 1919–1939', in *Socialism in India*, ed. B. R. Nanda (Vikas Publications, 1972), 192.
11. Chaudhuri, 192.
12. Ranajit Guha, ed., preface to *Subaltern Studies*, Vol. III (Delhi: Oxford University Press, 1984).
13. Ranajit Guha, 'On Some Aspects of the Historiography of Colonial India', in *Subaltern Studies*. Vol. I, ed. Ranajit Guha (Delhi: Oxford University Press, 1982), 1–8.
14. Chatterjee, 174.
15. Ibid., 177.
16. Ibid., 178.
17. Ibid., 179.
18. Ibid., 184.
19. Ibid., 192.

20. Ibid., 192.
21. Ibid., 193.
22. Ibid., 193.
23. Eashvarariah, 160.
24. Chatterjee, 200.
25. Eashvarariah, 163.
26. Ibid., 160.
27. Jawaid Sahail, 'The Naxalite Movement in India: Origin and Failure of the Maoist Revolutionary Strategy in West Bengal 1967–1971' (master's thesis, Brock University, 1978), 3.
28. Sahail, 3–4.
29. Anjali Ghosh, *Peaceful Transition to Power: A Study of Marxist Political Strategies in West Bengal 1967–1977* (Calcutta: Firma KLM, 1981). 70.
30. Tim Hanstad and Robin Nielsen, 'West Bengal's Bargadars and Landownership', *Economic and Political Weekly* 39, no. 8 (2004): 853.
31. Suhas Chattopadhyay, 'Operation Barga', *Social Scientist* 8, no. 3 (1979): 41–2, <doi:10.2307/3520390>
32. Ghosh, C37–C40.
33. Ibid., C37–C40.
34. Ross Mallick, *Development Policy of a Communist Government: West Bengal since 1977* (New York: Cambridge University Press, 1993), 171.
35. Mallick, 173.
36. Ibid., 188.
37. 'Lockouts overtake Strikes in West Bengal', *Business Line*, August 2002.

CHAPTER 8

From Fidelity to Creativity: Benegal and *Suraj Ka Satvan Ghoda*

Sudha Shastri

This aim of this chapter is to read Shyam Benegal's adaptation of Dharmavir Bharati's novel/novella, *Suraj Ka Satvan Ghoda* (*The Sun's Seventh Horse*), into a film of the same title, and attest to its role in the chronicling of Benegal's achievement as a filmmaker par excellence. This chapter is a study and a consideration of the book, its cinematic remake, questions of adaptation, and the outcomes of the changes made by Benegal while transcoding the text to cinema.

Bharati's book was first published in Hindi in 1952, and critically applauded for its formal and technical inventiveness. *Suraj Ka Satvan Ghoda* follows a narrative technique that, like an Escher diagram, confuses the contours of the narrative so that, depending on how one looks at it, the novel can be seen as comprising one story or three interweaving stories. Because of repeated entries into the same narrative from different points in time, which thereby challenges temporal sequencing, the three stories may well be the same story told three times. Two narrators, each framing the other in turn, make the novel self-reflexive.

In 1999, Bharati's novel was translated into English by Sachchidanand Hiranand Vatsyayan 'Ajneya' as *The Sun's Seventh Horse*.[1] In 1992, *Suraj Ka Satvan Ghoda* was made into a film by Shyam Benegal. It opened to mixed responses, as evinced in Sukanya Verma's 'Great film, no audience'.[2] But the audience was not to have the last word on the fate of this film, which perhaps predictably enough, went on to receive the year's (1992) National Film Award for best feature film in Hindi.

SHYAM BENEGAL

Born in 1934, Shyam Benegal shot to fame with *Ankur* in 1974. Meaning *The Seedling*, this film based on a real story became a milestone in the establishment of what is popularly known as parallel, or non-mainstream, Indian cinema. This was a genre associated with the well-known filmmaker Satyajit Ray, and is the genre within which many of Benegal's films find their feet. *Ankur* won three national awards among several others and starred stalwart actors like Anant Nag and Shabana Azmi playing out a rural drama of caste and feudalism. It was to herald the start of an illustrious career in cinema for a brilliant filmmaker.

Benegal's achievements straddle several domains, establishing his multi-faceted talents. Commercial success came arguably late in his career, but his passion for cinema dated back way earlier. He was related to the towering actor–director of Hindi cinema, Guru Dutt, and more pertinently, he was an admirer of the legendary Satyajit Ray. Thus, the two broad types of Hindi cinema, 'commercial' and 'art', were both influences for him. After a stint in advertising he started making films, chalking up an impressive total of 900 commercials and ad films, besides documentaries and corporate films. Notably, he was a teacher at as well as chairperson of the FTII (the Film and Television Institute of India) twice, from 1981–1983 and 1989–1992. He was conferred with a D.Litt (*honoris causa*) by Jamia Millia University in 2007, and a D.Litt by the University of Calcutta in 2012. He also served as a Member of Parliament in the Rajya Sabha from 2006 to 2012.

Benegal is widely deemed the inaugurator of realistic and issue-orientated cinema, variously known as New Indian cinema or parallel cinema. And yet, Benegal was not a niche filmmaker. While it is true that his films in parallel cinema, such as *Nishant* (*Night's End*, 1975) or *Manthan* (*The Churning*, 1976), established him as a peerless filmmaker and also gave Hindi cinema a generation of outstanding actors, he also explored other genres. *Junoon* (*The Obsession*, 1979) is colonial in its setting, and recounts the obsession of a rebel leader with a young girl he takes captive. There were others such as *Mandi* (*Market Place*, 1983), *Trikal* (*Past, Present and Future*, 1985), and *Zubeidaa* (2001), the last of which especially was a classic feature/commercial film. The ease with which Benegal negotiates the domains of 'art' and the 'commercial', almost challenging the disparateness between the two styles by the meticulousness and finesse with which he makes all his films, encourages one not only to use superlatives in the recounting of his achievement, but also think of genre-bending and genre-challenging insistently while encountering his oeuvre.

More pertinently to the concerns of this chapter, *Suraj Ka Satvan Ghoda* projects the heightened emotional drama one comes to associate with commercial cinema, and then deftly undercuts the melodrama with irony and self-reflexivity to push the limits of parallel cinema. Thus, while resting on many formulae familiar from mainstream cinema such as unrequited love, parental tyranny, and socio-economic disparity, it concurrently subverts them through a critical narrator whose narration is in turn critiqued by an even more critical narrator.

In this matter, the originality lies less with the film than with Bharati's novel. A brief synopsis of the text is in order here. Playing in a very cursory fashion, almost like an after-thought on the well-known mythological tale of the sun riding a chariot led by seven horses, the novel actually narrates the stories of the women Jamuna, Lily and Satti, via a narrator called Manik Mulla, who is both inside the stories in the way he influences their events, and outside them in the way he narrates them to a group of young male friends. Manik Mulla further alternates between the roles of narrator and character because he is inside the story (about him) narrated by the principal narrator of *The Sun's Seventh Horse*. The novella is extremely self-reflexive at many junctures, whether in the way the telling of these stories is punctuated by interruptions where teller and listener discuss the moral and meaning of these stories, in the way these morals are rendered parodic, or in the way the narrator's storytelling gift seems to be bigger than the stories he tells, suggesting the notion of a story for story's sake.

As an instance of the last, one of his listening friends picks up a knife at the beginning and *as* the beginning of Manik Mulla's story about the last of the three women who played important roles in his life. This woman is Satti. As a preamble to her story, Manik and his audience discuss narrative technique, and great storytellers of the world, and the discussion comes to rest on Chekhov. Proclaims Manik:

> Chekhov is reported to have said to a lady once, 'Telling a story is not difficult. You can place anything before me – for example, this glass, this ash-tray – and ask me to tell a story about it. Presently, my imagination will be roused; the life of many people connected with the objet would rise in my memory and a story construct itself.'[3]

So, as his listener flourishes the knife with the carved handle that has already been remarked upon as 'a strange object'[4] (one among many that litter Manik Mulla's living room with the sense of the exotic) and asks Manik if he can make the knife the pivot of the story he is about to narrate concerning Satti, Manik's response is typically disarming. He declares that this task would require no effort, as the knife is already the focus of Satti's story. But this piece of fortuitous coincidence nevertheless leaves the reader convinced that anything can become a 'story'; an idea suggesting that a story can be woven from anything, if only the storyteller were creative enough.

NOVEL BECOMES FILM

Fifteen years after the film was made, Sukanya Verma wrote in *The Sunday Magazine* of *The Hindu* acclaiming Benegal's masterly adaptation of Bharati's novel, observing the well-meaning advice given by Bharati's friends: '[w]ary of Bollywood's tendency to butcher literature, they advised its author against the adaptation. Bharati knew better and brushed aside their concerns, explaining, "I am entrusting my work to Shyam Benegal and not just any filmmaker. I have implicit faith in him."'[5]

It was a transcreative act born of mutual respect between two giants in their respective fields. Although Bharati was repeatedly approached by Benegal for involvement in the film, the former refused to, not seeing the need. His faith in Benegal was vindicated by the finished product, which won his and the critics' approval.

ADAPTATION

In Linda Hutcheon's oft-quoted words, '[a]daptation is repetition, but repetition without replication'.[6] In her comprehensive study, Hutcheon raises the uncomfortable question of adaptations being 'haunted at all times by their adapted texts',[7] thereby making comparisons perhaps inevitable, and inferentially, unnecessary. In this respect, the most valuable contribution by Hutcheon is the settling of, as it were, the fidelity debate. 'An adaptation's double nature does not mean, however, that proximity or fidelity to the adapted text should be the criterion of judgment or the focus of analysis',[8] she says. Dismissing the domination of fidelity criticism with scholarly support, Hutcheon establishes that it has been successfully contested.

Musing over what, then, ought to frame a theory of adaptation, if fidelity is to be dismissed, Hutcheon settles upon the dictionary meaning of to adapt, which is to adjust, alter, make suitable. Taking a cue from Hutcheon, this chapter will consider the ways in which Benegal transforms the text to cinema by making the transformation *suitable* to the target medium of film without losing the essence or the spirit of the text. In fact, the film closely follows the text, with a few, but distinctively notable, alterations with an eye to the changed medium.

SELF-REFLEXIVE NOVEL

In this as well as the next section of this chapter, I will study the ways in which self-reflexivity comes to be foregrounded in the novel and the film respectively. The comparison here is made only to show how Benegal's intervention is creative rather than simulative.

Self-reflexivity is a central concern in the novel, one which the film acknowledges in its own way. There are three remarkable ways in which the novel turns self-reflexive: one is in the frames that structure it. Thus, the story/stories of the three women that form the story of *The Sun's Seventh Horse* is/are narrated by Manik Mulla to a text-internal listener who in turn doubles up as a narrator addressing the reader. Since Manik Mulla is both a character in the stories that he tells as well as their narrator, this dual role could by implication complicate his recounting with the possibility of bias and partiality. This is corrected by his listener-turned-narrator who upon occasion can be critical of Manik, thereby demonstrating the need for a perspective on Manik's stories, as well as guiding the reader's interpretation of the story/stories. His presence in the book suggests that Manik's narration requires to be supervised. At the same time, by disclaiming all responsibility for whatever is amiss in the narration (attributing this to Manik Mulla), he also, paradoxically, abandons *The Sun's Seventh Horse* in the wilderness, as a narrative that he as the more trustworthy of the two narrators cannot vouch for.

Thus, right at the outset in the 'Curtain-raiser'[9] presented by the external narrator (who will henceforth be referred to as the narrator, to distinguish him from the inside narrator, who will be referred to by his name as Manik Mulla), the narrator concludes the introduction by stating:

> And if you find the style of narration colloquial and matter-of-fact, unlike my usual colourful pictorial manner, you must forgive me. For I am *only a compere*, the stories are Manik Mulla's, and are being offered as nearly as possible as he told them.[10]

And at the end, again, the narrator disclaims:

> In conclusion I wish also to make it clear that the praise or blame for the qualities of this piece of writing should all go to Manik Mulla, not to me, for *I am only an instrument*, a medium through which he has spoken. I now leave you free to form your judgment about Manik Mulla and his stories.[11]

That the styles of narration of the narrator and Manik Mulla differ from each other is also painstakingly established in the novel. As an instance, while narrating the story of 'Devasena, Princess of Malwa', Manik makes a preliminary observation to the narrator: '[t]hen in a sarcastic aside to me, "If the narrative style sounds like yours, don't blame me." Then he began the story.'[12]

The second self-reflexive turn that *The Sun's Seventh Horse* presents is in the question of the text's identity: whether it is a novel or a short-story collection. Supporting the latter position is the explicit arrangement of the stories as independent stories, each told on an afternoon by Manik Mulla to a group of friends, of whom the narrator is one. But as the stories succeeding the first story reveal, the characters that appear in it reappear later in the following stories. The decision to 'end' a story at a particular juncture of the narrative thus appears to be arbitrary. For instance, the story of the first afternoon, which revolves around Jamuna, reaches an end only because the audience, with some impatience, asks Manik Mulla, who has reached an event marked by iteration by commenting on how he and Jamuna met regularly: 'But how did it all end?'[13] Manik's response is in the nature of a retort:

> 'End?' said Manik Mulla sarcastically. 'What an intelligent lot you are! Is there a variety of ends to a love story. There is only one end. The heroine got married, Manik Mulla was left gaping. You can garnish it in any way you like.'
> But we did not like so ordinary an end of so interesting a story.[14]

Moreover, despite the token conclusion to this story that '[t]hus ended Manik Mulla's first love story with a moral',[15] we find in the story of the second afternoon a continuation of Jamuna's story, in how Jamuna got married and widowed. And yet the sentence, '[t]hat was the end of Jamuna's story', occurring in this continuation[16] is again belied as Jamuna's friendship with Tanna's wife becomes a curious addition to the story of the third afternoon.

In the story of the second afternoon, too, there are two claims to an ending. Manik Mulla first stops his narration at the point where Jamuna decides to hide the money she has brought from her husband's house lest she be obliged to help her father in his pecuniary difficulties. If she helped her father financially she would be depriving her future family from their rightful share, or so she reasons, and '[t]herefore, continued Manik Mulla, Jamuna thought of her future offspring and went back to her husband and continued to live happily. And that actually, is the end of her story.'[17]

But at this his audience protests, since this ending has not factored in the horseshoe that was the *raison d'être* of this story. Manik's response is that he was just testing their attention to his recounting, and he continues the story of Jamuna's motherhood and widowhood.

Thus, the stories end arbitrarily, challenging a claim made on behalf of Manik Mulla by the narrator in the curtain raiser:

> In the matter of technique his first proposition was that the modern short story inevitably missed one or other of the essentials – the beginning, the middle or the end. This was most undesirable. For completeness, he would assert, a story had to have a beginning in the beginning, a middle in the middle and an end at the end. These elements he defined thus: the beginning of a story is that which has nothing before it and the middle after it. The middle is that which has the beginning before and the end after. The end is that which has before it the middle *and after it the wastepaper basket*.[18]

The conclusion of the above excerpt as well as the fact that Manik Mulla unapologetically contradicts his own dictum about an ideal short story with blatant non-linearity testify to the subversive intent of the novel. This is underscored by the ending of *The Sun's Seventh Horse* where Manik Mulla says that '[h]is narrative really was a novel, a most ingenious novel . . .'[19] (rather than a collection of stories).

The third and overarching mode of self-reflexivity in *The Sun's Seventh Horse* consists of foregrounding the actual process of narration, such as questions of technique. This feeds into the larger metafictional domain of privileging storytelling over the story. The narrative structure of *The Sun's Seventh Horse* is aligned towards this reading by being a story told to us, the readers, of stories being recounted to listeners inside the novel, creating levels of embedded-ness and at the same time requiring us to examine it rather than lose ourselves by 'willingly suspending disbelief' into the world of the stories. Furthermore, each story is followed by a discussion of it, for the stories of the various afternoons are each of them separated by an interlude. The interludes comment on the stories critically, sometimes fantastically, so that the world of the stories is held up for scrutiny.

The reader's impulse to analyse rather than merge into the imaginative world of Manik Mulla's stories is further encouraged by the irony and parody that force themselves on the reader's notice. Manik Mulla is a firm believer in the point of a story: of a story having a moral. However, the moral that Manik Mulla wrests out of the very first story is liminal and irrelevant enough to the story to strike one as absurd. The story, for the most part, has been about the clandestine meetings between Jamuna and Manik, initiated by the heroine Jamuna, who is frustrated by a rigidly classified society that comes in the way of her making an advantageous marriage. Manik's visits to Jamuna's house had been necessitated by his sister-in-law's vow to feed a cow, since they did not own a cow and Jamuna's family did. From this, Manik Mulla draws the moral that 'there should be a cow in every home, so that the nation's cattle wealth improves and future generations have better health'.[20] Further, Manik brings the romantic angle in with the statement, '[u]neven distribution of wealth is the root cause of love. If they hadn't a cow I would not have gone there . . .'[21] The patent ludicrousness of the link made between the moral and the story works to produce a parodic effect, as if to ridicule the compulsion felt by readers to draw morals out of the stories they read.

SELF-REFLEXIVITY IN THE FILM

Benegal's *Suraj Ka Satvan Ghoda* does not depart from its novelistic predecessor in the points raised in the previous section. The conversations are more or less replicated in cinematic dialogue, and the structure of the film follows that of the novel with very little deviation. When departures do happen, they function as moments of epiphany and appear natural to the cinematic medium and not deliberate impositions of the book.

The novel begins with a curtain-raiser, which has the narrator introducing Manik Mulla to us as 'one of the celebrities of our part of the town. He was born there, he grew up there, found fans there and disappeared from there.'[22]

The concept of a neighbourhood or *muhalla* that is hereby broached in the novel is artistically recreated in the film by Benegal through a series of paintings that draw the narrator's attention. As the narrator gazes at these evidently non-realistic, almost surrealistic paintings, he pauses before the third, a portion of which seems to represent a neighbourhood, and launches into the story of Manik Mulla and his storytelling. The camera zooms into the painting as if trying to locate the neighbourhood of Manik Mulla and his friends inside it. The voice of the narrator can be heard saying that it feels as though the sounds of the neighbourhood (that he sees inside the painting) are reverberating in his ears.

Thresholds between ontologically distinctive worlds that are carefully hidden within realistic conventions of portrayal are flaunted wilfully in self-reflexive modes. Closely following on the incipit, the story of Jamuna performs just such a trompe-l'œil in Manik's narration. When his recounting of Jamuna's story reaches the juncture of her wedding, Manik is distracted by the sound of a wedding procession – in real time – outside his house and rises to look out through the window. He then calls his audience to join him, and what greets their as well as the viewer's eye is the wedding procession of Jamuna's husband.

Looking out of the window, Manik describes Jamuna's bridegroom from his story-world wedding procession rather than the procession that meets his gaze outside his window. 'With hardly a tooth in his head, and a few entrails in his belly, With half his hair gone, but money hides a variety of sins.'[23] The scene has by now cut seamlessly into the baraati or bridegroom's party making its way to her home, while a furious Jamuna, disappointed with her prospective husband's old age and appearance, stands on the terrace with an expression of frustration on her face (Figure 8.1).

This transition from one context to another through a link that is neither chronologically nor logically sequenced, but laterally so, is arguably a cinema-friendly rather than a text-friendly instance of disorientation leading to self-consciousness in narration. One way of describing this narrative move is to call it a collapsing of contexts, so that an isolated and general/universal event, a wedding ritual, becomes a connector of two vastly different times and stories. To clarify, the baraat that Manik Mulla looks at out of the window does not serve as a reminder of Jamuna's wedding, which would be a more natural connector within the demands of realism. Instead, this wedding becomes

Figure 8.1 Jamuna is filled with disgust at the thought of her prospective bridegroom.

that – Jamuna's – wedding, so seamlessly moving through what are in fact two unconnected episodes.

That this is a stylistic choice made deliberately by Benegal is evident from a second example that prefigures this, though less stridently, where Manik Mulla has just begun to narrate his sequence of stories to his friends. It is an informal setting and watermelons are being consumed. After they are done, Manik Mulla leans out of his window and throws the watermelon skins out, where they drop on a cow standing outside. The story that Manik begins to narrate is the story of Jamuna, which in his telling revolves around the cow that he had to feed to please his sister-in-law. 'Coincidence' is not quite the word to explain this linking of the two contexts through a cow; the point is that referents seem to connect without contextual support.

Both foregoing examples testify to Benegal's skill as a filmmaker from the way in which he has made the adaptation of text to film a process natural to the cinematic medium, which deals with the visual, with scenes rather than with words. Thus, the beginning of the film is an emphatic re-presentation of the process-rather-than-product trajectory usually taken by self-reflexivity. Benegal has given the narrator in his film a choice; an opportunity to exercise an option, of looking at extremely creative and artistic paintings to make an entry-point into his narration. This choice is not available to the narrator of the text, not merely because Dharmavir Bharati did not offer it, but because the medium of the text cannot make such an option appear natural to itself in the way a film can. Benegal's creative adaptation thereby takes medium into account while exercising his option – as only a gifted and highly original filmmaker can do.

ALTERATIONS/ADAPTATION

One of the ways in which the book signposts the continuity between the purportedly independent stories of six afternoons is through the device of anticipation. For example, the first intimation we get of Mahesar Dalal's involvement with Satti is in a digressive fashion, that there were 'strange rumours' about him that 'he was spending all his earnings on a soap-maker's daughter'.[24] That this marginal character would emerge as the central character of a later story seems counter-intuitive to conventions of novelistic structuring, but that is exactly what happens here.

Since characters tend to get repetitive portrayal, as in the case of Satti turning from a minor character in someone else's story to a major character in her own, events permit themselves to be narrated more than once. Again, this is a choice that the book makes consciously, sometimes to exploit suspense. In the same story of the third afternoon which is also Tanna's story, we are informed that the soap-maker's daughter was found dead, and the corpse disposed of. Ahead, the story of the fifth afternoon ends with the observation that Mahesar along with the soap-maker had strangled Satti. In the story of the sixth afternoon that dwells largely on Manik's self-loathing after betraying Satti, we are informed that Satti was in fact very much alive.

Suspense is of more than one sort. The cinematic medium stands at a disadvantage in the case of maintaining suspense about a character whose identity can be revealed only considerably after they first appear in the text. Unless by resorting to unimaginative modes of preserving secrecy like hiding the character behind a screen or inside a veil, the film being a visual medium cannot present a character to the spectator without showing who the character is. It is otherwise with a written text. Dharmavir Bharati can, and does, present Tanna's wife in his story without revealing that she is, in fact, the same girl Lily who fancies herself as being in love with Manik, by using a referent different from her name to hide her identity as a way of springing a surprise on the reader later with a grand disclosure. Thus she is referred to as 'Tanna's wife'[25] or bhabhi or 'sister-in-law' by Jamuna in the Hindi version,[26] a common mode of addressing a neighbour's wife in Northern India; and even when she is referred to by her name as 'Lily' or 'Lila',[27] the text succeeds in withholding her identity until Manik Mulla grandly declares, '[b]ut I can tell you one thing: this Lila was the very girl who was married to Tanna; that evening it was Mahesar the commission agent, who had come to see her', while concluding the story of the fourth afternoon.[28]

This device becomes wholly lost to the film as a medium. We have already seen Tanna's wife when Tanna makes his bride-seeing visit in the story of the third afternoon; later we see her entertaining Jamuna's visits. And then we see her with Manik Mulla as his 'Devasena', and we already know her 'future' in the narrative.

While Benegal gracefully acknowledges his loss in this particular case, he manages to generate the effect of suspense elsewhere in a manner that the book might have chosen to, but does not. This is in the manner of revealing information pertaining to the same event in increasing doses. An early example in the film is Jamuna's visit to her parental home for the first time after getting married, which is shown twice with incremental repetition. The first time when she enters her home, her mother talks to her about Tanna, saying that a match has been arranged for him. Jamuna replies that she is not interested (in Tanna). This is Benegal's creative intervention, not a part of the book, and it finds completeness in expression when this very scene is replayed later in the film, where for all her supposed indifference to Tanna, Jamuna goes up to Tanna and speaks to him, asking him if his fiancée is more beautiful than she is (Figure 8.2).

Figure 8.2 The visual medium potently suggesting the intimacy between Jamuna and Ramdhan.

In the book, there is no indication that it is during Jamuna's first visit home following her nuptials that she asks Tanna if his affianced bride is more beautiful than her. She does ask him this, but later. While the extreme non-linearity of the structure makes it difficult to assert the timeline of many events, in this case Bharati's narration is unambiguous. Indicating this as a different visit from the first to her mother's house, we are told that '[a]t the time of Tanna's betrothal she came again, even more elaborately dressed . . .'[29]

What does this change by Benegal achieve? Apart from adding one more layer to the non-linear trajectory, this change also establishes the character of Jamuna as duplicitous or wavering, depending on how judgemental the viewer is. This extra information, when it follows her remark to her mother that she is not interested in Tanna, becomes a way of adding complexity to her character more subtly than straightforward description. It also plays to the strength of the cinematic medium which is about showing rather than telling.

In a related fashion, Benegal also repeats scenes, by replaying them without addition, but with altered perspectives. These identical repetitions succeed in the objective to scatter the linearity of the timeline, by complicating, visually, the question of what came before and what came after. One of the striking instances of the same event playing twice in the film, proleptically and analeptically, is that of Satti warning the lecherous grocer to mind his behaviour in her presence. And yet the same scene comes to be located in two different narrative trajectories across its two presentations. The first time it is a part of Tanna's story and the second a part of Satti's story, thus forming a circular and a closed trajectory of its own.

The film plays another episode belonging to Satti's narrative two times. The second iteration concerns the disappearance of Satti from the scene. This is presented to us for the first time in a scene in which a man tells a crowd gathering outside a house that he had seen a horse-cart drive by with a corpse in it shrouded in white, which was in all probability Satti's, and that she had been murdered by Mahesar and Chaman. This is narrated within the larger story of Tanna and his wife. This very scene is nearly replayed at the end of Manik's narration of Satti's story.

It is noteworthy that despite deploying the technique of replay more than once in his film, Benegal makes each repetition unique and different from other instances of replay. In this case, the first announcement of Satti's probable death shows a man standing outside the locked door of a dwelling with a crowd gathered before it. In its second and last replay, the perspective of the scene is slightly altered. The man and his crowd of listeners are at a greater distance from the lens of the camera this time, so that the viewer's field of vision is able to take in the figure of Manik Mulla, walking past Satti's house in front of which the crowd is gathered. Manik is missing from the spectator's field of vision in the earlier presentation of the same scene.

Manik has in previous instances in the film played the role of a witness, as in the case of Jamuna meeting Tanna; but this time, he is as much an active player as a witness of the incident he is narrating, since in all likelihood it was his betrayal of Satti that led to her disappearance. Thus, the change made by Benegal in playing out this scene the second time makes it meaningful for the viewer's comprehension in a way that the earlier presentation could not manage.

While this chapter intends to make the point rather than list the various replays in the film, one more needs to be included before moving on to the next section. It is the repeated scene of the wedding vows of Tanna and Lily. The pheras as they are known, where the couple walks around the fire as sacred witness, are shown twice in the film; first, cursorily, while recounting the story of Tanna and his wedding, second, within the story of Lily, so that by now we know that Tanna's wife imagines herself in love with Manik Mulla and that she takes the vows with a broken heart.

The above instance as well as those concerning Satti, and Jamuna's visit to her parental home, use the technique of the replayed scene in such a way that the viewer watching the same scene again has, in the interval between the two depictions of it, acquired greater knowledge of the context surrounding it so as to be able to make a considered judgement on it. For example, in the case of Jamuna, the second portrayal shows us that contrary to her claim that she does not care for Tanna, which is all that we have been shown in the first portrayal, she cares enough for him to accost him about his impending wedding and reproach him with not having loved her. What we have also been shown in the meantime is the extent of the investment that Tanna and Jamuna have made in each other, allowing for the restrictions imposed by a rigidly moralistic middle-class neighbourhood.

In Benegal's words,

> [t]he novel had a series of stories and some of them were stories within stories. One required a form which would be fairly close to the literary form of Dharamvir [sic] Bharti [sic]. A film cannot take you to multiple actions simultaneously very easily as it manifests in terms of visuals and sound. The process is unlike writing where your experience is [sic] very internal one. The reader's imagination can work at different levels at the same time but when you manifest it in terms of visuals and sound then it becomes sequential rather than simultaneous.[30]

'So,' explains the writer of this piece, 'he shot the same scene from the points of view of different characters to "give it a sense of simultaneity".' This technique concurrently establishes non-linearity. The iterative mode of representation encourages a sense of circularity, which through self-referencing also establishes self-reflexivity.

On the flipside, the sense of non-linearity is also suggested by the way in which certain trajectories are left aside and picked up later with the narrative gap left vacant. A glaring case in point is the question of Jamuna's father's financial woes. He was to have gone to jail if he could not replace the money missed in the office accounting. Jamuna does not lend him the money and yet later in the story when we find him in her house at her husband's death, this question is not seen as important to be raised or resolved.

OTHER DIFFERENCES MADE BY BENEGAL

Some of the changes in the film are aimed at economy and some, as already pointed out, at taking advantage of the visual medium. The book attributes three sisters to Tanna; the film shows only two, eliminating the third sister who, in the book, is only 'used' by Mahesar's mistress to send to the market for purchases[31] and is thereby dispensable. Mahesar is reported to have died in the book,[32] but in the film, Manik Mulla only mentions that he disappears. Two cynical moments in the book, both misogynistic, are missing in the film. After Mahesar throws his mistress out of the house, his late wife's jewels are found to be missing,[33] and after Satti is taken away from Manik's house by Chaman Thakur and Mahesar, Satti's ornaments which she had brought along were gone. 'Manik suspected that his sister-in-law had taken and locked it up in her trunk, for safety's sake, but he never knew for certain.'[34] If his sister-in-law had indeed taken it, she was stealing what did not belong to her.

Among the noteworthy changes made by Benegal, one is in the relationship that he establishes for Mahesar's mistress with his children. In the Hindi version of the novel, Mahesar insists that his children address her as *bua* meaning 'father's sister',[35] thereby suggesting that their relationship is purely platonic. But the film changes her role to the less mistakable one of *mausi* meaning 'mother's sister'. The English version cannot make a closer point in this respect given that its use of 'auntie' is a general term that does not specify the exact nature of the relationship.

Also, passages in the novel that are implicit are made explicit in the film. In the novel, Jamuna's conduct towards Manik is narrated decorously to explain nothing beyond

> [w]hen finally she grew quiet she wiped her tears and had suddenly started saying the kind of thing that you find written in story books. I didn't like it one bit . . . I would want to talk about my school and my books but she would wipe her tears and start talking like magazine stories.[36]

The film more explicitly shows Jamuna laying her head on Manik's shoulder. Later she is shown embracing Ramdhan in an unrestrained manner, as he urges the horse to run faster, faster, leaving us in no doubt that he has fathered her son, a point over which the text maintains greater ambiguity.

LITERARY MOTIF

Aside from overt discussions of technique and references to other authors like Tagore, Premchand, Chekhov and Maupassant, the motif of *Devadas* in the film also adds to its self-reflexive character. The inclusion of *Devadas* in the film is not entirely Benegal's invention, but given that this famous novel by Sarat Chandra Chatterjee[37] is mentioned sparingly in the text only to be critiqued as irrelevant to contemporary times, its augmented presence in the film is Benegal's contribution. In both text and film, *Devadas* is the film that Lily and her friend Kammo go to watch, as Lily informs Manik Mulla, saying pityingly that Kammo could not understand its profundity. Lily, as Jamuna before her, effortlessly quotes lines from *Devadas* with great empathy and emotion, vicariously experiencing the emotions of the characters of *Devadas*.

Benegal uses it more extensively in his film and to the deployment of parody, showing how the influence of *Devadas* in the lives of its readers/viewers makes them incapable of discrimination by drawing them into sentimentality and rendering them incapable of distinguishing fiction from real life. Hence Jamuna quotes from *Devadas* to explain to Manik Mulla the reason why Tanna will not disobey his father. Again, Jamuna reads from *Devadas*, loudly enough for Tanna to hear, relevant excerpts about parental withholding of consent to the young lovers' marriage. The ability to interpret the mundane happenings of one's life from the perspective of a hugely sentimental novel is mocked by the film as the pitiable need of a middle-class girl to see her life as larger-than-life and tragic in a grand manner.

Benegal brings *Devadas* into the picture quite a number of times, also making a point about commercial Indian cinema, which has a history of having seen fifteen cinematic versions of this book.

> Sarat Chandra's popular novel has been adapted for cinema a record 15 times, in 7 Indian languages (Hindi, Urdu, Bengali, Telugu, Tamil, Malayalam, Assamese). There have been 2 loose adaptations (*Dev D* and *Aur Devdas*), and a silent version as well (1928).[38]

This article in fact begins with the startling proposition: '[a]ccording to popular legend, there are only 5 scripts in Bollywood. All other scripts are inspired by these 5 stock stories, give or take a few plot variations.' Topping this list is *Devadas*.[39]

BENEGAL'S GESTURES TOWARDS BOLLYWOOD CONVENTIONS OF COMMERCIAL CINEMA

Two major differences are executed in the film which mark its Bollywood identity unmistakably. The first is the death of Tanna. In the book he loses his balance at the door of the train he is standing in, when it gives a sudden jerk, and he falls down from it, losing both his legs, and then his life. Tanna's death is presented differently by Benegal. Not just that he dies by being hit by a train while standing on a track, but that he has just met a widowed Jamuna with Ramdhan on the station platform and he feels happy after a long time. He does lose his legs in the film as a result of the accident, but when he regains consciousness in hospital, in great pain, we find Jamuna by his side. It seems like a natural presence since she had watched him being hit by the train, but to ensure that there is no doubt regarding her feelings for Tanna, the film shows her weeping inconsolably when he dies. The visual effect of this scene is extremely powerful, since Jamuna is wearing a white saree, the garb of a widow. This scene associates her widowed status with the man lying dead, over whose body she is hysterically weeping, thus making a symbolic visual point about their emotional connect. Counter to the norm, consoling Jamuna is Tanna's wife, who seems to have exchanged roles with Jamuna. Rather than weep over the loss of her husband, she soothes the weeping Jamuna as if the latter were his wife.

This scene itself is picturised in a melodramatic manner reminiscent of Bollywood conventions of enacting emotion, and it testifies to the ease with which Benegal is able to bring together two styles of Hindi cinema typically perceived as mutually exclusive: 'commercial' and 'art'. The element of parody that the book already contains is useful for Benegal while turning commercial into art, since irony can transform a commercially oriented portrayal into an artistic one through additional layering.

The second and more significant Bollywood-isation of *Suraj Ka Satvan Ghoda* by Benegal is in the song sequence between Manik Mulla and Lily. This is a clearly heightened depiction of Bollywood romance, hyped by the romantic couple who cannot help seeing their story within the larger stories of *Skandagupta* or *Devadas*, and themselves as playing grand roles. The lyrics of this song are based on a poem by Dharmavir Bharati, which itself does not form a part of his novel.

In her article 'Celluloid Love Songs', Natalie Sarrazin studies love songs in Hindi cinema, the conventions that enshrine them and the multiple implications of their picturisation in film. Her classification of these songs includes the category of courtship songs, which are mostly duets. The main duet is a musical portrayal of 'love-in-union' and '[th]e principal duet is often picturised in pastoral settings involving nature, lush fields, and flowers. Cinematographically, a long shot and panoramic view capture the lovers in mountains, in fields, by oceans, waterfalls and other sensual settings.'[40] Citing Dwyer, she describes the romantic couple as 'always alone, highlighting both intimacy and commitment'.[41]

These discourse features stand out in the only song in Benegal's film. When after a bout of weeping, Lily goes to the window and looks at the drizzle outside, Manik tells her not to move away even though the rain drops fall on her. He exclaims at her wet cheek asking her not to dry them, then remarks on the beauty of a wet curl of hair, all of which pleases Lily, whose idea of romance originates from these stylised, even stale descriptions and dialogues. Manik subsequently joins her at the window, and they then spontaneously launch into song.

The song is a duet; scenically it is perfectly formulaic. His arm around Lily, Manik Mulla walks with her through a garden in a lightly drizzling rain. There is greenery and there are flowers, now in the foreground, and now in the background of the lovers. When Lily appears to be annoyed, Manik cajoles her with a red flower that he takes to her. At this point the scene cuts to their reflections in a pond, before moving upwards to their real not reflected selves.

THE ENDING

The endings of the text and the film differ markedly. The novel concludes with a greater sense of closure. After having ended Satti's story, Manik waxes eloquent about the eponymous seventh horse of the sun, calling it the horse of the future and of inspiration. Crediting Manik Mulla, therefore, for the unusual title of the novel, the narrator bids adieu to us, his readers.

The film, however, is markedly open-ended. Manik is addressing his audience, this time outside his house, talking of the seventh horse that leads all of us forward. The view to the audience is of a rapt Manik Mulla in the foreground while from the darkness behind him a figure slowly, suspensefully, emerges. Just as Manik tells his listeners that the horse of the future is the seventh horse of the sun, the figure coming from behind touches him and he turns back, shocked to see that it is Satti and shocking her equally. With an expression of stunned fury on her face, she clutches a little boy closer to her and, pushing aside Chaman Thakur, rushes away from Manik. After this, the two versions part ways. The film shows Manik, stupefied, walking as if beyond his volition behind Satti, following her until he disappears into the smoke, leaving his bemused listeners behind.

Then we cut to a scene where a horse gallops, after which the film comes full circle, with the narrator standing before the paintings of the first scene, saying that 'Manik babu', after this, simply disappeared. Open endings permit multiple interpretations, but one obvious conclusion here seems to be that Satti turned out to be Manik's seventh horse, and also his nemesis.

It is difficult to have the last word on Benegal's transformation of *Suraj Ka Satvan Ghoda* despite the near-miraculous fact that Benegal shot the film in a mere twenty days. This chapter has attempted to address some of the main queries raised in the film, and from the perspective of a viewer whose engagement with the film is coloured by their reading of the novel. What a reader would make of the film without a foreknowledge of the book is beyond the scope of this chapter, but arguably within that of another. Such is Benegal's talent that his creative interventions provoke questions endlessly.

Note: All dialogue translated by the author.

NOTES

1. This chapter is based on the English translation by 'Ajneya' of Dharmavir Bharati's novel originally written in Hindi and titled, *Suraj Ka Satvan Ghoda*. It was titled in English *The Sun's Seventh Horse*. The English translation does not include the subtitle in the Hindi version – 'a short novel of a new style'. Although I have read the text in both Hindi and English, typically all quotations and citations in my chapter are from the English translation. The exceptions are few, as seen in the use of the Hindi word *bua*, which cannot be translated into English without losing the specificity of its meaning; or in my translation of the subtitle of the text from Hindi, as the English translation does not have a subtitle.
2. Sukanya Verma, 'Great Film, No Audience', *The Hindu*, 17 September 2017, <https://www.thehindu.com/entertainment/movies/great-film-no-audience/article19691271.ece>, accessed 1 September 2021.
3. Dharmavir Bharati, *The Sun's Seventh Horse*, trans. Sachchidanand Hiranand Vatsyayan 'Ajneya' (New Delhi: National Book Trust, 1999), 66–7.
4. Bharati, trans. Ajneya, 2.
5. Verma.
6. Linda Hutcheon, *A Theory of Adaptation* (Informa, 2006), <https://books.google.co.in/books/about/A_Theory_of_Adaptation.html?id=79WNAgAAQBAJ&printsec=frontcover&source=kp_read_button&redir_esc=y#v=onepage&q&f=false>, accessed 1 September 2021.
7. Hutcheon, *A Theory of Adaptation*.
8. Ibid.
9. Bharati, trans. Ajneya, 1–5.
10. Ibid., 5, emphasis added.
11. Ibid., 94, emphasis added.
12. Ibid., 53.
13. Bharati, trans. Ajneya, 16.
14. Ibid., 16.
15. Ibid., 16.
16. Ibid., 27.
17. Ibid., 24.
18. Ibid., 3, emphasis added.
19. Ibid., 91–2.

20. Ibid., 16.
21. Ibid., 16.
22. Ibid., 1.
23. *Suraj Ka Satvan Ghoda*, directed by Shyam Benegal (1992; India: National Film Development Corporation of India).
24. Bharati, trans. Ajneya, 42.
25. Ibid., 43.
26. Bharati, *Suraj Ka Satvan Ghoda*, 44.
27. Bharati, trans. Ajneya, 54–61.
28. Ibid., 61.
29. Ibid., 43, emphasis added.
30. Anuj Kumar, 'The Best of Benegal', *The Hindu*, 20 July 2016, <https://www.thehindu.com/features/metroplus/The-best-of-Benegal/article14499342.ece>, accessed 1 September 2021.
31. Bharati, trans. Ajneya, 38.
32. Ibid., 44.
33. Ibid., 42.
34. Ibid., 78.
35. Bharati, *Suraj Ka Satvan Ghoda*, 40.
36. Bharati, trans. Ajneya, 15.
37. Ibid., 82n.
38. Nirupama Kotru, 'From Devdas and Beyond: Most Successful Book Adaptations in Indian Cinema', *The Indian Express*, 21 March 2017, <https://indianexpress.com/article/entertainment/bollywood/devdas-and-beyond-most-successful-book-adaptations-in-indian-cinema-manto-4578569>, accessed 1 September 2021.
39. Kotru.
40. Natalie Sarrazin, 'Celluloid Love Songs: Musical "Modus Operandi" and the Dramatic Aesthetics of Romantic Hindi Film', *Popular Music* 27, no. 3 (October 2008): 399, <http://www.jstor.org/stable/40212399>, accessed 1 September 2021.
41. Sarrazin, 399.

CHAPTER 9

Mammo and Projections of the Muslim Woman: Indian Parallel Cinema, Partition and Belonging

Omar Ahmed

INTRODUCTION

I was absolutely shattered. I never believed that we Indians were capable of something like that. These things have happened before in History. Temples have been destroyed, so have mosques at other times. But for a mosque to be destroyed as a clearly well-thought out political action – something like that had never happened.

Shyam Benegal[1]

Shyam Benegal's outrage at the act of mindless vandalism directed by Hindu *kar sevaks* against the Babri Masjid mosque in Ayodhya bears witness to a trauma that had long-term repercussions for Muslims in India. The first of three collaborations with journalist-turned-scriptwriter/director Khalid Mohamed,[2] director Shyam Benegal's 1994 film *Mammo* was the first in a series of interventionist films, four in total,[3] which addressed the plight and contemporary experiences of Muslim women in India. Although the film is set 'on the outskirts of Mumbai in the 1970s',[4] at the time of the film's release in 1994, the political landscape was changing quite dramatically. Events including L. K. Advani's *Ram Rath Yatra*[5] in 1990, the demolition of the Babri Masjid[6] in 1992, the pre-mediated Bombay riots in 1992 and the following retaliatory bombings of Bombay in 1993 created a disturbing climate marking Muslims as anomalous. Abdul Shaban writes, 'the dominant instrument of alienating Muslims from mainstream Indian society and the majority community is through construction of the identity of the "other"'.[7] The othering of the Muslim is made altogether detrimental when considering that 'Muslims are a socio-economically marginalised community'[8] in

India today experiencing high levels of poverty and unemployment comparable to the systemic social exclusion faced by Dalits.[9]

In this respect, it is imperative to recognise *Mammo* as a deeply personal riposte from Benegal against the persecution and marginalisation of Muslims living in India at a time of great social and political upheaval. However, Sangeeta Datta notes that 'Benegal turns away from the immediate history of violence to a tragic fate of an old woman trying to return to her land.'[10] At the same time, writer Shoma Chatterji argues that Benegal's decision to make *Mammo* was borne out of mob law violence he witnessed first-hand such as a 'Muslim bakery being set on fire by an angry mob'.[11] Given the concurrent tenor of heightened tensions between Hindus and Muslims, much of the antagonism stoked by a troubling neo-fascist populism[12] accords *Mammo* with prescience. This chapter explores how the representation of the Muslim woman[13] in *Mammo* is predominantly refracted through the politics of belonging and the Partition. Moreover, I will demonstrate how parallel cinema, a site of cultural resistance of which Benegal is a key pioneer, played a critical role in helping to open up a counter-representational space, which humanised Muslims.

Mammo[14] is structured as an extended flashback that is triggered by the memories of Riyaz, the nephew of Mammo. The flashback takes us back to a time when Riyaz was thirteen years old and living with his temperamental grandmother, Fayyazi (Surekha Sikri). Mehmooda Begum (Farida Jalal[15]), affectionately known as 'Mammo', arrives abruptly. We discover that Mammo left with her husband for Pakistan after the Partition. But after his sudden death, Mammo was expelled from her home in Pakistan and returned to India on a temporary visa to visit her sister Fayyazi. At first Riyaz resents Mammo, but gradually warms to her endearing personality, realising how Mammo is effectively an exile with no permanent abode, longing for a sense of belonging. Abandoned by his father, Riyaz shares a similar experience of separation and relates to the estrangement felt by Mammo, particularly when Mammo discloses her traumatic memories of the Partition. However, Mammo is also something of a nuisance, interfering in the lives of Riyaz and Fayyazi who both come to begrudge her. Eventually Mammo is forcibly taken away by the police and deported back to Pakistan. But at the end, twenty years later, as Riyaz is recollecting their memories of Mammo, there is a knock at the door and it is Mammo, eccentric as ever, who returns like a spectre and declares herself dead so that she can finally remain in India.

INDIAN PARALLEL CINEMA AND THE RECOVERY OF THE MUSLIM

This chapter explores how the emergence of parallel cinema as an alternative to mainstream and popular Hindi cinema helped to open up a new space for

Muslim representations and on-screen imaginings that had been interrupted after the Partition. There are four films in particular that I want to highlight for the purposes of this study. These include *Garam Hawa* (*Scorching Winds*, 1973, directed by M. S. Sathyu), *Salim Langde Pe Mat Ro*[16] (*Don't Cry for Salim, the Lame*, 1989, directed by Saeed Mirza), *Naseem*[17] (1995, directed by Saeed Mirza) and Benegal's *Mammo* (1994). Muslim representations in the past, notably the 1940s onwards, have tended to be most prominent in the exotic romantic milieu of the Muslim social, expressly the Islamicate imagery of the Mughal era as seen in *Pukar* (*The Call*, 1939, directed by Sohrab Modi). Ravi Vasudevan says the Muslim social emerged in the early 1940s as a response to the 'political demands for representation of community interests . . . through the prism of modern social reform'.[18] Rachel Dwyer[19] defines the Muslim social, which she labels broadly as the Islamicate film, as a pre-Partition development, a 'counterpart to the "social" genre as romances set in a roughly Islamicate world',[20] identifying the particular Islamicate iconography associated with the Muslim social. However, Dwyer contends, 'the Hindi film, outside the Islamicate genres, regards Muslims as the Other',[21] accentuating the fact that the stereotyping that proliferates in the imagination of the audience is one that is perpetuated by the mainstream media including popular Hindi cinema.

Rachel Dwyer, Ira Bhaskar and Richard Allen have argued convincingly for the Islamicate genres of Bombay cinema, which include the sub-genres of the Muslim historical, the courtesan film, the classic Muslim social and the new wave Muslim social. Dwyer along with Bhaskar and Allen go as far as to categorise *Mammo* as part of the new wave Muslim social, the final category of the Islamicate genre, and which they argue, 'eschewed the representation of an idealized *nawabi* culture that had formed the earlier genre.'[22] Given the impact of the Partition on the film industry and the representations of Muslims, the Islamicate genres chosen by Bhaskar and Allen point to large gaps in the chronology of this genre especially after the Partition. I would argue that the intermittent nature of the Islamicate films after the Partition point to the ways in which Muslims in Indian films became precarious to represent. After the Partition it was not until the 1970s that we witnessed a realist engagement with the social and political issues of Muslims living in India, expressly initiated by the critical success of *Garam Hawa* in 1973; a point raised also by Bhaskar and Allen. *Garam Hawa* inverted the traditional Islamicate iconography so that it took on a wider political resonance about what was the growing alienation and isolation of Muslims in India unable to cope with the trauma of the Partition.

Although I would argue that Dwyer, Bhaskar and Allen labelling films such as *Garam Hawa* and *Mammo* as an evolution of the Muslim social appears logical considering the Islamicate iconography on display, it is largely at the risk of displacing the interventionist role parallel cinema[23] came to play in helping to negotiate a new counter-representational space for the Muslim. Films like *Garam Hawa* that emerged as part of parallel cinema were directly concerned with the contemporary plight of Muslims living in India. This was relatively new ground and signalled a break from trying to situate the Muslim in a fixed historical era. Undeniably, few films have been made since the 1970s that directly engage with the contemporary Muslim experience, suggesting it is more appropriate to label films like *Garam Hawa* and *Mammo* as part of a transitory cycle indicative of parallel cinema rather than a new sub-genre of the Muslim social. Sangeeta Datta argues, 'Khalid Mohamed's script demystifies the Muslim family'[24] and presents 'Pakistani and Indian women as ordinary middle-class people'.[25] More specifically, a recurring theme seems to be the generational experience of Muslims living in India. In all four films we see the historical and cultural shift from an older Muslim generation who had lived through the trauma of the Partition towards a new younger generation of Muslims commonly represented as disaffected, marginalised and in many cases unemployed. Moreover, in both *Salim Langde Pe Mat Ro* and *Naseem*, communalism is critiqued as a concept propagated by political parties in attempts to sow discord among Hindus and Muslims.

It is important to recognise that the four films I have underlined were all supported by the FFC and later the National Film Development Corporation (NFDC).[26] This is significant because it expressed the state's wish to promote an inclusive social agenda in which the narrative of the Muslim was acknowledged and embraced as part of a wider dialogue. A distinctive feature of these four films is the exploration of Muslim characters in relation to the contemporary realisation of community, nation and family. And while seminal films like *Garam Hawa* privilege the Muslim male patriarch, *Mammo* reverses this traditional gender paradigm, foregrounding the ageing Muslim woman as the focal point and the main agent of the narrative. Bhaskar and Allen go so far as to describe Mammo as a proto-feminist, arguing that 'her struggle against the injustice of territorial borders that defy the wishes of the human heart is also a struggle against patriarchal injustices to women'.[27] Considering the near absence of the older matriarchal Muslim woman in contemporary Indian cinema, the character of Mammo becomes situated as exceptional compared to the narrow and limited representations of Muslim women offered up by Islamicate genres of the past; the courtesan remaining the most radical disrupter of gender norms.

The counter-Muslim representations in *Mammo* are not simply the creation of Khalid Mohamed, but were also influenced by the ongoing creative collaboration between Benegal and Shama Zaidi. Shama Zaidi, who has never been recognised for her significant contributions to many of the scripts Benegal worked on through the 1980s and 1990s, is an important component of *Mammo* since she is one of the few women Muslim scriptwriters to have worked so consistently in the film industry. Shama Zaidi alternated between working as a playwright, art director, costume designer and scriptwriter, having made her name adapting Ismat Chughtai's short story as a full-length screenplay that would become *Garam Hawa*. For Benegal, whose films[28] from as early as *Ankur* (*The Seedling*, 1974) expressed an affinity with female narratives, and who often referred to himself as a feminist, the involvement of Shama Zaidi brought an added resonance to *Mammo* because her Muslim heritage imbued the female characters with an ideological clarity and authenticity that had become characteristic of parallel cinema's pursuit of realism. Indeed, Muslim characters had featured in Benegal's films in the past, notably *Junoon* (*The Obsession*, 1979), a historical epic set during the time of the Indian Mutiny of 1857. And it was the capacity of parallel cinema to give a voice to those groups of people normally excluded from cinematic representations, narrating a history from below, which may explain why films like *Mammo* were exceptional at such a polarising moment in India's history.

In *Mammo*, Shyam Benegal establishes the Muslim milieu through the parochial image of *namaz*, performed by Fayyazi, sister of Mammo and grandmother of Riyaz. What is interesting about this representation of the Muslim, predictably associated with the devotion to Islam, is the unglamorous framing, challenging the overstated opulence of Islamicate genres in which Mughal architecture is used to codify Muslim identity. Fayyazi appears at a distance, behind curtains slightly open so that we can voyeuristically eavesdrop on the ordinariness of this moment. This shot sees Fayyazi eventually rise to her feet, folding the *namaz* mat and hobbling towards us, extenuating her old age. In addition, Fayyazi's praying is juxtaposed with Riyaz sitting at his desk using his typewriter.

As I noted earlier, this cycle of parallel cinema films that focuses on the Muslim experience extenuates the generational divide, a theme Benegal also restates, and in this case suggests that Riyaz conceals his Muslim identity from society. However, Riyaz's identity is a broadly progressive one, shaped by Fayyazi and Mammo, two resilient Muslim women. As we discover, the father is altogether absent, having abandoned Riyaz to lead another life. The displacement of the traditional patriarchal Muslim is characteristic yet again of Benegal's oppositional approach to narrative storytelling and the ways in which parallel cinema often celebrated and favoured women-centric narratives, subverting the customary gender paradigm. Furthermore, the absence of the father from the depiction of family, a recurrent motif in Benegal's work, strengthens the bonds between the female characters, creating a sense of camaraderie and resilience that defies the patriarchal system. However, it is important to note that the absence of the father is a theme that manifests itself in different ways through this cycle of films as a wider historical and political crisis concerning Muslim patriarchy and, relatedly, the family. In *Naseem*, the old patriarch is on his deathbed whereas in

Garam Hawa the dignified Salim Mirza (Balraj Sahni) wanders the streets like some phantom and in *Salim Langde Pe Mat Ro* the despondent father has been made unemployed due to a longstanding factory strike. In the context of this particular trajectory, the lack of a patriarchal figure in *Mammo* appears ideologically motivated since the displacement of the father in the family, and the fact that his place is never recovered, points to Hindutva's subjugation of the Muslim male.

Recovery is a key theme in *Mammo*. As Benegal notes, 'It's Mammo who he [Riyaz] wishes to recover'[29] from the past. The collision between the past and present, a recurring theme in the films of Benegal, strikingly dealt with in *Trikal (Past, Present and Future*, 1985), repeats itself in the recovery of the memory of Mammo. The device of recovery at a time when Muslims were increasingly under attack in the mainstream, expressly from Hindutva, reiterates how this cycle of films acts as a collective attempt to recover the Muslim in the imaginings of Indian cinema, which had become displaced and lost over time. Subsequently, the attempt to recover the Muslim and situate it more clearly in Indian cinema was an ideological intervention instigated by the inclusive social and political agenda of parallel cinema that also filtered through into subsequent mainstream representations of Muslims as seen in *Fiza*[30] (2000, directed by Khalid Mohamed). Recovery occurs instantly in *Mammo*. After Riyaz begins reading through the letters written by Mammo and which Fayyazi has been holding on to, the doorbell rings. Riyaz opens the door to reveal Mammo standing before him. But when we cut back to Riyaz, it is the younger version that is conjured before us, segueing seamlessly into a flashback. Through the letters, a tangible record of the past, Riyaz is quick to resurrect the memory of Mammo. This indicates that although the Muslim can be suppressed or demonised momentarily in the wider imaginings of a right-wing Hindu nationalist discourse, the Muslim can never really be erased completely from history or the nation because film as a cultural artefact, in this case parallel cinema, opens a new way for recovery and resistance.

BENEGAL'S WOMEN: THE MUSLIM WOMAN AS A VICTIM OF PARTITION

The recovery of the Muslim, first articulated in the opening to *Mammo*, is also closely linked with the Partition and the figure of the woman, since women 'were in most cases the worst sufferers'[31] of the Partition. Benegal's revisionist approach to history, a key thematic preoccupation of his oeuvre that forms the basis for many of his best films such as *Trikal* and *Bose* (2005), is also evident in *Mammo*. While the opening uses the flashback as narrative device to resurrect Mammo, the Muslim woman, the theme of the Partition, is brought into play straightaway with a compelling montage of fragmented images from the film.

This is not necessarily a strategy of foreshadowing but the fragmented style creates a dissonance in which the theme of separation seems most potent, a visual link to the history of the Partition that bears down on many of the Muslim characters. Moreover, the fractured editing style personifies the theme of the Partition. In this opening montage, Benegal wants us to feel an overwhelming dislocation, something that is experienced by Mammo on a continual basis. The conceptualisation of Mammo's alienation and exilic status is expressly signalled when the montage segues into the first rendition of the *ghazal* '*Yeh Faasle Teri Galiyon Ke*', which is juxtaposed with Riyaz waking in his bed. Now it becomes clear that everything we have just seen are the fractured memories of Riyaz who is haunted by Mammo, a symbolic link for the Muslim to a traumatic past, which remains intact. In this respect, Mammo's status as a Muslim woman is augmented by the Partition; the two are inseparable.

The sequence in which Mammo relays her memories of the Partition to Riyaz is an important moment in the film because it points to a historical rupture that re-organised communal relations between Hindus, Muslims and Sikhs, a traumatic wound that remains open. Mammo begins by telling Riyaz that she has experienced hell; this is the way she refers to the trauma of the Partition, announcing that she should never have to witness it again. Harenda writes, 'the whole act of Mammo providing her spoken testimony can be viewed in terms of double witnessing'.[32] Mammo talks of having left behind everything in the dead of night and making the arduous cross-border journey to Pakistan. This oral re-telling of Mammo's story of the Partition is one of the thousands of similar stories of suffering. The significance of the oral re-telling and passing of trauma to a new generation[33] is chiefly important because this is the primary way in which the memories of the Partition have been kept alive, confined to a personal, secretive and familial space:

> In passing on this story to Riyaz, the child of a new generation, Mammo bears witness to that woman's personal tragedy, a tragedy that implicated all who lived through those catastrophic times.[34]

This is also the first time Mammo refers to herself as a refugee, talking of the horrors of what she witnessed, expressly the suffering, fire, blood and looting:

> There were around five hundred of us. While we were crossing over from this side just as many were coming across the other. From this side, the people were Muslims, and from that side, Hindus and Sikhs. But both sides went through the same trauma. Abandoning their homes, property, loved ones. There was a woman walking along with me. She had two small children. They were in her arms. One died while in her arms. Where was the time for any burial? When we came to a river people told

her to dispose of the dead body in its waters. The poor woman was not in her senses. She threw the live baby into the river and held the dead child strapped to her breast. Her worn and beady eyes are still before me, and her shriek . . .[35]

The allegory of the traumatised mother as a victim of the Partition functions as a logical expression of Mammo's own experiences. And the imagery of madness conjured by Mammo to describe the lunacy of Partition links to Sadat Hasan Manto's famous short story *Toba Tek Singh* (1955) that revolves around lunatics in an asylum in Lahore on the eve of the Partition. Not to mention, Mammo's memories of the Partition are triggered by a conversation with Riyaz that talks of Manto as a writer. Rather than resort to an extended flashback that could have visualised the recollection, Benegal chooses to have Mammo positioned centrally in a medium close-up and talk directly of her experience (Figure 9.1), suggesting that it is a trauma from which she cannot escape. The use of smoke, a concrete link to the past, that drifts across the shot of Mammo as she speaks is an unexpected moment of magical realism, deepening the inescapable nature of the Partition that locks victims into re-living a personal trauma. By the same token, agency is critical; letting Mammo speak of the horrors she has experienced, significantly as a Muslim woman, reiterates Benegal's thematic commitment, which has been to articulate the voices of women often never heard or seen in Indian cinema.

Figure 9.1 Mammo recounts her memories of the Partition to Riyaz.

Indeed, the trauma of the Partition is not spoken in exclusive terms of the Muslim as victim, but speaks of a shared trauma that impacted Hindus, Sikhs and Muslims alike. In a sequence devoid of sentimentality[36] there are two pertinent shots that Benegal inserts into Mammo's recollection which anchor the witnessing of trauma as something tangible for the film spectator. The first is an obscure panning shot of people at night fleeing in desperation as fire rages in the background. In many ways, this first shot denotes rioting and exile, stereotypical of Partition literature and films, situating Mammo's story as part of a well-known historical narrative. But it is the second shot, a disturbing image, which is of real significance; 'a naked baby moves on the body of the raped and dead mother'.[37] Albeit the image of the naked baby connects metonymically with the story that Mammo relates of the devastated mother, it arguably points to a repression that underlies the notion of memory. It is important to note that Mammo never describes this image in her oral recollection to Riyaz; it is an image that Mammo shares only with us. Benegal seems to be suggesting how memory is fractured, incomplete and bound to the context in which it is recalled, an idea tied to narrative subjectivity that forms the basis of *Suraj Ka Satvan Ghoda* (*The Seventh Horse of the Sun*, 1992), Benegal's masterful take on the trope of the unreliable narrator and one of his most reflexive and open works.

A final means of framing the Partition is through a reflexive gesture. When Mammo, Riyaz and Fayyazi visit the cinema, the film they go to see is *Garam Hawa*. As noted earlier, *Garam Hawa*, written by Shama Zaidi, also contributed to the script of *Mammo*. The importance of cinema-going as a cultural ritual is an autobiographical aspect of both Benegal's and Mohamed's childhood and it is a motif evident in Riyaz's attempts to bunk off school to go and see Hitchcock films at the local cinema. Remarkably, the scene from *Garam Hawa* that Benegal chooses to use in *Mammo* is the one when the ailing matriarch dies in the ancestral house. Before her death, Salim Mirza pleads with the new landlord, an old friend, that his mother is very ill and wants to return to the ancestral home for a final time. The grandmother's desire to return to the home where she was born is mirrored in Mammo's similarly arduous plea to return home to India. Since the victim often has to relive the trauma of the event, the trauma of Partition that Mammo carries with her is symbolically re-enacted towards the end of the film. And it is the act of separation that resurfaces when Mammo is dragged out of her sister's home, led away by the police, forcibly put on a train and deported back to Pakistan. Priya Kumar argues that 'the film testifies to the enduring official inheritance of Partition which ensures that survivors like Mammo will not be allowed to transgress the boundaries that have been demarcated for them'.[38] Perhaps the only way to circumvent or counter the ways in which the Partition marks Mammo is through the total erasure of identity and her very existence, an area of discussion that will take up the final section of this chapter.

BELONGING AND CITIZENSHIP

> To me the irony is that she [Mammo] is accepted only when she becomes invisible.[39]

Much of the action shot inside the Bombay flat where Mammo comes to stay is framed around a fish tank that slices through the interior of the flat, separating Riyaz from Mammo. The fish tank is part of a *mise-en-scène* connected to Riyaz's childhood, working symbolically to extenuate themes of belonging and citizenship while playing a significant role in a critical moment in the narrative. Mammo organises a surprise birthday party for Riyaz. However, Riyaz reacts badly since he is somewhat embarrassed by his modest living conditions and does not want his friends coming to the flat. Riyaz confronts Mammo and accuses of her interfering in his life, reminding her that she is a guest. The sense of estrangement Mammo feels is summed up in her response, 'Those who don't have their own home have no home at all.' Since Mammo inhabits a cross-border identity, having shifted back and forth between India and Pakistan, the want for a home haunts her. Searching for Mammo in the city, Riyaz and Fayyazi find her taking refuge in the Haji Ali *dargah* and bring her back home. When Mammo returns to the flat, looking at the fish tank she remarks, 'No-one can take them away from their little home.' Bhaskar and Allen argue that the fish tank is used to suggest unity and integration of the family:

> What was previously a screen that isolated Riyaz from Fayyazi now becomes a metaphor for their integrated family life that Mammo herself has done so much to bring about.[40]

Although I agree with the analysis, I would posit that there is a further dimension here in which the symbolism of the fish tank is just one of many ways in which Benegal explores the intertwined themes of belonging and citizenship. Firstly, the fish in the tank, which have a sense of permanency, a fixed abode so to speak, remind Mammo of herself in an opposite condition, namely her exile, displacement and lack of belonging. Mammo might be right in saying that the fish cannot be taken away, but the fish are also helpless. Alternatively, the fish tank harbours an altogether provocatively coded thought related to the marginalised status of Muslims in India after Ayodhya; segregated, cut-off and hemmed into a space from which they cannot escape. The stateless Mammo personifies a crisis of citizenship for the Muslim. Where this statelessness finds a powerful rejoinder is in the removal of Mammo from the flat and the subsequent faking of her own death so that she can remain in India, but not as an official citizen. Both of these ideas are worth pursing further.

Towards the end of the film, the police arrive at the flat and arrest Mammo who is forcibly removed for not having a visa and put on a train back to Pakistan. Prior to this act of state intervention, Mammo on two occasions goes to renew her visa at the local police office and eventually resorts to bribing Inspector Apte (Sandeep Kulkarni) to extend her stay. Harenda notes that 'Mammo finds herself in opposition against the greatly expanded Indian administration system'[41] of the 1970s and the endemic corruption that plagued many civil institutions such as the police and immigration. Contextually, the bribery that Mammo is forced to resort to may in fact be indicative of the rampant corruption of the 1970s, but authorially the oppressed individual in conflict with the monolithic political system is a theme that runs through much of Benegal's best work beginning as early as *Ankur*. However, it is also important to recognise that corruption, a socio-political theme initially amplified by parallel cinema, found a striking correlation in the angry young man films of the 1970s, pointing to just one of the ways in which parallel cinema and popular cinema converged ideologically.

When the police arrive at the door with the deportation order, Mammo reasons with them, pleading that it is Eid tomorrow. However, the state accuses Mammo of 'hiding' in India under false pretences, effectively criminalising her and erasing her claim to citizenship. The sequence begins with a state official handing Mammo a deportation order. This is followed by a woman police officer berating Mammo for remaining in India without a visa and threatening to handcuff her. Surprisingly, Mammo maintains her welcoming demeanour throughout this initial exchange, hoping the situation can be resolved amicably. Harenda argues that Mammo 'does not have any feelings of hatred or intolerance towards the members of other religious groups'[42] and that 'she is above religious and caste divisions',[43] embracing a plural identity that echoes the secularist sentiments of a director like Benegal. Next, the police drag Mammo out of the flat, down a flight of stairs (Figure 9.2) and into the back of a police car. A distraught Fayyazi is helpless to do anything though, looking on as Mammo is taken away. At the train station Mammo continues to plead with the state authorities: 'My home is here. I want to be buried here,' she exclaims. By this time, a desperate Riyaz arrives at the station in the hope of saying goodbye to Mammo. Riyaz runs alongside the train as it moves out of the station, reaching out to touch Mammo who is literally caged behind the bars of the train window and separated indefinitely from Riyaz (Figure 9.3).

In many ways, this sequence repeats the trauma of the Partition, invoking the imagery of the train as iconographic of exile, encapsulating the contemporary mistreatment and dehumanisation of immigrants, refugees and migrants. Where Mammo found a sense of belonging from Riyaz and Fayyazi, her rejection by the authorities and banishment from her homeland of India indicates how callously the state erases citizenship and renders individuals near invisible.

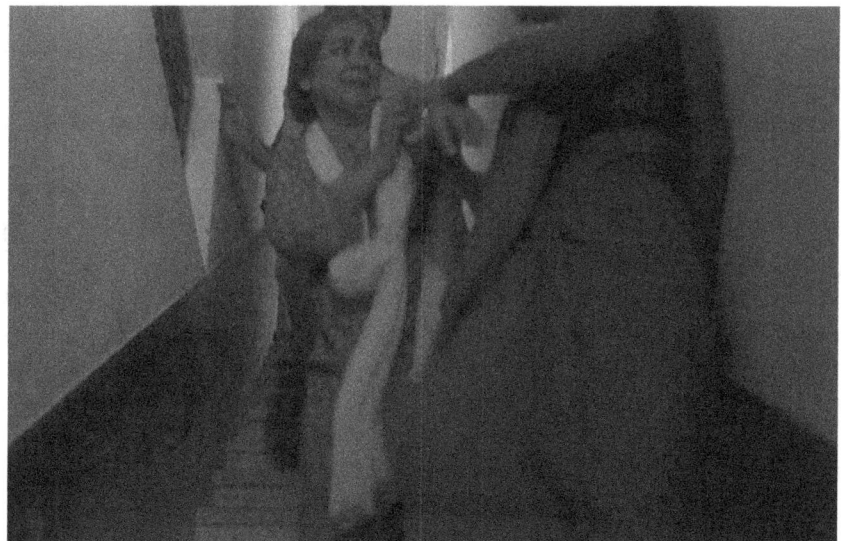

Figure 9.2 Mammo is dragged away by the police.

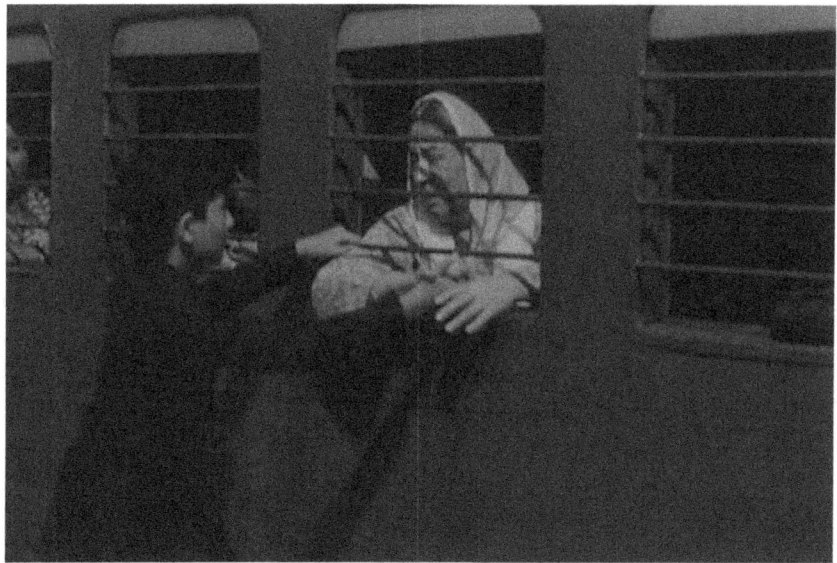

Figure 9.3 Mammo is deported from India.

The strange irony here is that invisibility is something Mammo has to pursue after she is deported; this becomes her only means of returning to India given the animosity that the Partition has created between the two nations. Ilsa Abdul Razzak notes, 'the protagonist declares herself dead on paper to become stateless and evade the imposition of bureaucratic violence'.[44] With Mammo banished from India, the flashback ends and we return to the beginning of the film with the older Riyaz. There is a knock on the door. Riyaz opens the door and Mammo reappears like a phantom, resurrected before our very eyes. Mammo is a lot older now but has lost none of her acerbic wit: 'I won't die so easily. There's strength still in these old bones,' she tells Riyaz. Paradoxically, the death certificate furnishes Mammo with a belated belonging and acceptance, allowing her 'to escape the clutches of citizenship'.[45] The fact that Mammo resorts to circumventing the tests of citizenship, which she cannot pass and which are made considerably worse because of her status as a Muslim, was indicative of the crisis faced by many Muslims at the particularly decisive moment in India's history which ushered in a post-Ayodhya context. By Mammo declaring herself dead, Benegal sustains an authorial trait first initiated in his early work, articulating 'narratives of marginalised females'[46] that are often suppressed in mainstream culture. There is a real despondency to Mammo's outcome though – having to render herself invisible and expunge her identity so that she can claim citizenship in the country in which she was born and of which she feels a part. Indeed, Mammo's exilic despair and desire for belonging is incarnated in the *ghazal* that Benegal redeploys at the end, reminding us of how her identity has been reshaped radically by the events of the Partition and that she and many like her are doomed to wander:

> *Yeh faasle teri galiyon ke*
> *Humse taya na hue* ...
> *(I never could cross the distance of your streets)*[47]

The *ghazal*, a deeply haunting refrain, emerges as a binding force used strategically to invoke an everlasting melancholy. The lyrics, expressly the line 'Who knows which soil was the earth of one's country?', personify the loss and exile felt by Mammo and many others like her who not only suffered the trauma of the Partition, but feel equally unwanted as Muslims in a changing post-secular India. But it has to be said that Mammo is in no way a pessimist – she is a rebel and disruptor.

FINAL THOUGHTS

The influence of a film like *Mammo* is still evident in the inadequate and intermittent humanised depictions of Muslims in Indian cinema. *Mulk* (*Country*, 2018, directed by Anubhav Sinha), a recent exception, starring Rishi Kapoor, that looks at the ways in which the Muslim community is collectively marked and demonised as the other, ends with a freeze-frame of a young Muslim boy

Figure 9.4 The final shot of *Mulk*.

leaping into the air (Figure 9.4). He is wearing a white *topi* cap and the No. 7 shirt of M. S. Dhoni, an icon of Indian cricket. There is pluralism at work; the co-existence of multiple identities that seems under threat right now in India. Although this ending could be questioned for its idealistic utopian longing, it situates Muslims as an integrated part of Indian society, reiterating that their citizenship should never be in question and taking its cue from the paradoxical ending of *Mammo*. At the end of *Mammo*, although Mammo is now officially dead, the final image, a three shot of Mammo, Fayyazi and Riyaz laughing together, signifies a unity and a reconstitution of the family (Figure 9.5). The belated optimism of this end shot harks back to the ending of *Garam Hawa* in which Sikandar (Farooq Sheikh), the son of Salim Mirza, decides to remain in India and join an anti-government protest taking place on their way to the train station. Moreover, there is a secularist refrain at work in the closing shot of *Mammo*, an ideal cherished by director Shyam Benegal, which shows a humanised re-imagining of the Muslim at a time when the demise of parallel cinema saw a marked shift in Indian cinema to an increasingly right-wing nationalism that permutated the cinematic unconscious.

Shyam Benegal's oeuvre stretches across four decades and is populated with a remarkable array of films many of which are key to parallel cinema. Retaining creative autonomy was critical to Benegal and he turned to financing for his films from divergent sources including private, co-operative and state sources. In the 1980s, Doordarshan created a new audience for filmmakers like Benegal. *Mammo*, a co-production between the NFDC and Doordarshan, was a work that many audiences would have encountered on television. However, working

Figure 9.5 The final shot of *Mammo*.

in this new institutional context for Benegal was a natural continuation of his earlier television production *Bharat Ek Khoj*[48] (*The Discovery of India*, 1988), also made for Doordarshan. In some respects, Benegal's dissenting voice was far more pronounced that Satyajit Ray, a director he has often been compared to, and *Mammo* demonstrates a political anger that was consistent with his earlier work and resonated with contemporaries like Mrinal Sen. To humanise the Muslim and expressly the Muslim woman at a time when Muslims were being vilified and overtly situated as the enemy of the state, is a testament to Benegal's heroic effort to intervene and question the status quo. Undeniably, the triumph of *Mammo*, to never sloganise or fall into the trap of sentimentality, is not an isolated act but part of Benegal's overarching restraint as a filmmaker.

Note: All dialogue translated by the author.

NOTES

1. Shyam Benegal, 'Issues and Censorship in Indian Cinema', *Monsoon* 24, no. 2/3 (1997): 293.
2. Khalid Mohamed is a film critic-turned-filmmaker. His story about his grand aunt published in the *Times of India* caught the attention of Benegal who asked Mohamed if he would write an original screenplay based on the story.
3. *Mammo* (1994), *Sardari Begum* (1996), *Zubeidaa* (2001) and *Well Done Abba* (2009) form a quartet of films that explores Muslim identity and women in Indian society.

4. Olivier Harenda, 'The Scent of One's Own Country: The Partition of India as the Unprocessed Cultural Trauma in Shyam Benegal's *Mammo*', *Theoria Et Historia Scientiarum: An International Journal for Interdisciplinary Studies* 16 (2017): 126.
5. A political and religious rally, much of it anti-Muslim, led by L. K. Advani and organised by the Bharatiya Janata Party (BJP) that consolidated the rise of Hindutva.
6. Hindu nationalist groups demolished the ancient Babri mosque in Ayodhya, arguing that the mosque had been built on the site of a temple of Ram.
7. Abdul Shaban, ed., *Lives of Muslims in India: Politics, Exclusion and Violence* (London: New York: Routledge, 2018), 7.
8. Maidul Islam, 'Rethinking the Muslim Question in Post-Colonial India', *Social Scientist* 40, no. 7/9 (2012): 64.
9. Islam, 64.
10. Sangeeta Datta, *Shyam Benegal* (London: BFI, 2002), 173.
11. Shoma Chatterji, 'Shyam Benegal's *Zubediaa*: Memory as Voice', *The South Asianist* 3, no. 2 (2015): 54.
12. Leftist Indian scholars like Romila Thappar and Tanika Sarkar have openly criticised the rise of Hindu nationalism and how it has impacted the everyday facets of life in India.
13. Harenda contends that Mammo's status as a practising Muslim cannot be applied to Riyaz or Fayyazi. I would agree with Harenda on Riyaz who, as a writer alluding to Manto, is probably suspicious of religion. However, in the opening scene when we are first introduced to Fayyazi she is clearly reading *namaz*, thereby consolidating her status as a practising Muslim.
14. Harenda (2017) writes that the film takes place in the 1970s but this is never really made explicit other than with the screening of *Garam Hawa* which arguably could have been a special screening or re-release of the film.
15. Farida Jalal has acted in films for over forty years and has received the best actress Filmfare award for her performance in *Mammo*.
16. *Salim Langde Pe Mat Ro* (*Don't Cry for Salim, the Lame*), directed by Saeed Mirza (1989; India: NFDC). Director Saeed Mirza has said that the 1984 Bhiwandi riots were a catalyst for both the anti-Muslim sentiments portrayed in the film and the emerging communal politics of the late 1980s that was being shaped by the rapid ascent of Hindutva violence.
17. *Naseem*, directed by Saeed Mirza (1995; India: NFDC). The final sequence of *Naseem* is by far the most moving, with director Saeed Mirza staging the death of the ailing secularist patriarch (played by lyricist Kaifi Azmi) to the demolition of the Babri Mosque. In many ways, Mirza posits the demolition of the Babri Mosque as a turning point in the history of new India, signalling the erosion of co-existence, the intensification of communalism and an age of uncertainty for Muslims who live in India.
18. Ravi Vasudevan, 'Film Genres, the Muslim Social, and Discourses of Identity c. 1935–1945', *Bioscope* 6, no. 1 (2015): 41.
19. Rachel Dwyer, *Filming the Gods: Religion and Indian Cinema* (London; New York: Routledge, 2006), 97. I agree with Dwyer's important distinction, arguing how Islamicate films 'are in no way Islamic' and are 'concerned with religion as part of everyday social and cultural life among Muslims, rather than with religion and religious belief per se'.
20. Dwyer, 123.
21. Ibid., 126.
22. Ira Bhaskar and Richard Allen, *Islamicate Cultures of Bombay Cinema* (New Delhi: Tulika Books, 2009), 91; Dwyer.

23. See Omar Ahmed, 'Re-claiming Indian Parallel Cinema', *Silhouette Magazine*, last modified 4 June 2016, <https://learningandcreativity.com/silhouette/indian-parallel-cinema> Here, I discuss at length my position on parallel cinema, arguing for its political, aesthetic and historical significance.
24. Datta, 176.
25. Ibid., 176.
26. Ibid., 173. Datta notes that in the 1990s 'the NFDC entered into a strategic collaboration with Doordarshan to produce films' and that *Mammo* was made on a low budget.
27. Bhaskar and Allen, 96.
28. Benegal's films have often been categorised as part of 'Middle Cinema', a term that is used to describe a type of cinema that emerged in the mid-1970s and which was seen as a compromise between Indian art cinema and the mainstream.
29. William Van der Heide, ed., *Bollywood Babylon: Interviews with Shyam Benegal* (London: Berg, 2006), 174–5.
30. *Fiza*, directed by Khalid Mohamed (2000; India: Pradeep Guha). Written and directed by Mohamed, *Fiza*, starring Hrithik Roshan and Karisma Kapoor, explores the issue of Islamic terrorism in a mainstream context.
31. Rabia Umar Ali, 'Muslim Women and the Partition of India: A Historiographical Silence', *Islamic Studies* 48, no. 3 (2009): 427.
32. Harenda, 128.
33. Ibid., 128.
34. Priya Kumar, 'Testimonies of Loss and Memory', *International Journal of Postcolonial Studies* 1, no. 12 (1999): 213.
35. *Mammo*, directed by Shyam Benegal (1994; India: NFDC/Doordarshan).
36. Harenda.
37. Bhaskar and Allen, 310.
38. Kumar, 'Testimonies of Loss and Memory', 213.
39. Benegal, 'Issues and Censorship in Indian Cinema', 285.
40. Bhaskar and Allen, 314.
41. Harenda, 132.
42. Ibid., 131.
43. Ibid., 131.
44. Ilsa Abdul Razzak, 'The State and the Subaltern: Bureaucratic Violence and Agency in Partition Cinema', paper presented at the Saida Waheed Gender Initiative in Lahore, 2018, 1–15, <https://swgi.lums.edu.pk/sites/default/files/user376/panel_1_the_state_and_the_subaltern.pdf>, accessed 1 September 2021.
45. Razzak, 12.
46. Datta, 172.
47. Bhaskar and Allen, 306.
48. *Bharat Ek Khoj (The Discovery of India)*, directed by Shyam Benegal (1988; India: Doordarshan). *Bharat Ek Khoj* was an epic undertaking for Benegal. Made for Doordarshan, the series comprised fifty-three episodes and covered the history of India from the Vedic era to independence. The cast and crew featured many of the names associated with parallel cinema including Om Puri, Vanraj Bhatia, Shama Zaidi and Naseeruddin Shah.

CHAPTER 10

Adapting Gandhi/Kasturba in *The Making of the Mahatma*

Vivek Sachdeva

Mahatma Gandhi has inspired various political activists, writers and filmmakers across the world. Mark Robson's *Nine Hours to Rama* (1963), Richard Attenborough's *Gandhi* (1982), Shyam Benegal's *The Making of the Mahatma* (1996) and Feroz Abbas Khan's *Gandhi, My Father* (2007) are all well-known films about Gandhi, and Rachel Dwyer lists a few short films and documentaries as well. These constitute a list of cinematic works through which different aspects of Gandhi's personality have been explored. Likewise, Louis Fischer and Joseph Lelyveld have authored books on Mahatma Gandhi, and various visual artists have paid tribute to him through their art. However, in our patriarchal world, artistic representations of Mahatma's wife, Kasturba Gandhi, are few and far between. She, who had participated in the freedom struggle along with Mahatma Gandhi, has been under-explored and under-represented to the extent of neglect. Except for a couple of plays[1] and books on Kasturba Gandhi, for example, Neelima Dalmia Adhar's *The Secret Diary of Kasturba* (2016), Arun Gandhi's *The Forgotten Woman: The Untold Story of Kastur, Wife of Mahatma Gandhi* (1981) and N. C. Beohar's *Kasturba Gandhi: The Silent Sufferer* (2018), few books about her exist. Vinod Ganatra[2] proposed to make a documentary about Kasturba Gandhi's life, but his proposal was rejected by the Films Division of India. This rejection was unequivocally criticised by the filmmaker and by Tushar Gandhi, Mahatma Gandhi's great-grandson.[3] Kasturba Gandhi suffers from a serious intellectual and creative neglect by Indian society. Arun Gandhi, the son of Manilal Gandhi, Kasturba's second son, depended upon oral histories to reconstruct his mother's narrative for the book he wrote about her. With few historical or literary works available, Kasturba Gandhi, as a historical figure, stands marginalised in historiography and cultural studies. The present chapter looks at the representation of Kasturba Gandhi in Benegal's film *The Making of the Mahatma* (1996) and through it attempts to compensate for her intellectual neglect.

Acknowledging cinema as an influential art form, the Indian state intervened in its production by establishing the Film Finance Corporation (FFC) and the National Film Development Corporation (NDFC) to promote cinema in the country. The Indian New Wave films carried out the socialist agenda of the state.[4] The filmmakers of the Indian New Wave, which started as a movement in the late 1960s and early 1970s, presented a different image of women and India on screen. Shyam Benegal, an important filmmaker of the Indian New Wave or New Cinema, in his long career spanning over more than forty years, has made films on various questions, challenges and issues that India as a nation-state has had to confront since Independence. Through his realist aesthetics, Shyam Benegal has made socially relevant and politically charged cinema focusing on the issues of the lower castes, women and other minority groups of India. Despite the fact that most of Benegal's films were not sponsored by the FFC and NDFC, unlike films of other filmmakers of the Indian New Wave, his work has been understood as carrying the state's modernising and developmental agenda.[5] He has made films to 'address the need for women's emancipation, a casteless society, an end to feudal relationship',[6] the exploitation of the Dalits, the status of women in the Indian society and the empowerment of the downtrodden. His films are known for their 'sustained engagement with dynamics of power and powerless, domination, and subordination'.[7] His films do not glorify India, nor do they indulge in jingoism. Rather from the vantage point of the margins, his films offer alternative imaginaries of India as a nation-(state).

Benegal offers myriad images of India as a nation-state from the point of view of the lower castes and women in his cinema. He has told stories of the lower castes and women in feudal society and has also dealt with the question of the identity of women in the wake of modernity in India. In mainstream Hindi cinema, women were portrayed as being subservient to men in most of the narratives and were given stereotypical roles such as the ideal mother, ideal wife or idealised suffering mother, or as submitting to the pressure of the dominant male gaze and voyeurism in cinema. As such, they are desired as objects. Moreover, the sexualised female body is shown as 'a sexual *subject* who articulates her sexuality through image, values, behavior and desires in Indian cinema'.[8] But in Benegal's cinema, women confront Indian patriarchy, they struggle for their identity and are given agency to resist the oppressive patriarchal structure.[9] Compared with Satyajit Ray for his masterly control over the medium, ever since *Ankur* Benegal has narrated stories of the marginalised, oppressed and silenced sections of Indian society. Through his progressive cinema, he has questioned the existing oppressive social and political order and has lent a voice to the voiceless. Benegal, while telling stories of men in different layers of Indian society, has portrayed women sensitively in his films. In films like *Ankur* (*The Seedling*, 1974), *Nishant* (*Night's End*, 1975), *Manthan* (*The Churning*, 1976), *Bhumika* (*The Role*, 1977) and *Mandi* (*Market Place*, 1983), he has focused on the problems faced by women in rural, urban and in *moffussil* (suburban) spaces. *Ankur*, *Nishant* and *Manthan* are the narratives of women's oppression and exploitation in rural spaces. *Bhumika* is a narrative of a woman's search for identity in a male-dominated urban space and *Mandi* portrays the challenges faced by courtesans in a small town near Hyderabad in the wake of social and economic changes.

Made in 1996, *The Making of Mahatma* stands out for two reasons – first, it tells the story of Gandhi's stay in South Africa, which is a lesser known narrative in the popular nationalist imagination in India; second, the filmmaker has given Kasturba Gandhi's voice and point of view to the narrative while telling the story of Mahatma Gandhi, which is important from a narratological point of view. It would be erroneous to generalise that the film focuses primarily on Kasturba Gandhi – it does not, as Mahatma Gandhi enjoys centrality in the narrative – but even so, Kasturba Gandhi's portrayal in the film invites critical attention. Made immediately after the period of apartheid in South Africa, the film is based on the book *Apprenticeship of a Mahatma* by Fatima Meer (1970), an academic and anti-apartheid writer. Immediately after the apartheid period was over, Fatima Meer approached Shyam Benegal to make a film about either Nelson Mandela or Gandhi. Shyam Benegal agreed to make a film about Mahatma Gandhi. This chapter will first discuss the relation between films and history, and second compare the representation of Kasturba Gandhi as it appears in the book to her role in the film, within the frame of adaptation studies.

Horizons of film adaptation have grown wider over a period of time. From an initial focus on the adaptation of a literary work – a novel or a play – into film, now an increasingly wide range of narrative forms, such as memoirs, autobiographies, real incidents, or the life story of a famous historical personality, are being adapted to the screen. Films based on historical personalities or their biographies tend to adapt not only the book but also history,[10] placing history in the domain of popular culture. All kinds of writings have their own aesthetics and relationship with history. Despite the ontological differences between aesthetics and history, historical biographies narrativise history while telling the story of a historical personality. They are an important source in postmodern historiography. Films based on the life story of famous historical personalities, which I call Historical Biopics,[11] structure their narrative around a historical personality and thus contribute to the ever-growing narrative of history. J. Dudley Andrew's question, 'Why not treat historical films as adaptation?'[12] and Thomas Leitch's idea of the 'adaptive nature of historiography'[13] make a plausible argument to treat Historical Biopics as adaptations of history. Through Historical Biopics, the filmmaker simultaneously engages with narratives at three levels – one, the narrative of the source book; two, the narrative of history; and three, the narrative of the film, which becomes the medium and the site of negotiations with earlier narratives. The tripartite model is helpful to understand the engagement between the author (of both book and film), the narrative (of both book and film) and the history. By offering a new perspective and interpretation to history, a filmmaker also writes history with a camera. Establishing a critical bond with the camera, these adaptations try to fill 'gaps, silences, absences' and complement 'patterns revealed over long periods of time'.[14]

Different schools of historiography, such as the Anglo-American school, the *Annales* school, the semiologist school and the narratologist school, have deliberated on the relationship between narratives and history, expressing their diverging views on the subject. Hayden White, while commenting on the ideas given by narratologists like Genette and Barthes, emphasises the importance of studying narrative discourse even while doing history. Narratologists like Todorov, Genette and Roland Barthes agreed that narrative is a discourse, and Gadamer and Paul Ricoeur have studied narrative as a discourse of a 'special kind of time-consciousness'.[15] Narratology, as a discipline, would prefer to see film adaptation as an engagement with a narrative at the level of discourse. Adaptations, within the frame of narratology, are seen as creative and critical engagements with the narrative discourse, and not seen in terms of being primary or secondary. Since verbal text also has the visual dimension while the visual image of cinema has the sayable dimension, Jacques Rancière's concept of 'the sentence-image' understands adaptation in terms of negotiations between two kinds of images in verbal and cinematic texts. The sentence-image moves between the visible and the sayable to explore possibilities in the field of aesthetics and truth[16] across media.

In this chapter, using Linda Hutcheon's ideas of adaptation as interpretation, Historical Biopics are seen as an interpretation of not only the source book, but also of history. By offering a new understanding, the filmmaker contributes to the continuum of history, which is in a constant state of becoming. The relation between history and film has moved away from what has been criticised by historians as a 'misrepresentation of history'. This relation is not understood in terms of fidelity or accuracy; rather it is important to see what 'kind of historical thinking [. . .] takes place on the screen'.[17] The narrative of a film thus becomes the site where a new historical thinking, a reinterpretation of history and a re-writing of history, takes place. The real worth of the narrative does not lie in its form, but in its content. Through structuration of events in time and space, narratives offer a new viewpoint on history and a new meaning, which destabilises the monolithic and fixed discourse of history. Every narrative, fictional or non-fictional, verbal or cinematic, is the 'instrument with which the conflicting claim of the imaginary and the real are mediated, arbitrated, or resolved in a discourse'.[18] Questioning the notion of finality, every re-telling of history or historical narrative contributes to the pre-existing narrative of history either to fill gaps or to extend the discourse. Based on a book by Fatima Meer, *The Making of the Mahatma* by Shyam Benegal is a Historical Biopic. This chapter attempts to see how Shyam Benegal engages with Fatima Meer's narrative through his medium. The endeavour shall be to see how the film-maker's ideology influences representation of characters with special focus on Kasturba Gandhi and to discover what function this narrative plays in the cultural politics of India.

The adaptation of Fatima Meer's book in *The Making of the Mahatma* exhibits Shyam Benegal's ideological leaning towards giving voice to the voiceless. The film primarily narrativises events in the political, moral and spiritual growth of Gandhi. The film contributes to the body of work on Gandhi's life and ideas by telling a lesser known narrative of Gandhi's life. Nevertheless, Shyam Benegal has told Gandhi's story from Kasturba's point of view as she witnesses Gandhi's transformation from an ordinary man and a stumbling lawyer to the leader of India's struggle for independence. It was in South Africa that Gandhi found his spirit of struggle and mode of protest against British imperialism and the film narrates Gandhi's confronting of colonial injustice, racism and violence there. His experiences in South Africa were instrumental in his transformation. Finding his voice of truth, its strength and righteousness in the struggle against the injustice of the British Empire, Mohandas Karamchand Gandhi eventually became Mahatma Gandhi. Gandhi's stay of twenty-one years in South Africa was his journey of self-discovery, during which he came face to face with racism and the violence inherent in the enterprise of European colonialism. Gandhi had gone to South Africa to solve a family feud between two brothers, but came back to India a mature leader, ready to solve the problems of India under the rule of the British Empire. By telling the story of the father of the nation, Shyam Benegal has paid a rich tribute to a great personality. By telling a lesser known narrative of Gandhi's life, the film contributes to the larger narrative of Gandhi's contribution to India's struggle for independence. Kasturba Gandhi was with him on his journey, and witnessed the evolution of Mohandas into Mahatma, but his personal chemistry with his wife brings to the surface contradictions in the personality of the great Mahatma. Although Benegal gives us a narrative of a man who evolved into the Mahatma, the filmmaker also highlights his weaknesses and limitations. Gandhi's confrontations and constant negotiations with Kasturba were equally instrumental in his spiritual growth. Kasturba in the film is not a submissive, docile wife who would keep her lips sealed and follow the great man; rather, she is shown as a woman who expresses her disagreements with Gandhi on various issues. Using her vantage point, the filmmaker deconstructs the great political leader to bring to the surface contradictions in his personality.

Fatima Meer begins her book with the family background and childhood of Mahatma Gandhi, establishing connections between Mahatma Gandhi's personality and the values he had inherited from his father and grandfather, who were 'shrewd in statecraft'.[19] His grandfather had a 'technique in politics, as he had a passion for justice and his trait was strong in his son Kaba,[20] and would pursue Mohandas to the end of his life'.[21] The man who later played a decisive role in the history of a country was, as a child, scared of the dark. His fear of the dark assumed many shapes such as 'thieves and serpents and ghosts'.[22] The scared child would be comforted by repetition of the name of Rama. Fatima Meer recounts events from Gandhi's childhood to his marriage, studies in England and his struggle to establish himself as a lawyer before going to South Africa. Shyam Benegal's film, on the other hand, does not give any information about Gandhi's childhood. It begins with Mohandas Karamchand Gandhi[23] getting an invitation from Seth Dada Abdullah in South Africa. The opening shot of the film shows Mohandas Gandhi reading a letter of invitation aloud, sitting on a swing almost in the centre of the frame, while Kasturba Gandhi is sitting to his right (Figure 10.1). The *mise-en-scène* establishes the patriarchal order of the society that Mahatma Gandhi was a part of. Kasturba disapproves of Mohandas Gandhi's going to South Africa as he'll be no more than a *munshi* or a clerk there. In their relationship, Kasturba voices her opinions freely and fearlessly with a certain commanding tone in her voice. A loving wife, Kasturba doesn't want Mohandas Gandhi to leave India. Mohandas is able to have his way. While expressing her opinion, she walks and takes a seat next to Gandhi on the swing. The opening scene establishes the social order in which Gandhi and Kasturba will operate; one which empowers men. Simultaneously, it also hints at Kasturba's subjectivity; someone who can negotiate her space in the patriarchal order.

In the next scene, Gandhi is in South Africa and his tryst with history begins. The short opening scene sets the tone, giving viewers a glimpse into the dynamics of Mohandas and Kasturba's relationship. Shyam Benegal has not made a hagiographic narrative glorifying Mahatma Gandhi in his film, nor has he portrayed Kasturba Gandhi in a linear fashion. In the film, Kasturba Gandhi is an assertive and strong-willed woman with independent views. Despite the baggage of values of a Hindu wife that she carries and according to which she is supposed to follow her husband, she is not a completely meek and submissive woman. She has a mind of her own and asserts her

Figure 10.1 Gandhi reads out the letter to Kasturba.

individuality whenever required. Ironically, despite these qualities, she lives in the shadow of her husband. In some narratives Kasturba Gandhi has been portrayed as one who had completely surrendered before Mahatma Gandhi, losing her individuality to the overpowering personality of her husband. Arun Gandhi admits in his book that his grandmother had been misrepresented by Mahatma Gandhi and other biographers. According to Arun Gandhi:

> I find that Bapu has done Ba a disservice in his autobiographical writings by his frequent depictions of her as meek and submissive. Such characterization of Ba have widely been accepted and repeated by Gandhi's biographers. But in my view she was never as spineless and long suffering, as tolerant of abuse, as altogether helpless and long-suffering, as Bapu (and his biographers) would have us believe.[24]

It is the same image of Kasturba Gandhi as a meek and submissive woman that is found even in Richard Attenborough's film *Gandhi*, in which she is more of a silent follower of Mahatma Gandhi, with almost no agency. Yet Kasturba Gandhi in the narratives of Arun Gandhi, Fatima Meer, Neelima Dalmia Adhar and Shyam Benegal's film emerges as a different woman. She is not a 'silent sufferer', but a firm and confident woman. Fatima Meer makes clear distinctions between Mohandas Gandhi's and Kasturba Gandhi's personality, even when they were children. Following the traditional customs, they were married at a very young age. In the early days of their marriage, when passion was the driving force, the young Mohandas Gandhi in the spasm of aggression

> wished to possess and control her. But Kastur or Kasturba was not easily controlled. Besides, while the young Gandhi was a boy, loitering with other boys; she was a woman who had assumed adult responsibilities and become a junior partner with his mother in running the household.[25]

Mohandas Gandhi, as a child, was scared of the dark, whereas Kastur would remain unperturbed. Knowing his fear of the dark, she would rather smartly put out the light to keep the young husband away from her.

Kasturba Gandhi, or Kasturba or Ba, was brought up according to the traditional Hindu ethos of Gujarat. Her parents' family also lived in Porbandar and their house was very near the house of the Gandhis. In traditional Indian society in which family rather than individual values take the driving seat, Kastur kept her individuality intact even while following the traditions. According to Arun Gandhi, she was 'always proud and free. Those who remembered her have testified that Ba would never allow anyone to dictate to her – not even her husband'.[26] Arun Gandhi's description of Kasturba challenges the stereotype of traditional Indian women who are believed to have surrendered their individuality to their husbands. By contrast, Kasturba Gandhi had the strength to question and challenge her husband when she felt he was in the wrong. In the film, she voices her dissentious opinion to raise fundamental questions about her status in the family 'Just because I am your wife . . . I have put up with this non-sense?'[27] (Figure 10.2), or about acknowledging her work at home as labour and service to the society: 'Here I work night and day. Is it no service?'[28]

Arun Gandhi narrates another incident in which his grandmother questioned Gandhi and challenged his self-proclaimed position of authority. It happened when Kasturba, a newly wedded bride, was only thirteen years old. Mohandas Gandhi had instructed Kasturba to not go anywhere without informing him. But the very next day, Kasturba had gone to the temple along with her mother-in-law and other women. On being berated by Mohandas, Kasturba defied her authoritative husband and left him speechless by asking a simple and fundamental question: 'Are you suggesting that I should obey you and not your mother?'[29] On various occasions, she questions Gandhi and disagrees with him. An intelligent and perceptive woman, Kasturba Gandhi noticed each and every change coming about in Gandhi's personality, be it Mohandas Gandhi's romancing the idea of educating Kasturba, his experiments with meat-eating under the

Figure 10.2 Kasturba saying to Gandhi, 'Just because I am your wife . . . I have to put up with this non-sense?'

influence of Sheik Mehtab, his losing interest in studies after marriage, or the changes in his personality following his father's death. It cannot be denied that Kasturba was living under the towering personality of Mahatma Gandhi, which meant that her own personality wasn't allowed to bloom to its fullest, yet in spite of Gandhi's great presence, Kasturba Gandhi was able to carve out some space for herself. She exercised her limited agency in both personal and public spheres. Hers is a story of constant negotiations between individuality and customs. Her identity embodies the conflict between two centres. She represents the constant conflict between her free spirit and the ideal of a good Hindu wife that she was expected to live up to. Seen from Kasturba Gandhi's point of view, Mahatma Gandhi's own weaknesses and shortcomings are revealed. As shown in the film, in the interpersonal equation between Mohandas Gandhi and Kasturba, paradoxes in the former's personality come to the surface. Mohandas Gandhi, who practises the passive non-violence method in the public sphere, acts like an autocrat, self-imposing and sometimes in a completely unreasonable manner, in his personal sphere. In the public sphere, Gandhi is 'open to negotiations with his opponents',[30] but in his personal sphere, he is a rigid, 'hard and uncaring man'.[31] Driven by rage, Gandhi once tried to throw Kasturba out of the house, and on another occasion, imposing his whims and ideas onto his wife, he forced her to clean the chamber pot. On yet another occasion, Gandhi announces that he has taken a vow to practice complete abstinence from sex while being married. Being a Hindu wife, Kasturba agrees to the idea, but her pain is shown by the filmmaker when she turns her face. The close-up shows the sting and unhappiness Kasturba felt on the de-sexing their marriage and on not having been consulted on a matter that concerned both the husband and the wife equally. Neelima Dalmia Adhar sums up Kasturba's emotions with, '*it was your decision to ravage my body at will; now it is your decision to ravage my mind. So be it Mohandas, so be it. Brother and sister we shall be.*'[32] In the power dynamics between Gandhi and Kasturba, Mahatma acquired the position of superiority and authority by exercising abstinence and penance. The high moral position empowered Gandhi to dominate his wife and also gave him the strength for his political struggles. Gandhi is shown to be focused more on his political battles, and the inner growth needed to fight these battles, than the price he was asking Kasturba to pay.

Kasturba, less educated than Gandhi, had a very simple understanding of religion. She could not understand the complex thought process behind Gandhi's mixing religion with new morality and politics. According to her, Mohandas's views were not in the line with conventional religion, and she became disturbed when Mohandas brought his newly found morality into the household. Kasturba found it difficult to accept the intrusion of Gandhi's ideas into her space to defile 'it in a manner she found intolerable'.[33] Whether it was Gandhi's attitude towards untouchability, the issue of cleaning the chamber pot or keeping the jewellery given to her by people in South Africa, Kasturba was always on tenterhooks with Gandhi. Despite their differences, she supported him in his struggle and in practising his ideas. She supported him out of her own convictions, not because as an ideal wife that was what she was supposed to do. 'I was not emulating him in his predefined passions and goals, I was merely being loyal to the essence of my calling and soul, a truth that he would never know.'[34] In fact she 'eventually became his most devoted disciple, but did create space for herself. She didn't allow him to walk over her'.[35]

Shyam Benegal has explored different dimensions of Kasturba Gandhi's personality while telling the story of Mahatma Gandhi. As with female protagonists of his other films, Shyam Benegal in *The Making of the Mahatma* does not portray Kasturba in a monochromatic fashion. Kasturba Gandhi suffers at the hands of Mahatma owing to his temper, whims and ego, which reveal contradictions and human weaknesses in Mahatma Gandhi. Kasturba, being his wife, witnesses his growth and also survives him. Instead of glorifying the figure of the father of the nation, Shyam Benegal provides a critical understanding of Mahatma Gandhi's character from Kasturba Gandhi's point of view. Kasturba Gandhi has multidimensional subjectivity. She is a confrontationist; she contests, resists, while being an understanding mother and a compassionate wife. As a mother, she understands her elder son's sentiments better than her husband does. She and Hari Lal are sailing in the same boat when it comes to having an opinion about Gandhi as a father, while she empathises with Gandhi's thoughts and situation as well. As a wife, she does not succumb to the whims and temper of Mahatma Gandhi just because she was expected to play a good Hindu wife. She asserts herself on various occasions to preserve her dignity. Through her moments of conflict with Gandhi and the limited space given to her in the film, the filmmaker has succeeded in critiquing patriarchy through a focus on Mohandas Gandhi's ventures.

Kasturba is an important character in the film. While adapting a book authored by a female writer, Shyam Benegal has given Kasturba's voiceover to the narrative – replacing the female point of view of the author with the female voice in the film. Kasturba is a witness to as well as the narrator of Gandhi's transformation from an ordinary man to an extraordinary man. Kasturba witnesses Gandhi changing, growing and 'mutating along with these historically shifting contexts'[36] and while witnessing Mohandas Gandhi grow into Mahatma Gandhi, Kasturba Gandhi also grows as an individual. Their stay in South Africa results in the growth of their respective moral and spiritual beings. Initially, as described by Kasturba in the film, Gandhi's ways were not easy 'either on the children or me'.[37] She begins to understand her husband and his ways better. Historically speaking, Kasturba Gandhi was not merely a witness to history in the making, she was also an active participant in it. She grew as a political activist. When Mahatma Gandhi was in jail, she would take charge of the activities of *satyagraha*. She became one of the first women *satyagrahis* to go to prison in South Africa; a role she continued to play in India too. She emerged as an inspiring personality in South Africa.

The narratives by Meer and Benegal 'are implicitly proposing an understanding of historical narrative in which the primacy of truth claimed by facticity yields to equally pressing claims of interior life'.[38] The image that emerges in the narrative of Fatima Meer's book, and Shyam Benegal's adaptation of the same, contributes to the narrative of history not by adding to the existing body of factual information on Mahatma Gandhi's life, but by sharing with the readers and viewers an alternative perspective on this life. Through adaptation, there are constant negotiations between the verbal narrative and the cinematic narrative through the image, which both narratives embody. Both narratives bring a lesser known narrative of Mahatma Gandhi's life in South Africa into the public domain. The female author behind the biography of Mahatma Gandhi understands and imagines Kasturba Gandhi from a woman's point of view, which puts the image of Kasturba in conflict with the image of Kasturba Gandhi as found in Mahatma Gandhi's autobiography and Richard Attenborough's movie, *Gandhi*. Shyam Benegal's film establishes a complex relationship between 'subject, author and reader'[39] by looking at Gandhi from a different angle. Historical thinking in the biography as well as the film is the result of dialectical thinking between earlier available narratives and the film. The film provides the 'instrument of the angel'[40] to look at an important historical personality from a different point of view.

Seen from Kasturba Gandhi's perspective, Gandhi had many personality flaws. Kasturba, who was never a weak and submissive person as a child, had a mixed relationship with her husband. Although illiterate, she had a tremendous understanding of human nature and impressive leadership qualities. She participated in the freedom struggle and organised women's participation in the *satyagraha*. The paradox lies in the fact that whatever space she carved out for herself was provided to her by her husband. Even while living in the shadow of her husband, on various occasions she asserted herself strongly in front of him. Benegal portrays the intriguing personality and testing circumstances of Kasturba Gandhi, proving her strength in her reticence. Gandhi was gradually rising in political stature, empowered by his notions of dharma and righteousness in the public and private sphere. His position was further strengthened by patriarchy, which disempowered Kasturba Gandhi. Shyam Benegal, in his film, has shown the tensions between the powerful and the powerless in the domestic sphere where, as a woman, Kasturba Gandhi is constantly fighting for her space and identity while negotiating with the surname Gandhi attached to her own. The film is as much Kasturba's narrative as it is Gandhi's.

Note: All dialogue translated by the author.

NOTES

1. Examples of plays on Kasturba Gandhi include, *Jagdamba* directed by Sanjay Maggirwar; *Kasturba*, a Gujrati play directed by Aditi Desai; *Kasturba aur Gandhi* directed by Arvind Gaur.
2. Vinod Ganatra is the director of *Heda Hoda* (2003), *Lukka Chuppi* (2006) and *Harun–Arun* (2009).
3. Tushar Gandhi came out clearly criticising the decision of the Film Division, saying that Kasturba Gandhi has been 'criminally neglected'. For details, please see Bharti Dubey, 'Film on Kasturba Gandhi fails to Get Nod', *The Times of India*, 8 March 2013, <https://timesofindia.indiatimes.com/india/Film-on-Kasturba-Gandhi-fails-to-get-nod/articleshow/18857740.cms>, accessed 1 September 2021.
4. For details, please see M. Madhava Prasad, *Ideology of the Hindi Film: A Historical Construction* (Delhi: Oxford University Press, 1998).
5. M. Madhava Prasad and Ashish Rajdhyaksha have studied Shyam Benegal's cinema with said perspective. For details, please see Prasad and Rajadhyaksha, *Indian Cinema in the Time of Celluloid: From Bollywood to the Emergency* (New Delhi: Tulika Books, 2009).
6. Anuradha Dingwaney Needham, *New Indian Cinema in Post-Independence India: The Cultural Work of Shyam Benegal's Films* (New York: Routledge, 2016), 3.
7. Needham, 2.

8. Shoma A. Chatterjee, 'The Evolution of Representing Female Sexuality in Hindi Cinema 1991–2010', in *Routledge Handbook of Indian Cinemas*, ed. K. Moti Gokulsing and Wimal Dissanayake (New York: Routledge, 2013), 180.
9. No doubt, early mainstream Hindi cinema has portrayed a wide variety of female characters. Films such as *Achut Kanya* (directed by Franz Osten, 1936), *Pyaasa* (directed by Guru Dutt, 1957), *Naya Daur* (directed by B. R. Chopra, 1957), *Andaz* (directed by Mehboob Khan, 1949), *Aurat* (directed by Mehboob Khan, 1940) and *Mother India* (directed by Mehboob Khan, 1957) have shown different dimensions of women on screen, yet the ideology of patriarchy can be seen working in the undercurrents of these films, and also determines their characterisation and narrative patterns.
10. Hayden White, *The Content of the Form: Narrative Discourse and Historical Representation* (Baltimore, MD and London: Johns Hopkins University Press, 1990). Along the lines of White, History here is taken as a narrative.
11. As historical movies and biopics are two established genres of film, I propose to call films telling the life story of historical personalities Historical Biopics, as this encompasses both dimensions. In Historical Biopics, an individual's life story is intertwined with a historical narrative. The term makes such films distinct from what are commonly known as biopics.
12. J. Dudley Andrew, 'Adapting Cinema to History: A Revolution in the Making', in *A Companion to Literature and Film*, ed. Robert Stam and Alessandra Raengo (Malden and Oxford: Blackwell, 2004), 191.
13. Thomas Leitch, 'History as Adaptation', in *The Politics of Adaptation: Media Convergence and Ideology*, ed. Dan Hassler-Forest and Pascal Nicklas (Basingstoke: Palgrave Macmillan, 2015), 7.
14. Kathryn Millard, 'Projected Lives: A Mediation on Biography and Cinematic Space', in *Screening the Past*, ed. Tony Barta (London: Praeger, 1998), 231.
15. White, 31.
16. Truth here is not understood as empirical or scientific truth. It also entails political, social and moral truth with which art engages.
17. Robert A. Rosenstone, *History on Films/Films on History* (London and New York: Pearson Longman, 2006), 15.
18. White, 4.
19. Fatima Meer, *Apprenticeship of a Mahatma: A Biography of M. K. Gandhi, 1869–1914*, 2nd rev. ed. (Durban: Institute of Black Research/Madiba Publishers, 1994), 2.
20. Mahatma Gandhi's father, Karamchand Uttamchand Gandhi, was also known as Kaba.
21. Meer, 2.
22. Ibid., 3.
23. Mohandas Karamchand Gandhi is the full name of Mahatma Gandhi. In this chapter, Mohandas Gandhi will be preferred over Mahatma Gandhi as the film tells events of his growth from Mohandas Gandhi to Mahatma Gandhi.
24. Arun Gandhi, *The Forgotten Woman: The Untold Story of Kastur Gandhi* (USA: 1998, 2007, 2015; Kindle), 52.
25. Meer, 9.
26. Gandhi, Chapter 3, Loc 440.
27. *The Making of the Mahatma*, directed by Shyam Benegal (1996; India), 00:46:30.
28. *The Making of the Mahatma*, 00:55:40.
29. Gandhi, Chapter 3, Loc 448.
30. Needham, 136.
31. As opined by Kasturba in the film. *The Making of the Mahatma*, 00:55:58.
32. Neelima Dalmia Adhar, *The Secret Diary of Kasturba* (New Delhi: Tranquebar Press, 2016), 176. Emphasis in the original.

33. Meer, 47.
34. Adhar, 147.
35. Benegal to William Van der Heide, *Bollywood Babylon: Interviews with Shyam Benegal* (Oxford: Berg, 2006), 157.
36. David Martin-Jones, *Deleuze and World Cinema* (London and New York: Continuum, 2011), 74.
37. *The Making of the Mahatma*, 00:44:10.
38. Janet Sternburg, 'Long Exposures: A Poetics of Film and History', in *Screening the Past*, ed. Tony Barta (London: Pragaer, 1998), 239. Sternburg has developed her argument of relation between history, film and memory in a different context. I am aware that the phrase 'interior life' in Sternburg's writing means something different as it borders on experiences of life and memory. However, in the present chapter the phrase has been retained to connote Mahatma Gandhi's personal life, which may not have direct connections with memory.
39. Millard, 232.
40. Sternburg, 245.

CHAPTER II

In Search of Zubeidaa

Ramit Samaddar

The anti-Muslim sentiment that engulfed India in the early 1990s, following the demolition of Ayodhya's Babri Masjid by right-wing Hindu militants on 6 December 1992 and the subsequent Hindu-Muslim riots in Bombay, prompted Shyam Benegal to articulate his profound compassion for the Muslim minority through the medium of cinema. Shaken to the core, the secular-minded auteur made three critically acclaimed films – *Mammo* (1994), *Sardari Begum* (1996), and *Zubeidaa* (2001) – relating the soul-stirring tales of three Muslim women. The eponymous protagonist of each film is doubly marginalised as a Muslim and a woman. Although Benegal competently dramatises this double marginalisation, it is not the feature that renders these films significant. Rather, the significance of each film lies in its remarkable delineation of the strength of spirit that characterises its heroine. Mammo, Sardari Begum and Zubeidaa are women who strain against the stifling barriers set around them. They are rebels who dare to carve out their own destinies, for better or worse. Together, they remind us that Benegal, celebrated as the trailblazing father of parallel cinema, is a progressive feminist who unflinchingly prioritises agency-seeking women in his meaningful cinema, delving deep into their complex psyches with exemplary sensitivity. While the Bollywood industry is crowded with liberal male filmmakers winning plaudits for churning out women-centric classics, no one, in the opinion of a Benegal aficionado like me, matches Benegal in his clear-sighted exploration of the position of women in modern-day India.

Although the present chapter focuses on *Zubeidaa*, some mention must be made of *Mammo* and *Sardari Begum*, especially because both Mammo and Sardari Begum make brief appearances in *Zubeidaa*. *Mammo* revolves around Mehmooda Begum aka Mammo (Farida Jalal), a dynamic veil-clad Muslim widow, who suddenly arrives in Bombay from Pakistan to reside with Fayyazi

(Surekha Sikri), her sister, and Riyaz (Amit Phalke), the adolescent grandson of Fayyazi. The film engagingly chronicles the day-to-day life of Mammo and her tireless attempts to extend her visa as a foreign national. Misfortune strikes when Mammo is unceremoniously deported to Pakistan by the police as she has overstayed her terms of visit. The film, however, concludes with Mammo's miraculous return to Bombay after many years to an aged Fayyazi and adult Riyaz (Rajit Kapoor) and her strategic declaration of herself as dead – she stages her own demise through a fabricated death certificate – so that she can continue to stay in India thereafter. Like *Mammo*, *Sardari Begum* depicts the life of a feisty Muslim woman. It deals with the relentless endeavours of Sardari (Smriti Mishra and Kirron Kher), a classical singer, to emancipate herself from the shackles of oppressive gender norms as she single-mindedly pursues a musical career. The film is structured around the recreation of Sardari's unusual life, after her accidental death during an incident of communal violence, through the recollections of a host of characters, either known to her personally or associated with her professionally. Besides Sardari, there are two other important female characters in the film: Tehzeeb Abbasi (Rajina Raj Bisaria), Sardari's niece, who, like her aunt, evinces a striking independence from moth-eaten social mores, and Sakina (Rajeshwari Sachdev), Sardari's daughter, who vehemently resists incorporation into her mother's vocation only to become a singer after Sardari's untimely passing.

Zubeidaa, a period drama, required a budget much larger than what Benegal raised for *Mammo* and *Sardari Begum*. Benegal initially approached Plus Channel, which produced *Sardari Begum*, to hire prominent Bollywood stars for the cast. However, most A-list male actors rejected the film because of the female-centric plot and Benegal's nascent plan with Plus Channel came to nothing. In 1999, Benegal was introduced to Farouq Rattonsey, who had produced only two films before and who conceded to finance the ambitious project. The hunt for a capable actress willing to essay the titular role came to an end when Benegal signed Karisma Kapoor, the premier Bollywood actress of the time. Kapoor charged a surprisingly low fee for the film, the reason being that she did not want to miss out on the rewarding opportunity of working under the ace direction of Benegal in a challenging role that would showcase her acting prowess. For her incredibly nuanced performance, Kapoor won the coveted Filmfare Critics Award for Best Actress in 2002. Casting a mainstream actress like Kapoor as Zubeidaa also ensured a touch of glamour for Benegal's film, something further accentuated by the crew's spectacular creation of the bygone era needed for the film's early 1950s setting. Benegal's keen eye for historical accuracy is patently evident in the film reminding us of the famous words of Lionel Trilling: 'pastness is a factor of great importance'.[1] Describing the period-authentic *mise-en-scène* of *Zubeidaa*, Shoma A. Chatterji remarks:

The ... setting on location for *Zubeidaa* was Ram Niwas Mahal in Jaipur for the Jodhpur segment in 1999. The walls of the original palace were re-worked to give them a touch of historical authenticity. The walls had been decorated and painted with intricate motifs, old sepia-tinted photographs of royal hunts were put up on the walls, and a portrait of the prince ... dominated one end of the room.[2]

Clearly, *Zubeidaa* was mounted on a grander scale than other Benegal movies. Rajan Kothari, a noted cinematographer who shot the film within a relatively short span of time, is of the opinion that the allotment of a bigger budget enabled him and Benegal to turn *Zubeidaa* into an aesthetically pleasing cinematic product:

> Shyambabu likes to use modern technique. We used a lot of crane and trolley shots. He is extremely good with *mise-en-scène*. We had four-to-five minute shots in single takes. We used filters to get the period look without looking dated. *Zubeidaa* does not look like it was shot in fifty days ... He is extremely disciplined and gives precise instructions so there is no spillover. He is also very good at incorporating suggestions in his scheme of things. I do a lot of work in the mainstream industry, but doing a film with Shyam is like rejuvenation every time.[3]

Yet, despite being one of his costliest ventures, *Zubeidaa*, according to Benegal, remains true to his 'creative sensibilities':

> Whatever the genre of cinema, you cannot go beyond or against your own creative sensibilities. The range of your vocabulary can be flexible, but you can't defy your sensibility. If something does not move you as a film-maker, it is unlikely to move the audience.[4]

Zubeidaa had one of the biggest releases of 2001, including an international premiere. Yash Raj Films distributed the film simultaneously in India and abroad. It ran for twelve weeks in the UK. alone, grossing around £1,75,000.[5] The film also earned praise with its screenings at several film festivals across the world and is now readily available on DVD and online.

Zubeidaa marks Benegal's third successive collaboration with Khalid Mohamed. After penning well-wrought screenplays for *Mammo* and *Sardari Begum*, Mohamed wrote the script of *Zubeidaa* loosely modelled on the real-life story of his late mother, the starlet Zubeida Begum. A Shia Muslim, Zubeida voluntarily converted to Hinduism, following monotheistic Arya Samaj rituals to marry Maharaja Hanwant Singh of Jodhpur in 1950, adopted the name Vidya Rani and shifted to Jodhpur leaving behind Mohamed (her son from her first marriage) with her mother in Bombay. Two years later, she was killed in an air accident along with her husband at Godwar, Rajasthan. Mohamed was brought up by his maternal grandmother, and he had very limited information on his mother while growing up. He merely heard about her in bits and pieces from others. He never had a complete picture of the woman who birthed him. This fragmentary knowledge generated in him the overwhelming desire to undertake a journey into his mother's past, a woman who forayed into the alluring world of celluloid, but left her career and her infant son behind for love, a love that snatched her life instead. Benegal's film is a quasi-biographical rendition of the eventful story of this unconventional woman. For Mohamed, 'this autobiographical script was a process of therapy; for Benegal, it offered the trappings of a grand romance with a tragic end'.[6]

Zubeidaa centres on Zubeidaa's gown-up son Riyaz's (Rajit Kapoor) search for his dead mother, a sentimental subject tailor-made to suit the taste of an Indian audience brought up on a staple diet of maudlin melodramas. Riyaz attempts to solve the mystery that shrouds his mother by gleaning information about her from multiple sources. As a result, the narrative progresses through flashback sequences presenting slices of Zubeidaa's tumultuous life from her formative years to her unfortunate death. However, despite these long flashbacks, the narrative manages to march forward at a captivating pace. Riyaz's search brings him into contact with six individuals who knew Zubeidaa at various stages of her life. As Zubeidaa's mother, Fayyazi (Surekha Sikri) is an important figure in her life. She is a traditional Muslim woman who never disagrees with her authoritarian husband Suleiman Seth (Amrish

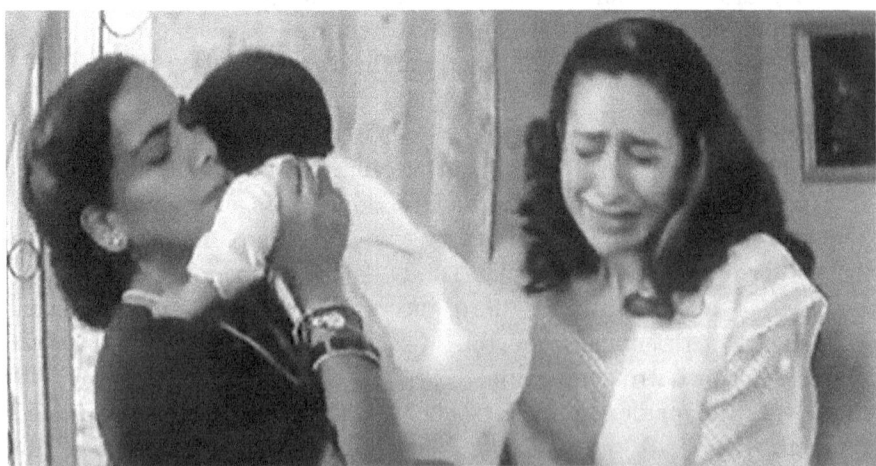

Figure 11.1 Fayyazi forcibly takes baby Riyaz from a visibly distraught Zubeidaa.

Puri), a film studio owner. Fayyazi's servile passivity is the root cause of her perennial unhappiness. Yet it is Fayyazi who takes the crucial decision of permitting her divorced daughter to marry Maharaja Vijayendra Singh (Manoj Bajpayee) of Fatehpur, also known as Victor, on the condition that Riyaz is left with her. The ever-submissive Fayyazi is thus responsible for driving a wedge between Zubeidaa and her infant son as she is against the idea of raising Riyaz in a Hindu household. Her old-fashioned value system alienates a mother from her child, although she believes herself to be acting on grounds that are morally right (Figure 11.1). It is from Fayyazi that Riyaz learns about his ill-fated mother's initial years.

Two other characters familiar with Zubeidaa before her second marriage are Hiralal and Rose Davenport. Riyaz's mission brings him to Hiralal (Shakti Kapoor) quite early on in the film. Once a sought-after choreographer, Hiralal has fallen on hard times and is living a hand-to-mouth existence. But despite his personal difficulties, he warmly reminisces to Riyaz about how he directed a teenage Zubeidaa for her only song-and-dance number in the unreleased, incomplete film *Banjaran Ladki* (*Gypsy Girl*). Like Hiralal, Rose (Lillete Dubey) hails from the film industry. A former actress (of Anglo-Indian descent) who enjoyed the patronage of Zubeidaa's father as his kept mistress, Rose is reduced to a cantankerous alcoholic who spends her idle hours talking to her cats in her tumbledown apartment. Chatterji offers an apt summarisation of her fascinating character:

> White-skinned and English speaking, Rose finds access to elitist social clubs, parties and polo matches graced by royalty smooth and easy. She is almost as free spirit [*sic*] as Zubeidaa is but not as much, since she accepts the position of 'keep' to her employer Seth, in whose B-Grade films she performs. It is like a pre-condition of her work in his films. When Riyaz comes to meet her, she is a ghost of her former self, without work or identity because post-Independence, the Anglo-Indian was gradually falling out of favour of the newly formed Indian government.[7]

Rose informs Riyaz that she extended a hand of friendship towards Zubeidaa because she understood Zubeidaa's needs more clearly than Fayyazi did. She tured out to be the architect of Zubeidaa's destiny when she introduced the latter to the already-married Victor during a polo match.

Significantly, Fayyazi and Rose are not the only women who tell Riyaz about his mother. Riyaz meets Victor's widow, Maharani Mandira Devi (Rekha) when he travels to Fatehpur. Mandira fondly recounts to Riyaz those early days when Zubeidaa entered the palace as a wide-eyed bride of the king. An epitome of majestic elegance, Mandira speaks flawless English and is perpetually dressed in exquisite chiffon saris matched with tasteful jewellery. Her nickname, Mandy (like Vijayendra's Victor), has a British ring to it, suggestive of the impact the coloniser's Western way of life had on the family. She commands great respect from her subjects, which proves that she is a beloved queen. Nevertheless, Mandira leads a restricted life within the high walls of the palace, playing her part of a quintessential 'angel in the house' – a term that comes from Coventry Patmore's 1854 poem of the same name, which extols domestic femininity as ideal womanhood. Her world is comprised of her husband and two children. Mandira stands as a hapless bystander when her husband takes a younger second wife who belongs to a different faith and has no royal credentials. Does she approve of this unexpected foisting of a *souten* (co-wife) on her after spending so many years of conjugal togetherness with her husband? Strangely enough, Benegal's film does not provide a definitive answer to this question.

Interestingly, Mandira's narrative about Zubeidaa is set against two male narratives. On the one hand, there is the account of a certain aide-de-camp, Girivar Singh (Ravi Jhankal), who is now the caretaker of the palace, which has been converted into a magnificent hotel. On the other hand, there is the narrative of Victor's dissolute brother Raja Uday Singh (Rahul Singh) who supervises the hotel business. While Girivar confides to Riyaz that Zubeidaa was a woman of loose morals who seduced their king and caused his premature death in a plane crash, Uday – who once made forceful sexual advances towards Zubeidaa demanding she have an illicit affair with him – barefacedly denies the very existence of Victor's second wife, thus pointing to the sheer effacement of Zubeidaa from the history of the Fatehpur royal dynasty. Although Riyaz's interactions with these diverse characters help the narrative forward, what these secondary but fully developed characters serve to illustrate is Benegal's remarkable insight into the complexities of human nature. Riyaz's interactions with these characters provide him with an array of biographical details which fill in some of the gaps in the intriguing tale of the life and death of Zubeidaa.

Benegal's heroine inhabits many subject positions throughout her life. First, she is the only child of an affluent Bombay-based Muslim family that consists of an overtly dominating father and a spineless mother who prevail over her and do not care for her. Both parents are demanding in their own ways: Suleiman expects Zubeidaa to strictly abide by his rules while Fayyazi pressurises Zubeidaa to unquestioning consent to whatever Suleiman does. For example, when Zubeidaa expresses resentment at her father's sudden announcement of her marriage to his friend's doctor son Mehboob Alam (Vinod Sharawat), Fayyazi coaxes her into accepting Suleiman's decision instead of siding with her: 'Don't behave childishly. You know we've to do as he wishes . . .

He is your father. When I got married, my father never asked me.' When an angry Zubeidaa protests, a crying Fayyazi emotionally blackmails her:

> Is it all my fault? Isn't it enough that he [Suleiman] takes his ire out on me? Now you too want to trouble me? Zubie, don't torture me – I can't bear all this. For God's sake ask for your father's forgiveness.

Zubeidaa cannot help but relent: 'Don't weep mother. I'll ask for father's forgiveness tomorrow, for your sake.'

Second, Zubeidaa is an aspiring actress enamoured by the colourful world of filmdom to which her father is professionally attached. She pines to partake in it so that she can demonstrate her potential as an artiste and may be also to impress her father. But her aspiration is nipped in the bud by her father. A man with a patriarchal mindset, Suleman believes that girls from respectable families do not work as actresses in films. According to him, working actresses disobey social propriety and are therefore immoral, although it is very ironic that the mistress he publicly flaunts is a flamboyant actress. Small wonder, then, that when he finds out that Zubeidaa is shooting for a song-and-dance sequence under the guidance of Hiralal, he rudely pulls her away, turning a deaf ear to her livid protestations.

Third, Zubeidaa is a wife and a mother. After being compelled to marry against her wishes – a fuming Zubeidaa even tries to commit suicide by threatening to shoot herself in the head with her father's loaded pistol, only to be stopped by her aunt Mammo – she goes through a degrading divorce procedure initiated by her cowardly husband. What leads to the dissolution of the marriage is the roaring fight between Suleiman and Zubeidaa's father-in-law Sajid Masud (S. M. Zaheer). As Zubeidaa settles into her married life, learning to love her husband, Sajid plans to move to Pakistan owing to the racial discrimination he faces as a Muslim in Bombay. Sajid wants his son and daughter-in-law to accompany him. This annoys Suleiman and he quarrels with Sajid. Soon after Riyaz's birth, Zubeidaa is divorced by her husband on Sajid's instruction; clutching a newborn Riyaz in her arms, a heartbroken Zubeidaa listens to her husband as he pronounces triple *talaq* (a form of Islamic divorce) in the presence of a presiding *kazi* (judge). She loses all contact with her husband after he moves to Pakistan, throwing her life into complete disarray.

Fourth, Zubeidaa is a co-wife. Her journey to becoming a royal co-wife is nothing short of a fairy tale. When she sinks into depression after her divorce, Rose offers her a magic antidote in the form of a strapping Victor. Courtship follows and the couple tie the nuptial knot, with Zubeidaa hoping to start life anew with her knight on a white charger. She expresses her newfound freedom

Figure 11.2 Zubeidaa argues with Mandira over royal conventions.

while melodiously singing '*dheeme dheeme gaoon*' ('I sing slowly'), a song-and-dance sequence Benegal shot on the Western Ghats mountain range. However, Zubeidaa's happiness disappears when she enters the Fatehpur palace only to be told by Mandira that she must live according to royal conventions. Zubeidaa finds it rather difficult to come to terms with these binding conventions. For instance, during a woman-only ceremony when commoners dance at the palace, Zubeidaa impetuously joins in, only to be reprimanded by Mandira who is deeply embarrassed by Zubeidaa's lack of self-control (Figure 11.2). But instead of apologising for what is decidedly a transgressive behaviour, Zubeidaa abruptly storms out of the gathering, defiantly refusing to live like a 'prisoner': 'I'm tired of these customs. Don't do this and don't do that. I'm sick and tired of it all. I will do as I please . . . I don't want to live like a prisoner here.'

Further crises occur when Zubeidaa gradually discerns that politics, not romance, is Victor's priority. A shrewd political animal, Victor understands that with independence after nearly 200 years of British rule, princely states like Fatehpur will soon be integrated into the democratic republic of India. So, in an effort to retain his power, he decides to participate in the nation's first general elections. This dramatic entry of Victor into the very public world of politics leads to the gradual breakdown of his private world with his second wife and marks the ascendency of his first wife in his life. It is Mandira, not Zubeidaa, who accompanies the victor on his electoral campaigns; Mandira even wins over largely illiterate, naive voters with her eloquence in their rural dialect. Feeling deserted, Zubeidaa inwardly marvels at why Victor behaves the way he does. She wonders whether it is because his fascination with an independent-minded Muslim woman has waned, or because he is ashamed of openly acknowledging her as his legitimate partner, having acknowledged Mandira as his spouse already. Benegal's heroine never finds the answers to these questions. She becomes increasingly frustrated as she realises that whenever Victor needs support, he invariably leans on Mandira. Matters get complicated to such an extent that when Victor, after winning the elections, is about to board a plane with Mandira to visit Delhi for a meeting, a hysterical Zubeidaa intervenes unannounced, insisting that she will go along with the king on his trip to the national capital. Humiliated, Mandira sidesteps, allowing Zubeidaa to accompany Victor. The two-seater tragically crashes as soon as it takes off, ending the turbulent saga of Zubeidaa and Victor.

In *The Other Side of Silence*, Urvashi Butalia opines that 'so much depends on who remembers, when, with whom, indeed to whom and how . . . the way people choose to remember an event, a history, is as important as what one might call the "facts" of that history.'[8] Zubeidaa is remembered not only by the people who choose to remember her and tell various aspects of her history. Her memories are also conveyed through a *dupatta*, a photo album, a monochrome footage, and a journal. Collectively, these items contribute to Riyaz's process of piecing together the story of his deceased mother. The *dupatta* (long scarf) that appears during the opening credits is a metonym for Zubeidaa to whom it belonged. Bright red in colour, it emblematises the vitality of spirit that characterised Zubeidaa. Red being the colour of courage, the *dupatta* symbolises Zubeidaa's courage in flouting norms. Made of chiffon-like material, the shapeless *dupatta* is so lightweight that it fleetingly glides across the azure sky, embodying the sense of unrestraint that typified Zubeidaa during her lifetime. The presence of the *dupatta* is complemented by a pathos-laden song sung by Lata Mangeshkar, the 'Nightingale of India', set to music by A. R. Rahman. Javed Akhtar's haunting lyrics, '*So gaye hain, kho gaye hain, dil ke afsaane/Koi tohaata, phir se kabhi inko jagaane*' ('They have slept, they have gotten lost, the stories of my heart/I wish someone would've come to awaken them'), suggest that Zubeidaa desires someone, probably her son, to 'awaken' the 'lost' and sleeping 'stories' of her 'heart'. She wants her son to remember her.

Like the *dupatta*, the photo album rekindles memories of Zubeidaa. Gifted by Mandira to Riyaz at the closure of the film, the photo album is precious to both characters. It is precious to Mandira because it makes her nostalgic for the camaraderie she enjoyed with Zubeidaa, or 'M', as she affectionately called her. Although she had to share her husband with Zubeidaa, Mandira is sensible enough not to harbour any ill will against Zubeidaa. This is also the reason why she preserves the photo album and hands it over to Zubeidaa's surviving son, as she understands how desperate Riyaz is to have access to it. The photo album is precious to Riyaz because it is an heirloom containing traces of the hidden past. When he glances at the photos, the life his mother had in Fatehpur unfolds before his very eyes. Commenting on the importance of the album, Chatterji notes:

> The photographs in the album offer a glimpse into the only period in life Zubeidaa was truly happy and thrilled in the fresh flush of love and marriage. It is the only private record of her brief life as co-wife of Vijayendra Singh.[9]

Riyaz receives another valuable item from Mandira: the black-and-white footage of the gypsy song-and-dance number performed by his mother for a film that never saw the light of day. Riyaz watches the footage in a private theatre with his grandmother shedding tears of joy; he sees his youthful mother happily gyrating as the liberated soul that she was. Her animated face and electrifying dance moves show that she had all the potential of reaching the pinnacle of fame.

Finally, there are Zubeidaa's handwritten journals through which she speaks in her first-person voice. They are kept hidden from Riyaz as Fayyazi does not want her grandson to know certain things about his mother. She is of the view that the secrets of those who have departed the mortal world are best left alone because they are no longer alive to shield those secrets. So, when Riyaz demands to see the journals, Fayyazi refuses to hand them over to him and hides them in her bedroom *almirah*. However, when Riyaz attempts to steal them and his grandmother catches him in the act, she decides to give them to him against her better judgement. Reading the journals makes Riyaz realise that his mother was not a wilful woman, but a thorough romantic at heart, capable of articulating her inner thoughts on the pages of the journals with poetic exuberance. Her philosophical introspection about the incidents in her life makes Riyaz realise that Zubeidaa had a great clarity of mind. This renders the journals the most significant items in defining Zubeidaa's identity.

Yet, all these items and the face-to-face interviews that Riyaz collects in his quest to understand his late mother do not help him grasp the true essence of Zubeidaa. At the end, Riyaz fails to succeed in fully comprehending the enigma that was his mother. There is always something that slips out of his reach just when his apperception of Zubeidaa seem possible. The mystique about what she wanted from life remains unfathomable. Towards the finale of the film, an exhausted and confused Riyaz asks Fayyazi: 'After all, what did mother want?' Every viewer of *Zubeidaa* is bound to ask the same question about Benegal's elusive heroine.

Note: All dialogue translated by the author.

NOTES

1. Lionel Trilling, 'The Sense of the Past', in *Literary Criticism: A Reading*, ed. B. Das and J. N. Mohanty (Calcutta: Oxford University Press, 1985), 260.
2. Shoma A. Chatterji, 'Shyam Benegal's Zubeidaa: memory as "voice"', *The South Asianist Journal* 3, no. 2 (2015): 57–8.
3. Quoted in Sangeeta Datta, *Shyam Benegal* (New Delhi: Roli Books, 2008), 208.
4. Quoted in Datta, 206.
5. Datta, 208.
6. Datta, 201.
7. Chatterji, 61–2.
8. Urvashi Butalia, *The Other Side of Silence: Voices from the Partition of India* (Durham, NC: Duke University Press, 2000), 8.
9. Chatterji, 66–7.

CHAPTER 12

Subversive Heroism and the Politics of Biopic Adaptation in *Bose: The Forgotten Hero*

Sneha Kar Chaudhuri

Shyam Benegal directs *Bose: The Forgotten Hero* at a juncture in his career (the film was released on 13 May 2005 in India)[1] when he has already garnered a lot of experience, maturity, critical acclaim and popular recognition for his trademark parallel films on Indian rural lives and its problems related to caste, gender and economy. Besides, he had behind him the experience of making successful documentaries in television series (for example, *Yatra* meaning 'journey', in 1986 and *Bharat Ek Khoj*, a TV adaptation of Jawaharlal Nehru's *The Discovery of India*, in 1988), as well as a biopic on Mahatma Gandhi (*The Making of the Mahatma*, 1996) and a bio-documentary on Satyajit Ray (1985). All these experiences and directorial maturity helped him mould an ambitious project such as *Bose* with an astute clarity and measured eloquence of a veteran filmmaker. *Bose* as a historical biopic is a grand film that runs for nearly three-and-a-half hours and represents the important historical facts and events in three parts (Faith, Unity, Sacrifice) related to Subhas Chandra Bose's magnificent attempts to undo British rule in India from 1940 till his controversial death in 1945. It is, perhaps, the first biopic that adapts on screen significant portions of Subhas Chandra Bose's life and career and tries to reinstate his image in the popular imagination as a subversive hero of India's freedom struggle against the British.

Before going to a detailed discussion of the film it is equally important to briefly discuss the critical discourses related to biopic adaptation studies. The popularity of biopic as a film genre can be found in every big or small film industry all over the world. But the emergence of a coherent constellation of theories to explain such an interdisciplinary (written biography/real-life accounts to film narrative) act is relatively recent and, therefore, the term 'biopic adaptation studies' appears quite novel and unique in itself. For several years, biopic adaptation studies and the critical field of adaptation studies in general has grappled with the problem of 'fidelity criticism',[2] as the critics have always placed the principle of authenticity as the benchmark of a good film based on a famous person's life. This staunch adherence to issues of historical fidelity and textual authenticity was challenged by most poststructuralist critics of biopic adaptation studies. Most notably, Brian McFarlane in *Novel to Film* (1996) takes his cue from Roland Barthes's structuralist views and took a narratological approach to adaptation.[3] He considers all kinds of film adaptations to be not mere imitations and derivations of the original texts/biography/real lives but rather cinematic texts as narratives which add to the latter several important intertextual, cinematic and cultural connotations and thereby enrich them. Screen adaptation involves a dynamic transformation from the written and/or lived experiences to the visual forms of mimetic representation. This approach found support with adaptation studies scholars like Robert Stam, Kamilla Elliott and Deborah Cartmell who used postmodern critical tools such as Bakhtinian dialogism and Gérard Genette's concept of 'hypertextuality' to underscore the strong creative and original approach of the film as a contributive discourse in the inter-art exchange between the media of literature/biography and film.[4] These theoretical re-orientations have profoundly impacted the burgeoning field of biopic adaptations. In the field of biopic adaptations of a well-known person's life and career, there are similar such critical and theoretical postulates to explain this complex and ambiguous interchange between a person's life experiences or autobiographical and/or biographical representations and their screen or cinematic narrativisations.

Biopic adaptation studies is a pretty new field in the parlance of adaptation studies that focuses on how notable and remarkable lives of individuals are presented on screen throughout the world. A biopic as defined by Tom Brown and Belen Vidal (2014) is

> a fiction film that deals with a figure whose existence is documented in history, and whose claims to fame or notoriety warrant the uniqueness of his or her story ... Unlike in other film genres placed at the intersection of fiction and history, such as the epic, the costume film, the docudrama – all of which can feature historical characters and biographical tropes – in the biopic the individual's story comes to the fore. Personality and point of view become the conduit of history in stories that often boil down complex social processes to gestures of individual agency.[5]

According to this definition, biopic concentrates on enlivening particular historical events through the protagonist's life and their perspectives and the exclusive focus is on the rise and fall of the hero/heroine and their unique life circumstances. In other words, a biopic is a historical film that grows out of the micro-narrative and minoritarian perspective of the protagonist experiencing the forces of the meta-narrative of history. The narratological focus of the film becomes selectively individual and unfurls the real events filtered through the personal encounters of the protagonist with the impersonal flow of time and events around them. Thus, Brown and Vidal also claim that 'the biopic trades on a sense of authenticity that stems from the actor's body himself'.[6] This involves a cinematic process of screen 'monumentalisation' of a character chosen as the focal point of the narrative and provides the lead performer with tremendous scope to enact an author-backed role of a lifetime that unfurls before the spectators from the actor's perceptions, thoughts and ideologies. It is the role and presence of the lead actor that gives power and force to the flow of the narrative and determines the quality of the cinematic representation. For Deborah Cartmell and Ashley Polasek, the biopics were 'a form of personal and especially national myth-making in their early days'.[7] It can also be said that biopics of famous people have often intertwined the ideological thrust of the nation with that of the individual protagonist's complicated engagement with it. This is true of political biopics, where the professional contribution of the central character is often measured in relation to their volatile involvement with the issues that defined their nation during their lifetime. Marta Minier and Maddalena Pennacchia pun on the word 'biopic' and call it 'bio(e)pic'; they define it as a film that 'while offering an intimate approach to history through the life of some notable historical character also bends towards the epic genre'.[8] For them the biopic is a cross between a biography and an epic, where history is used for both national myth-making and the formation of national identity.

Biopics have tended to be critically denigrated by historians and orthodox film critics, even though in the last decade biopic films have achieved sustained commercial success and critical acclaim, encouraging new and old filmmakers to make more and more such films in this sub-genre. As Brown and Vidal indicate, 'the biopic's bad reputation echoes the prejudices against literary biography among the historians. Biography and biopic carry, in parallel ways, the stigma of backward modes of storytelling.'[9] Purist historians and scholars do not find commercially popular biopic to be an authentic account of a person's life; rather they think that in the course of a biopic there are attempts to, variously, sensationalise the subject, blow things out of proportion, resort to exaggerations and hyperbole and, thereby, distort the real and mundane course of events in the protagonist's life. Most of these mainstream 'impure narratives' resort to these convenient techniques to attract commercial success and cheap popularity. Though resorting to formulaic means is never a guarantee of commercial success, and despite compromising with the textual and historical authenticity of the biopic content, plot and narrativisation, many such potboiler films fall prey to rejection by the masses and critics alike.

However, Shyam Benegal's *Bose: The Forgotten Hero* (2005) is a serious and conscientious celluloid tribute to one of the most controversial political leaders of India during the fight for independence against the British in the 1940s. It foregrounds the qualities of leadership, courage, honesty and wisdom in Netaji Subhas Chandra Bose's character and tries to create a space for him in the popular imagination. It belongs to those films Benegal made in the recent past that negotiated the boundaries of mainstream and arthouse cinema. Benegal sought to make a seriously documented film that would make Bose more popular among the common Indian cinegoer, but which did not resort to any cheap thrills and factual distortions to make his political hero more attractive and acceptable. Though popular in Bengal as the greatest of the Indian leaders, Bose's image in the rest of India is often quite shaky due to his fundamental political differences with Gandhi, regarded as *Bapuji* or the 'father of the nation'. The film deftly shows Bose or *Netaji*'s (meaning 'leader') respect for Gandhi, his visionary qualities as a leader and his inability to reconcile himself with the passivity of Gandhi's non-violent resistance of the British.

The disclaimer at the beginning of the film states: 'This film is a fictional representation based on historical facts'. This clearly shows Benegal's reliance on thorough text-based historical research to represent with historical authenticity the last five years of Bose's life till his mysterious death/disappearance in 1945. He is careful enough to infuse his narrative with a sense of mimetic and historical fidelity as is characteristic of any traditional biopic that tries to depict historical records without any attempts at distortion or hyperbolism. The proper balancing of the personal and political in Bose's life and the balanced use of history in the fictional format of the film enlivens the intensely dramatic political adventures of Bose. Benegal attempts to project the right political image of Bose without 'either diluting or distorting history to serve his ends', and his historical documentation has the right amount of 'intellectual honesty'.[10]

It is also a film that does not experiment with the alternative and psychoanalytically informed ways of storytelling that are quite popular in Western biopics like *Iris* (2001) and *Sylvia* (2003) among others and which attempt to bring out the complexities in the celebrity's mind regarding their life experiences. *Bose: The Forgotten Hero* does not much explore the biopic protagonist's mental world or the psychological nuances of his life and career using surreal techniques of cinematic storytelling, but like an orthodox biopic uses a historical–realist format to enliven the various aspects of Bose's personal and political experiences. Hence, the narrative is divided into three neat segments – Faith, Unity, and Sacrifice – so as to impose a chorological and teleological pattern on the plot. The protagonist's political career moves in three narrative sections that describe the historical and diachronic events in his life from 1940 to 1945.

This film has certain populist features, as it narrates the life of a well-known politician using music and action sequences that might attract a larger audience, but is essentially committed to 'an aesthetic of "alternative cinema" (another name for parallel cinema) or of a realist Hindi cinema that reflects his [Benegal's] socially conscious yet deeply humanistic mind'.[11] It is a film project that casts light on the life of 'the controversial leader' Subhas Chandra Bose and 'looks at the nationalist movement and the problems of leadership in the freedom fight'.[12] However, for Benegal, Bose wasn't 'a violent figure', and he thinks that the representation of Bose as a figure of revenge was 'a complete distortion' of his image.[13] In the section 'Interview 8: Present and Future' of *Bollywood Babylon: Interviews with Shyam Benegal* (2006), Benegal discusses this film with great enthusiasm and in great detail. His views on Bose are worth quoting as they establish the cinematic points of view from which he was trying to reimagine Bose's political contribution in the history of Indian nationalism. Benegal says that,

> Yes, it's a *great adventure story*. But he's also a remarkable figure in the Indian nationalist movement because he found a way that would have prevented Partition, if he had lived that long. So he's a fascinating figure of Indian history.[14]

He also says about Bose that, 'He was what one might call a very modern Indian, like Nehru. He could be called a *cosmopolitan nationalist*, because he was capable of accepting a great deal beyond the narrow confines of nationalism.'[15]

The film starts *in medias res*, at a point in Subhas Chandra Bose's life when he has been elected president of the Indian National Congress in the Tripura Convention of 1939. The first scene depicts a very historically significant conversation between Mahatma Gandhi and Bose in the presence of Jawaharlal Nehru as the listener-interlocutor (Figure 12.1). It is a crucial scene in the sense that it strikes the keynote of the film and the hero's character – his argumentative and subversive nature that makes him challenge Gandhi's non-violent means of national resistance against the British and leave the presidential post on grounds of ideological differences with Gandhi on the issue of the Indian freedom struggle. This is a scene that shows Bose resolutely defending his own political ideologies and opposing the father of the nation, and this thread is repeated in his interactions with other influential world political leaders like Adolf Hitler in Germany and Prime Minister Tojo of Japan at other crucial points in the film's narrative. The leadership qualities and resolute character of this unique hero enable him to raise a full army against British imperialism in India. It is important to note that the basic narratological thrust is to represent the narrative of the Indian freedom movement from the political perspectives offered by Bose. It is his point of view that drives and controls the historical narrative of the freedom struggle in the film, and it is depicted as a historical movement that gained its most outstanding dimension in the leadership of Bose and his political vision. It also, however, shows that due to Bose's political

Figure 12.1 Bose in conversation with Gandhi and Nehru after he is elected president in the Tripura Convention, 1939.

differences with the then major leaders of Congress like Gandhi and Nehru, his achievements were never mainstream approaches to the cause of India's freedom struggle against the British. It allows, therefore, an alternative cinematic myth-making that foregrounds the solitary endeavours of Bose to bring about India's freedom through the means of war and active resistance against the British Empire in the Indian sub-continent.

In the first section, entitled 'Faith', we get to see how Bose makes his solitary attempt to escape his home as he moves towards Afghanistan to cross the border and enter Russia to seek help against the British. This section has a narrative suspense and pace as we see how Bose manages to contact the Germans and Italians and negotiate many petty hurdles and risks involved in the course of his trajectory. It is interesting to see Bose taking up different disguises in order to escape; first he is the insurance agent Ziauddin who is not even recognised by one of his family members, and then an ordinary Pathan in Peshawar and Kabul trying to extract diplomatic help from the Russian embassy. Meanwhile, the British in India, particularly Calcutta, are very intrigued by his mysterious disappearance and fail to figure out his real whereabouts. Even most of his family members, except Sisir Bose and Ela Bose, are not aware that he has left and only later learn that he has become a hermit. This is one of the most gripping sections of the film where the audience is unable to figure out how Bose will actually move to Germany amid so much adversity, confusion and diplomatic manoeuvring of the foreign embassies. Then, we find him taking up the disguise of Count Orlando Mazotta to enter Germany, getting help from the Italian embassy in Kabul. The second section, 'Unity', has three important episodes – Bose's attempts at creating an army with the help of the Germans and the Japanese; his negotiations with the German dictator Adolf Hitler; and his transit from Germany to Japan in a German submarine. It also contains the account of his personal life and brief relationship with his secretary Emilie Schenkel that ends in inevitable separation as he has to give preference to his nation over his family. In this segment, it is important to note how Bose's subversive side emerges as he is unable to reconcile himself with the biased political views of the self-obsessed Hitler and is deeply dissatisfied with the latter's poor estimation of the Indian nation and its necessity for independence (Figure 12.2). Bose's strong personality enables him to see the ideological loopholes of senior and more established leaders like Gandhi and Hitler and he is not scared to express his disillusionment and discontent with them. These moments of disagreement in the narrative strongly reinforce Bose's recalcitrant individuality and his strong commitment to honesty and selfless political activism for the good of the nation. In these scenes, Benegal outlines the ideal trajectory of a biopic's ideological and generic imperative – the hero's unusual choices, perspectives and actions that not only establish his individuality and uniqueness but also enable the storyteller to emplot the history of the Indian freedom struggle from his point of view and experiences, however transgressive and anti-normative they might appear. The third section of the film, entitled 'Sacrifice', is a broad account of the struggles and endeavours of the *Azad Hind Fauj* or Indian National Army under the stable

Figure 12.2 Bose's interactions with Hitler in Germany as he seeks help against the British in India, 1942.

and inspiring leadership of Bose, and the many resource limitations it suffered due to bad weather, petty internal skirmishes and dwindling help from the Japanese. The scenes which show Bose holding public meetings to garner popular support, taking important diplomatic decisions as the army general, and solving petty provincial differences among his soldiers all highlight his powerful individual presence as a towering political personality. This section finally ends with Bose's disappearance in the Saigon plane crash, the trial of the surrendered INA soldiers at the Red Fort in Delhi, the Indian Navy rebellion, and the coming of Indian independence in 1947. There is a lot of detailing of battle scenes and makeshift army barracks, army encounters and face-offs that are handled deftly by National award-winning art director Samir Chanda. However, the solitary greatness of Bose's contribution is not overshadowed; rather his achievement as a leader is highlighted as much as possible.

The film charts the political and public career of Netaji with a strong mimetic fidelity and historical precision, but does not remain oblivious with regard to his personal and family life. The family scenes have been inserted intermittently to show the audience some of the reactions of the family members to his disappearance, his political conquests and his sudden death. Bose is shown to have a high regard for and fond attachment to his widowed mother; the brief mother–son scenes are very evocative and underscore Bose's regard and love for the elderly members of the family. He is also very emotionally attached to the younger generation in his family, such as Ela Bose and Sisir Kumar Bose. They also hero-worship him, and go to any extent to help, protect and champion his cause. Ela and Sisir aid him in fleeing the city and later also protect the secret from the rest of the world so that Bose can leave the Indian sub-continent without being tracked by the British. The family scenes involving the near and dear ones in Bose's family establish his ability to love and to share strong family bonds. Unlike many power-hungry political leaders all over the world, as an Indian man Bose is presented as a political figure who was very affectionate and homely and nurtured very healthy family values that hardly contradict or clash with his political values. However, at all points in his life, he had to sacrifice the personal for the sake of the country's cause.

The episodes concerning Bose's affair with his secretary Emilie Schenkel (they first meet in Berlin in 1934) is given a brief but substantial space in the narrative (Figure 12.3). The memory of Emilie pre-occupies his mind even in the most difficult and critical times, when he is at his most forlorn and disappointed. Images of Emilie come to him in flashbacks when he is questioned by the homely wife of Uttamchand Malhotra, Ranu, in Kabul as to whether he has any thoughts of settling down in life, and when he leaves Emilie and their young child Anita to stay in the battlefield camp. The brief but meaningfully romantic interactions between Emilie and Bose are given plausible emphasis and a credible context. Emilie is portrayed as a more simple and confident woman

Figure 12.3 Bose with his wife Emilie and daughter Anita before leaving Germany in 1942.

who impresses him with her honesty and intelligence, while she is enamoured by him as a great leader and an extraordinary human being. Being a woman brought up in a progressive Western society, she does not deny him physical intimacy and wants to get married only after she conceives. She wants a proper Hindu ceremonial marriage; and their marriage is solemnised by a ritual ceremony as Hitler had outlawed inter-racial marriages in Nazi Germany. When confronted by Adam von Trott zu Solz on her choice of partner she boldly declares that she has not married him for his high connections or to live in luxury, and would have accepted him even if he were a pauper. She merely wants some glass bangles from India as a gift and goes to Vienna to give birth to her child. The parting scene between Emilie and Bose before he leaves Germany is brief, but quite evocative and poignant. Bose promises that he will come back and asks her to follow his last order as his secretary and post the letter he has written to his family members in which he confides to them that he has married Emilie and wants her and her child to be treated with the same love and respect as they have given him. After the Germany episodes, Emilie has just one more scene, towards the end of the film. As she bravely and hopefully waits for them to be reunited, she is shattered by the news she hears on the radio about Bose's supposed death in the plane crash, and hurriedly clutches her daughter to her, shedding tears of sorrow and loss. There was a lot of controversy surrounding this particular episode in the film. The Calcutta premiere had to be cancelled because of protests from the Forward Bloc party regarding Bose's relationship with Emilie, which they alleged was falsely depicted in the film. The biopic trying to show a romantic side of Bose based on proper historical documents was found to be unacceptable by his party members who always wanted to see him as an unattached Bengali bachelor dedicating his life solely to the country. This episode interfered with their entrenched image of Bose as the ideal and quintessential Indian politician incapable of building a family with a foreigner and thereby indulging in racial inter-breeding. The essentialist image of Bose as an asexual and immaculate character in the Bengali psyche received a big jolt from this fact-based projection of a personal chapter in his life.

Sachin Khedekar as the actor embodying the historical legend that is Bose had a lot of responsibility placed on his young shoulders. Benegal chose him for the role as he had a strong background in theatre and resembled Bose in appearance and height. The body of the actor that is often 'monumentalised' in a biopic has the crucial power to establish the protagonist's true worth as the heroic narrative nerve-centre of the film and must justify the film's ideological imperative of political mythicisation. Khedekar's role is as grand as that of Ben Kingsley in Richard Attenborough's *Gandhi* (1982) and he does full justice to it frame by frame, through his lucid and thorough understanding of the character, its mannerisms and body language. Khedekar is able to deliver a performance that establishes the solitary power and strong individuality of Bose as well as his easy-going manners and accommodating nature. He appears to be a formidable and gritty political personality with an affable human warmth and sense of goodwill. Khedekar's Bose humanises the remote and impersonal political image of Bose and adds the necessary touch to the depiction of the character to render a sense of the familiar to this heroic persona. There is also a sense of firmness in the body language of the actor that makes him appear prominent and heroic in the role – a role of a lifetime that required tremendous dedication and resourcefulness on his part. Benegal astutely chose an actor who could deliver rather than one with great star power but mediocre acting talent. Bose's character is the focal point in this serious and dense narrative and it is never meant to play to the gallery.

Benegal admitted that he decided to replace his long-time music director Vanraj Bhatia, music director of most of his early films, with the extremely talented and popular A. R. Rahman because he wanted the soundtrack of this film to have a popular appeal. A. R. Rahman had also composed the music for *Zubeidaa* (2001) with great innovativeness and mass appeal, and hence was entrusted with making a soundtrack for *Bose* which would be in tune with the patriotic feel and the gravity and momentum of the historical situations depicted. The first song, which plays in the background time and again while Bose is trying to get help from the anti-British nations all over the world to crush British imperialism in India, is '*Desh ki Mitti*' ('The soil of the motherland'), sung very soulfully by Sonu Nigam. It has powerful lines such as '*Tanha Raahi Door Chalta Jayega*' ('The lone traveller will keep moving far'), which appears as a leitmotif that reinforces the central idea of the film – Bose's solitary and resolute struggle against the British Empire in India. Well-known songs of the INA ('*Kadam, Kadam Baraye Jaa*'/'Keep going on step by step') are used at appropriate moments in the film, with the soldiers either singing them or the songs playing in the background while they are fighting. Moreover, the song '*Subhashji, Subhashji*' sung by Sonu Nigam, in which Bose is referred to as *Shaan-e-Hind* (the pride of Hindustan), is inserted as a tribute to his legendary contribution to the Indian nation. In such a powerful and well-researched biopic, the importance and uniqueness of the title character is underlined by the melodious jingoism of the film's music and background score.

The film foregrounds the qualities of leadership, courage, honesty and wisdom in Netaji Subhas Chandra Bose's character and tries to create a space for him in the popular imagination. It belongs to those films Benegal made in the recent past that negotiated the boundaries of mainstream and arthouse cinema. Benegal appropriates the tropes and conventions of political celebrity biopics in Indian cinema and makes a film that highlights the goodness of Bose even as a subversive hero who challenges the British by creating his own army, the Indian National Army. The complexities and contradictions of Bose's life depicted in this war film both challenge and reinforce the popular perceptions about him in the Indian cultural imaginary. It is an epical attempt to re-establish Bose's achievements in the Indian mass imagination through serious cinematic depiction of the extraordinary nature of the hero and his remarkable achievements. An October 2019 Bengali regional film entitled *Gumnaami* directed by Srijit Mukherji examines intensively the various theories about the death and disappearance of Bose and tries to establish, following the proceedings of the Mukherjee Commission in 2005, that Bose did not die in that Saigon plane crash but returned to India as an ascetic known as 'Gumnaami Baba'. The character of Bose/Netaji was played by veteran and popular Bengali actor Prosenjit Chatterjee and was a runaway hit at the box office. The film draws heavily on Benegal's film and tries to create an inspiring narrative about Bose's life and political ideologies in exactly the same spirit as Benegal does in *Bose*. Hence, *Bose* has become an iconic biopic as far as the screen representation of Netaji/Bose is concerned. Future filmmakers wanting to tackle this subject for the big screen are likely to look to Benegal's film for inspiration.

Note: All dialogue translated by the author.

NOTES

1. *Bose: The Forgotten Hero*, directed by Shyam Benegal (2005; Mumbai, India: Ultra Videos Ltd, 2005), VCD.
2. See George Bluestone, *Literature and Film* (Bloomington and London: Indiana University Press, 1973); J. Dudley Andrew, *Film in the Aura of Art* (Princeton, NJ: Princeton

University Press, 1986) and Jack Jorgens, *Shakespeare on Film* (New York: University Press of America, 1991).
3. See Brian McFarlane, *Novel to Film* (Oxford: Clarendon Press, 1996). I have also discussed these issues in two of my recent book chapters on adaptation studies. See Sneha Kar Chaudhuri, 'Tagore's New Woman and the Contradictions of Patriarchy: Adapting *Char Adhyay* as *Elar Char Adhyay*', in *Tagore's Ideas of the New Woman: The Making and Unmaking of Female Subjectivity*, ed. Chandrava Chakravarty and Sneha Kar Chaudhuri (London, Los Angeles and New Delhi: Sage and Stree Samya Books, 2017), 256–72, and Sneha Kar Chaudhuri, 'Postmodern Subversion and the Aesthetics of Film Adaptation: The Example of *Tasher Desh*', in *Rabindranath Tagore's Drama in the Perspective of Indian Theatre*, ed. Arnab Bhattacharya and Mala Renganathan (London and New York: Anthem Press, 2020), 167–79.
4. See Kamilla Elliott, *Rethinking the Novel/Film Debate* (Cambridge: Cambridge University Press, 2003); Deborah Cartmell and Imelda Whelehan ed., *Adaptation: From Text to Screen, Screen to Text* (London and New York: Routledge, 1999); Robert Stam, *Literature Through Film: Realism, Magic, Art of Adaptation*. (Malden and Oxford: Blackwell, 2005); Deborah Cartmell and Imelda Whelehan eds. *The Cambridge Companion to Literature on Screen* (Cambridge: Cambridge University Press, 2007) and Deborah Cartmell, *A Companion to Literature, Film and Adaptation* (Oxford: Wiley-Blackwell, 2012) for more on this literature/film debate.
5. Tom Brown and Belen Vidal, *The Biopic in Contemporary Film Culture* (Oxford and New York: Routledge, 2014), 3.
6. Brown and Vidal, 11.
7. Deborah Cartmell and Ashley D. Polasek, *A Companion to Biopic* (Oxford: Wiley-Backwell, 2020), 2.
8. Marta Minier and Maddalena Pennacchia, *Adaptation, Intermediality and the British Celebrity Biopic* (London and New York: Routledge, 2014), 5.
9. Brown and Vidal, 8.
10. 'Cellouid Tribute to a National Hero', *The Hindu*, 20 May 2005, <https://www.thehindu.com/todays-paper/tp-features/tp-fridayreview/celluloid-tribute-to-a-national-hero/article28583086.ece>, accessed 1 September 2021.
11. Sangeeta Datta, *Shyam Benegal* (New Delhi: Roli Books, 2008), 1.
12. Datta, 2.
13. William Van der Heide, ed., *Bollywood Babylon: Interviews with Shyam Benegal* (Oxford and New York: Berg, 2006), 200.
14. Van der Heide, 198. Emphasis added.
15. Ibid., 199. Emphasis added. Benegal also says very pertinently, 'He [Bose] and Nehru were rivals, yet Bose was a Congressman till the very end even after he was expelled. But he considered Gandhi to be his leader, although he criticized him for his poor political tactics. He felt that Gandhi always lost out, because he was too concerned about converting his opponent to his point of view. Bose felt that he was behaving like Buddha and Jesus and that he was unable to achieve political outcomes. He felt that everytime Gandhi brought the British to their knees, he lost the initiative, because he allowed the British to play upon the diverse interests of Indians' (199).

CHAPTER 13

The Rural in the Glocal Intersection: Representation of Space in *Welcome to Sajjanpur* and *Well Done Abba*

Aysha Iqbal Viswamohan and Sayanty Chatterjee

INTRODUCTION

With the advent of globalisation, the constant negotiation between Western globalising 'modernity' and local 'traditions', resulting in culturally hybridised and contingent social formations, has provided an interesting contour to the socio-cultural and political zeitgeist of rural India. Globalisation as a process 'generates contradictory spaces, characterised by contestation and internal differentiation'[1] that brings about a shift in our understanding of topographical paradigms of space. The idea of a 'global' space vis-à-vis a confluence of the global and the local space or the 'glocal' has been contested in the theoretical understanding of globalising spaces. The change in the landscape and the mindscape in the aftermath of globalisation has brought forth an intersection between 'globalisation' and 'glocalisation' as George Ritzer has argued.[2] He has located the origin of globalisation in the capitalistic endeavours of multinational companies and the modern nation-states to wield power. The boom of market economies in the post-liberalised world plays a major role in this accomplishment. Such processes resulted in the diffusion of non-distinctive social formations, such as credit cards and McDonald's restaurants – in Ritzer's words, 'nothing' – which remained identical from culture to culture, leading to cultural homogenisation. On the other hand, glocalisation is the 'interpenetration of the global and the local', which emphasises how indigenous agents can appropriate global influences for unique and unpredictable ends.[3] In the course of this chapter, we strive to understand how the influences brought forth by the globalising processes in the space of the rural get appropriated in the realm of the local. We will be discussing representation of space in two of acclaimed Hindi cinema director Shyam Benegal's later films. Through the analyses of the *mise-en-scène*[4] in *Welcome to Sajjanpur* (2008) and *Well Done Abba* (2009), the focus of the study is to perceive the socio-cultural and political context of rural India on the cusp of globalisation and how the social space is produced through the various spatial networks.

SHYAM BENEGAL AND HINDI CINEMA

Shyam Benegal was born in 1934 in Hyderabad. His father, a still photographer by profession, instilled a passion for films in his son. Benegal grew up watching a lot of films, ranging from American cinema to the social and nationalistic films of India, particularly the ones produced by Prabhat (located in Pune, a city to the south of Mumbai) and New Theatres (Calcutta). This early childhood exposure to films of a specific kind set the course of Benegal's trajectory as a filmmaker who invests in the making of socially meaningful cinema.[5]

In the 1960s, with the establishment of the Film Finance Corporation (FFC), the New Indian Cinema movement was set in motion with its initial two films, Mrinal Sen's *Bhuvan Shome* (1969) and Mani Kaul's *Uski Roti* (*Other's Bread*, 1969). It is in this environment of the proliferation of parallel cinema outside the realm of mainstream popular cinema that Shyam Benegal, an advertising executive at that point, made his first feature film, *Ankur* (*The Seedling*, 1974). Although *Ankur* bears the signature style of parallel cinema with its representation of realism and the 'oppression of rural subaltern women and a landless peasantry under feudal social arrangements',[6] the film (and also Benegal's later films) has been defined as 'middle cinema', a term Benegal himself rejects.[7]

Shyam Benegal's first three films, *Ankur*, *Nishant* (*Night's End*, 1975) and *Manthan* (*The Churning*, 1976), often dubbed the 'emblematic rural trilogy',[8] constituted three interconnected tales of the oppressed underprivileged section of rural Indian society and with its unabashed brand of realism posed a revolutionary challenge to the existing status quo of the feudal set-up. There is a stark polarisation when it comes to the critical stature of Shyam Benegal among Indian critics. While critics like Chidananda Das Gupta or Aruna Vasudev consider him one of the major filmmakers in India, who creates socially significant and aesthetically pleasurable films, another group of critics such as Ashish Rajadhyaksha and M. Madhava Prasad argue that his works are compromising on account of being an instance of 'an evolving developmental aesthetic employing a statist realism'.[9] According to them, Benegal's inclination towards nationalist propagandising narratives and advertising stylistics takes away from his films the 'socio-cultural significance of the Bollywood cinema and the formal-cultural importance of filmmakers like Mani Kaul and Kumar Shahani'.[10]

While talking about the 'cumulative cultural significance' of Benegal's rural trilogy, M. Madhava Prasad writes in a chapter of his book *Ideology of the Hindi Film* entitled 'The Developmental Aesthetic' that the movement these three films come to symbolise is a 'movement towards the consolidation of a developmental aesthetic allied to the contemporaneous stage of the passive revolution'.[11]

Shyam Benegal supported his preoccupation with a nationalistic reformist agenda in an interview conducted on 16 March 2006 by stating, 'Of course my films reflect my interest in ongoing national debates; issues relating to what defines us as Indians are an important-seminal-point of reference for my films.' In the same interview he remarked that the idea of India that he endorses is a Nehruvian one – the idea, fuelled by a liberal mindset, that from its inaugural moment of independence in 1947 to Jawaharlal Nehru's death in 1964, India sought to establish 'a constitutional style of governance' and committed itself to 'secular principles, economic programmes of centralised planning', whose 'strategies for peaceful social revolution moderated the fundamental tension between the strong state and representative democracy'.[12]

Both Rajadhyaksha and Prasad view Benegal's films from this period as conforming to what Rajadhyaksha calls the 'aesthetics of state control'. The critics who evaluate New Cinema favourably de-link it from the state's activities during the Emergency and see it instead as participating in the 'disenchantment of people with established institutions whose validity got deeply eroded in the seventies'. For them, 'the new Indian cinema attempted to come to terms with aspects of the emerging social reality', which included a decade of social and political strife 'leading to a critical re-evaluation of the country's most fundamental institutions, traditions and values'.[13]

On being asked about his relationship to Indian cinema, Shyam Benegal has described his relationship with Hindi cinema as 'somewhat tenuous'. Benegal felt that due to its more generalist nature, Hindi cinema lacked the 'character of the place', unlike South Indian regional cinemas which had a very specific regional context, 'a connectedness to the soil'. He has remarked, 'Hindi cinema has always functioned essentially as parable, and when you have something that functions as a parable, particularly a moral parable, you don't necessarily locate it geographically.' Benegal has always been interested in representing the specific idiom, appearance and language of a region, much as in the films of Satyajit Ray whose influences over Benegal's cinematic career have been paramount. Hence, the signs, the signals and the symbols that emerge from his films have a geographic situatedness.[14]

From *Ankur* onwards, Benegal's films have been lauded and rewarded by the nation-state. Both his feature films and his documentary films have received National Film Awards and have been frequently selected to represent India at various international platforms. Benegal himself has been the recipient of some of the nation's most prestigious honours. He received the Padma Shree in 1976, Padma Bhushan in 1991, the Indira Gandhi Award for National Integration in 2004 and, finally, the Dadasaheb Phalke award in 2005. Due to Bengal's direct connection with the state as a member of the Rajya Sabha from 2006 to 2012, Anuradha Needham argues that possibly his films from this period 'represent a set of concerns whose ideological investments the state welcomes and/or wishes to call its own'.[15] Incidentally, the two films in question here fall into this time period. Whether the films subscribe to and promote a state-mediated ideology of governance and a propaganda of various welfare schemes is open to debate. By situating the two films within the oeuvre of Benegal's works, we will try to understand the vantage point from which these particular films are speaking to the audience.

RECONCEPTUALISATION OF SPACE: SOCIO-POLITICAL CONVERGENCE

The concept that we generically refer to as the 'social space' is not a singular entity. We are rather confronted by 'an unlimited multiplicity or uncountable set of social spaces' that are intertwined together. Lefebvre puts forth the argument that 'no space disappears in the course of growth and development'. Multiple social spaces can co-exist together. Hence, no matter how contested the negotiation is, the global does not 'abolish the local'.[16]

Ashis Nandy, in his seminal book *An Ambiguous Journey to the City*, expostulated that the pre-eminence of city, in the village-versus-city dynamic in place since the conception of the superiority of the metropolis, is largely a colonial construct. There are two distinctly opposite viewpoints pertaining to the dichotomous position of the city and the village. On one hand, the city offers anonymity and a freedom from the caste-ridden social system of Indian society. At the same time, it reeks of self-indulgence and vice. The village, on the other hand, is uncivil and intrusive, but is the 'depository of traditional wisdom and spirituality, and of the harmony of nature, intact community life and environmental sagacity'.[17] Nandy has posited the village as the 'self' and the city as the decadence of that self in the 'absence of self-restraint'.[18] In the postcolonial framework, this dichotomy garners more complexity. The imagination of the village as a 'serene, pastoral landscape'[19] replete with an almost 'Gandhian austerity'[20] has gained more currency in post-Independence India with multitudinous models of Nehruvian developmentalism. With the spatial rearrangement of the postcolonial rural landscape, the village is not seen as a counterpoint to the city. Rather, with the thrust of globalisation, the spaces in the village and the city undergo a significant transformation, to the extent of influencing each other.

After a couple of decades of romancing and projecting the 'modern', urban, middle-class Indian population in order to expand the diasporic viewership, Bollywood finally sets on its journey to explore the 'authentic national consciousness'[21] in the rural-scape in the latter half of 2010s. Benegal, with his rendition of village life and living, becomes one of the precursors of that wave of 'focus on the local'. With the visual representation of the 'contested'[22] socio-political space of the rural, Shyam Benegal tries to portray the nuanced image of the 'real' India.

The very idea of a visual representation operates on the concepts of locale, space, setting, site and so on. According to Edward Soja, a 'site' is a space that is churned by the meeting of historical and global processes.[23] In both films, Benegal has represented the village as a microcosm of the nation-state, a 'site' where the nuanced socio-political reality of the postcolonial and the post-liberalised world are being played out.

WELCOME TO SAJJANPUR (2008)

After *Charandas Chor* (*Charandas, the Thief*, 1975), *Welcome to Sajjanpur*, released in 2008, marks Shyam Benegal's late venture into comedy. The film chronicles the journey and growth of Mahadev from an unemployed aspiring writer to a published novelist. The backdrop of the film is a small village in the northern part of India where Mahadev, with a Bachelor of Arts degree from Satna College, is forced to live with his mother. Mahadev, being one of the few literates in a space where the literacy rate is strikingly low, takes up the vocation of letter-writing to help out the people of his village. The story revolves around the various 'customers',[24] a 'colourful palette of characters'[25] whom Mahadev encounters in the course of his profession as a letter-writer. Although the narrative is mediated from Mahadev's perspective, it portrays the story of the place and the several characters inhabiting the space simultaneously. The opening scene starts with a folksy anecdote with regard to the nomenclature of the place as the camera overviews the locale. It points to the post-Independence politics of re-naming as Mahadev mentions the transition from 'Durjjanpur' to 'Sajjanpur' and the underlying irony in it. Nandi Bhatia conjectured in the essay '*Welcome to Sajjanpur*: Theatre and Transnational Hindi Cinema' that the name of the film is possibly 'inspired by Sarjanpur, near Azamgarh, Uttar Pradesh or Shahajanpur'.[26] The subsequent narration indicates the grim realities of the village. Mahadev describes the place as a 'full-fledged developed village, but [with] no formal education, mode of communication or technology of information'[27] available in the space. Right at the outset, we learn of Mahadev's aspiration to go to the city of Mumbai to become a writer. He is in search of a subject for his writing and finds a lack of material in the village. Yet, he acknowledges that even in the city, there is a lack of subjects. The film, on many occasions, engages with the dialectic opposition of the village and the city as the Western-educated Mahadev tries to navigate the myriad 'spatial practices'[28] of the rural-scape. As the film invokes the nostalgia of an idyllic past through the pastoral landscape of the place, we also get acquainted with the almost lost art of letter-writing and cannot help romanticising the very idea. Mahadev has set up his 'shop' under a banyan tree, beside the post office, which eventually becomes the locus of the identity of the village (Figure 13.1). It is to be noted here that the idea of having a common space where everyone from the community will gather together and chat is a quintessentially Indian thing which has its origin in the ancient Indian rural villages. Benegal has retained the spatial uniqueness of the village by symbolising the space around the *bargad ka ped* (banyan tree) as the common social space of the village. Thus, by occupying the common social space, Mahadev, too, assumes the position of centrality, around whom the various incidents unfold.

Benegal has explored a wide array of socially relevant issues via humour and satire in this film. From the staggering ratio of unemployment, the myriad forms of superstition that pervade the rural existence, to the supposedly illicit, 'modernising' idea of widow's remarriage and women's education, *Welcome to Sajjanpur* traverses the margins and raises some significant questions with regard to the hegemonic power structure of the place. Mahadev's childhood crush, Kamla, was forced to drop out of school by her father because of her epileptic seizures. Vindhya, who later becomes Mahadev's wife, has to negotiate with the superstition of her mother who has arranged for her marriage to a dog, on account of her being a *mangalik* (a person cursed according

Figure 13.1 Mahadev reads a letter in the open space under the banyan tree of his rural village.

to Hindu astrological beliefs). Although she is an educated and rebellious young woman, riding through the village on her scooter, the negation of the importance of education for women by society makes us question whether village life really does stand for all that is good and right.

The crowing of the rooster, the cows mooing, the mud oven in Mahadev's house, the cow dung on the walls, the hand-built pottery – all heighten the authenticity of the *mise-en-scène* in the film. The language used in this film contributes to the *mise-en-scène* of the village as well. The entire film is replete with mythological and folkloric references, which in turn accentuate the vivacity of the dialect. In a review of the film, Khalid Mohamed has remarked that 'the spine of Shyam Benegal's *Welcome to Sajjanpur* is its rustic, colloquial dialogue'.[29] Written by Ashok Mishra in a mixture of Hindi and Awadhi, the screenplay hails back to the glorious heritage of India's mythological past with references to Ram, Sita, Hanuman and so on. Kamla, whose husband Bansi has been staying in Mumbai for the past four years, compares herself to Sita who had to stay away from her husband Ram for a long time. To infuse his letters with greater dramatic effect, Mahadev starts filling them with his own emotions, borrowing references from Shravan Kumar (an obedient son who served his blind parents with utmost devotion), as well as from Ram and also Shah Rukh Khan's popular dialogues from Bollywood films. It is probably in the tradition of Bollywood that Mahadev hatches a devious plot as he intervenes in the course of Kamla and Bansi's marriage when Kamla comes to seek his assistance in writing letters to her husband. By fabricating the contents of Bansi's letters and sending prodding and rude replies to him, Mahadev tries to antagonise Kamla against Bansi and have her for himself. He constantly discourages Kamla from harbouring any hopes for her husband. Towards the end, however, Mahadev realises the implication of his selfish misdemeanour when he finds out that Bansi is going to sell his kidney in order to take Kamla to Mumbai. Bansi's letters unravel the sad realities and hardships of migrant workers in the cityscape as they escape the rural-scape in order to realise the dream of a better life. Mahadev helps the couple by arranging the money for them without their knowledge and becomes a catalyst in their reunion in Mumbai. Thus, the film has all the traits of a classic popular Bollywood film and is replete with intertextual references to Hindi cinema. Incidentally, *Welcome to Sajjanpur* is Benegal's take on a commercially viable popular Hindi comedy film, a genre he had refrained from until that point.

The proliferation of the politics based on caste, class, religion and gender is another interesting point of inquiry in the film. The conversations between Mahadev and Yamuna *bai*'s husband, Ram Singh, give us an insight into the political structure of the village and the country in general as the director presents the space of Sajjanpur as a microcosm of the country. Religion plays a pivotal role in the dynamics of the space and the unfolding of the politics. Ram

Singh makes Mahadev write a letter to the collector in order to prevent Salim Mohamed's wife from standing against his wife, Yamuna *bai*, in the upcoming election. He instigates the possible threat of a Hindu-Muslim riot if any Muslim candidates stand for the post of *sarpanch* (head of a village). Salim Mohamed laments to Mahadev that politics has no place for a good person. However, much along the lines of Madhava Prasad's argument of 'statist realism',[30] the film tries to portray a balance between corruption and positivity in Indian democracy. Hence, the inclusion of a third gender in the realm of popular politics and the benevolent aegis of the bureaucracy to Munni *bai*, followed by her win as the villagers rejoice, projects a somewhat optimistic vision. The interpersonal relationship and the proximity of the inhabitants to each other is a unique feature of the rural social space. In contrast to the more modern form of campaigning, Munni's electoral campaign projects a rural existence that incorporates the social space of the villagers into a more political one. Hence, through this confluence of social and political space, Munni *bai* expands her field of achievements, winning the election against the position of centrality epitomised by Yamuna in this case. Though a scathing satire on the political system of India, the song in this film, '*raja gayi, rani gayi, ab to prajatantra hai*' ('monarchy is over; we live in democracy'), romanticises the idea of a democracy in India as opposed to other South Asian nation-states like Pakistan.

One of the most important tools of social change that the film rather glosses over is the performance of a street play written by Mahadev entitled '*Aaya Toofan*' ('Cometh the Storm'), which discusses the issues of capitalistic ventures and the promises of industry, construction of a mall and the subsequent generation of employment naturally resulting from the requisition of lands. The incorporation of meta-theatre and elements of theatricality is what ascribe to the film, according to Nandi Bhatia, its effectiveness 'as an agent of social change', beyond the overall 'hegemonizing impulse' of Bollywood cinema.[31]

As Lefebvre has argued, the emergence of the 'global does not eradicate the local'.[32] The instances of co-existence of the globalising process and the traditional mode of life and living are an interesting point of entry into the film. A close study of the *mise-en-scène* shows us the presence of an STD, ISD and PCO[33] in the bazaar space, the presence of a television in Mahadev's house in the same frame as the post office and the lair of Mahadev's letter-writing business. It indicates two different teleological spaces cohabiting in the same territory. Similarly, Mahadev's fascination for the ink pen as opposed to the modern ball point pen, the co-existence of *mobile-chithhi* (text messaging) along with the physical letters, the colourful nylon *saree*-draped Kamla with her glass bangles and making handmade pottery as opposed to the *salwar-kameez*-clad, scooter-riding Vindhya signify a constant interaction and negotiation between the global and the local, resulting in 'unpredictable ends'[34] of a new 'glocal' existence. Subedar Singh's approval of the match of compounder, Ramkumar, and his widowed daughter-in-law, Shobha, is a sign of the undercurrent of that change – a change in the form of supporting the love marriage of a widow in the rural space. Although tragedy ensues – the community members lynch the couple as they do not approve of a widow remarrying – the hope lives on.

Both Ramkumar and Mahadev take off on a flight of fantasy as they dream about engaging in two equally clandestine relationships, the former with a widow and the latter with a married woman. This flight becomes important in the context of the space which otherwise does not allow such mobilisation. Shantanu Moitra's music represents the romantic fantasy of the duo in classic Bollywood tradition. In his fantasy, while riding the bike with Kamla, Mahadev dreams of them riding a motorbike, driving a fancy car, and even flying in a plane. He imagines Kamla driving the car, with both of them clad in Western attire. (It is also noteworthy that the dialect of the songs is that of standard Hindi.)

The chasm between fiction and reality becomes clear when, towards the end of the film, Mahadev meets with his publisher after his novel has been published. Mahadev with his faculty of writing becomes the locus of the rural life. The prevalence and predominance of the written word is once again established as the creative imagination of Mahadev becomes the creator of the picture called *Sajjanpur*.

WELL DONE ABBA (2009)

Based on *Narsayyaki Bavdi* (*Narsayya's Well*) by Jeelani Bano, *Phulwaka Pul* (*Phulwa's Bridge*) by Sanjeev and *Still Waters: A Screenplay* by Jayant Kripalani, *Well Done Abba* is a 2009 Hindi film primarily intended as a political satire, released in India in 2010. The story is about a Muslim car driver, Arman Ali, working in Mumbai, who returns to his native village after asking for a month's leave. The narrative progresses in retrospective, through continuous flashbacks as Arman Ali, upon his return to his workplace, explains to his employer how he got entangled in the harrowing web of rural governance and administration.

In contrast to the exposition in *Welcome to Sajjanpur*, *Well Done Abba* makes a transition from the skyscrapers of the cityscape to the rural areas of Chikatpally, a fictional village in Andhra Pradesh, which is Arman Ali's native village. Under the guise of humour and satire, the film unveils the issue of acute water crises in the rural villages of India. While in *Welcome to Sajjanpur* Benegal explores the socio-political space of the rural, in *Well Done Abba* the director documents Arman Ali's journey through the bureaucratic obstacles he faces in his attempt to get a *bavdi* (well) with the help of a government-sponsored welfare scheme. Apart from the involvement of the same screenplay writer (Ashok Mishra) and music director (Shantanu Moitra), there are certain overlapping issues that both films concern themselves with, illiteracy being one of them. In both films, the high rate of illiteracy brings home a sad reality of the rural space. At the same time, the lack of awareness and nonchalance with regard to the importance of education among the village politicians hints at a problematic aspect of the rural political sphere. The issue of the minority community both in terms of religious and economic categories, referred to in passing in *Welcome to Sajjanpur*, is taken up in a more exhaustive manner by Benegal in *Well Done Abba*. The director has carefully constructed the *mise-en-scène* in order to situate the story in a recognisably rural setting. The astute use of wall-hoardings as an apparatus to generate both political and social awareness apparatus is deployed in the film to serve the agenda of 'statist realism'.[35] It comes as no surprise that the film was bestowed with the National Film Award for Best Film on Social Issues in 2009. The film constantly shifts between the city and country spaces. The interpolation of the cityscape of Hyderabad and Mumbai into the rural-scape heightens the grim realities of village life.

Well Done Abba explores a beautiful father–daughter relationship between Arman Ali and his daughter, Muskan. He has come home, besieged by his twin brother Rehman Ali and his wife Salma, to get Muskan married off. Muskan is an intelligent young woman who always speaks her mind and wants to study further. She is articulate and has an affinity for flying kites instead of being cooped up in a *burkha*. This becomes a hindrance in finding a good match for her since the 'spatial practices'[36] deem her undesirable as a housewife. Unable to get her married off, Arman Ali bypasses the hierarchical order of the bureaucracy to get a *bavdi* (well) under *Kapildhara Yojana*, a welfare initiative offered by the government for the underprivileged sections of society. Following the advice of the government officials, Arman Ali enrols himself as belonging to the below poverty level (BPL) category, since the weakened economic status garners several government facilities such as getting a free home under the *Indira Amma Awas Yojana* (Housing Plan). However, on his trip from Balamma, the *sarpanch* of his area, through to the *Tehsildar* office to the sub-engineer and the contractor, Arman Ali realises the inefficacy and the unscrupulousness of the people belonging to the system. Apart from the harassment and humiliation, the funds he was supposed to receive for the digging of the well get extorted by the various officials in the form of bribery. As would happen in a theatre of the absurd, the well remains unfinished. Throughout this film, Benegal strongly critiques the political and administrative space of the nation-state as hugely unsupportive of and unco-operative with the poor, contrary to its claim to have successfully implemented various welfare schemes for the underprivileged. Muskan being the social agent of change tries to challenge the hegemonic power structure of the bureaucracy. With her infectious streak of optimism, Muskan files a police case for the never-built well as being 'missing'. The investigation takes place with regard to the same theft of the well. The entire administration falls prey to its own misconstrued creation. Arman Ali tries to grapple with the reality as the different spheres of bureaucratic spaces ensnare him in a loophole.

Mass mobilisation and protests are initiated by the villagers under the leadership of Arman Ali, Muskan and Arif in order to get back what is rightfully theirs. After much protest and pressure from all fronts, the minister *garu* comes to visit the space of the 'stolen' *bavdi* and promises to conduct a thorough investigation into the matter. The minister strives to politicise the issue in order to dip into the minority vote-bank to facilitate his win in the upcoming election. Arman Ali, Muskan and Arif swear not to drink water unless they get their stolen *bavdi* back (Figure 13.2). The space of Arman Ali's unfinished *bavdi* thus becomes a space for protest and a tool to demand justice for the downtrodden and exploited villagers. The involvement of the digital space and media helps in realising their cause further. According to the orders of the upper levels of the administration, all the supposedly stolen *bavdis* of the village were finally constructed. The ultimate farce inherent in the political space is seen in the conferring of awards to the same system that prevented the construction of the *bavdi* in the first place. But, in a humorous and ironic stroke, the entire stage prepared for the award ceremony comes crashing down, taking those same corrupt officials and others involved in the embezzlement along with it.

The influences of the globalising processes are more prevalent in this film as compared to *Welcome to Sajjanpur*. Arman Ali gifts Muskan a mobile phone after coming back from Mumbai, which can be seen as an act of incorporating global elements in the local plane. Similarly, the act of typing messages in

Figure 13.2 Arman Ali and Muskan sitting on the site of their unbuilt *bavdi*.

Hindi can be seen as an attempt to indigenise globalised devices into a localised form. The mobile phone here stands for a socialising and at the same time mobilising tool. Later on, technology comes to the rescue while Arman Ali is running from pillar to post to make his *bavdi* happen.

It is interesting to note the concept of privacy and how it gets lost for most people inhabiting the space. Rural space necessarily assumes a predominance of common space over the private. For instance, when Arif receives a message on his phone, the customer in his auto repair shop constantly peeks at the screen. This also serves as a comment on the enchantment created by technological networks, the mobile phone being a case in point.

Amid a corruption-ridden system of state machinery, the secondary role of the *sarpanch* to her male counterparts reveals the true position of a woman in the sphere of hierarchical and patriarchal politics. The misconstrued and conservative notion of the importance of household chores over engagement in a public space for a woman has been established and subsequently debunked in this film.

Being able to quench your neighbour's thirst is an important part of the Indian traditional value system. When Arman Ali is unable to give drinking water to the rickshaw-*wallah* who comes to drop him at his home, therefore, he is visibly upset. Later in the film, when he struggles to get his *bavdi* dug, his earnest wish is to give a glass of drinking water to whoever comes to his home.

As a juxtaposition to the corrupt, lackadaisical work culture of the various institutions, Arif demonstrates an essentially modernistic philosophy of work ethic. When Muskan comes to repay the money that her uncle and aunt have borrowed from Arif, she finds him working on the holiday of Eid. As a representative of the new generation's work ethic, Arif believes in '*kaam karke Eid manana*' ('celebrating the festival with work'). Arif was educated in the city, but had to come back to the village after his mother's death. He is represented as the common stakeholder in the endeavour of social change as he navigates between both spaces.

The common strand of disenchantment with the city – or with its globalising dreams to be more precise – binds Mahadev, Bansi, Arif and Shakeena together. Shakeena is married off to an Arab sheikh who turns out to be abusive and kicks her out of his house. Her failed marriage in the big city and the subsequent loss of their globalising dreams makes Arman Ali realise that in a negotiation between the global and the local, the local always constitutes the space of familiarity, a social space of mutual trust and solace. He agrees to Muskan's wish to get married to Arif, despite not knowing anything about his actual lineage (he was abandoned during riots as a baby and found shelter with a benevolent Muslim family).

In a review of the film in *Outlook* magazine, Namrata Joshi has remarked that in its claim to portray a successful implementation of the government-sponsored welfare programme, the film gets lost. The plot becomes 'too long-winded, a web hampered by a dull and awkward narrative'.[37] The film has a full gallery of cast and characters, but this at times works to its disadvantage, resulting in it only scratching the surface of the various issues being examined.

At the end, Arman Ali seeks justice by putting himself in jail for an hour for bribing the venal officers and being a passive accomplice in the falsification of government documents. In his discussion of *Manthan*, Madhava Prasad criticised the revolution shown in that film as 'passive' and not challenging the political order in a radical fashion.[38] Although the same argument can be raised in terms of the reformist ideals of *Well Done Abba*, the very notion of the existence of the *bavdi* at the film's conclusion makes for an optimistic vision of state welfare, no matter how delayed the process might get.

CONCLUSION

For Appadurai and Breckenridge in *Consuming Modernity: Public Culture in a South Asian World*, 'film is perhaps the single strongest agency for the creation of a nationalist mythology of heroism, consumerism, leisure, and sociality'.[39] The cultural significance of Benegal's films, with their propagation of socially relevant messages, is similarly indisputable. Although Benegal's tryst with the rural thematic in his earlier films is indelibly etched in the psyche of the Indian audience, the treatment of the rural space on the cusp of globalisation in the two films discussed here is unique. While in his earlier rural trilogy, Benegal shot the films on location in order to ascertain the 'authentication of Indian reality',[40] both *Welcome to Sajjanpur* and *Well Done Abba* were shot in film cities across the country, where the rustic space was recreated by the director's imagination. As Thomas Elsaesser professed in *Early Cinema: Space Frame Narrative* (1990), the question is not 'how real that which is being filmed actually is, but whether the system that governs its representation is intelligible to its viewer'.[41] Hence, the importance of representation is significant in these two films. In addition, Sangeeta Datta has mentioned in her definitive book on Benegal that the idea of shooting on location in that period had also to do with 'the economics of film production'.[42] She says, 'It proved far more economical to take a film unit into a village and shoot for four to six weeks than reproduce this setting in a studio.'[43] The scenario has changed since then with the emergence of film cities where the cost of producing the reimagined space of a village is significantly lower than actually going through the hassle of shooting on location. Therefore, it is interesting to observe how Benegal represents and retains the authenticity of the rural space through the incorporation of the '*dehati* Hindi' and 'Dakhhini Urdu' dialects (in *Welcome to Sajjanpur* and *Well Done Abba* respectively), through the exploration of everyday relations and by engaging with spatial practices. However, we cannot deny that films like *Ankur*, with their 'understated and entirely credible performances by its new, mostly FTII-trained actors',[44] differ significantly from these two satires and their representation of the space by way of the melodramatic, exaggerated (to some extent, unbelievable) and comic portrayal of the characters by an ensemble cast largely belonging to the system of commercial Hindi cinema.

Both films engage with the utopia of an idyllic village life, free from the Jeffersonian idea of the 'pestilential character of big cities'.[45] When it comes to execution, of the two films *Welcome to Sajjanpur* manages to do greater justice to portraying a realistic picture than *Well Done Abba*. People coming together as a community to formulate a common social space that can challenge the existing power structure is the common thematic strand in both films. No matter how idealistic and passive that challenge is, these two directorial ventures by Benegal pave the way for a particular wave of films that engage with the representation of the 'real' and '*desi*' India. Benegal's so called 'middle cinema' thus becomes the true precursor to commercially successful and socially relevant films like Subhash Kapoor's *Jolly LLB* (2013), Shree Narayan Singh's *Toilet: Ek Prem Katha* (*Toilet: A Love Story*, 2017) or R. Balki's *Padman* (2018), to name just three, over the next decade.

Note: All dialogue translated by the author.

NOTES

1. Saskia Sassen, quoted in Barbara Mennel, 'The Global City and Cities in Globalisation', in *Cities and Cinema* (London and New York: Routledge, 2008), 195.
2. George Ritzer, introduction to *The Blackwell Companion to Globalisation* (USA: Blackwell Publishing, 2007), 18.
3. George Ritzer, as cited in *Bollywood and Globalisation: The Global Power of Popular Hindi Cinema*, ed. David J. Schaefer and Kavita Karan (London: Routledge, 2012), 110–11.
4. *Mise-en-scène* is the setting or surroundings of an event. The term is borrowed from a French theatrical expression, roughly meaning 'put into the scene'. In other words, *mise-en-scène* describes the stuff in the frame and the way it is shown and arranged. The major elements of *mise-en-scène* in a film production are the setting, lighting, costume and staging.
5. William van der Heide, ed., *Bollywood Babylon: Interviews with Shyam Benegal* (Oxford: Berg, 2006), 1–2.
6. Anuradha Dingwaney Needham, introduction to *New Indian Cinema in Post-Independence India: The Cultural Works of Shyam Benegal's Films* (London: Routledge, 2013), 1.
7. Van der Heide, 3.
8. Needham, "The Places Occupied by Women': Gender, Subalternity and the (Nation-)state in *Ankur* and *Nishant*', in *New Indian Cinema in Post-Independence India*, 19.
9. M. Madhava Prasad, introduction to *Ideology of the Hindi Film: A Historical Construction* (Delhi: Oxford University Press, 1998), 25.
10. Van der Heide, 5.
11. Prasad, *Ideology of the Hindi Film*, 196.
12. Needham, 3.
13. Aruna Vasudev, quoted in Needham, *New Indian Cinema in Post-Independence India*, 7.
14. Van der Heide, 39–40.

15. Needham, 3.
16. . Henri Lefebvre, *The Production of Space*, trans. Donald Nicholson-Smith (USA: Blackwell Publishing, 1991), 86.
17. Ashis Nandy, *An Ambiguous Journey to the City: The Village and Other Odd Ruins of the Self in the Indian Imagination* (New Delhi: Oxford University Press, 2001), 13.
18. Nandy, 13.
19. Ibid., 13.
20. Ibid., 13.
21. Nandi Bhatia, '*Welcome to Sajjanpur*: Theatre and Transnational Hindi Cinema', in *Travels of Bollywood Cinema: From Bombay to LA*, ed. Anjali Gera Roy and Chua Beng Huat (New Delhi: Oxford University Press, 2012), 200–1.
22. Sassen, quoted in Mennel, 195.
23. Edward W. Soja, *Postmodern Geographies: The Reassertion of Space in Critical Social Theory* (London and New York: Verso, 1989).
24. Rajeev Masand, 'Masand's Verdict: *Welcome to Sajjanpur*', *Rajeev Masand.com: Movies that Matter*, accessed 3 January 2019, <https://www.rajeevmasand.com/uncategorized/masands-verdict-welcome-to-sajjanpur>
25. Masand.
26. Nandi Bhatia, 215.
27. *Welcome to Sajjanpur*, directed by ShyamBenegal (2008; Mumbai: UTV Spot Boy Motion Pictures).
28. Lefebvre, 16, 18, 33.
29. Khalid Mohamed, 'Review: *Welcome to Sajjanpur*', *Hindustan Times*, accessed 3 January 2019, <https://www.hindustantimes.com/movie-reviews/review-welcome-to-sajjanpur/story-Qf5cXupZj3Df41eMWZEhkN.html>
30. Prasad, 25.
31. Bhatia, 213.
32. Lefebvre, 86.
33. Subscriber Trunk Dialling; International Subscriber Dialling; Public Call Office.
34. Ritzer, 18.
35. Prasad, 25.
36. Lefebvre, 16, 18, 33.
37. Namrata Joshi, '*Well Done Abba*', *Outlook*, accessed 5 January 2019, <https://www.outlookindia.com/magazine/story/well-done-abba/264911>
38. Prasad, 216.
39. Arjun Appadurai and Carol A. Breckenridge, 'Public Modernity in India', in *Consuming Modernity: Public Culture in a South Asian World*, ed. Carol A. Breckenridge (Minneapolis: University of Minnesota Press, 1995), 7.
40. Sangeeta Datta, *Shyam Benegal* (London: British Film Institute, 2002; New Delhi: Roli Books, 2008), 74.
41. Thomas Elsaesser, 'Introduction to Early Film Form: Articulations of Space and Time', in *Early Cinema: Space Frame Narrative*, ed. Thomas Elsaesser and Adam Barker (London: British Film Institute, 1990), 12.
42. Datta, 74.
43. Ibid., 75.
44. Needham, 1.
45. Thomas Halper and Douglas Muzzio, 'It's a Wonderful Life: Representations of the Small Towns in American Movies', *European Journal of American Studies* 6, no. 1 (Spring 2011), accessed 30 October 2016, <http://ejas.revues.org/9398>

CHAPTER 14

Shyam Benegal in Conversation with Anuradha Dingwaney Needham[1]

Anuradha Dingwaney Needham (AN): *From what you have mentioned in our earlier conversations, you come from a lively, intellectually vibrant family that encouraged debate and arguments on political, social and cultural subjects and included a fair number of artists/creative people like your cousin Guru Dutt, himself an influential filmmaker. Could you please speak about this family background and its impact on your own work?*

Shyam Benegal (SB): My father was a professional photographer. He had an excellent reputation as a portraitist. In his free time, he would shoot films with his 16mm camera usually featuring his children. He had a huge collection of these films. He had raised a large family – we were ten children in all – and since each child merited a film he would make one devoted to that child until the next one arrived. There were films made on each one of us apart from some others that he had made on different subjects. I was made aware of the cinema from as long back as I can remember. Photography and films were central to our lives from the very beginning. Our after-dinner entertainment usually consisted of watching the films made by my father accompanied by a running commentary volunteered by one of the children, which added a comic edge to the show. That's how my involvement with the cinema began and eventually led me to become a professional filmmaker. It helped that there was a 16mm movie camera that belonged to my father which was available to me, if I ever wanted to use it, which I did when I was around twelve years of age. I made a film about my siblings and cousins coming together during the summer vacation. It was called *Chhutiyon mein Mauj Maza* (*Fun and Games during Holidays*). This was the first film I made.

There was a cinema catering largely to an army garrison close to where we lived, in the cantonment area of the city of Secunderabad/Hyderabad. Since it was primarily meant for the army, there was a change of programme almost every other day – films in different Indian languages with an English-language film being shown on the weekend.

I saw practically every film that was shown there, having befriended the projectionist. Since cinema was a constant presence, I guess it was quite natural for me to become a filmmaker, although I don't believe anyone in my family thought I would become one as I had shown no real interest while at school. It was only much later after having done my MA in Economics and having started my career as a lecturer that I gave it all up and went to Bombay, having decided to follow my instincts and get into filmmaking as quickly as I could. The quickest was for me to join an advertising agency where I got an opportunity to make film commercials, although this was not my original plan. My original intention was to join my cousin Guru Dutt who was already a well-known filmmaker living in Bombay at the time. However, it did not quite work out like that. If anything, he tried to dissuade me, saying that being an assistant to a director was not necessarily the best way forward. Making advertising films gave me an opportunity to learn everything there was to learn on how to make films beginning with ideation, writing scripts, making breakdowns, casting, shooting, editing, recording, mixing and so on – the whole gamut of filmmaking. Within a couple of years, I had made close to 200 films. By the time I gave up advertising films and began my first feature fourteen years later, I had already made upwards of 750 to 800 advertising films and between twenty and thirty documentaries.

AN: *Shyam, let's go back a bit: I remember from our earlier conversations that you talked about your family and how you grew up in this family where argument and debate were often part of the whole way of being...*

SB: I was already over twelve years of age when India became independent. My family was very nationalistic in their outlook. During the early part of the twentieth century, my father was very much involved in the home rule movement. He had left his home near Mangalore in South Karnataka to make a career for himself in Delhi where he found his first job as a photographer's assistant. He got involved in the home rule movement of the time and participated in a number of agitations called by the Congress. Apparently in his youthful enthusiasm, he made a public speech that caught the attention of the British CID. He fled Delhi before the police could apprehend him. The safest place for him to go to was a native state where the colonial police couldn't arrest him. He went to Hyderabad where he became a photographer and started his own studio. All these experiences of his made him a very politically conscious person.

When I was growing up in my parents' home, my father was very particular that the whole family should eat at least one meal a day together. The subject at meal times would usually be politics and my father loved to argue and debate at the table, which was invariably with my older brothers whose opinions were always at odds with one another – particularly my eldest brother who was more than a decade older than me and had gone off to Kolkata to become an artist, where he studied painting at the Kolkata School of Arts.

AN: *He was the one that Guru Dutt went and joined, is that correct? And Guru Dutt stayed with him?*

SB: Guru Dutt and he were very close. My aunt – Guru Dutt's mother – lived with her family in Kolkata. The family lived a fairly modest life there, often helped along financially by my uncle (father's youngest brother). My uncle ran a successful commercial arts studio and had famous clients such as Uday Shankar, the well-known dancer, among them. He also did a lot of publicity designs for American films – hoardings, posters and so on. Uday Shankar's dance troupe had become very well-known, particularly in the United States, and he had Sol Hurok as his promoter in the West. Knowing of Guru Dutt's passion for dance, my uncle who knew Uday Shankar recommended Guru Dutt to him. Soon Guru Dutt became a valuable member of Uday Shankar's dance troupe. When Uday Shankar's troupe dispersed, he helped Guru Dutt find a job as a dancer/choreographer for Prabhat Film Company. Soon, however, Guru Dutt graduated to become a film director. Around that time my oldest brother was living in Kolkata with my uncle and worked with him at his commercial art studio. This was the time a little before India became independent and the Second World War was coming to an end. Bengal was recovering after the great famine and the country appeared to be lurching from one crisis to another. Our dining table at home became a site for heated debates on contemporary politics of the time.

There were votaries of different political ideologies around our dining table. Our father represented a pro-Congress nationalist view. My oldest brother was strongly left of centre, my second brother was close to the RSS in his thinking. There was an uncle who had made his way back to India by foot from Burma when the Japanese invaded Burma. He was largely non-political and engaged in conversations related to literature and the arts, which he felt passionately about. It was at evenings around that dining table that my learning began; more than in the classroom in school.

AN: *Given your almost five-decade long career as a feature and documentary filmmaker; given, moreover, the sheer range of subjects – political, social and cultural concerns – your films engage, what have been some of your most abiding preoccupations? How have they developed over the course of your career in different films? Why do they matter and/or what impact do you see them having on your viewers? So, starting with your career as director from 1974 . . .*

SB: I began my working career soon after finishing my MA. Not finding anything worthwhile in Hyderabad, I came to Mumbai and managed to join an advertising agency as a copywriter at the princely salary of Rs.175/- per month. Fortunately, I managed to find a job with much better pay with Lintas after a few months. This offered me an opportunity that I was looking for all along – to be able to make films; although in this case they were advertising films. Three years later I left Lintas to join yet another advertising agency as the Head of the Film Department. This was a huge step forward as it allowed me to make a large number of advertising films and also gave me enough time to make documentary films independently. It was from here that I took the final step to become an independent, full-time filmmaker.

AN: *Let's focus on your feature films. How do you see your development as an artist and director? You often write your own screenplays, you're very involved with your films, so if you could talk about that arc of development.*

SB: I've held a left-of-centre view of Indian politics from the very beginning. And I have often felt that cinema has a role in helping to initiate social change. At the time of Indian Independence, there was great diversity in the political views and ideologies where I was growing up in Hyderabad, which was a feudal state. A militant communist movement was on at the time against the ruler. When Hyderabad joined the Indian Union, the movement turned into an insurrection against the Indian state. The Communist Party at that time had taken what they called their 'maximum agitational position'. It took the Indian army to quell the revolt. A large number of students and young people were hugely influenced by this; they felt that it was essential to overthrow feudal state structures. This insurrection came to be known as the Telangana movement, which started in 1946, but grew in strength between 1948 and the mid-1950s when it finally petered out. By then, the Communist Party had turned into a regular political party and took part in the first democratic election of independent India. Until that time, however, the Communist Party was underground, fighting – actually at war with – the Indian state. This was the Telangana movement. I was growing up in the middle of all that. The air was thick with politics, the times were very alive, very electric, and much of that atmosphere influenced my early filmmaking. So, there was *Ankur* (*The Seedling*, 1974), *Nishant* (*Night's End*, 1975), and later *Manthan* (*The Churning*, 1976). They dealt with change – social and to some extent political. They also dealt with women's issues. This found centrality in a film like *Bhumika* (*The Role*, 1977). Obviously, my views were influenced by the political atmosphere of the time. I had a fairly individual point of view. This compelled me to write my own scripts – certainly the first draft so that the structure of the film would be clear to the writers who were brought in to detail the scripts with finished dialogues and so on.

AN: *And then, once you go past these films – you also have films like* Trikal (Past, Present and Future, *1985) and* Junoon (The Obsession, *1979) and, you know, the two you made for Shashi Kapoor.*

SB: All this got me seriously interested in our own evolution and history, in Indian history – particularly the history of the last century and the feudal system, which carried on even after India was colonised. I was reading everything that I possibly could, fiction, historical writing, memoirs. This had a lot to do with the kind of subjects I chose to make my films. If you look at my films from 1973 onwards, you will notice rural subjects set in the Indian countryside dealing with near contemporary events set between the 1950s and 1970s. Of course, I went further back in history with *Junoon*, which was set in 1857, and explored the ambivalent relationship that we've always had with the British, who had colonised us for about 200 years. We never viewed them entirely as monsters, as some other countries under British rule did. As much as we hated being their subjects, we appreciated several aspects of their rule and borrowed a great deal from them.

AN: *And then* Trikal *and* . . .

SB: Apart from the British, who colonised most parts of India, there were other European powers that had colonial enclaves in India. The Dutch and the Portuguese. Goa, Daman and Diu were colonised by the Portuguese for almost 500 years, bringing Roman Catholicism with them. I became fascinated with the way in which the Portuguese colonised Goa, which was very different from the way the British had colonised the rest of India. Portuguese termed Goa a part of metropolitan Portugal. They also went on a conversion spree to make Goans totally Christian and Roman Catholic. The British never really cared to convert Indians to Christianity. There were, of course, British missionaries in India, but that was it. Portugal, of course, was keen on making Goa a Christian land. This aspect interested me a great deal. The result of this was my film *Trikal*. It was, in a way, a biography of a house, a seventeenth-century mansion in central Goa. There were lots of comings and goings of Portuguese – functionaries of different kinds, including the Portuguese governor to the mansion over the centuries. The mansion belonged to the family of Mario Miranda, the brilliant cartoonist and caricaturist. Mario belonged to an old patrician family of Goa, who built and owned the mansion and lived in it for over 300 years, and so it was an integral part of his familial memory. Everything in that house had an accumulation of memories of over three centuries. Mario was still living at the time when I planned the film. Sadly, he had passed away when I actually made the film. But his wife was still living and had made the old mansion her home. My fascination with the subject was also because of the language of Goa, which is Konkani. Konkani also happens to be my home language although I speak a dialect as spoken in Mangalore by Hindus, while the Konkani in Goa has been influenced by both Portuguese and Marathi. I felt that I shared a common background particularly with the caste system in Goa which was much like the caste system in Mangalore – you had the Brahmins and the other castes below them – the way it was constituted was very similar. The Portuguese did not attempt to break up the caste system, instead they attempted to convert the Brahmins so the castes below them would automatically follow. The British in India, on the contrary, began the conversions with castes at the bottom of the pyramid. The Portuguese felt that if Brahmins became Christian, it would be far easier to convert the rest of the community. And so, in Goa they created a patrician class of Brahmin Christians who spoke Portuguese even in their homes. And the caste system got easily transposed into the Roman Catholic community in Goa. You had Brahmin Christians and other types of Christians in a hierarchical order who followed some of the social rituals very much the way Hindus did, despite the fact that they were Christians. When you see *Trikal*, you have references to all of that.

AN: *What about the films you made on the epics, for example,* Kalyug (The Mechanical Age, *1981).*

SB: For me, *Kalyug* was a contemporary re-telling of the *Mahabharata* battle between the Pandavas and Kauravas as a contest between two warring industrial families. Such battles were quite common in the pre-corporate industrial period. A contest between cousins in an extended family who are fighting and competing to create their own industrial empires.

AN: *How many films did you make with Shashi Kapoor or for Shashi Kapoor, for his banner? You made* Junoon *and . . .?*

SB: Well, I made only two: one was *Junoon*, the other was *Kalyug*.

AN: *What strikes me is that they're both adaptations –* Kalyug *is based on a very famous epic and* Junoon *is based on a Ruskin Bond story.*

SB: Ruskin Bond had written a story titled *A Flight of Pigeons* based on events that took place in Shahjahanpur in UP during the mutiny of 1857. I had mentioned to Ruskin that I wanted to make a film based on it, and asked him where the events in his story had taken place and he had mentioned Shahjahanpur. I followed up on that and went to Shahjahanpur, where I found the Labadoor (the protagonists) family graves in the cemetery. I looked at the church records for that period and found a lot of the missing links – it was like putting together a crossword puzzle.

AN: *Did you take ideas for these films to Shashi Kapoor and he said, they sound good, or did he approach you with those ideas?*

SB: Shashi Kapoor offered to produce one of my films. I was delighted. He added that he would also like to involve his family in it, which meant that it would be him, his wife, and children since they were a family of actors. Anyway, he said, 'Why don't you think of a subject in which the family could participate.' I mentioned that if Jennifer, his wife, who was English, had to be in it, the story would have to be set (at the time) when the British were still in India. That's when I came upon this particular story, and I felt it was perfect because Jennifer could also feature in it. The children could also be included in the film. I had the daughter Sanjna and her brothers, Kunal and Karan – all three of them in the film.

AN: *One of the things that strikes me is that, as you move from one subject to another, it's not as if the films are sort of clustered, it's not like you decide now I'll make historical films, I'll make films about oppression; when you're looking at the arc – I'm going back to the arc of your career – what kinds of films do you see yourself making now, your more recent ones?*

SB: It depends on what is of interest to me at any given moment. I follow an idea that I find interesting – and the subject emerges from that. If you look at the films I've made from the very beginning until now, they've always had to do with my state of mind at that particular time and the environment in which I have found myself. They could be historical or contemporary subjects – they were always connected to the environment in which I was at the time. That's how it's been all along; there have been long periods of time when I did not make feature films, but worked on other things that engaged me: a fifty-three episode series on Nehru's *Discovery of India* or the series on the Indian Constitution, the ten-part television series *Samvidhaan (The Making of the Indian Constitution)*, which was the last big thing that I did apart from *Jang-e-Azadi (The Battle for Freedom)*, which was the last film I made. It dealt with the history of Punjab. It was a commissioned film. To tell the history of Punjab itself was exciting because Punjab is very different from other parts of India, and has had a somewhat different history particularly from the time of Maharaja Ranjit Singh to the present day – with the Partition clearly being the most traumatic event in the life of Punjab – the entire personality of contemporary Punjab has eventually resulted from the division of Punjab, each part belonging to a different nation.

AN: *'It is always the women who steal the show.' Your viewers rightly make much of your focus on women – the range of female subjects and subjectivities they address,*

Figure 14.1 A scene from *Mandi* (*Market Place*, 1983).

their deep insight into the complex, even tortuous routes to female emancipation. What do you see as the basis for this extended and significant concern? Why, in other words, does it matter to you and why should it matter to your viewers? What kinds of subjects/issues does this concern enable you to foreground and address? A related question: in as much as this preoccupation has also resulted in your introducing some very powerful female actors (Shabana Azmi, Smita Patil) to Indian cinema, how have these actors, in turn, had an impact on the portrayal of female subjectivities so central to your films?

SB. That's very easily answered. When we talk of Indian tradition, there are two distinct sides and aspects. The world of the home and the world outside of the home. If you recall, A. K. Ramanujan translated and often transcribed classical Tamil poems – dealing with the two aspects of living: one concerned with the world of domesticity and the other concerned with the world outside the home – *akam* and *puram*. Traditionally, the world outside is seen as a man's world and the world of the home is seen as a woman's world, and together they complement each other. That complementarity is necessary for a balanced society – the yin and yang as it were. Today, that balance no longer exists; once you enter the modern world, you no longer are in the world of complementarity, you are in the world of competition. You have women doing jobs that traditionally were meant only for men and you have men doing jobs that traditionally were supposed to be reserved for women. In a situation like this, when it is assumed that it's a man's world out there – women being relegated to second place is no longer acceptable. Contemporary lifestyles and societal arrangements, particularly relating to urban living, force women to take up two jobs – one of sharing the economic burden of earning or living and the second of running the home and rearing a family. There are two sets of responsibilities while the male has the single responsibility of going out and finding a job and feeding the family. The woman has to deal with both: to look after the home, bear children, nurture them *and* also work outside the home and be a wage earner. This dual responsibility forces Indian women to be much stronger than their men folk. So, it is, in my films, whether it's *Ankur* or some of the others, it wasn't that I had planned to represent women in this way. It was actually the experience of women in India collectively. And this got spotlighted in the films I made at the time. It was far more unconscious than a conscious choice. And then, of course, there were biographical films like *Bhumika*, based on the autobiography of a Marathi film actress, Hansa Wadkar, whose feminist views emerged from her own personal experience. That was probably one of the reasons why women took centre stage in several of my early features. This was reinforced by my own predilection towards creating strong women characters. As far as Indian cinema is concerned, this was not the norm, as you well know. Typically, it would be a male who would be the main protagonist while women are brought in to add charm and beauty to the scene, but were not necessarily central to the story. And, in my case, as I said, it wasn't that I chose to do that: the kind of stories I wanted to tell just happened to have strong central characters who happened to be women, whether it was in *Ankur, Nishant, Manthan* or *Bhumika*. If you look at most of the films, particularly the earlier ones, you'll find that it's something that kept happening, without my even being conscious of it. This put the spotlight on several talented women performers, and actors – for instance, Shabana Azmi, Smita Patil, one after the other – and soon female actors found centrality in Indian films as never before.

AN: *Complementing this centrality of women, there are other considerations; in* Ankur, *it is feudal oppression in general as, too, in* Nishant, *and in* Bhumika, *of course, it is more focused on her biography as a woman, but it was also your interest in certain other questions that helped you to foreground women, would you say?*

SB: Yes, she is making her way in what was considered a man's world; being an actress, she didn't find it easy. For male actors, it was quite easy to function, but for women, it's always been a problem. You'll find that we've had so many actresses who were absolutely at the very top of their profession – but most of

Figure 14.2 A scene from *Bhumika* (1977).

them had one problem or another; either they became alcoholics or something unfortunate happened to them. And a large number led very unhappy lives, not because they wanted to but because they were forced into that situation. If you look at the Indian film industry, you will find that the change accelerated between the 1950s and the 1980s. It was a time when India itself was changing much faster than before. Today it is no longer a man's world out there. Times have changed and Indian society itself is changing quite rapidly. Women are becoming far more aware of their own rights now, whether it's in rural or urban India. At the time I was making my earlier films, depicting the everyday experience of women in our society, they had barriers to cross and hills to climb that men never needed to. Whether I liked it or not, they became the centre of the story.

AN: *I want to press you a little bit on that because you keep saying, 'I did not choose to do so, but the stories I wanted to make all had strong women, and women inevitably became the focus' – it makes it sound as if it were something that just happened, whereas the fact that you were choosing the stories themselves says something about your investment in women as characters, right?*

SB: Yes, that too is very easily explained. If you look at my own family for instance, my mother brought up her ten children, kept them all in good health until their adulthood, held the family together and did not crack up under the strain while my father was busy working to make two ends meet. This is something I witnessed at very close quarters and something I saw around me generally: women shouldered responsibilities that were far greater than what men were taking on. When you see this every day in India, it becomes part of your consciousness. This often comes to the fore when you're choosing stories, creating characters, or working out plots quite subconsciously.

AN: *People say this about New Indian Cinema in particular – I'm not trying to label your films necessarily, but you're all considered part of a group concerned with these things – that it not only focused on all sorts of oppressions, you know, economic oppression and feudal oppression, but also women's oppression at a time when women were very active against their own subjection, and that had a significant impact on films made by, for example, Girish Kasaravalli, Girish Karnad, Mrinal Sen, you – that this focus on women was sort of a preoccupation of this group of filmmakers. Do you agree with that, do you see yourself as part of that?*

SB: Up to a point. Not entirely, but up to a point, yes. But I will take some of the credit because I didn't wish to portray women as victims, though it would have been very easy to do so. The moment you start to look at women only as victims of Indian social and traditional circumstances, you are not giving them the credit they deserve – you don't recognise their own strength, the strength they actually have. I was looking at their strength rather than at their victimhood: their strength to fight back, their strength to stand up on their own two feet, that sort of thing. That was something, I think, quite new in Indian cinema at the time.

Yes, women have been at the centre of many film stories of Indian Cinema; they were mainly seen as victims, as being victimised, but I was looking at this from another point of view. They were fighting their victimhood, by fighting and struggling against oppression, not just sitting there and bemoaning their victimhood. If you look at most nineteenth-century/early twentieth-century Indian literature, you'll find that women are seen languishing in their victimhood.

AN: *Can you speak a little bit about how you went about choosing the stories? Ankur, for example – I know, you said how you had carried the short story around for a long time – and* Nishant, *because, again, that says something about how particular kinds of stories interested you.*

SB: Stories emerged from real events. *Ankur* was based on a real incident, and *Nishant* was based on what occurred during the Telangana movement in a village uprising against a feudal landlord. And this is true for stories I chose later as well. For example, *Mandi* (*Market Place*, 1983) was based on a well-known

Urdu short story, which in turn was based on a real event that took place in the 1920s in a neighbourhood in Allahabad. Jawaharlal Nehru's father lived in a neighbourhood that skirted the red-light district of the town. He wanted that whole neighbourhood cleared of the woman who plied their trade there. This incident was the basis of that short story. *Ankur* was based on an incident that took place not far from where we lived in the 1950s, and *Nishant* was based on a local rural uprising in the late 1940s. *Manthan* was contemporary to the time of the film's making, and *Bhumika*, of course, was based on an autobiography written by a Marathi film actress. So, you see, they were all based on real incidents. There was a great amount of fiction in them, but also a great amount of fact. You could say that these films were based on what was happening in our society; it was something that I could relate to. I think this was also the case with the actors in those films as well, particularly the actresses you referred to who played strong women characters with such conviction. Take, for instance, Shabana Azmi – she's been an active feminist, as was Smita Patil.

AN: *I know that directors and writers make/do things for themselves, that they are moved by ideas, but surely, you're also thinking about these films as having an impact on spectators, the viewers who go to the films?*

SB: When you are making a film, you are trying to tell the story in the best way possible. While filming, you're not really thinking whether it would appeal to a particular audience or not. Nor do you consider the kind of audience it will appeal to – all that happens after the film is made. At that time, you are trying to tell your story in a way that would appeal to anyone who might want to see that film. That's how you work on it. Later on, after you've made the film, then you start to consider who you think it will appeal to; that's when you're marketing the film and that's really when your distributors and exhibitors start to place the film in a particular way in the marketplace. They may feel a certain film appeals to women more than to men, or to a largely urban audience or a metropolitan audience and not a semi-rural audience and so on. When you're making a film, you're not thinking of any of these things; you're attempting to make it as well as you can.

AN: *People sometimes think about your career in terms of two or three films on the same subject; for example,* Ankur *and* Nishant *both are about the country and a particular region at a particular moment. I'm wondering if having chosen one female character as central had an impact, and you kept on returning to that as a way of intensifying that focus, or was that not a consideration?*

SB: If you think about it, *Ankur* and *Nishant* are situated in the same kind of milieu. They are set in Telangana at a certain time in contemporary history – between the late 1940s and the mid-1950s. This was when feudal attitudes were giving way; being challenged. It was no longer comfortably settled in the feudal ways the way it had been for almost half a millennium. Times were changing, and that change manifested itself in the characters of the story as well. Later, when India became independent, other changes started to take place – both economic and social. Development through co-operative action is one such example. And so, there's *Manthan*, a story relating to the creation of milk cooperatives. How poor farmers owning single cows living on the margins come together to create co-operatives to pool and market their products, improving not only their own collective existence but improving the environment around them as well. This, too, was based on what was happening at the time.

I have always been very interested in looking at change elements in our society, those that have made a huge difference to communities and transformed them. All my films are concerned with some element of change.

AN: *I think about films like* Bhumika *and* Sardari Begum *– and I know that you and I probably are not on the same page about this – that obviously are looking at changes because they are recording the changes happening in a society at a time a little before the moment of the films themselves, but I'm thinking of how they look back to an earlier set of concerns around performing women or prostitutes or actresses, which engages a different kind of history – different from the history, let's say, in* Junoon, *and the other historical films you made.*

SB: *Junoon* deals with larger history, but my interest is cantered more on what is happening on a micro level, on individuals and how they are affected. If you look at *Mandi* and *Sardari Begum*, they too deal with history, not with major events, but with history, nonetheless. *Mandi* is the story of displacement due to changes taking place in modern India; the government decides to build a dam at a catchment area affecting a number of villages, displacing people living there and then the problems related to their rehabilitation. Physical, psychological, environmental. These are all problems arising from change, problems that concern us all. Stories emerging from such situations have always been of great interest to me.

AN: *Earlier, when you spoke about* akam *and* puram, *I thought about Ray's* Home and the World. *When you made your documentary on Ray, you did most of it on the set of this film. Why Ray, and why that particular decision to film it on set? Was it a strategic, deliberate choice, or did that simply happen to be the time and place that he was available to you?*

SB: It was quite coincidental. It just happened that Ray had chosen a particular short story of Tagore's to make into a film – *Home and the World*. Ray, too, was looking at the world much like Tagore did – the domestic world and the larger world outside of the home; *akam* and *puram* as it were. I was making a documentary on Ray at the time and was filming with him while he was shooting his film *Ghare-Baire* (*The Home and the World*, 1984). It was easy for me to make the film on him because he trusted me. At that time, I saw myself as a kind of *chela* (disciple) of his. So, it was an easy film to make; he was not guarded, openly expressing his opinions. He was relaxed and informal and the work was much easier than I expected. I think he was quite happy with the way the film turned out. I say this because we were supposed to make a twenty-minute film for Films Division. I ended up making a film that was over two hours long. I didn't wish to cut it down and, when Ray himself saw the film, he was very happy with it just the way it was. He only had one comment to make. 'One of the problems with this film', he said, 'is that there's too much Ray and too little Benegal.' But that's how it was supposed to be, that's what I thought it had to be, although I guess he expected I'd put more of myself in the film since I was the filmmaker.

AN: *And, of course, other people were involved in the film like Jennifer Kapoor, who had worked with you. She was on the set, at least during the scene that the documentary foregrounds, the one in which she's teaching the piano to Bimala . . .*

SB: It was on that particular set [of *Ghare-Baire*] that my interview with him began, although it took me almost a year and a half to complete the film because I could only do short spells of shooting with him from time to time since he was very busy at the time and I had to find moments when he was free to speak to me, whether in Calcutta, or Bombay, or wherever else he could find time for me. I think it worked out reasonably well because my film on him is the only definitive film on him and his work. Nobody else has made such a detailed film on Satyajit Ray; it's become part of the collection of the British Film Institute as well as collections in the United States and Europe. I am very happy with it because it gives you a fairly comprehensive view of Satyajit Ray as a person and a filmmaker and the kind of films he made.

AN: *Let's talk about your making of the* Discovery of India; *the reason I bring this up is because you imported a lot of new information into it. For example, when you wanted to talk about Gandhi, you used R. K. Narayan's novel and then you also used different sorts of cultural forms, including classical dances and theatre. Why did you make that choice? Because that's not necessarily how Nehru approaches the* Discovery of India, *the overarching history of India that he presents.*

SB: I was using Jawaharlal Nehru's *Discovery of India* merely as the spine of the story. It really was the Story of India, an overarching view of India as a whole. Of course, Nehru's was a very useful point of view for the very simple reason that he was not a professional historian – he looked at his country as a committed citizen. He was but a politically involved person who was fighting to make India independent of colonial rule, and that was the basis on which he started to write *Discovery of India*. In the beginning, he wrote letters to his daughter introducing her to her nation. She was young and he was in jail. And as there was no parental connection with the child during the long periods of time he spent in jail, he wrote her letters to augment her education, offering her a view of the world, which really was his own worldview. Later he continued with the practice, writing longer letters for and to her, as she was growing up, in greater detail, which were compiled and published as the book, *Glimpses of World History*. The first set of letters became the book *Letters from a Father to his Daughter,* written when she was a child, and after that, *Glimpses of World History* written to her when she was in her early teens, and finally a comprehensive story of India titled *Discovery of India*, written while he was in Ahmednagar jail during his last incarceration and his daughter was already a young woman. All these three books constituted the spine of my story. I used Jawaharlal Nehru as the narrator. But I wanted the series to be more than the subjective view of a single person. So, I consulted several historians of our country to create a more objective point of view (this viewpoint is articulated by Om Puri) and then I added a third point of view, which was my own. So, we had three points of view from which we viewed our history. For instance, you referred to R. K. Narayan. I brought in literary works from different period of India's history. There were medieval texts from Rajasthan, there were the great epics from the classical period, different literary works from different parts of India, so that you got a culturally comprehensive picture of India; not just its political history, but its cultural history as well – the history of Indian music, the historical evolution of its poetry and poetic forms, and so on. It was a massive project for me. Needless to say, it was an extremely enriching experience. The series became an important one for Indian television; it was repeated several times over the years. And the Government of India decided that they would use the series for teaching history in government schools in different parts of India. So, eventually the TV series *Discovery of India*, which was titled *Bharat Ek Khoj* in Hindi, found many uses.

AN: *Could you comment on your engagement with iconic figures of India's history – for example, Gandhi in* The Making of the Mahatma; *Nehru in the three-hour documentary for Films Division,* Bharat Ek Khoj *about which we have spoken already, and Subhas Chandra Bose in* Bose: The Forgotten Hero? *How did you go about deciding what the treatment of a particular figure should be? And to what end? Could you also please comment on your interest in these figures in particular? In other words, why these?*

Figure 14.3 A scene from *The Making of the Mahatma* (1996).

SB: Well, *The Making of the Mahatma* is one of them. It was a co-production between the Government of India and the newly formed Government of South Africa, soon after apartheid had been abolished and the new government was formed with Nelson Mandela as the new president. At that time, the South African government felt that of those countries that had supported South African majority rule, India was among the most important, since it had been steadfast in its support. Soon after South Africa got rid of the apartheid, the South African Broadcasting Corporation, which ran the main TV channel of South Africa, wanted to make a film on Nelson Mandela. About that time, I had been invited to South Africa by Fatima Meer, an eminent anti-apartheid activist who had written a book called *The Apprenticeship of the Mahatma* on the young Gandhi in South Africa. It told the story of a young Gandhi who arrived in South Africa to try and earn a living as a lawyer as he found it difficult to get briefs in India. He thought it better to pursue a career in South Africa where there was a fairly large Indian population. But when he went to South Africa, he got involved in the politics of South Africa of the time and started to fight for the cause of the majority of South Africans, who were the black and coloured communities including indentured labour from India shipped there to work on plantations. Fatima Meer's father worked closely with Gandhi at the time. When I was invited to South Africa, her original intention was to ask me to make a film on Nelson Mandela. However, I felt that I was not the right person to make a film on Nelson Mandela. It would make more sense for a native South African to make such a film. I may have known enough about contemporary South African history, but didn't really know the complexity of South African politics, to make a truly credible film on the subject. I suggested to Fatima that I would rather make a film based on her book, since I could easily relate to Gandhi. The South African Broadcasting Company was willing to co-produce such a film and, in fact, Nelson Mandela also agreed to the proposal, so my film on young Gandhi became the very first film that the first black majority Government of South Africa decided to produce. I wrote the script and shot the entire film in South Africa. Nelson Mandela was extremely supportive. It was an immense honour when he presented the film both in Durban and Johannesburg. We made the film, had it presented, and released it there with the participation of the South African Broadcasting Corporation, so the entire nation of South Africa saw the film. We titled the film *The Making of the Mahatma*. It didn't get much of a release in India, but it turned out to be far more successful in South Africa.

Before making the film on young Gandhi, I had already made a three-hour long documentary on Jawaharlal Nehru. It was shown in three parts on the 100th anniversary of his birth in 1989. A Government of India project, it was presented by the president of India at the Rashtrapati Bhawan in Delhi. Nehru was my idol, and since my childhood, like many of my generation, I had grown up reading his books. When I was about nine or ten years of age, I was presented with a copy of *Letters from a Father to His Daughter*, a book made up of letters that Nehru had written to his daughter from jail at the time she was starting her schooling. After that, I read his *Glimpses of World History*, a much more expansive work dealing with all of world history. *Glimpses of World History* was a very important book for me; I learnt a great deal from it and it helped me acquire a worldview. A lot of orthodox historians do not consider it as particularly good history. For me however, it was revelatory. My interest in history deepened greatly on account of it. There was a third book Nehru wrote while in jail – when he found the time to write: *Discovery of India*. It was the book I dipped into to make my fifty-three-hour television series *Bharat Ek Khoj*. I later made a biographical film on Subhas Chandra Bose which was produced by Sahara India. I shot the film in Calcutta, Myanmar and Southeast Asia, that is, Singapore and Malaysia. That was the third biopic I made about our nationalist leaders after Gandhi and Nehru. There was also a biographical film I made on a film actress of the 1930s and 40s, *Bhumika* in 1976. Altogether, I made four biographical films: *Bhumika* based on the life of Hansa Wadkar and three others on Jawaharlal Nehru, Mahatma Gandhi and Subhas Chandra Bose.

AN: *Of course, their texture is different in each case.* Bhumika *is also, as you have said, about the early history of cinema in India.*

SB: Yes, it deals with the development of Indian cinema from the silent era through to the sound era. It is as much the story of the evolution of Indian cinema as it is the story of Hansa Wadkar.

AN: *Let's move to – I have a list of films over here* – Kondura *(The Sage from the Sea,* Hindi version, *1978)/* Anugraham *(The Boon,* Telugu version, *1978);* Suraj Ka Satvan Ghoda *(The Sun's Seventh Horse, 1992); and, then, of course, what is called your Muslim women trilogy (*Mammo, Sardari Begum *and* Zubeidaa*); and* Hari-Bhari *(Fertility, 2000). The film that stands out among all these is* Suraj Ka Satvan Ghoda *because there, unlike the other films where you're sort of interested in a particular thematic political strand, you seem to be experimenting with the narrative itself, right?*

SB: Dharamvir Bharati wrote a story, based on which I made *Suraj Ka Satvan Ghoda*, creating multiple narratives from different points of view on a single set of events, which I found both challenging and exciting to make as a film. It was to use seemingly objective visual images in subjective ways. I filmed the story in the same way Dharamvir Bharati had written it. He and I spoke about it and he seemed somewhat sceptical about it working out. He felt it was far too experimental. He offered me another book of his to make instead. However, it was the experimental aspect that I found challenging and exciting. I was very worried that it might not work, but eventually it did because audiences seemed to have negotiated their way through the film's narrative successfully. It was one of my experiments that actually worked.

AN: *And the bilingual one? Why did you choose . . . ?*

SB: *Anugraham/Kondura? Kondura* is an outstanding Marathi novel set in the Konkan. The novel was based on local lore and is outstanding. I felt it would make a wonderful film, but no one seemed willing to put up the money to produce *Kondura*. None of my producers were particularly interested in it. Then one day, a Telugu film producer came up to me, and suggested that I make the film in Telugu. I felt I could make two versions, in Telugu and in Hindi. I felt he could release the Telugu version and perhaps find a distributor to release the Hindi adaptation. So, we shot two versions of the film, the Telugu version was called *Anugraham*, and the Hindi version was called *Kondura*, the title of the novel. I shot both simultaneously. The main actor, Anant Nag, who is Hindi-speaking and a wonderful performer, learned to speak Telugu so that he could do the Telugu part himself. Vanisri, a very well-known Telugu actress at the time, also played both parts. However, in some cases, I had to use two separate actors – one for the Hindi version and a different actor for the Telugu version. In the case of Vanisri, however, the Hindi version was dubbed, which did not work too well because each language comes with its own body language. However, both language versions were made; the Telugu version did fairly well in the marketplace, but the Hindi version collapsed, despite the fact that Smita Patel had a very important part in it, and at that time, she was already a well-known star because of *Bhumika*, for which she had won the National Award. But the fact was the film didn't work at all in Hindi as it did in Telugu.

AN: Arohan *(*The Ascent, *1982) was a little bit like* Manthan, *because it too was produced by a co-operative?*

SB: As you know, Bengal went through a very volatile time in the late seventies with the Naxalite movement and frequently changing governments: a United Front government that brought communists into the government for the first time in Bengal was soon brought down. However, it was replaced by a Left Front government in which the communists dominated. When the Left Front was in power, they decided that films should mirror the reality of Bengal – and deal with the problems and challenges of accelerated social, political and economic change – land reforms being one of them. As you know, land reforms were causing a great deal of social and economic churning in the countryside and the Left Front was very keen that the land reforms being undertaken by the government should find cinematic depiction. The Bengal government contacted Mrinal Sen, M. S. Sathyu and me, asking us whether we would like to make films on the radical changes taking place in Bengal. There was no other brief. Sathyu, Mrinal Sen and I made our separate films. Mine was based on a report written by a Deputy Commissioner of one of the districts of Bengal. It was an interesting case of a peasant farmer trying to get back his rights to the land on which he was working. He was being forced to work as a tenant farmer even though the land he worked on actually belonged to him; the landlord had taken control of the land as the farmer owed him money. The farmer became a kind of a serf of the landlord on land that was his own and not the landlord's – this system was known as *bargadari*. I decided to make a true-life story written by the Deputy Commissioner of that particular district into a feature film. The leftist government of the time agreed. The film was to be made in Hindi (not Bengali) because I wanted it to be shown all over the country. The other two filmmakers made their films in Bengali. My film won the National Award for being the best film of the year, and the government of West Bengal itself released the film in Bengal, but it didn't get a good release in the rest of India. It also won Om Puri (who played the dispossessed farmer) the best actor award not only in India, but also at the Karlovy Vary International Film Festival in Czechoslovakia. This was his first International award. His performance was noticed on an international level and opened doors for him in international cinema, where he gained an excellent reputation as an actor, particularly in the UK and the US.

AN: *And* Hari-Bhari, *which Shabana calls one of your 'cause-related' films – that was supported by a co-operative of some kind, no? Or am I mistaken there?*

SB: No, no. Not *Hari-Bhari*. Actually, the film had Shabana in it. Somehow it didn't seem to work as well as I would have liked it. It deals with problems in a Muslim family – one of the big problems in India cinema is that our films rarely deal with communities other than the majority Hindu community. The moment one tries to make a film in a Muslim setting or with the Christian community, there is a general perception that it will not be of mainstream interest. The Indian film industry by and large makes films about the Hindu community because they feel that films about the Muslim minority may not appeal to the majority community. And when they do make films about the Muslim community, it's usually for exotic reasons. I wanted to break that; I didn't want to make a film that seemed stereotypically exotic. Subsequently, I made three films dealing with Muslim families over the years. In 1985, I had made a film called *Trikal* about a Roman Catholic Christian family in Goa.

AN: *Let's try to round it up by talking about two things, films you recently made –* Welcome to Sajjanpur *and* Well Done Abba *(*Well Done Father, *2009) – and films you've thought about making –* Carmen *and a film on Noor Inayat Khan that you've sometimes mentioned. Maybe we could end with that?*

SB: *Welcome to Sajjanpur* and *Well Done Abba* were based on human interest stories that were published in local newspapers as reports of events in different parts of the country. For instance, *Well Done Abba* was about a farmer who dug a well single-handedly because he needed water to irrigate his little farm. Stories like that, done in a comic way, but dealing with serious problems and real issues. Both turned out quite well. In fact, both were reasonably successful, having covered their costs and made a little profit for the producers.

Of the projects I've been wanting to do, one is a Rajasthani adaptation of *Carmen*, which is presently a screenplay waiting for someone to produce it. Then I have two other scripts that have also been sitting around for a while. One is called *Holi*, which deals with *Lathmar Holi*; *Lathmar Holi* is celebrated in the Mathura/Agra area of Uttar Pradesh on the day of Holi, when women are allowed to beat the hell out of men, the one day of the year they have permission to do so. In traditional Indian society, women generally tend to be subservient to men, but on this one day of the year, the position gets reversed. This is in compensation for all they have suffered through the year.

AN: *Carnival. It's like carnival where you invert social hierarchies for one day, there's an inversion of roles.*

SB: Yes. There is a reversal of traditional roles: women beating the hell out of men with lathis – I mean it's not play acting – they actually beat the men who are made to run all over the place, to avoid being hit with staves. At the same time other women throw colour and douse them with water. *Holi* is based on that, but it also deals with some of the incidents in the great Sanskrit classic *The Gita Govinda* (*The Song of Govind*). I have used a lot of the original poetry from the classic. That's another script I'm hoping to film. And, of course . . .

AN: *Noor Inayat Khan.*

SB: *Noor* . . . I no longer feel hopeful about it. I've tried very hard over a considerably long time. I have done a lot of research, went to England to find a financier, but it never really worked out. It was a fairly expensive proposition since it needed to be shot in Britain and France, and was a period piece – the period during the Second World War when Noor Inayat Khan became an indispensable spy for the British in Europe under German occupation until she was arrested by the Gestapo and put to death in a concentration camp in Germany.

AN: *So, what do you see in the near and far future in terms of what your filmmaking career will be?*

SB: Well, I'm not quite sure really, because it depends, you know. There are two things that work against me at this moment. One is age, because a lot of people probably feel that I should really be retiring from all this. I don't wish to retire, of course, but in the film business, the moment you cross eighty everybody thinks, why do you persist in wanting to do this kind of work? – It takes a lot out of you to make a film – that sort of thing. But, I will continue to persist. There still are people who have shown interest in some of the films I have mentioned; every two weeks, someone or the other calls: why don't you do it like this or that? All this goes on. But I haven't made a film for the last two-and-a-half years. Well, if it happens, it happens, and if it doesn't there is nothing I can do about it. But I do have these scripts with me, and I hope that I will be able to turn at least one of the scripts into a film.

NOTE

1. This conversation with Shyam Benegal was conducted by Anuradha Dingwaney Needham over three 45–55-minute periods on 10, 11 and 12 August 2018.

Index

Note: *italic* indicates a figure, n indicates a note

Abbas, Ghulam: 'Anandi', 73, 82n32
Abbas, K. A.: *Dharti Ke Laal* (*Children of the Earth*), 119–20
adaptation studies, 196–8
Adhar, Neelima Dalmia: *The Secret Diary of Kasturba*, 171, 177, 180
Advani, L. K.: *Ram Rath Yatra*, 154
Agache, Mohan, 34
agrarian relations, 120–4; *see also* feudalism; land system
'Ajneya' (Sachchidanand Hiranand Vatsyayan), 135
Ali, Nafisa, 92
Allahabad, 234
Allen, Richard, 156, 163
alternative cinema, 12, 199–200
Ambedkar, Dr B. R., 51, 52, 53, 54, 59
Anand, Chetan: *Neecha Nagar* (*The Lower Depths*), 119–20
Anderson, Benedict, 106–7
Andrew, James Dudley, 13, 173–4
Ankur (*The Seedling*), 1, 12, *18*, 226, 231–2, 233

awards, 136
beating scene, 24–5
card game scene, 22
caste discrimination, 14–16, 20, 25, 120
consecration rituals, 34
and contemporaneity, 101
feudalism, 48, 103, 120, 209, 234–5
language, 39
as middle cinema, 209
mirrors and mirroring, 16, 17
modernity, 22, 29
origins, 234
as parallel cinema, 135–6
patriarchy, 14–15, 18, 22, 23, 26
plot, 15–16
production, 34
protest metaphor, 21, 22, 23–5, 26
realism, 13, 14
subalterneity, 15, 17, 18, 23
technology, 104
themes, 15, 16, 18–19, 23
as third cinema, 14, 32
trial scene, 19–20, *19*

window symbolism, 25
women, 172
Anugraham (The Boon), 240, 241
Appadurai, Arjun, 220
Arohan (The Ascent), 120, 125–32, *126, 127*, 241
art
 and imperialism, 85
 tamasha (folk art), 65–6
Asad, Talal, 35
Attenborough, Richard: *Gandhi*, 177, 181, 205
Azmi, Kaifi, 102, 169n17
Azmi, Shabana, 5, 14, *35, 40*, 99n42, 103, 136, 234, 242

Babbar, Raj, 105
Bachchan, Amitabh, 1
Bahadur Shah Zafar, 91, 92
Balibar, Étienne, 108
bandh see *hartal*
Banerjee, Victor, 105
Bangabandhu, 4
Bano, Jeelani: *Narsayyaki Bavdi (Narsayya's Well)*, 216
bargadars, 125, 127–8, 129, 130, 132
Barker, Thomas Jones: *The Relief of Lucknow* (painting), 85
Barnes, Julian: *England, England*, 83 (epigraph), 97
Barnwal, Pramod Kumar, 6
Barthes, Roland, 174
Basu, Jyoti, 131–2
Bates, Crispin, 90, 96
Bazin, André, 13
Beato, Felice, 85
Benegal, Sadanand, 2
Benegal, Shridhar, 2, 223, 224–5
Benegal, Shyam
 and advertising, 12, 209, 226
 awards, 4, 135, 136, 210–11, 217, 241
 on Babri Masjid mosque, 154

 on *Bose: The Forgotten Hero*, 200
 and children's film, 4
 and children's television, 3
 choice of stories, 233–4
 and class, 120
 and comedy, 212, 214
 creative sensibilities, 187
 documentaries, 3, 53, 168, 196, 224, 229, 235, 236–9
 early career, 3, 136, 224, 226
 early life, 2, 209
 education, 2, 3
 and the female psyche, 20–1
 and feminism, 26, 158, 185–6
 and feudalism, 103–4, 227
 films *see* names of individual films
 financing of films, 167
 future projects, 243
 and Hindi cinema, 210
 honorary degrees, 136
 and humour, 213
 influences, 136, 229
 introduction to film, 2–3, 223–4
 on *Junoon*, 85
 and language, 227–8
 and the local, 212
 on *Mahabharata*, 110
 and materialism, 114
 and 'Middle Cinema', 170n28
 and past and present, 159
 and politics, 25, 48, 136, 226
 and realism, 172, 209
 and 'reform', 8In7, 210
 and regional-nationalism, 12–13
 and rural spaces, 220
 and satire, 213
 and scriptwriting, 226
 on social morality, 111
 studies of, 5–7, 12
 'Talkies, Movies, Cinema' essay, 53
 as a teacher, 3, 136
 and women's issues, 172–3, 229–33

Bengal
  agrarian relations, 120–4
  communists, 127
  Left Front (LF) government, 129, 131–2, 241
  Naxalite movement, 125, 128, 241
  strikes, 132
Bharat Ek Khoj (*The Discovery of India*), 4, 168, 229, 236–7, 239
Bharati, Dharmavir *Suraj Ka Satvan Ghoda* (*The Sun's Seventh Horse*), 135, 137–8, 144–5, 146, 147, 148, 240
Bharatiya Janata Party (BJP), 169n5
Bhaskar, Ira, 156, 163
Bhatia, Nandi, 212, 215
Bhatia, Vanraj, 170n48
Bhiwandi riots (1984), 169n16
Bhumika (*The Role*), 4, 66, 226, 231, 232, 239–40
  caste discrimination, 66–8, 69–70
  contemporaneity, 101
  female liberation, 73
  as feminist cinema, 65
  origins, 234
  patriarchy, 65, 66, 68–9, 70, 71–3, 78
  prostitution, 65, 74
  and social change, 235
  technology, 104
  women, 172; labour of, 65–73, 74, 79
  writing credits, 102
Bijlani, Mohan, 39
biopics
  actors, 205
  adaptation studies, 196–8
    definition, 197–8
    historical, 173–5, 176–82
    political, 198
  see also *Bhumika*; *Bose: The Forgotten Hero*; *Making of the Mahatma*, *The*
Bisaria, Rajina Raj, 186
Blaze Advertising Agency, 12, 34
Blaze Films, 39

Bobby, 1
Boehmer, Elleke, 84, 89, 93–4, 96
Bollywood, 212, 214
Bombay riots (1993), 154, 185
Bond, Ruskin: *A Flight of Pigeons*, 83, 84, 86, 90–1, 95, 96, 228
Bose: The Forgotten Hero, 4, 201, 202, 204
  as alternative cinema, 201
  as a historical biopic, 196, 198–206, 239
  role of Bose, 205
  soundtrack, 205–6
Bose, Jagadish Chandra, 116n3
Bose, Subhas Chandra see *Bose: The Forgotten Hero*; *Gumnaami*
Boucicault, Dion: *Jessie Brown, or the Relief of Lucknow*, 95
bourgeoisie, 118–19
Brahmins, 228
  Saraswat Brahmins, 10n5
Breckenridge, Carol A., 220
British Empire 84, 175, 227, 228; see also Pax Britannica
Brown, Tom, 197, 198
Brunsdon, Catherine, 87
Butalia, Urvashi, 193

Calcutta *see* Kolkata
Canning, Charlotte, 85
Carmen, 242
Cartmell, Deborah, 197, 198
caste discrimination, 51, 172, 228
  Ankur (*The Seedling*), 14–16, 20, 25–6
  Bhumika (*The Role*), 66–8, 69–70
  Manthan (*The Churning*), 48, 49, 50, 54–5, 57
  in villages, 52, 59
  and women's liberation, 64–5
  see also untouchables
Cawnpore, siege of, 92, 95
Chakrabarty, Dipesh, 62n16

INDEX

Chanda, Samir, 203
Charandas Chor (Charandas, the Thief), 4, 101–2
Chatterjee, Dhritiman, 125
Chatterjee, Partha, 120, 121, 122
Chatterjee, Prosenjit, 206
Chatterjee, Saibal, 10
Chatterjee, Sarat Chandra: *Devadas*, 149
Chatterji, Shoma, 155, 187, 189, 194
Chaudhuri, B. B., 121
Chekhov, Anton, 137
Child of the Streets, 3
Chopra, Samir, 6
Christianity, 227, 228; see also Roman Catholicism
Chughtai, Ismat, 102, 158
Chuttiyon Mein Mouj Mazha (Fun in the Holidays), 3
cities, 211, 213
class conflict, 118, 133
   Arohan (The Ascent), 120, 125
   Bengal, 120–4
   Sen and, 125
   see also caste discrimination
co-operative movement, 49, 52, 53
Collins, Wilkie see Dickens, Charles and Collins, Wilkie
colonialism, 94, 227; see also British Empire
Communist Party of India, 30, 44n4, 226
communists, 127, 241; see also Maoists
Congress Party, 128, 132
   'Settlement Operation' programme, 130
consecration rituals, 33–6

Dalits, 14–15, 19, 61n2
Dasgupta, Chidananda, 119, 209
Datta, Sangeeta, 5–6, 12, 32–3
   on *Ankhur*, 25, 39
   on *Kalyug*, 113
   on location shooting, 220
   on *Mammo*, 155, 157

D'Cunha, Jean, 75
De Sica, Vittorio, 14
democracy, 48, 52, 59–60, 118, 119, 120, 124, 125, 131, 133, 210, 215
   Committee for the Protection of Democratic Rights, 44n4
Deshpande, Anirudh, 118–19
'design-made films', 2
*devdasi*s, 66, 67, 68
Dhanagere, D. N., 36
Dickens, Charles and Collins, Wilkie: *The Perils of Certain English Prisoners*, 84
disclaimers, 44n3
Doane, Mary Ann, 26
Doordarshan (television network), 4, 167, 168
Dubey, Lillete, 189
Dubey, Satyadev, 34, 35, 86, 101, 102
Dutt, Guru, 3, 12, 136, 224, 225
Dwyer, Rachel, 156

Ektara Collective: *Turup (Checkmate)*, 80
elites, 60, 112, 122
Elliott, Kamilla, 197
Elsaesser, Thomas, 220
Englishness, 85
epistemicide, 89, 90

family planning, 63n23
Fanthome, J. F.: *Mariam*, 83
feminism
   Benegal and, 20, 26, 158, 185–6
   Dalit, 62n20
   early films, 26
   and patriarchy, 64
feudalism, 41–2, 48, 103–4, 120, 209, 226, 227, 234–5; see also land system
film adaptations, 137–8, 173–4; see also intertextuality
Film Finance Corporation (FFC), 12, 33, 157, 172, 209

film societies, 119
folk songs, 37, 38–9, 42
Formalists, 13
Forster, E. M.: *A Passage to India*, 95

Gadamer, Hans-Georg, 174
Gama, Vasco da, 89
Ganatra, Vinod, 171
Gandhi, Arun, 171, 177, 178
Gandhi, Indira, 60, 115, 128
Gandhi, Kasturba, 171, 177, 180; *see also Making of the Mahatma, The*
Gandhi, M. K.
  books about, 171, 173, 176
  Bose and, 199
  in *Bose: The Forgotten Hero*, 200, 202
  films about, 171; *see also Making of the Mahatma, The*
  and villages, 51, 59
Gandhi, Tushar, 171
gender discrimination, 51
  Manthan (*The Churning*), 55–6, 57–8, 60
Genette, Gérard, 86, 174, 197
geographies, imaginative, 89
Ghatak, Ritwik, 119
gherao, 132
girls: as slaves, 36
globalisation, 208
glocalisation, 208
Goa, 227–8
Goldblatt, David, 87
'good cinema', 119
Gopalarishnan, Adoor, 119
Guha, Ranjit, 121

Habermas, Jürgen, 35
Hall, Catherine, 85
Hangal, A. K., 105
Hanwant Singh, Maharaja, 188
Hardy, Thomas: *Tess of the d'Urbervilles*, 88

Harenda, Olivier, 169n13, 169n14
Hari-Bari, 242
hartal (*bandh*), 132
Henty, G. A.: *A Pipe of Mystery*, 84
Hindi cinema, 210
Hindu, The (newspaper), 137–8
Hindus and Hinduism, 87, 122, 228, 242; *see also* Brahmins; *Holi*
Hindutva, 159, 169n5, 169n16
historiography
  colonial, 89–90
  postmodern, 173–4
  schools of, 174
historiophoty, 42, 43, 44n8
history films, 30–1; *see also* biopics: historical
Holi, 242–3
Hood, John W., 32
Hutcheon, Linda, 137–8, 174
Huyssen, Andreas, 96–7
Hyderabad, 226
hypertextuality, 197; *see also* intertextuality

illiteracy, 217
imperialism, 85, 87, 94; *see also* British Empire
Inden, Ronald, 87, 90
India
  Constitution, 52, 107, 118
  'discovery' of, 89; *see also Bharat Ek Khoj*
  Independence, 13, 60, 95, 122, 175, 193, 199, 202, 210, 226
  Partition: and film industry, 156; *Jang-e-Azadi* (*The Battle for Freedom*), 229; Muslim women and, 159, 160–2; shared trauma of, 162
  Proclamation for India (1858), 97n9
  and Western imagination, 87–8
Indian Institutes of Management (IIMs), 112

INDEX 249

Indian New Wave films, 172
Indian People's Theatre Association (IPTA), 119
individuation, 73
International Film Festival, 14
intertextuality, 86–7, 96; *see also* film adaptation; hypertextuality
Islamicate films, 156

Jalal, Farida, 155, 186
Jang-e-Azadi (*The Battle for Freedom*), 229
Jhankal, Ravi, 190
Joshi, Namrata, 219–20
*jotedar*s, 121–2, 123, 124, 125, 127, 128, 129
Junoon (*The Obsession*), 4, 91–6, *93*, *94*
    adaptation of, 83–4, 228
    Benegal on, 85, 235
    cast, 103
    circularity of narrative, 91–2
    dialogue credits, 102
    Dubey on, 86
    mirrors and mirroring, 91–2
    Muslim characters, 158
    plot, 92–3, 95–6, 136
    as a postcolonial narrative, 96, 227
    production, 229
    setting, 91
    success of, 100
    trans-temporal ventriloquism in, 87

Kalyug (*The Mechanical Age*), 4, *114*, *116*
    dialogue credits, 102
    feudalism, 120
    good and evil, 105
    kinship, 101, 102–3, 108–15
    legitimacy, 105–6
    as a machine age movie, 100–1, 104–5, 112–13
    Mahabharata narrative, 102–3, 228
    as a materialist critique, 114–15
Kambara, Chandrashekara, 41
Kanpur *see* Cawnpore

Kapoor, Jennifer *see* Kendal, Jennifer
Kapoor, Karisma, 186–7, *189*, *192*
Kapoor, Raj, 1
Kapoor, Rajit, 186, 188
Kapoor, Rishi, 166
Kapoor, Shakti, 189
Kapoor, Shashi, 83, 92, *94*, 103, 105, *109*, *114*, 228–9
Karnad, Girish, 5, 13, 34, *35*, 41, 101, 102, 104, 233
    Kaadu (Forest), 29
Kasaravalli, Girish, 233
Katha Sagar (*A Sea of Stories*), 4
Kaul, Mani: *Uski Roti* (*Other's Bread*), 209
Kendal, Jennifer (Jennifer Kapoor), 92, *94*, 229, 236
Kharbanda, Kulbhushan, 92, 105
Khedekar, Sachin, 205
Kher, Kirron, 186
Khosla, G. D.: *The Last Mughal*, 96
Khubchand and Sons, 115
Kolkata, 119
Kondura (*The Sage from the Sea*), 240–1
Kothari, Rajan, 187
Kripalani, Jayant: *Still Waters: A Screenplay*, 216
Kumar, Arun, 6

land system, 36, 130, 131; *see also* agrarian relations; feudalism
Le Beau, Bryan F., 30–1
Lefebvre, Henri, 211, 215
Left Front (LF) government
    manifesto (1977), 131
    Operation Barga, 129–30, 132
    and Socialism, 132
Leitch, Thomas, 173–4l
literature
    and cinema, 86–7, 92, 96, 137–8; *see also* intertextuality
    Victorian, 83, 84–5, 88, 95

location shooting, 220
love songs, 150–1
Lundgren, Egron, 85
Lutgendorf, Philip, 115

McFarlane, Brian, 197
Mahabharata, 102–3, 109, 110, 111
Mahayra, Raahul, 190
Majumdar, Neepa, 81n7
Making of the Mahatma, The, 4, 173, *177, 179, 237, 238*
    as a historical biopic, 175–82
    Kasturba Gandhi's portrayal in, 172, 173
    making of, 238, 239
Malgonkar, Mahonar: *The Devil's Wind*, 96
Mammo, *161, 165, 168*
    belonging and citizenship, 163–6
    ending, 167
    as an interventionist film, 154, 159, 185
    mirrors and mirroring, 119
    Muslims' representation, 158, 159–62
    and new wave Muslim social, 156
    plot, 155, 186
Mandela, Nelson, 238–9
Mandi (Market Place), 4, *75*, 136, 230
    as feminist cinema, 65
    origins, 233–4
    patriarchy, 65, 73–4, 77–8, 79, 80
    prostitution, 74–8
    and social change, 235
    women, 73–80, 172
Mangalore, 228
Manthan (The Churning), 4, 13, 48–61, *50, 55*, 136, 226
    caste discrimination, 48, 49, 50, 53, 54–5, 57
    contemporaneity, 101, 235
    and Emergency (1975-1977), 60
    feudalism, 48, 209
    financing, 49
    gender discrimination, 55–6, 57–8, 60, 172
    origins, 234
    plot, 48, 49–50
    production, 34
    technology, 104
    as third cinema, 32
    writing credits, 102
Manto, Sadat Hasan: *Toba Tek Singh*, 161
Maoists, 132–3
Marx, Karl, 71, 88, 89–90, 118
masala films, 10n1
Mazumdar, Charu, 124
Meer, Fatima, 238, 239
    Apprenticeship of a Mahatma, 173, 176, 177–8, 180
Meher, Sadhu, 103
Mehra, Prakash: *Zanjeer (Shackles)*, 1
Mehta, Ketan: *Mirch Masala (Hot Spice)*, 80
middle cinema, 5, 170n28
middle class *see* bourgeoisie
Minier, Marta, 198
Miranda, Mario, 227–8
mirrors
    Ankur (The Seedling), 16, 17, *18*
    cinema as, 119, 241
    Junoon (The Obsession), 91–2
    Mammo, 119
    and memory, 83
Mirza, Saeed
    Naseem, 156, 157, 158–9
    Salim Langde Pe Mat Ro (Don't Cry for Salim, the Lame), 156, 157, 159
Mishra, Ashok, 214, 217
Mishra, Smriti, 186
modernity and tradition, 208
Modi, Sohrab: *Pukar (The Call)*, 156
Mohamed, Khalid, 154
    Fiza, 159
    on *Welcome to Sajjanpur*, 214
    Zubeidaa, 188

Mohammed Quli Qutub Shah, 40
Mohanty, Chandra Talapade, 15
Moitra, Shantanu, 216, 217
Morley, David, 87
mosques: Babri Masjid, Ayodhya, 154, 169n17, 185
Mukherji, Srijit: *Gumnaami*, 206
Mulvey, Laura, 15
Murray, Dr John, 85
Muslims
  anti-Muslim sentiment, 185
  Bengal, 122
  films about, 242
  othering of, 154–5, 156
  representations of, 155–9, 166–7, 168
  segregation of, 163–6
mutinies, 90, 91
  in fiction, 84, 86–8

Nag, Anant, 34, 103, 105, 136, 240
Nair, Bandu, 15
naming, 88–90
Nana Sahib, 92, 95, 96
Nandy, Ashis, 116n3, 211
Narayan, R. K., 237
narratology, 174
National Film Development Corporation (NFDC), 33, 157, 167
nationalisation, 131
nationalists and nationalism
  Hindu, 159
  kinship and legitimacy, 106–8
  regional, 12
  right-wing, 167
  and villages, 51
  and women, 60
nationhood, 111
Naxalite movement, 124, 125, 128, 241
Needham, Anuradha Dingwaney, 6, 211
  on *Ankur*, 17–18, 20, 22, 24
  and Benegal in conversation, 223–43
  on *Bhumika*, 69

on *Mandi*, 77–8
on *Manthan*, 60–1
on *Nishant*, 32
Nehru, Jawarharlal
  Benegal's documentary on, 3, 239
  formation of government (1952), 14
  and villages, 51, 52, 53, 59
  writings: *Discovery of India, The*, 4, 236–7, 239; *Glimpses of World History*, 237, 239; *Letters from a Father to his Daughter*, 237, 239
New Cinema movement, 101
New Indian Cinema, 2, 43n1, 209, 210, 233; *see also* parallel cinema
new wave films *see* Indian New Wave films
Nigam, Sonu, 205, 206
Nihalani, Govind, 5, 91
Nishant (*Night's End*), 4, 13, 226, 233
  consecration rites, 33–6
  contemporaneity, 101
  feudalism, 48, 120, 209, 234–5
  historical realism, 30
  languages: English, 35; Telugu, 37, 38, 39
  modernity, 38, 42–3
  origins, 234
  as parallel cinema, 136
  patriarchy, 30, 49
  plot, 34, 37
  production, 34
  songs, 39–41
  studies of, 32
  and time, 29–30
  women, 41, 172
Noor Inayat Khan, 243

Osten, Franz: *Acchut Kanya* (*Untouchable Maiden*), 25

Pabna Revolt (1873), 121
panchayati system, 52, 54, 129

Pandey, Mangal, 91
parallel cinema, 12, 29, 31–2, 48–9, 135–6
  class struggle in, 118, 119
  locations, 13
  and Muslim representation, 155–9
  'women-oriented', 65
  see also New Indian Cinema
Parciack, Ronie, 33, 39, 40
Pathans, 98n40
Patil, Smita, 5, 234, 241
Patmore, Coventry, 190
patriarchy, 172
  Ankur (*The Seedling*), 14–15, 18, 22, 23, 26
  Bhumika (*The Role*), 65, 66, 68–9, 70, 71–3, 78
  and exploitation, 72
  and feminism, 64
  Gandhi and, 178–80, 181
  Indian nationalists and, 62n16
  and law, 62n20
  Mandi (*Market Place*), 65, 73–4, 77–8, 79, 80
  Muslim, 158–9
  Nishant (*Night's End*), 30, 49
  and prostitution, 75
Pax Britannica, 90
peasants
  Bengal, 120–2, 124, 129, 132
  land rights, 131
  mistreatment of, 31, 37
  Telengana peasant struggle (1946–51), 13, 30, 31, 37
  West Bengal, 123
  see also bargadars
Pennachia, Maddalena, 198
Phalke, Amit, 186
photography: and imperialism, 85
Pillai, Manu S.: *The Ivory Throne: Chronicles of the House of Travancore*, 89
Piñera, Walfredo, 14

Plus Channel, 186
Polasek, Ashley, 198
Ponzanesi, Sandra, 85
Portuguese colonisers, 227
postmoderrnism, 86
poststructuralism, 86
Prabhat Film Company, 225
Praja movement, 122
Prasad, M. Madhava
  on *Ankur*, 13, 25
  on Benegal, 209, 210
  on *Manthan*, 60–1, 220
  on *Nishant*, 17, 32
Progressive Writers Association, 119
prostitution
  Bhumika (*The Role*), 65, 74
  legislation, 74–5
  Mandi (*Market Place*), 74–8
Punjab, 229
Puri, Amrish, 34, 188
Puri, Om, 5, 112, 125, 170n48, 241

race
  and cultural identity, 85
  and language, 95
Raghavendra, M. K., 14
Rahman, A. R., 205
Rahman, Sheikh Mujibur, 4
Rajadhyaksha, Ashish, 15, 43n1, 119, 209, 210
Rajan, Sundar, 24
Ramanujan, A. K., 230
Rancière, Jacques, 174
Rao, Benegal Dinkar, 2
Rattonsey, Farouq, 186
Ray, Satyajit
  Benegal's documentary on, 3, 235–6
  and film societies, 119
  Ghare-Baire (*The Home and the World*), 235–6

influence of, 210
interviews, 5
and parallel cinema, 136
Pratidwandi, 125
realist aesthetics, 13, 14
Razzak, Ilsa Abdul, 165–6
realism, 13
 neo-, 14
 statist, 217
 see also parallel cinema
Rege, Sharmila, 62n20
Rekha, 105
Religion, and morality, 180; *see also* Christianity; Hindus and Hinduism; Roman Catholicism
Ricoeur, Paul, 174
Ritzer, George, 208
Roman Catholicism, 227, 228, 242
Roy, Bimal, 14, 119
 Sujata, 25–6
Rushdie, Salman
Midnight's Children, 86
 Moor's Last Sigh, The, 89

Sachdev, Rajeshwari, 186
Sachdeva, Vivek, 6
Sagar, Preeti, 104
Said, Edward, 89
Sambad Prabhakar (periodical), 120
Samvidhaan (The Making of the Indian Constitution), 229
Sangari, Kumkun, 73, 74
Sanjeev: *Phulwaka Pul (Phulwa's Bridge)*, 216
Sardari Begum, 2, 4, 168n3, 185, 186, 235
Sarkar, Tanika, 169n12
Sarrazin, Natalie, 150–1
Sathyu, M. S., 241
 Garam Hawa (Scorching Winds), 156, 157, 159, 162, 167

Satyajit Ray, 3, 235–6
Sawant, Shivaji: *Mrityunjaya (Victory Over Death)*, 106
scopophilia, 15
Scott, Paul: *The Jewel in the Crown*, 95
secularism, 35
Sen, Mrinal, 233, 241
 Bhuvan Shome, 209
 Calcutta 71, 125
 and film societies, 119
 Padatik, 125
sentence-images, 174
Sepoy Rebellion (1857), 84, 90, 91, 92, 94, 95, 96
Shaban, Abdul, 154
Shah, Naseeruddin, 5, 34, 91, *93*, 170n48
Shahjahanpur, 91–2, 228
Shankar, Uday, 225
 Kalpana (Imagination), 119–20
Sharawat, Vinod, 191
Sharpe, Jenny, 94, 95
Sheikh, Farooq, 167
Sikri, Surekha, 155, 186, 188, *189*
Sinha, Anubhav: *Mulk (Country)*, 166–7, *167*
sisterhood, 82n35
slaves, 36
social spaces, 211
 Welcome to Sajjanpur, 213, 215
 Well Done Abba (Well Done Father), 219
socialism, 52, 132
Soja, Edward, 212
solidarity, 82n35
song-and-dance spectacles, 39, 192
South Africa, 238–9
Stam, Robert, 13–14, 26, 86, 197
Sternburg, Janet, 184n38
strikes *see hartal*
subalterneity, 15, 17, 18, 23
Sundarayya, P., 36

Suraj Ka Satvan Ghoda (*The Sun's Seventh Horse*), 4, 136–7, *145*
  as an adaptation of Bharati's novel, 137–8, 240
  Bollywood identity of, 150–1
  compared with novel, 141–4, 145, 146–9, 151–2
  ending, 151
  parody in, 149
  self-reflexivity in, 137–41, *143*, 149

Tagore, Rabindranath: 'Karna Kunti Samvaad', 106
Tanvir, Habib: *Charandas Chor* (*Charandas, the Thief*), 101
Taylor, Charles, 35
Taylor, Miles, 84
Telangana movement, 13, 30, 31, 36, 226
Tendulkar, Vijay, 30, 41, 44n1, 44n4, 102
Tennyson, Alfred, Lord: 'The Defence of Lucknow', 84–5
Thappar, Romila, 169n12
third-world cinema (third cinema), 14, 32
Thirumali, I., 36, 37
Todorov, Tzvetan, 174
Trevelyan, G. O.: *Cawnpore*, 92
Trikal (*Past, Present and Future*), 4, 120, 136, 227–8, 242
Trilling Lionel, 187

Uberoi, Patricia, 81n11
Unquiet Revolution, The, 53
untouchables, 52, 53, 54

Valicha, Kishore, 32
Van der Heide, William, 5
Vanisri, 240–1
Varavia, Freni, 39
Vasudev, Aruna, 13, 209

Vasudevan, Ravi S., 15, 156
Vatsyayan, Sachchidanand Hiranand *see* 'Ajneya'
ventriloquism, 83, 84, 85, 86, 87
Verghese, Dr, 49
Verma, Sukanya, 137–8
Victoria, Queen, 84, 85, 91
Vidal, Belen, 197, 198
Vidya Rani *see* Zubeidaa Begum
villages, 50–3, 59, 88, 211, 212–13, 216

Wadkar, Hansa, 65, 81n7, 231; *see also* Bhumika
Welcome to Sajjanpur, 4, 212–16, *213*, 242
  as a comedy, 214
  dialogue, 214
  fiction and reality, 216, 221
  illiteracy, 217
  mise-en-scène, 214, 215
  music, 215, 216
  politics, 214–15
  social change, 215
  social space, 213, 215
  superstition, 213–14
Well Done Abba (*Well Done Father*), 4, 168n3, 216–20, *218*
  critiques of, 219–20
  fiction and reality, 221
  globalising processes, 218–19
  illiteracy, 217
  mise-en-scène, 217
  National Film Award, 217
  plot, 216, 217–18, 242
  social spaces, 219
  women's roles, 219
  work ethic, 219
White, Hayden, 44n8, 174
White Revolution, 49
Winterbottom, Michael: *Trishna*, 88, 90

women
  Dalit, 14–15, 19
  education of, 213–14
  empowerment of, 64, 79, 101, 185, 192–3, 194–5
  and Holi, 242–3
  identity of, 172, 176–8, 179, 229–33
  in Indian New Wave films, 172
  and labour, 65–73, 74, 79, 80
  liberation of, 73
  marginalised, 166
  and marriage, 191–2, 217
  Muslim *see Mammo*
  and prostitution *see Mandi*
  and rape, 94–5
  and sexuality, 21, 30, 32, 41, 74, 172, 180
  sisterhood and solidarity of, 82n35
  see also feminism; gender discrimination

Yashraj Films, 188
Yatra (*Travel*), 4

Zaheer, S. M., 192
Zaidi, Shama, 102, 157–8, 162, 170n48
*zamindar*s, 122, 124
Zavattini, Cesare, 13–14
Zubeidaa, 2, 4, 136, 168n3, 185, 186–95, *189*, *192*
  casting, 186–7
  distribution, 188
  male narratives, 190–1
  memory, 193–4
  mise-en-scène, 187
  music, 192, 194
Zubeidaa Begum (Vidya Rani), 188

EU representative:
Easy Access System Europe
Mustamäe tee 50, 10621 Tallinn, Estonia
Gpsr.requests@easproject.com

www.ingramcontent.com/pod-product-compliance
Lightning Source LLC
Chambersburg PA
CBHW070322240426
43671CB00013BA/2333